Stanisław Umiński, Jarosław M. Nazarczuk (Eds.)

Regions in International Trade

Stanisław Umiński,
Jarosław M. Nazarczuk (Eds.)

Regions in International Trade

Managing Editor: Konrad Sarzyński
Language Editor: Michael Evans

DE GRUYTER
OPEN

Published by De Gruyter Open Ltd, Warsaw/Berlin
Part of Walter de Gruyter GmbH, Berlin/Munich/Boston

ISBN: 978-83-958150-3-4
e-ISBN: 978-83-958150-4-1

The book is a part of the project entitled "Regional exporting activity. Assessment of determinants in light of contemporary foreign trade theory for Poland and Spain" financed by the National Science Centre in Poland under the grant no. 2015/19/B/HS4/01704.

Bibliographic information published by the Deutsche Nationalbibliothek
The Deutsche Nationalbibliothek lists this publication in the Deutsche Nationalbibliografie; detailed bibliographic data are available in the Internet at http://dnb.dnb.de.

Managing Editor: Konrad Sarzyński

Language Editor: Michael Evans
www.degruyter.com

Cover illustration: © 2019 Stanisław Umiński

Contents

Part I: Region and Trade

Part II: **State of Art**

Part III: **Empirical Analyses of Regions' Foreign Trade**

Part IV: **Policy Implications and Possibilities**

Part V: **Concluding remarks of the book**

List of contributing authors

Stanisław Umiński

Faculty of Economics, University of Gdańsk, Sopot, Poland

e-mail: stanislaw.uminski@ug.edu.pl

Institute for Development, Sopot, Poland

e-mail: s.uminski@instytut-rozwoju.org

Introduction

Chapter 1, 4, 5, 7, 8

Concluding remarks of the book

Jarosław M. Nazarczuk

University of Warmia and Mazury in Olsztyn, Poland

e-mail: jaroslaw.nazarczuk@uwm.edu.pl

Introduction

Chapter 7, 12

Concluding remarks of the book

Anna Fornalska-Skurczyńska

IMC University of Applied Sciences Krems, Krems an der Donau, Austria

e-mail: anna.fornalska@fh-krems.ac.at

Chapter 1

Tomasz Brodzicki

Faculty of Economics, University of Gdańsk, Sopot, Poland

e-mail: t.brodzicki@ug.edu.pl

Institute for Development, Sopot, Poland

e-mail: t.brodzicki@instytut-rozwoju.org

Chapter 2, 3, 6, 8

Tomasz Jurkiewicz

Faculty of Management, University of Gdańsk, Sopot, Poland

e-mail: tomasz.jurkiewicz@ug.edu.pl

Chapter 7, 12

Laura Márquez-Ramos

Department of Economics, Universitat Jaume I, Castellón de la Plana, Spain

e-mail: lmarquez@eco.uji.es

University of Adelaide, Adelaide, Australia

e-mail: laura.marquez-ramos@adelaide.edu.au

Chapter 8, 9

Tony Cavoli

School of Commerce, University of South Australia Business School, Adelaide, Australia

e-mail: tony.cavoli@unisa.edu.au

Chapter 9

Dandan Lin

School of Commerce, University of South Australia Business School, Adelaide, Australia

e-mail: dandan.lin@mymail.unisa.edu.au

Chapter 9

Clinton Uzobor

Faculty of Economics, University of Gdansk, Sopot, Poland

e-mail: clintuzo@yahoo.com

Chapter 10

Krystyna Gawlikowska-Hueckel

Faculty of Economics, University of Gdańsk, Sopot, Poland

e-mail: k.gawlikowska@ug.edu.pl

Institute for Development, Sopot, Poland

Chapter 11, 12

List of abbreviations

AIT – Agreement on Internal Trade
CAP funds – Common Agricultural Policy funds
Comecon – Council of the Mutual Economic Assistance
CUSFTA – Canada-United States Free Trade Agreement
DD – Dutch disease
ELG – export-led growth
FDI – foreign direct investment
FOE – foreign-owned entity
FTA – free trade agreement
GTF – global technology frontier
HME – home market effect
H-O – the Heckscher-Ohlin (H-O) theorem/theory
IIT – intra-industry trade
IV approach – instrumental variables approach
MAR externalities – Marshall-Arrow-Romer externalities
MEGA – metropolitan European growth areas
MNE – multinational enterprise
MS – member states (of the EU)
NAFTA – North American Free Trade Agreement
NEG – new economic geography
NMS – new member states (of the EU)
NNEG – 'new', new economic geography
OLI – ownership, location, internalisation (OLI) model/framework
PLC – product life cycle
PPML – Poisson pseudo maximum likelihood
RPO – regional operational programme
SMEM – semi mixed-effects model
SOE – small open economy
SWOT – strengths, weaknesses, opportunities, and threats (analysis)
SUR – seemingly unrelated regressions

Introduction

Export activity has been traditionally analysed for countries. Its regional dimension was somewhat neglected or not noticed. The main premise of our research is that exports are strongly diversified regionally. The imperative to conduct such research stems from constatation that exports do not come from an undefined space, from a country treated as a single point – but rather from particular locations. For a long time, international economics has not been interested in what is inside the exporting countries in terms of their lumpiness. The question "where do exports come from" was not asked. While the regional distribution of economic activity, as such, was subject to profound research by geographers, economists and regional scientists – exports were not. International economics is, however, changing. It has incorporated a geographical component, which is represented by the New Economic Geography (NEG), and heterogeneity of firms, that have different productivity, while higher productivity positively contributes to exports. The regional analysis of exports represents a domain in which heterogeneity of regions and heterogeneity of firms meet.

This book continues the research done by the group of economists focused on international economics and regional issues (Brodzicki, 2016a, 2017a; Gawlikowska-Hueckel and Szlachta, 2014; Gawlikowska-Hueckel and Umiński, 2013a, 2013b, 2016; Márquez-Ramos, 2016a, 2016b, 2016c; Nazarczuk and Umiński, 2018b). The research cooperation created the possibility to share experience, confront results and verify hypotheses in a broader context. The novelty brought in our analysis stems from extending the examination beyond Poland and including the regions of Spain. We fill the gap in the literature by making a comprehensive inquiry in the sphere of regions' foreign trade, reviewing main theoretical threads and empirical research.

This book presents the results of the research financed by the National Science Centre, Poland, within the project "Regional exporting activity. Assessment of Determinants in Light of Contemporary Foreign Trade Theory for Poland and Spain", under the research grant 2015/19/B/HS4/01704.

The research done within the project resulted in several publications focused on such issues as gravity panel data analysis model on the role of metropolises and path dependency (Brodzicki and Umiński, 2017), distribution of exporters and the role of ownership (Nazarczuk, Umiński, & Brodzicki, 2019), the role of specialisation (Nazarczuk, Umiński, and Gawlikowska-Hueckel, 2018), patterns and determinants of Intra Industry Trade (IIT) (Brodzicki, Jurkiewicz, Márquez-Ramos, and Umiński, 2019), consequences of Brexit (Nazarczuk, Umiński, and Márquez-Ramos, 2020), as well as determinants of the regional export base (Brodzicki, Márquez-Ramos, and Umiński, 2018). The comprehensive information thereof can be found on the ResearchGate website.[1]

This book comprises four parts. Part one "Region and Trade" introduces the concept of region as a small open economy (SOE) and treats regions as something "in-between", between a whole nation level and disaggregation of statistical data, for particular firms. In part one, much attention is put on presenting selected theoretical concepts useful in exporting activity interpretations from regions' perspective. Not only international trade theory is referred to, but also foreign direct investments (FDI), NEG and NNEG as well as the heterogeneity of firms. The role of openness in the economic growth of regions is depicted thoroughly, with particular attention on the perspective of NEG, evolving into NNEG. Also, the principle of subsidiarity is mentioned, as a concept that justifies any action taken at the regional level, aimed at exports promotion.

Part two "State of Art", reviews the empirical literature on the sophisticated nexus between trade and other aspects of openness, and economic growth performance. The studies at the regional level are depicted. Also, the role of FDI is presented. A separate point is focused on Dutch Disease (DD), which we treat as an interesting phenomenon linking regional and international economic problems. This part also includes the comprehensive overview of research on regions' foreign trade, structured into main issues tackled, such as examples of the early research on regions' exports, the role of FDI, exports promotion, measurement problems, agglomeration of exporters and border effect.

Part three presents the results of the empirical analysis of foreign trade in Poland's and Spain's regions. Trade openness is assessed, the primary taxonomy of exporting parameters is presented, including geographical and product structures, their concentrations, the quality of exports and the role of FDI. This part also embraces the inquiry into the determinants of regions' foreign trade, broken into orthodox and non-orthodox factors. Apart from Polish and Spanish regions, Australian and Canadian cases are presented.

Part four, "Policy Implications and Possibilities", concentrates on the understanding of competitiveness concept, applied to regions and their exporting activity, and shows the possibilities of exports support at a regional level. Because smart specialisation has become an important concept used in stimulating regional development and improving competitiveness, the role of smart specialisation-related exports in overall regional exports has been assessed.

---

1 https://www.researchgate.net/project/Regional-Exporting-Activity-Assessment-of-Determinants-in-Light-of-Contemporary-Foreign-Trade-Theory-for-Poland-and-Spain

Acknowledging the limits and imperfections of our research, methodology and datasets used – by preparing the book and publishing other research results of the project in scientific journals, we aimed at inviting researchers from Poland, Spain, Australia, Canada and other countries to participate in the discussion related to the nexus between regional and international economics. Regions have become more open. Their economic situation and labour market trends, in particular, depend on the sphere of foreign relations. We are sure that this kind of analysis will flourish, also because more comprehensive datasets for regions are available.

As mentioned, the book represents the results of work performed in the years 2016-2019 by a team comprising: Tomasz Brodzicki, Anna Fornalska-Skurczyńska, Krystyna Gawlikowska-Hueckel, Tomasz Jurkiewicz, Laura Márquez-Ramos and Jarosław M. Nazarczuk, and supervised by Stanisław Umiński. The Australian and Canadian cases contribution was possible due to cooperation with Tony Cavoli, Dandan Lin and Clinton Uzobor.

Stanisław Umiński
Jarosław M. Nazarczuk

Part I: **Region and Trade**

Stanisław Umiński, Anna Fornalska-Skurczyńska

1 Region as a small open economy and an exporter

1.1 Region as "something in between"

Our approach to the analysis of exports and imports is not common in literature, as most of the research is performed at country or sectoral level. The theories and concepts applied to the analysis of international trade as such, have been created for the trading countries, not regions. Therefore, for an economist, it is challenging to make a serious inquiry into the nature of regions' foreign trade activity, based on the solid theoretical background. The solution is treating the region as a small open economy (SOE), which enables the transposition of most of the international economics apparatus into the regions' world.

In the literature, a region understood as an SOE is treated as "something in between" (Eswaran, Kotwal, Ramaswami, and Wadhwa, 2007; Siebert, 1969), an intermediate category, situated between an aggregated economy (in which the spatial dimension does not exist) and highly disaggregated system, understood as a set of places in space. The conceptual approach proposed by Siebert (also represented by Cassey (2011b)) enables to choose the most appropriate level for aggregation of statistical data for economic entities (firms). The proper level of data aggregation is essential, for instance, in the analysis of intra-industry trade (IIT). If a highly disaggregated product classification level is used, accompanied by low-level territorial units – unnaturally low values of IIT indices could be expected (Umiński, 2014; Yoshida, 2008). It sheds appealing light on the problems with transposition of international economics apparatus to the regional level of analysis. Siebert (1969) noticed that in the classical economic models, the deductive process was based on the prerequisite of a one-point economy, having no spatial dimension. Therefore, the main questions, such as how to produce, who produces, who is the consumer – were interpreted in a non-spatial, distanceless world, with non-existent transport costs.

1.2 International trade theories – they are changing

Several essential prerequisites can be exemplified, once we look for relevant theoretical concepts explaining regions' participation in international trade:

(a) international trade theories have been changing. Besides concepts strictly related to trading countries (i.e. H-O theorem), far more universal apparatus has been applied, such as the gravity model,

(b) undoubtedly a question can be formulated how far this universalism reaches. According to Cieślik (2005) and Findlay (1995), there appears an integrated general theory of localisation, relative factors endowment and international trade in conditions of increasing returns to scale – which is composed of new economic geography (NEG) and the international trade theory. NEG evolves in the micro-heterogeneity direction, thus incorporating the firm's heterogeneity in productivity, a crucial element in contemporary research on international trade. However, NEG has been severely criticised by geographers, for whom many aspects of NEG cannot be accepted because of the high contextuality of regional analysis,
(c) also, some elements of international economics seem to have become less critical. For instance, there is no need to bother so much with foreign currency exchange issues, while analysing trade within the currency union, such as the eurozone. It simplifies the regions' foreign trade analysis, as the number of trade determinants can be reduced,
(d) another question is to what extent does international trade resembles interregional trade, once it happens within the internal market of the EU (in the eurozone in particular), with no trade obstacles,
(e) the fundamental question, however, is how seriously we treat assumptions present in international trade theories. A vivid example is H-O theorem, in which strict assumptions have been formulated related to differences between trading partners resulting from differences in factors endowment and factors' mobility. Shall countries be treated as flat (Krugman, 2015) or lumpy (Courant and Deardorff, 1992)?

Acknowledging that in empirical studies, we observe acute differentiation of regions' export profiles is a substantial prerequisite for further considerations and search for theories that can be applied to regions' participation in foreign trade. Those differences inspire us to use the international trade apparatus, theories and models to interpret a region's exports. Yet, many concepts originated from international trade theory have much broader, universal application, a perfect example being the comparative advantage rule that is widely used in regions' competitiveness assessments. A permeation of regional and international economics is a fact.

Our intention is not to provide the reader with the fully-fledged, comprehensive inquiry into the theory of international trade applied to regions. We instead focus on the selected, most interesting theoretical concepts, which in our opinion, clarify of the nexus between the region and the global economy. These are mercantilism, absolute and comparative advantages within the standard model of international trade, factor endowment within H-O theorem, IIT, demand-side related theories, FDI and concepts incorporating technological dimension. NEG is only briefly mentioned, as it is described in a detailed way in section 2.3. Also, the gravity model is not discussed because it is presented in section 8.

1.3 Mercantilism – an almost forgotten, but useful concept

This old, almost forgotten concept that has been the solid background for the economic and foreign trade policy between the early 16th and the mid-18th centuries still seems useful for regions, as SOEs, participating in the global market (Landreth, Szeworski, Godłów-Legiędź, Dzionek-Kozłowska, and Colander, 2013). The fully-fledged application of the concept of mercantilism to regional analysis is difficult because its important component are monetary issues – and monetary policy as such is not performed at the regional level. Mercantilism postulated positive trade balance, available also through active foreign trade policy. Such policy is obviously not conducted at the regional level, as it belongs to the exclusive competences of the EU. Regions are, however, not wholly deprived of the possibilities to influence their trade balance, which is often perceived as a primary indicator of competitiveness. As mentioned, the promotion of exports is often transposed to regional agencies/institutions, and their aim is explicitly defined as improvements in competitiveness, regions' foreign trade balance, and – generally – the promotion of export base and regional exporters (see sections 11 and 12, where policy-related issues are undertaken). A similar approach may be adapted to regions competing over the EU structural and investment funds or export subsidies. Promotion of a region's exports is perceived as a tool to increase employment. If a region hosts a substantial number of firms which are the key players in a particular sector of the economy and their market position is threatened by foreign competitors, these firms may postulate the introduction of antidumping or anti-subsidy procedures. In that way, a region – or a group of regions having similar production or trade profile (in section 7.7 regions are grouped into clusters, comprising similar units in terms of exports) – can influence the EU common commercial policy. Summing up, mercantilism, although not perfectly suited for analysing trade of regions, is an interesting concept, suitable for understanding the regions' participation in world trade.

1.4 Standard model of international trade

Within the standard model of international trade, two approaches can be identified, which are the absolute or comparative advantages. Both theories, formulated by A. Smith and D. Ricardo respectively, are well described in the literature; therefore there is no need to elaborate on their assumptions and predictions (Batabyal and Nijkamp, 2015, p. 4). In fact, they have become the most important concepts in economics. Both are used in the discussion related to how regions' competitiveness shall be perceived. The comparative advantage rule, applied to regions, brings an important and optimistic conclusion that although a region may not have any absolute advantages due to high costs of production or low productivity, there are products in which the comparative advantage can be found, making foreign trade beneficial. As mentioned by

Batabyal and Nijkamp (2015, p. 4), the main drawback of the Ricardian concept is that in the model trade does not affect the distribution of income, which in the real world produces clear winners and losers.

The comparative advantage rule has its important practical and empirical application, which is the variety of measures, such as revealed comparative advantages or location quotients indices, intensively used in the assessments of competitiveness (see section 7 for an empirical application). In both – absolute and comparative advantage – the benefits from trade are shown as an equilibrium in an open economy (with trade) compared with an equilibrium in the state of autarky. In the model, there is a state of autarky, which is a problematic issue because, in the real world, it is hard to find a country representing a closed economy. Regional economies are "closer" to the autarkical state, primarily if a region's economy is dominated by an industrial sector characterised by low export intensity. In other words, it is easier to find an almost autarkical region, than a country, especially if the analysis is performed at a low level of regions' delimitation. In this respect, section 6 deals with rational trade openness, while in section 7, differences in exports per capita are addressed.

1.5 Factor endowment

According to the Heckscher-Ohlin (H-O) paradigm (applied to regions), it is highly probable that a region relatively well abounded with labour will specialise in production and exporting of labour-intensive goods and will import goods that require intensive use of the scarce (and relatively expensive) factor. Another region will specialise in production and export of capital-intensive goods. It is a simple transposition of the H-O theory to the situations of regions engaged in international trade. Factor endowment constitutes a source of competitiveness that enables the region to benefit from international trade and the division of labour and capital. The H-O theory was extended to include not only capital and labour, but also differentiated factors (such as qualified and unqualified labour).

H-O theorem is rigorous in its assumptions. One of them is the factors' immobility: they are only mobile, as being embodied within the products being traded. It is problematic in the analysis focused on regions. In reality, factors do migrate between regions and the more mobile they are, the less region's foreign trade is determined by its indigenous factors' abundance. This problem is signalled by Krugman (2015), who points to the narrowing factor-price differences, which reduces the reason to trade. Whether the countries are flat or differentiated (lumpy) – it will remain the question of the debate. According to Krugman (2015, p. 29), the world cannot be regarded as flat, but America – due to the high mobility of ideas, people and capital – can. The alternative point of view was presented by Armington (1969), according to whom customers differentiate the products by their attributes, which are specific to the place of origin. In other words: a customer pays attention if, for instance, wine comes from the Chianti region, or from other regions, which stops the world from becoming flat. Products traded are not "the same".

H-O theory rests on the assumption that trading partners are different; the essential difference is related to factor endowment. There are two possible approaches on how to perceive those differences, which undoubtedly is a rather casual interpretation of the basic H-O theorem: (i) a region can be compared to other regions within a country, participating in international trade; (ii) or it can be compared to the "rest of the world", which obviously would require the much more comprehensive and large dataset to be included in the analysis. In fact, flexible approaches can be found in empirical research, H-O being one of the most important conceptual frameworks, constituting the fundament of international trade analysis.

The question is, how useful is H-O theory for the analysis of contemporary foreign trade, in which trade shifts towards more similar ("less different") trading partners. It implies that other theories will gain importance, for instance, IIT conception. Still, for Poland and Spain, H-O theorem holds its usefulness for the interpretation of trading partners with countries that are different in terms of the level of development etc.

The so-called missing trade problem shall be mentioned, as often trade intensity between partners turns out to be less intensive than predicted by H-O theory-based models. The missing trade problem is one of the reasons for the gravity concept (see section 8 for an empirical example of its use) to become useful in trade interpretations (Brodzicki and Umiński, 2017), as it focuses on the explanation of factors that hamper trade.

Courant and Deardorff (1992) formulated a lumpy country concept, which introduces regional differences to the initial H-O model. Each of the country's regions can specialise in exports and imports of different products, which implies that factors' proportions do not necessary equalise. It has an important consequence: regions' trade specialisation can be idiosyncratic. If a nation's foreign trade is dominated by a few regions, it is very likely that the structure of their trade is similar to that of the whole country. The remaining regions (having lower shares in the nation's trade) can reveal significant idiosyncrasies in their trade characteristics. According to Courant and Deardorff (1992), a nation's foreign trade in which factors are equally distributed among its regions will be different to a situation, in which there are significant inequalities among regions in terms of their factors endowment. The main conclusion formulated by Courant and Deardorff (1992) is that regional inequality in factor endowment determines a nation's foreign trade. Thus, regional inequalities shall be considered. Ceteris paribus, a nation tends to export a good, production of which requires more intensive use of the factor, which is lumpier (more unevenly distributed). If differences in factors endowment are large, regions may reveal complete specialisation (in one product), which rarely happens at a country level. A paper by Courant and Deardorff (1992) shall be perceived as a serious invitation to treat regions as SOEs that have their own distinct factors endowment and therefore reveal specific trade patterns.

The H-O model was also complemented by a group of neo-technological theories, in which the importance of technological differences was highlighted. Schumpeter (2013) and Marshall (1919) investigated the relationship between technological advancement and international trade. First, the interdependence of innovation, imitating technological progress and foreign trade was emphasised. Marshall focused on methods of technology transfer between countries and their impact on comparative advantage. Based on these considerations, Posner (1961) formulated the outline of the technology gap theory, explaining the way in which technological progress and technology transfer affect the development of international trade.

Hufbauer (1970) (1966) and Krugman (1979) contributed to the theory stating that different levels of specific knowledge and technology advancement ("ladder of countries"), as well as limited possibilities of fast and free access to technical knowledge from other countries, are responsible for observing international trade. Regions can be ranked according to their technological development: the higher the level of technological development, the higher the products are at the scale of production capacity, which is also the scale of comparative advantage. In *Rethinking International Trade* (Krugman, 1990), pointed to the process of "closing of the gap", that is to decreasing superiority of industrial nations. The set of neo-technological theories is often referred to when analysing trade flows of regions. They may be applied to regions that can be ranked on a "technological advancement ladder". The differences in the technological advancement of production might be observed between regions, constituting the base of competitive advantages.

1.6 Intra-industry trade

IIT explains the overlap between exports and imports, while differentiated products from the same product group are traded, being close substitutes in production or consumption. IIT is a type of trade that happens predominantly between "similar" countries, in terms of their level of development, in which customers demand "variety". The "love for variety" is a factor that stimulates the growing role of IIT. Product differentiation (heterogeneity), economies of scale and imperfect competition are traditionally regarded as factors constituting the base for IIT. However, in the more up-to-date literature, production fragmentation between countries has been identified as a factor that intensifies IIT (ABS, 2019a; Cieślik, 2008; Krugman, 1979; Marrewijk, 2008; OECD, 2002; Yoshida, 2008, 2008), which stems from FDI (mostly MNEs) activity (Cieślik, 2008). Two main types of IIT can be distinguished: horizontal (goods are differentiated by attributes) and vertical (goods are differentiated by quality). The distinction between the two types of IIT is made with the use of unit value criterion (Krugman, 1979; Greenaway, Hine, and Milner, 1995). IIT theory was formulated for countries. Therefore, benefits stemming from it traditionally were discussed for country-level of analysis. As regards regions, the gains from IIT were not particularly reviewed yet, and they undoubtedly deserve attention and more profound research.

With respect to IIT analysis for regions, the following issues shall be considered:
1. At the regional level, high intensity of IIT reflects not so much “love for variety”, but production fragmentation, often driven by FOEs activity. If IIT is a result of FDI, then all the possible consequences of FDI inflow disclose in the regional economy. They are positive and negative, as FOEs are “multidimensional creatures” (Forsgren, 2008).
2. FOEs often co-localise, which draws our attention to agglomeration processes. If agglomeration embraces firms from the same industry, it increases vulnerability, because the regional economy becomes more specialised. On the contrary, “differentiated” agglomeration (embracing firms from different industries) may decrease vulnerability.
3. IIT is driven by economies of scale, which as such are positive, as they constitute a base for trade. However, ceteris paribus, they make the regional economy more specialised, which – again – increases vulnerability.
4. Agglomeration and specialisation lead to new resources being attracted to the region, incl. human resources. It changes regions’ position against other regions.
5. IIT is more intense between spatially closer trading partners. Due to cumulative causation, proximity contributes to furtherly intensified trade relations (that is what gravity teaches us), as trade costs matter.
6. Due to IIT, a region’s positioning on a trade quality ladder is settled. It depends on the type of IIT, whether it is horizontal or vertical (low quality/down market or the high quality/high market).
7. Intensive IIT takes place in relations among integrated partners, which eliminated trade barriers. It reduces the likelihood for a regional economy to be hit by an unanticipated implementation of trade barriers. It positively contributes to economic stability in the region.

After an extensive overview of theoretical IIT underpinnings, Brodzicki (2016b) concludes that the structure of IIT and its directions are highly unpredictable. The question why the particular region is engaged in the IIT is even more difficult to answer. Regions are different, and their foreign trade profiles are different, described by geographical, product patterns, trade intensity per capita etc. Regions’ IIT overall intensity inequalities, may stem from specific IIT intensity of particular products groups. However, concrete outcome results from a combination of industry-specific and regional-specific factors. Different IIT intensity of regions’ trade may reflect industry branches’ specific capability to generate IIT. Some industries generate higher IIT, in others IIT intensity is lower, or even H-O type of trade dominates.

1.7 Demand-side related theories

In the standard model of international trade, demand-side of the market is ("sooner or later") introduced. Offer curves (or reciprocal supply/demand curves) illustrate market equilibrium: the quantity offered and demanded by trade partners. If regions are treated as SOEs, reciprocal demand curves could have some usefulness. Originating from international economics literature, they draw our attention to the question of demand. If for instance, indifference maps can be created not only for an individual customer but also for nations (as it is done in international economics literature), they could also be constructed for regions.

Linder's (Linder, 1961) concept of preference similarity is used in international economics as a useful instrument for interpretations of trade in industrial goods. It does not pretend to be a comprehensive theory of international trade, because it, in fact, ignores the supply side of the market, therefore depressing the significance of factor endowment. The main prediction of the Linder (1961) model is that in countries with a similar demand, the same (or similar) industries will develop. The so-called representative demand appears, and it stimulates trade between countries. Producers seek the market, in which they can satisfy demand, which resembles the one they know from their domestic market. Therefore, the similarity in the structure of demand positively contributes to trade intensity. GDP per capita was suggested by Burenstam-Linder as a proxy of demand preference similarity. If markets are similar, the so-called transfer costs associated with expansion to these markets can be reduced (for instance, the scope of necessary products' adaptation is lower).

Brodzicki and Umiński (2017) indicate that preferences similarity concept in region-country framework is related to gravity. The distance between the trading partners shall, therefore, be understood more broadly. Not only in terms of distance stemming from the structure of demand but also in terms of many other factors that reduce demand (i.e. cultural, linguistic, institutional, legal differences, etc.). According to the gravity concept used in international economics, they all can be responsible for "missing trade".

Among demand-related theories, also Armington (1969) type preferences shall be mentioned (already presented in the section on factor endowment).

1.8 Region as small open economy interpretations

The region as an SOE concept has also been used for interpretations of the relation between the regional and the world economy by Llop and Manresa (2007), focused on exports and foreign trade multiplier for Catalonia. The study of the Karela region in India (Harilal and Joseph, 2003) proves that any analysis must take into account that a region is a part of a world economy and is subject to its rules. Also, for India, Barua and Sawhney (2015) conclude that more impoverished regions gained in income growth from greater openness; however, the gains were not significant enough to offset the increasing regional disparities. For the Catalan economy, (Llop and Manresa, 2007) pay attention to multiplier effects, including the foreign-oriented sector of the regional economy.

The SOE concept of a region supplements various spheres, through which a region can be perceived, which according to Tomaszewski (2007) are: legal, geographic, economic, societal, ethnic and politological. These spheres affect the way in which a region functions within the global economy. The econometric models that search for countries' and regions' foreign trade determinants (Kepaptsoglou, Karlaftis, and Tsamboulas, 2010) prove how many factors exert an effect on the intensity and patterns of trade relations, including specific variables from the spheres listed by Tomaszewski (2007). However, Tomaszewski (2007) does not mention the role of region as an exporter. The concept of a region as an exporter is rarely mentioned in the literature in an explicit way. It has, however, been noticed by Florida (1995) that the most important linkages of regions are the ones with the global economy – not with host nations. According to Florida (1995), regions create effective points of entry into the global economy, and their characteristics differ. Domański (2013) underlines that each region has its individual, economic profile. The concept of a profile accommodates a wide variety of structural characteristics that in an empirical way are used to make the assessments of regions' competitiveness, investment attractiveness or any other inquiries, including the analysis of foreign trade relations.

The administrative sphere in which a region is placed shall be recalled here. According to Głąbicka and Grewiński (2005), a region is defined as an inseparable part, in cultural, societal and economic spheres. However, this administrative division may not have been done optimally, meaning that some parts of a region may have traditionally been strongly linked to the neighbouring regions. This problem has also been presented by Krugman and Venables (1995) with reference to the seamless world concept, in which international spatial specialisation evolves in a natural way.

Umiński (2012) distinguishes two main aspects of a region's participation in the international economic processes. In the first one, a region is perceived as being dependent on the international processes, such as exports, imports, capital transfers, migration of people. A region is thus a recipient of processes occurring in the international environment. The changes in the business cycles trends, economic and technological shocks affect the regional economy. These changes are finally reflected in the situation on the regional labour market; however, these are also within-regional factors that influence the labour market trends. In the second one, a region is perceived as able to influence the international markets, which obviously is an attribute of competitive, core regions from competitive countries. They are hosts for transnational corporations and are the source of lobbying that influences other economic agents. If such a region hosts large importers, their monopsonist position may affect the demand on the world market and the prices thereof.

A region can influence the international economic environment, especially if its size is relatively big. In the particular segments of the market or niche products, this influence can be substantial, even if a region's size is not that big. That is a case of highly specialised exporting firms, located for instance in the coastal areas, producing maritime transport equipment.

Referring to foreign trade policy, enterprises from such a strong region may initialise the antidumping procedures or disseminate new technologies or innovative solutions. Umiński (2012) concludes that each economic process does not take place in an undefined space, but rather in concrete locations. Interpreting it in the context of international economics, a transaction that is registered as the one occurring between countries occurs between specific places (or regions). It occurs between firms (economic agents), located in particular locations, performing various functions, which makes it difficult to unequivocally determine where the "export journey" begins. It can be the place in which the product has been manufactured, or substantially modified; or a place from which the shipment to foreign market begins; or alternatively a place in which the decision-making functions are performed, decisive for a firm's ability to export (Brodzicki and Umiński, 2017; Coughlin and Mandelbaum, 1991; Coughlin and Pollard, 2001; Coughlin and Wall, 2003; US Department of Commerce, 2013).

1.9 Heterogeneity of regions and firms

As already noticed, the role of a region as an exporter is relatively new. It has developed and strengthened with the increasing globalisation, deeply embracing various aspects of the regions' economies. Regions' heterogeneity thus gained a new dimension, so far neglected, which is the sphere of foreign trade. The recognition of this heterogeneity resulted in a spectrum of possible studies that, with the use of the international economics apparatus, assess the export performance of regions. Those inquiries are a part of the regional competitiveness assessments. However, also more focused and in-depth analysis is possible, for instance, related to the IIT. In section 7, we present selected aspects of this heterogeneity, referring to the structural characteristics of Poland's and Spain's NUTS 2 regions as well as the observed trends thereof.

The increasing globalisation has revealed the uneven competitiveness of regions. The highly competitive ones, hosting the most dynamic and productive firms, are those predesignated to get the most benefits from functioning within the open economy. It means that globalisation may increase already existing inequalities in regional development. Much depends, however, on the firms' and regions' characteristics. According to the heterogeneity concept by Melitz (2003), only the most productive firms become exporters; both theoretical and empirical literature shows a widespread consensus on it. It has been expected that the learning by exporting effect also exists, meaning that once a firm becomes an exporter, its productivity increases further – but it has not been proved in most of the research conducted. At the regional level of the inquiry, other mechanisms can be identified that increase regional inequality. Firms tend to agglomerate, meaning that the presence of an exporting firm in the region attracts other firms, including exporters. This effect has been well documented in the theoretical literature within NEG and NNEG. Exporters tend to agglomerate because of the learning, sharing and matching effects. They reduce the costs associated with exporting as well as decrease the risk of expansion on foreign markets. Baldwin and Okubo (2006) have identified the sorting and selecting effects. Accordingly, the most productive firms locate in the most competitive regions, which – as already mentioned – increases the already existent regional inequalities.

According to Florida (1995, p. 531), regions "can be distinguished by the level and extent of their insertion in the international economy and by their willingness to participate in global trade". While it is generally acknowledged that presence of exporting firms in a region brings positive consequences and proves a region's high competitiveness (understood as an ability to sell and to export), the question can be asked if there is a maximum level of openness, that can be regarded as "safe" for the region's economy. In fact, openness brings both positive and negative effects. Too much openness may cause instability and may result in the volatility in the economic situation of the region (Baldwin and Brown, 2004; Brodzicki, 2017b; Coulombe, 2007; Cronovich and Gazel, 1998; Hirose and Yoshida, 2018; Leichenko and Silva, 2004; Paluzie, Pons, and Tirado, 2001; Rodríguez-Pose, Tselios, Winkler, and Farole, 2013).

These negative consequences usually stem from a crisis (such as the one from 2008 and the following years) and from the strategies of the multinational enterprises, whose production relocations processes influence regions' economy in a severe way. For instance, for southern areas of Poland (Śląskie and Dolnośląskie), heavily dependent on exports on the FOEs' activity (predominantly in the automobile industry), the 2008 crisis has revealed the necessity to diversify the structure of production and exports, in terms of structural and geographical patterns, and also in terms of ownership. The question if openness brings stability or rather volatility to the regional economy, and its labour market, in particular, is also frequently asked by the authorities responsible for regional development policy.

There are several interesting aspects of the regions' heterogeneity that shall be mentioned. For instance, changes in the foreign trade policy instruments (incl. alterations in customs tariffs) and effective protection have a heterogeneous effect on regions, once their export and import structures differ. Fluctuations of the exchange rate of a national currency vs EUR or USD (Poland is not a member of the eurozone) are expected to have heterogeneous effects on regions' situations, depending on their export and import geographical structure and – which is most important – trade balance.

Once regions function in an open economy and the scope of their openness differs, any economic shock that happens in the global markets is likely to exert heterogeneous effects on regions' economies. Given regions' different structures of production, innovativeness capacity, productivity, product and geographical structure of exports as well as its technological advancement, regions display heterogeneous sensitivity to globalisation (OIR, 2011). The 2008 crisis and its consequences have clearly shown the pros and cons for regions of being strongly linked to global markets. Regions' competitiveness differs. Adaptive capacity is essential since it facilitates adjustments of regional economies to the changing global situation and the alterations stemming from the activity of MNEs.

Factors that influence regions' economic situation not only belong to the sphere of economics but also politics. The global situation has become highly unpredictable and uncertain. Shift of the position of the of US vs. China as the leading power in the global economy, the increasing competitiveness of the Indian economy, the uncertainty about the future of the integration processes within the European Union and the consequences of Brexit (if it will materialise at all), trade wars (that prove the rebirth of protectionism) and possible currency wars, a shift from multilateralism to bilateralism in global trade and investment arrangements – are the main factors contributing to the increasing uncertainty that already has and will have effects on regions' open economies. It makes a region's economies adaptive capacity an important category that facilitates structural adjustments to shocks and mitigates the consequences of sensitivity and vulnerability.

1.10 The principle of subsidiarity

An interesting perspective and theoretical background for the analysis of exports at the regional level is provided by the principle of subsidiarity, which became a part of the EU's acquis communautaire. In its profound meaning, it relates to the delegation of decision-making rights, which can also be used in the interpretations of exports and exports promotion in particular. According to Delsol (1993), subsidiarity refers to socio-political order, in which competences or prerogatives are preliminarily assigned to the social actors. Only if they turn to be inefficient or ineffective, the necessary action shall be taken by higher-level agents/institutions. These can be regional or national bodies. Once they prove to be ineffective, the EU level involvement can be justified. It is an example of the down-top transfer of competences. In the case of exports, we rather think of a top-down approach, in which for instance, promotion of exports – traditionally performed at country level – is transposed to regional agents. According to the principle of subsidiarity, exports promotion at the regional level can be more productive. Agency/institution responsible for promotion is "closer" to the firms, which need assistance. Therefore, their needs can be better inquired and assisted. According to the UE legislation, commercial policy belongs to the exclusive competences domain of the EU's institutions; however, the export promotion rules have not been harmonised in practice, and member states (MS) have much freedom in the way how intensively and in which form exports is promoted, at country or region level.

Subsidiarity is often understood as a tool to improve social structures and procedures. Practically, what matters in the light of our divagations is the effectiveness of exports promotion. Any existing bottlenecks in a region's exports can more easily be identified by a regional promotion agency, which is "closer" to the problems of local firms. Regional vs national promotional agents/agencies could have different priorities regarding exports promotion. A region could reveal a particular pattern of export links. For instance, Pomorskie region in Poland shows intensive trade relations with non-EU countries, many of which represent relatively small markets, from the perspective of the whole country's trade relations. However, Pomorskie has revealed distinctive comparative advantages, which from the perspective of the region's exporters, shall be promoted and strengthened.

Moreover, the promotion of a region's exports needs to be a part of a broader, regional, general economic policy scheme, of which smart specialisation and regional innovation strategies are the key elements (section 12 deals with the issue of smart specialisation). As stems from the firms' heterogeneity concept, well documented in the theoretical and empirical research, there is a clear nexus between innovativeness, productivity and export performance. However, it is not clearly reflected in smart specialisation strategies.

The subsidiarity principle assumes that the problems shall be solved as close to the citizen as possible. Translating it to the exporting activity, decision and actions shall be taken as closely as possible to the level that they apply to. It also relates to the promotion of a region as an attractive place for FDI. FOEs are expected to benefit from the advantages possessed by the foreign owner, which often represents the MNE. It is generally acknowledged in the literature that FOEs have higher productivity, compared to indigenous firms, which translates into higher exports (Helpman, Melitz, and Yeaple, 2004).

1.11 Foreign direct investment

Openness has many faces. Several channels can be listed through which the impulses from the global economy are transmitted to the regional one. These are foreign trade, migrations, technology transfer and last but not least global value chains (Abreu, Groot, & Florax, 2004; Bentivogli, Ferraresi, Monti, Paniccià, and Rosignoli, 2018). Processes occurring within each of these channels are highly interrelated. The literature relevant to analyse each of the channels is enormous, allowing thorough interpretations, especially if one applies the SOE concept.

A critical channel is FDI. FOEs contribution to exports varies among countries and their regions. Their share in particular regions' exports can be very high. The inflow of FDI, and FOEs activity thereof, significantly determines the dynamics of many regions' exports and imports, as well as their product and geographical patterns. The inclusion of FDI theory in the analysis of a region's foreign trade activity seems crucial. Processes observed in a region's trade often turn out to be better explainable and understood, if FDI-related theories are used, and statistical data on FDI's role is included on the list of the independent variables. FOEs' crucial role in trade is especially visible in transition or post-transition countries, in which economic growth and transition process have been financed, to a large extent, from foreign savings.

Mayer and Ottaviano (2008) show FOEs' higher inclination to engage in international transactions vs domestic firms. Through externalities, FOEs exert influence on indigenous firms, also positively contributing to their performance (although a negative impact can also occur). The multidimensional character of FOEs shall be recollected, which is essential in the formulation of expectations and conclusions related to FDI presence in regions' economies. Forsgren (2008) describes the multinational firm as a "beauty and a beast", stating that there are many conflicting views on its nature. He defines the functions that can be assigned to multinational firms. They are dominators, having serious market power. They also perform the coordination role, with a focus on cost efficiency, possible through internalisation. Multinationals can be regarded as knowing firms, taking part in the knowledge creation and exchange process. They also serve as designers and networkers, engaged in creating business networks. Multinationals also perform a politicising role.

According to the classical view on FDI by Dunning and Lundan (2008), FOEs possess ownership advantages, which is one of the components of the OLI paradigm (Ownership, Location and Internalisation). The ownership-specific advantage stems not only from tangible assets as capital, natural resources endowment or workforce. It also embraces a package of intangibles, such as technological capabilities, marketing and managerial skills and favourable access to intermediate goods. Also, another component of the OLI paradigm deserves attention, which is internalisation, which usually embraces economic activity dispersed among many parts of the MNE, localised in various nations (production fragmentation). It contributes to a region's IIT, as already mentioned.

Although it was stated that at a regional level, the significant positive inflow of FOEs on exports and imports is identified, the nexus between FDI and trade, in theory, is not that obvious. Complementarity or substitution between trade and FDI is frequently discussed in the literature. If the purpose of FDI is to "jump" over tariffs, the indigenous market of the country in which investment was made is the target, and FDI substitutes trade (Blomström, Globerman, and Kokko, 2002). On the other hand, Helpman (1984) and Helpman, E. and Krugman, P. R. (1985) predict FDI to be complementary to trade if there are significant differences between countries in terms of factors endowment. FOEs make use of their ability to internalise the market and draw benefit from different locations' advantages. For instance, labour-intensive activity (part of the value-added creation chain) is located in labour abounded countries/

regions, capital intensive in capital ones, etc. It creates trade (IIT in particular), as the final product embraces components coming from many locations.

In proximity-concentration models, firms invest abroad in order to avoid trade costs. From the fact of being close to the market, that is served, proximity benefits occur. This results in the establishment of FDIs. On the other hand, avoidance of duplicating fixed costs (associated with plants located in many countries), encourages a firm to concentrate production in one (or in few) countries/locations. Concentration benefits arise, which creates exports; however, FDI is not done (or is done at a smaller scale). Therefore, if concentration advantages dominate over proximity advantages, trade substitutes FDI (Brainard, S., Lael, 1993; Markusen, 1984).

Also, the motives of investment done in foreign markets matter. FOEs can be looking for the resources, market efficiency or strategic assets and capabilities (Behrman, Jack, N., 1972; Dunning and Lundan, 2008; Iammarino and McCann, 2013; Jensen, 2002). The consequence of the different motives driving foreign investment activity can be that even if an investor possesses ownership advantages, they do not necessarily translate into higher exports.

From the point of view of research on the region's exports nature, the character and the size of the export premium that FOEs have over non-FOEs – matters. The premium can be measured, for instance, as the propensity to export (the likelihood that a firm becomes an exporter), export intensity (exports share in total sales) or, for instance, the intensity of IIT. A FOE can rely on its ownership advantages that it possesses over the indigenous companies in a host country. They manifest in higher productivity (Antras and Yeaple, 2014), which, according to heterogeneity theory, increases the probability of exporting. As regards export intensity, the influence of foreign ownership has not been clearly identified empirically. Dunning and Lundan (2008, pp. 493–495) performed an extensive inquiry of the empirical research on the differences between FOEs and their indigenous counterparts, regarding export intensity, covering publications for the period 1958-2006, for both developing and developed countries. Accordingly, definite conclusions cannot be formulated due to the methodological differences between the studies inquired. Much depends on the combination of particular motives that drive FOE's activity and the structure of the given OLI (Dunning and Lundan, 2008; Estrin, Meyer, Wright, and Foliano, 2008; Forsgren, 2008).

1.12 FDI early theories reinterpreted

Stephen Hymer's (1960/1976) doctoral dissertation is regarded as a pioneering contribution to the theory of FDI. It showed the differences between portfolio and direct foreign investment, by focusing on the specific ownership advantages, possessed by a multinational firm. It is Hymer, who pointed out that FDI is not only capital being transferred through investment done in another country, but a group of resources, including entrepreneurship, technology, marketing, skills etc.

The thorough interpretation of Hymer's contribution to the understanding of location choices was provided by Iammarino and McCann (2013). According to Hymer's law of increasing firm size, as the company develops and transforms into the multinational enterprise, a pyramidal structure evolves, with three different levels of hierarchy. The lowest level is production; the higher one is an intermediary, performing control and coordination. The highest one performs top-level management and makes strategic decisions. According to the "correspondence principle", the hierarchical structure of multinational enterprise translates into the hierarchy of locations (Iammarino and McCann, 2013). The highest level of the hierarchy is located in global cities. The lowest one remains relatively evenly spread among locations, reflecting their attractiveness (described by resources offered, like labour, raw materials, etc.). The intermediary level is clustered around big cities, providing sufficient communication networks and qualified labour (Hymer, 1972).

Hymer's "correspondence principle" shows that FOEs activity contributes to uneven regional development. By "assigning" different roles to the locations, the interesting interplay between industrial and regional structures is developed by the FOEs. One of these roles is production, dedicated to export markets, making a particular location an exporter.

Another "early" theory of multinational enterprises that can be useful in the analysis of a region's exports is the product life cycle (PLC) by Richard Vernon. It shall be reviewed jointly with the comparative advantage concept (applied to regions). The PLC (Vernon, 1966) is one of the main concepts used in international economics. Referring to the microeconomic perspective, acknowledging market imperfections, Vernon sees innovation-related advantages as a result of technological gaps. At each of the stages of the life cycle that a product "passes" through, specific assets are needed. For instance, when an innovative product is born, it is sold on the domestic market, offering high demand, large enough to cover high production costs associated with risky, innovative production. Production is not yet performed at a larger scale that would enable economies of scale to occur. When exports arise, products are directed to similar countries, representing comparable demand conditions. In the second stage, FDI is done with the purpose to serve the local markets directly. In the standardisation stage, production is moved to low labour costs countries, and the home market is supplied through imports. PLC theory links multinational enterprise activity with particular locations through a hierarchy of requirements stemming from the ownership advantages. For instance, in the first stage of the PLC, production is performed in locations that are metropolises in the most developed countries. Innovations are generated in such places. A variety of available resources (mainly human capital and the required business services) in these locations reflects what has previously been performed within (internally) the company. As the product cycle progresses, production is moved from the initial agglomeration (metropolis) and spreads to similar location in terms of demand conditions. In the standardisation (mature) stage, intense price competition and high demand for low-skilled labour, shift production to locations in the developing countries. Iammarino and McCann (2013) present possible criticism of the nexus between PLC and regional (or urban) analysis. Accordingly, innovation shall not be treated in a simplified way, as being linear. Secondly, internal (firm-level) and external circumstances reach beyond cost activity dimension of multinational firm activity. Especially if one acknowledges many possible "configurations" of MNEs functions (Forsgren, 2008) and motives (Lall and Mohammad, 2007), the specific allocation of a FOE's activity to particular locations is far from being easily predictable.

1.13 Technological dimension of FDI – a regional point of view

Both the PLC and internalisation concepts have been criticised by Cantwell (1995), who formulated an international production theory, linked to innovations and technological accumulation. Cantwell extended the theory of FDI to accommodate new elements, related to agglomeration processes and clustering of the economic activity. He also paid attention to a regional dimension of FOEs' activity, as well as to the dynamic aspects of technology and knowledge accumulation that constitute the comparative advantage. According to Cantwell and Piscitello (1999), transnational corporations tend to disperse technological competencies across locations to draw competencies from alternative locations. Locations differ, for instance, in terms of institutional settings. The authors point of view on the changes that happened within the largest MNEs underlines their role as "networkers". Cantwell and Iammarino (2010) assessed the character of linkages of the UK regions with other locations in and outside the UE that are established by the MNEs. The authors proved that there is a conformity between the technological pattern of specialisation of FOEs affiliates and regions' position in the host country "locational hierarchy".

Cantwell and Iammarino (2001) showed the character of interactions between local and global processes. The activity of FOEs in the host countries results in the increased regional inequalities. The "first rank" regions' position is improved, while the less attractive (less competitive) regions are marginalised. The activity of MNEs creates chances that can be utilised by host country regions (by their firms). It implies, for instance, a possibility to cooperate and to become a part of international production (or value-added) networks. Regions with the most advanced technological profiles are able to become part of the technological cooperation networks. Spillover effects stemming from the activity of the FOEs are determined by the character of the host region, its technological position and industrial structure. Processes of technology accumulation by FOEs – propellered by cumulative causation – lead to increased regional inequalities. Moreover, as stipulated by Cantwell, they are limited to the concrete, competitive locations.

If the technological dimension of FOEs activity is taken into account together with the regional context, a region can be a part of a global network in which skills and competencies are exchanged. It shows that competencies originating from a particular location – through FOEs operations and coordination – can be used in other places. The combination of a region's characteristics with a FOE's ones gives a large number of idiosyncratic interactions that are dynamic. These interactions shall be perceived as having a location-specific context. We do not refer to the gravity concept here (please refer to section 8), and NEG (sections 1.14 and 2.3).

1.14 NEG – an integrating theoretical concept

As regards the interpretations of the relations between the global and regional economies, much help comes from NEG, which synthesises location theory with international trade theory into a comprehensive, universal analytical tool (Cieślik, 2005, p. 124). NEG perfectly suits the analysis of foreign trade performed at the regional level, as it tackles the mechanics of agglomeration processes. It is particularly useful for the interpretations of the agglomeration of exporters and exports (in terms of volume) in the metropolitan areas and in the regions located close to the most important export markets (due to lower trade costs). Venables and Krugman's (1990) reference to NEG has shown the consequences of the establishment of the EU internal market for the reallocations of economic activity in the EU. The concentration in the core regions has deteriorated the position of the peripheral regions, from which many firms were "washed back". Brakman, Garretsen, Gorter, van der Horst, and Schramm (2005) show the risk for the peripheral regions to hold on to the economic activity. Moreover, large infrastructural projects financed by the EU structural funds can have an adverse impact on peripheral regions, as they can be more easily serviced from the core ones. Krugman and Elizondo (1996) for Mexico and Tomiura (2003) for Japan show an interesting effect of dispersion of economic activity due to increasing imports, in a situation of initially highly regionally concentrated industrial structure. The increasing import penetration alters the already existing cooperative links and leads to spatial de-concentration of economic activity. The above-given examples of the empirical research show how difficult it is to predict the actual trends in the distribution of the economic activity and foreign trade (Gil, Llorca, and Serrano, 2008) in space. Much criticism has been formulated against NEG by geographers (Martin, 1999a).

Over the years, the NEG has evolved and shifted from the macro-heterogeneity (Ottaviano, 2011) of locations, to micro-heterogeneity of firms, once the Melitz heterogeneity concept has become the fundament for the international trade analysis. An example of empirical research is provided by Forslid and Okubo (2018) for the 49 Japanese prefectures, who have inquired the trade liberalisation effects, showing the concentration of the most productive multiproduct firms in the large markets. The frontiers of NEG have been presented by Fujita and Mori (2005), one of the theoretical frontiers being multi-unit firms and spatial fragmentation (Fujita and Gokan, 2005; Fujita and Thisse, 2006).

The evolution of NEG into new-NEG that embraces more of the micro-heterogeneous aspects related to firms' performance shows how complex relations between the region and the global economy are. They are determined by the agglomeration forces, changing trade costs and last but not least by firms' productivity. Trade activity that we focus on is not the only, but definitely the most important channel that links the regional and global economies. Trade activity is the one in which regional and firms' heterogeneities meet, which makes the region's exports worth a serious inquiry. In the above paragraphs, NEG has only been signalled. It is interpreted in a thorough way in part 2.3.

Tomasz Brodzicki

2 The role of openness in the economic growth of regions

2.1 The perspective of economic growth theory

The extent of openness understood as the level of integration with the global economy is one of the so-called deep determinants of economic growth. The nexus between openness and economic growth is complex, and the issue gets even more complicated if we acknowledge the existence of heterogeneous regions within the body of the nation-state. The flows of goods, services as well as production factors or technology thus happens within a given region (intraregional), between regions of a given state (interregional) and last but not least internationally. The last dimension is obviously of principal significance.

The traditional growth theory is applied to the level of nations. However, regions can be treated as SOEs. In his seminal paper, North (1955) pointed to "*A fundamental difficulty ... that the theory of regional economic growth had little relevance for the development of regions*". A spatial approach of the main branch of models being a major disadvantage. At the same time, authors pointed that for instance the concept of the regional export base has significance but is only one of the large number of determinants of regional economic growth that should be investigated (Tiebout, 1956).

The emergence of NEG models, especially of dynamic type (incorporating the evolution of the economic system over time and space), allowed some progress to be made – in particular incorporating the spatial perspective; however, in highly simplified systems. The most recent development is the inclusion of firm heterogeneity.

2.2 The role of openness in economic growth theory

The nexus between openness and economic growth is one of the most important areas of academic analysis both on the theoretical and empirical front. The issue has been and still is addressed by various fields of inquiry such as classical and new growth theory, international economics or economic geography, and finally NEG.

In the neoclassical growth theory (Solow, 1956; Swan, 1956) openness does not matter in the long-run as growth is independent of economic policy. It can only lead to the so-called level effect just affecting the level of the real GDP per capita in the steady-state and not the growth rate. In the short-run, capital deepening is the major source of growth as income per capita is directly proportional to the level of capital per capita. The level of real GDP per capita in the steady-state is a positive function of the rate of saving (and thus investment rate) and a negative function of the population growth rate and depreciation of capital. The technological progress of exogenous character affects the level positively. The only factor affecting the long-run growth rate is the rate of exogenous technological progress. Namely, it is equal to the rate of technological progress. In this setting, the impact of an increase in the extent of openness due, for instance, to changes in trade policy on economic growth is only temporary. Neoclassical growth theory predicts, furthermore, that regions will converge in the long run under the assumption of perfect competition (absolute β convergence or the catching-up level).

In an augmented model of Mankiw, Romer, and Weil (1992), human capital accumulation and the human capital endowment are considered, additionally. The model can better explain the observed variation in the level of economic development. It does not, however, modify the prior conclusions. The augmented neoclassical model by Brodzicki (2015) takes further the impact of infrastructure into account. In the model, following Mincerian tradition, the average level of education may be specified as a function of average years of schooling and average years of experience Bils and Klenow (2000).

Camacho, Carmen, and Zou (2004) proposed a spatial version of the Solow model in continuous time and space. With a standard neoclassical production function, the steady-state exists, and convergence gradually takes place. If one assumes homogeneity of space, then at the steady-state, all locations have the same level of physical capital. However, if spatial heterogeneity is introduced at the level of the technology or savings rate, regional differences persist, and there is no convergence.

The emergence of the endogenous growth and new trade theories (Aghion and Howitt, 1990, 1998; Lucas, 1988; Romer, 1986, 1990) has led to the reopening of the debate on the role of trade and more general the degree of openness in determining economic growth in the medium and long-term. The models of the first and second generation endogenised the rate of growth of technology either by allowing for the impact of human capital or introducing a separate R&D sector purposefully producing knowledge in the form of patents. It is worth pointing out, however, that even in a semi-endogenous model of Ben-David and Loewy (2002), openness to trade through its impact on the process of accumulation of knowledge and technology transfer (knowledge diffusion) leads to endogenisation of the economic growth process.

The new growth theory models of Rivera-Batiz and Romer (1991) or Grossman and Helpman (1995) lead to different policy conclusions. A policy shift leading to a greater extent of openness (such as trade liberalisation), creates a permanent effect – the long-run growth rate is affected but not only positively, an adverse impact is also possible. In brief, the balance of costs and benefits of greater openness (liberalisation) depends on the nature and the exact product structure of trade – in other words, it's not merely related to the intensity of trade but also its composition (what exactly a given region produces, exports and imports).

Greater openness to trade affects the rate of accumulation of knowledge, mostly through imports. They work as a channel allowing absorption of more advanced knowledge positively affecting the overall efficiency and thus the growth rate. Rivera-Batiz and Romer (1991) show, however, that whether the effect is positive or adverse depends on the distance of economy from the global technology frontier (GTF) and the nature of diffusion of knowledge (perfect versus imperfect). Imperfect knowledge flows, coupled with openness can harm underdeveloped states or lagging regions.

Barro and Sala-i-Martin (2004) or Aghion and Howitt (2009) emphasize the role of technology diffusion in both absolute (the catching up effect) and conditional beta-convergence. It is mostly because imitation and implementation of innovation are cheaper than initial innovation. Imitation and adaptation still entail substantial costs which can be however lowered through more intense trade (mostly imports) or superior human capital and skills base. Nelson and Phelps (1966) stress that followers tend to grow faster; the greater is the initial gap from the leader. The gap diminishes over time, and thus the followers' growth rates tend to decrease alongside. In the steady-state, the leader and the follower grow at the same rate. Nelson and Phelps (1966) argue that education could positively affect the speed of adoption of new technologies. They distinguished the theoretical (potential) level of knowledge from the prevailing (existing) level of technology.

Benhabib and Spiegel (1994) extended the original model by adding an extra innovation term that controls for the impact of own capacity to develop knowledge on top of the ability to absorb external knowledge. Abreu et al. (2004) further accounted for potential spatial dependencies between bordering economies. Ciołek and Brodzicki (2017) in their empirical model, extend it even further by including two potential channels for technology diffusion through imports and FDI inflows and testing it for Polish regions. The two aforementioned channels find support in many empirical studies.

In their seminal study, Coe and Helpman (1995) studied the impact of trade on technology diffusion and found that international R&D spillovers were related to imports and in particular to the composition of imports. Furthermore, a strong correlation between R&D embodied in (bilateral) trade flows and total factor productivity (TFP) growth was identified. Coe, Helpman, and Hoffmaister (1997) endorsed the impact of domestic and foreign R&D capital stocks on the TFP even after controlling for human capital. They extended the analysis by the inclusion of institutional variables, allowing for parameter heterogeneity based on institutional characteristics. The results suggested that institutional differences were significant determinants of TFP, and they had an impact on the degree of R&D spillovers. In the context of the second channel considered, Hejazji and Safarian (1999) identified significant R&D spillovers through FDI from the largest industrial countries to smaller OECD Member States. Xu (2000), in contrast, found that the technology transfer of US multinationals contributed to productivity growth but only in the group of developed economies.

According to Keller (2002), for most countries, foreign sources of technology are crucial (they account for 90% or more) in productivity growth. They are, at the same time, more valuable for small and relatively poorer countries. It could be related to the significance of the variation in domestic R&D investments. There is no indication that the process of international diffusion, and thus learning is inevitable, simple, or automatic. Imports are the primary channel of international technology diffusion with no indication of learning-by-exporting effects. FDI effects are, however, present, but the impact is highly asymmetric. Keller (2004) points out that technological knowledge spillovers appear to be resulting from a deliberate commitment to learning and matching international performance standards through ongoing interactions with foreigners. At the same time, local efforts seem to be necessary for successful technology adoption.

It could, therefore, mean that technology diffusion is not only spatially bounded but also not-universal. The follower must have a minimum level of endowments in order to be able to absorb technology. Technological change can thus be skill-based which could lead to technology-skill mismatch and thus non-convergence in the TFP levels (Acemoglu and Zilibotti, 2001).

Eaton and Kortum (2001) constructed in turn a model of innovation, growth, and trade with technology spillovers which pointed to convergence in income levels. The benefits of the larger market can be exploited by an innovator through exports. However, the innovator, in an open economy, must compete not only with domestic rivals but also with imported technologies. These are two offsetting forces. If they offset completely, only static gains from trade arise with no dynamic gains through technology accumulation. Decreased barriers to trade stimulate research activity characterized by the presence of scale effects. Real wages depend on the productivity of workers but also the size of the population. In the extreme case of autarky, relative real wages in the model depend on relative labour forces weighted by research productivity. Decreasing barriers to trade, however, benefit smaller economies to a large extent. On the other extreme, with zero gravity (a costless trade), relative real wages depend solely on relative research productivity with the size of the economy playing no significant role.

In an extension, Eaton and Kortum (2002), construct a Ricardian model accounting for realistic geographic features where bilateral trade is a function of absolute advantages, trade-promoting comparative advantages, and trade-resisting geographic barriers. The concept of trade gravity is thus fully integrated and accounted for.

Howitt (2000) in a multi-country endogenous Schumpeterian growth model, shows that due to technology diffusion, only R&D-performing countries grow in the long run and converge to similar growth paths, while non-R&D-performing countries stagnate. In this framework, an increase in the investment rate or the R&D-subsidy rate in any R&D-producing country can increase the overall growth rate. In an extension, Aghion, Howitt, and Mayer-Foulkes (2005) attribute the emergence of convergence clubs in income to R&D potential and knowledge diffusion. In their stylized model, countries sort themselves into three groups: members of the highest group converge to a steady-state where they perform leading-edge R&D (at the GTF), while the intermediate group converges to a steady-state where they only implement technologies developed elsewhere. High and intermediate group countries share the same growth rates in the long run as a result of technology diffusion; nonetheless, inequality between them in terms of development levels, increases. Economies of the lowest group grow at a slower rate and are unable to converge due to their inability to absorb knowledge from the GTF. In this set-up, the initial distance to the technological frontier matters and countries lagging by a significant distance can be entrapped. This model can be easily adapted to the regional context with innovative regions, catching-up regions, and lagging or falling behind regions.

It is also worth addressing the direction of causality between openness and economic growth. If openness affects growth than we deal with the so-called export-led growth (ELG) process through the channels described above. The term was introduced by Balassa (1978) and later investigated, among others by Marin (1992). Some theoretical work was conducted on the related concept of learning-by-exporting (Grossman and Helpman, 1995; Krugman, 1980b) or more recently at the firm level (Helpman, Melitz, and Yeaple, 2003; Melitz, 2003). The initial evidence was weak, and the general agreement to the existence of ELG is sometimes challenged (Dreger and Herzer, 2013).

On the other hand, the causality could be just the opposite – going from the growth to greater openness. Higher productivity in the larger domestic market (home marker effect, HME) could lead to greater international competitiveness and a subsequent increase in regional exports. At the same time, the demand for imports increases in the size of the regional economy. Thus, a bidirectional relationship is likely to exist if the processes described above hold simultaneously (Liu, Song, and Romilly, 1997).

It is worth stressing that in the new approach, Rodrik (2002) perceives openness or as he puts it the extent of integration as one of three deep fundamental determinants of economic growth alongside the quality of institutions and geographical conditions. Openness is treated here as a semi-endogenous factor shaped by purely exogenous geographical conditions (in particular of the first nature of geography) as well as institutional factors. Nonetheless, it, directly and indirectly, affects the shallow determinants of growth – related to the endowment of basic factors of production and the process of their accumulation as well as the overall productivity of the economic system.

Summing up, the initial literature review, from a theoretical standpoint, openness affects growth through several channels:

(a) first of all, it leads to the reallocation of factors of production to more productive sectors and thus to specialisation in accordance with the comparative or competitive advantage thus resources are allocated efficiently;

(b) it leads to increased diffusion and accelerated absorption of knowledge and technology (technology transfer) in particular through imports (Coe and Helpman, 1995) or inflow of FDI (Branstetter, 2006);
(c) it stimulates the rate of innovation as it is frequently associated with an increase in the expenditures on R&D;
(d) it allows better utilisation of scale economies and agglomeration externalities as a result of greater specialisation. At the same time, it leads to enhanced accumulation of factors of production;
(e) it stimulates competition in national and international markets, thus forcing companies to be more innovative.

2.3 The perspective of NEG

Further insight into the nexus linking openness to growth can be brought by the NEG literature. The NEG brought the issue of space into the mainstream economic theory. The seminal paper by Krugman (1991a) is generally regarded as the foundation of the NEG. It is an extension of the standard new trade theory model (Krugman, 1980a), allowing for interregional mobility of factors of production on top of the trade in final goods. Breinlich, Ottaviano, and Temple (2014) stress the fact that NEG theory is based on trade theory. Thus the relationship between external trade, internal economic geography, and regional disparities, is at its core. Fujita, Krugman, and Venables (2001) suggest that openness could work to disperse the manufacturing industry as a whole, but also lead to the spatial clustering of specific industries. External trade thus affects spatial patterns of activity and thus of trade by changing market access considerations (Hanson, 1996).

Incorporation of space into the theoretical framework and at the same endogenization of location choices requires moving beyond the neoclassical paradigm. It is crucial to reject the assumptions of the zero transport costs and allow for the presence of increasing returns to scale (both internal and external to a firm (plant)).

From a modelling point of view, NEG theories can be considered as an extension of new trade models allowing for simultaneous flows of goods as well as factors of production (capital and/or labour) and knowledge flows.

Fujita and Thisse (2004) state that there are three important assumptions in spatial modelling NEG:

(a) space is heterogeneous, which leads to the presence of comparative advantages in technology, natural resources, facilities or the presence of transport hubs or markets;
(b) externalities exist in both production and consumption – agglomeration forces arise from the bottom-up as a result of the non-market interactions between market agents - enterprises and households; classic Marshallian effects (Marshall, 1890; Marshall and Marshall, 1879) arise and specialisation

related to the snowball effect in the event of the concentration – we deal with external economies of scale and scope;

(c) markets are imperfectly competitive; thus firms are endowed with some degree of market power – shaping the price above marginal costs because of the utilisation of internal economies of scale; with respect to these two possibilities exist:
   - monopolistic competition – many companies, lack of strategic interaction, the product is diversified;
   - partial oligopolistic competition (few actors with similar market power, strong strategic interactions, the existence of the Nash equilibrium – game theory).

Combes, Mayer, and Thisse (2008) show that the choice of the above modelling strategy has significant implications for the results obtained. Approaches 1, 2, and 3a from the macro perspective bypass the role of individual companies. Approach 3b considers strategic interactions between agents. The first approach generates a solution that is socially efficient in the sense of Pareto, and the remaining models lead to socially inefficient solutions. Combes et al. (2008) state that the classic NEG model chooses the third approach, where location decisions become endogenous at the expense of assuming the homogeneity of space (thus omitting the first nature of geography).

The basic model of the NEG of Krugman (1991a, 1991b) with a typical core-periphery structure (CP) is based on the concept of the monopolistic competition of Dixit and Stiglitz (1997). NEG models focus on the relationships between three factors determining location decisions of market agents: agglomeration benefits, non-zero costs of transport, and interregional migration (Fujita et al., 2001; Fujita and Thisse, 2004).

The cost of transport (resistance to overcome space) is primarily a function of the distance between trading parties but may also be a function of institutional barriers.

A key feature of the NEG models is the endogenization of the location decisions, and thus endogenization of location and distribution of economic activity in space (Brakman, Garretsen, and Schramm, 2004; Brülhart, 2001). Endogeneity of the location decisions means that market players and households consciously decide on the selection of their location in order to maximize profits (firms) or their total utility (consumers) based on the information (including prices) generated by the market system.

The market structure in the NEG models gradually evolves in the spatial domain under the influence of such factors as the size of the economy of individual regions; the costs of transport; the scope of internal economies of scale associated with the size of the production in individual production plants; the scope of the external economies of scale related to the degree of concentration of economic activities in the different sectors (the classic Marshallian externalities); the presence of linkages (ascending and descending or forward/backward linkages) in value-added chains; the significance of HME; the intensity of competition in a market is a function of the number of firms and their size-distribution (market size and economies of scale, competitive effect) as well as the interaction between them (e.g. the existence of restrictive collusion or exclusionary competition).

The degree of spatial concentration or dispersion of economic activity depends on the balance between centripetal (pro-agglomerative) and centrifugal (pro-dispersal) forces. It is worth noting that various NEG models differ in the direction of the effect and the significance of particular forces. For instance, external economies of scale are a natural pro-agglomeration force leading both to the creation of within-sector concentrations of firms (industrial districts or clusters) or multi-sectoral agglomerations of firms or households (cities).

In the standard NEG model with monopolistic competition, we deal with a differentiated product, homogeneous companies specialize in the production of its specific varieties, firms pose a certain degree of market power, and the nature of competitive rivalry is thus imperfect. At the same time, the number of enterprises in the market is large enough to get rid of the problem of potential strategic interactions characteristic for oligopolistic models. The framework is quite often criticized for oversimplification, and some authors try to take account of the strategic interactions in the location decisions of agents, for example using the Cournot oligopoly model (Combes and Lafourcade, 2011).

In NEG models we typically deal with multiple equilibria of unstable or stable character (as evidenced by the so-called tomahawk diagrams). Several corner solutions are possible:

(a) the total concentration of production activities in one of the two regions concerned (catastrophic agglomeration);
(b) total dispersion of production activities (the symmetric layout, equal shares of both territorial units);
(c) intermediate asymmetric equilibria of typically unstable character.

Furthermore, in NEG models, short- and long-term equilibria can be distinguished. The long-term allows for structural changes in the economy and thus adjustment in the location of economic agents.

An important role in regional development processes plays a level of mutual openness (in other words, the degree of integration of the regional economy) which is by definition linked to the level of transport costs. The transport costs are typically modelled as the so-called ice-berg transport costs (Samuelson, 1954) in which transport costs linearly relate to distance, and they work by extracting from the arriving volume.

Transport costs reflect the specific resistance of space, leading to concentration or dispersion of production. Recent studies have proven the relationship between the level of transport costs and the degree of concentration of business to be non-monotonic and nonlinear having the shape of an inverted U (Ottaviano, 2008). High transport costs lead to the dispersion of economic activity. As transport costs fall to medium levels, we observed gradual concentration. If they fall further to low levels, dispersion of economic activity emerges once again.

The lowering of the cost of the exchange is the result of among others:
(a) technological progress through the use of more efficient means of transport, better organisation of logistic processes, etc.;
(b) utilisation of economies of scale in transport that leads to a decrease in the unit costs;
(c) improvement in the transport infrastructure leading to increased inaccessibility of the regions;
(d) reduction in the level of protection of the relevant market, and thus an increase in the level of mutual openness of the economies in the region.

In this framework, one can explore the impact of integration (asymmetric reduction in trade costs) on the location of economic activity. For example, Hanson (1994) examined the effects of a fundamental change of the trade policy regime in Mexico from protectionist to liberal in 1984, on the location of the processing industry within the country. In a relatively short time from trade liberalisation, it led to a significant contraction of the prior concentration of manufacturing industry around Mexico City (the so-called Mexico City manufacturing belt) which initial emergence was related to the implementation of the costly policy of import substitution. Liberalisation resulted in the relocation of production plants to the regions directly on the border with the US. We thus deal with interregional adjustment in location and production/export capacity within a single economy as a result of the shock – trade liberalisation.

The results of empirical studies indicate that the integration processes within the framework of the EU also affect the location of business activity – leading to an increase in the degree of spatial concentration of production activities (Amiti, 1999; Brülhart, 2011; Midelfart-Knarvik and Overman, 2002). The flow between the core and peripheral regions of the EU depends on the specific circumstances of each sector (including the intensity of economies of scale, dependence on transport costs, and the intensity of the backward and forward linkages) and we observe heterogeneity in this area. Furthermore, each new enlargement leads to an adjustment in the location decisions of firms and an adjustment in the structure of individual markets due to mergers and acquisitions. Brülhart (2001) believes that at the aggregated level, the core-peripheries system, characteristic for the European Union, seems to fade away gradually. Midelfart-Knarvik and Overman (2002) state that the equalisation-oriented structural policy of the EU has a significant impact on the location of economic activity, not necessarily leading to the efficiency of the block taken as a whole.

Models of NEG, aiming to resolve the problem of the analytical burden, typically assume the existence of two regions and two sectors (2 x 2). In reality, both the number of regions and sectors is significantly higher with multi-region and multisector framework. In reality, we are also dealing with the subset of multiproduct and multiplant firms (with dispersed activities).

Behrens, Lamorgese, Ottaviano, and Tabuchi (2004) point out that in the multi-regional system even the static location of companies is determined by mutually reinforcing spatial effects (accessibility) and non-spatial effects (attraction), which affects the overall distribution of demand in all the regions concerned (third-country/party effect). The economic potential of a specific region is a function of not only the size of the region but also its relative accessibility within the framework of the multi-regional system (hence the popularity of the market potential approach).

However, even the most advanced models of spatial equilibrium, for instance for France (Combes and Lafourcade, 2001, 2011), taking into account the problem of strategic interaction (Cournot competition) in the location decisions of agents, or Teixeira (2006) for Portugal, have a static character and thus ignore the problem of growth dynamics. NEG models trying to explain the evolution of the location of activities in space simply overlook the problem of the economic growth process.

Combes and Lafourcade (2011) state that they cannot tell whether France is close to a short- or long-run spatial equilibrium. They note that from a regional perspective, France is gradually moving from the system with one core (Ile de France – Paris) to a system with two cores – the other one emerging in the south-eastern part of the country.

These complex scenarios, including endogenous location choices and endogenous growth, are only possible in models combing static NEG with postulates or mechanisms characteristic for the previously described new growth theory, the so-called dynamic NEG models. This subset of models includes Fujita and Thisse (2006), Martin and Ottaviano (1996) or Baldwin and Forslid (1999; 2001).

Dynamic NEG models with endogenous growth assign a significant role to externalities arising from human capital accumulation or the broader concepts of knowledge. The externalities' effects are decreasing in the distance, which means that they are localized (Hanson, 2001). The same factors that determine the location of economic activity in the context of dynamic models of NEG are the same ones that are responsible for the endogenization of economic growth.

Baldwin et al. (2011) distinguish three types of dynamic NEG models. These are core-periphery models (CP); footloose entrepreneur models (FE); footloose capital models (FC).

The standard NEG model in the Dixit-Stiglitz-Krugman formula includes the following structure and set of assumptions:

(a) two regions – developed North (N) and the underdeveloped South (S);
(b) two sectors of the economy – agriculture (A) and the manufacturing industry (M);
(c) two factors of production – physical capital (K) and labour (L);
(d) one of the factors of production is mobile, and the second is immobile;
(e) A sector – Walrasian agricultural sector with perfect competition producing a homogeneous product with constant economies of scale;

(f) M sector – manufacturing sector producing n varieties of a differentiated product in the presence of increasing economies of scale within monopolistically competitive market;
(g) each of the varieties of the differentiated good is produced by another company which within this given variety possess market power – a monopolist rent, and thus sets prices above of marginal costs;
(h) firms are however homogeneous (representative firm model) or symmetric;
(i) preferences of firms and households are homogeneous;
(j) regions share the same level of technological sophistication.

A typical mainstream NEG model, a la Krugman (1991a, 1991b), is characterized by the following features:
(a) circular causality on the demand side (which offset production moves) and on the supply side (production costs, offset production affects the level of costs);
(b) hysteresis in the location of economic activity, that is, the present distribution in space depends on the preceding situation (path-dependency);
(c) the occurrence of multiple stable or unstable equilibria;
(d) the presence of symmetric (N = S, dispersed equilibrium) as well as severely unbalanced equilibria (the tomahawk diagram);
(e) the bell-shaped chart depicting the evolution of regional development;
(f) the presence of catastrophic agglomeration due to the homogeneity of preferences;
(g) the presence of HME;
(h) the existence of the so-called spatial structure of wages reflecting the variation in productivity;
(i) non-linearity (non-monotonic character) of many associations, such as the impact of transport costs on the level of the spatial concentration of economic activities.

In dynamic models, in contrast to static approaches, processes have a temporal dimension, which creates a fundamental difference. In terms of the medium-term, changes (shifts) in economic policy result is a one-time adjustment of capital, which is the flow and allocation of capital between regions, although the rate of accumulation is unchanged – we thus deal with the level effect. In the long-run, economic policy changes can affect the pace of capital accumulation, and thus we deal with the rate of a growth effect.

Effects for the overall level of prosperity in the case of models with a fixed level of capital (K) are as follows:
(a) the effect of prices on the border – the decrease in import prices rises prices in exports which causes an increase in the prosperity of the region N according to the classic definition of the terms of trade effect;

(b) the effect of location on the cost of living – if the number of varieties of differentiated good n is constant, the dislocation of the production of one variety of the differentiated good from the region S to N causes an increase in the prosperity of the region; the significance of the effect increases with the increase in transportation costs;
(c) the effect of migration depends on the type of model, in CP and FE models an inflow of mobile capital K raises real income; in the FC model, it has no impact on the level of prosperity.

In the case of dynamic models with capital accumulation, the capital accumulation occurs until the steady-state level is reached, for which the value of an additional unit of capital aligns with the cost of its production. In the steady-state, further accumulation of capital bring zero effects for the general welfare.

Baldwin et al. (2001) distinguish two NEG models with an accumulation of capital: (a) the constructed capital (CC) model (Baldwin, 1999); (b) localized (LS) or global (GS) spillover models.

In the CC model, with the accumulation of capital, each new unit of capital is associated with the emergence of a new variety of differentiated goods. The increase in the number of available varieties is thus the manifestation of technological progress, by analogy with the horizontal differentiation models of endogenous growth literature. The process of accumulation of capital thus translates into an increase in several available varieties. It causes a progressive decline in the general level of prices, and therefore a gradual increase in the real product and real wages.

LS and GS models also allow for the endogenization of economic growth. The key feature is the adoption of a broad definition of capital – physical capital, human capital, and knowledge considered together bypasses the problem of diminishing returns through the incorporation of learning curve effects in the production process. Thus, the cost of broadly defined capital decreases in time. Capital of this type may spill into adjacent areas (imperfect diffusion, LS – localized spillovers) or globally (perfect diffusion, GS – globalized spillovers).

Knowledge diffuses primarily within individual economic sectors (intra-sectoral spillovers, the so-called MAR externalities) and to a more limited extent between sectors (inter-sectoral spillovers, or the Jacobian externalities). The localized spillovers are the main forces responsible for the spatial concentration of sectors or overall spatial agglomeration of economic activity and population, explaining the phenomena of industrial districts, clusters, and the emergence and development of cities and metropolitan centres.

In the LS models, we are dealing with a perfect diffusion of knowledge between enterprises in a given region (for example, within a single cluster) and hindered interregional knowledge diffusion. The scale of localized diffusion location choice has an impact on the long-term growth rate.

In the GS models, knowledge defuses between firms from different regions. In this setting, capital accumulation can lead to catastrophic agglomeration. Spatial considerations do not affect the long-term growth rate; however, they have an impact on the level of development (through transitional effects).

In the LS and GS models, private atomistic innovators overlook the presence of externalities in their activities and thus the impact of their activities on the evolution of the general price levels. At the same time, the learning effect occurs in the innovation sector. The apparent market failure leads to the socially suboptimal growth rate in the Pareto sense and thus creates an opportunity for a potentially favourable public intervention (e.g. R&D subsidy). The dynamic NEG models with knowledge spillovers include models of Martin and Ottaviano (1996). Baldwin and Forslid (1999), Baldwin et al. (2001) Baldwin and Martin (2004).

Endogenization of growth in the NEG model requires similarly to models of the new growth theories, the extension of the concept of capital and taking into account externalities in its accumulation, or endogenization of the technological progress by the introduction to the structure of the model of an R&D sector responsible for the creation of new knowledge and innovation. In the process of knowledge generation, knowledge diffuses to the neighbouring regions.

From the theoretical point of view, diffusion of knowledge can be perfect (global and immediate diffusion) or imperfect (spatially restricted or localized). Numerous empirical results confirm that the diffusion of knowledge is imperfect and is strongly localized, despite the progress in the field of information technology (Ciccone, 1996; Coe et al., 1997; Eaton and Kortum, 2001; Jacobs, 1970; Jaffe, Trajtenberg, and Henderson, 1993; Keller, 2002, 2004; Thompson and Fox-Kean, 2005; Zucker et al., 1998). The recent evidence for Poland also points to the localized character of knowledge diffusion (Ciołek and Brodzicki, 2016, 2017). The localized knowledge spillovers are in brief due to the tacit character knowledge which diffusion requires direct face-to-face interaction.

Dynamic NEG models are far from ideal. They are foremost, not able to fully capture the complex nature of space or the interactions between actors (Zaucha, 2008). To some extent, they represent a compromise between the desire to capture as much of the spectrum of conditions and factors and the objective limitations on the modelling side.

NEG models cannot be considered as exhaustive coverage of spatial issues in the analysis of economic growth. They are excessively one-sided and respond to the question on the role of space in the process of economic growth, refer only to the cost of tackling space. In this situation, spatial concentration is the factor, which promotes development. The alternative approach is the postulate of space without the cost of its overcoming. The NEG, however, omits the costs of "density", which may negatively impact the growth rate of GDP through congestion (Zaucha, 2007, 2008).

Fujita and Krugman (2003) stated that future models must have even richer microeconomic foundations, rely to a greater extent on the results obtained through empirical analyses, and relate directly to the consequences for the well-being of individual societies, and therefore, generate better recommendations for economic policy.

The newest theoretical models a la Melitz (2003) move away from the traditional assumption of firm homogeneity (representative company models) and consider the actual heterogeneity of firms in terms of, e.g. productivity, size, or scope of activities. These models, taking into account the stochastic distribution of productivity, lead to meaningful and new theoretical postulates, for example on the cause of the occurrence of the exporters, competitiveness, internationalisation, and innovation, but at the same time lose the simplicity and thus transparency characteristic for former models and thus lead to unambiguous economic policy recommendations.

Ottaviano (2011) notes that future NEG models should account for both macro-heterogeneity across locations and micro-heterogeneity across firms within sectors and people with various preferences. Taking the firm heterogeneity into consideration leads to the emergence of the next generation of models – the so-called new NEG (NNEG) models. Ottaviano states: "still based on the pillars of scale economies and imperfect competition but with a stronger emphasis on how individual heterogeneity across people and firms maps into aggregate behaviour".

For instance, Baldwin and Okubo (2006) built a model of the NNEG-type integrating a heterogeneous firm's Melitz-style model of monopolistic competition with a simple NEG model obtaining several interesting results. First, only the most productive firms can benefit from reallocation to larger regions. The selection effect exists, decreasing the extent of traditional agglomeration economies. Furthermore, a spatial sorting effect arises that induces the highest productivity firms to move to the core and the lowest productivity firms to the periphery. Furthermore, the HME is weaker due to firm heterogeneity. According to Ottaviano (2011), in the model firm heterogeneity acts as an additional centrifugal force – the greater, the larger are the trade costs and the larger the substitutability between firms' products.

Forslid and Okubo (2010) extended the Baldwin and Okubo (2006) model by introducing different capital intensities among firms (that can move between regions) and sectors. More productive firms were assumed to be more capital intensive. As a result, the model postulates sorting to the large regions from both ends of the actual productivity distribution (Pareto or log-normal distribution of TFP is observed in the actual firm-level data). Specifically, firms with high capital intensity and high productivity as well as firms with very low productivity and low capital intensity tend to relocate to the core (core region premium). Using Japanese data, authors provide some evidence for the predicted two-sided sorting and in particular in high capital intensity sectors. The early NNEG models include as well the works by Baldwin and Okubo (2009), Nocke (2006) or Okubo (2009).

In a recent paper, Forslid and Okubo (2019) proposed an NNEG model incorporating firm heterogeneity in which multiproduct firms can relocate between regional markets (core and periphery). In the framework, the product scope of a firm increases in the market size and simultaneously, the product scope of a firm increases in its productivity. The most productive firm has, at the same time, the highest incentive to deviate to the core region. Trade liberalisation in this framework thus leads to relocation of the most productive firms to the larger market (core region), where they further expand their product scope (given the relocation costs). The less productive firms with a smaller product range located in the smaller market contract their product range due to increased competition. The above effects are magnified with the productivity of the migrating firm. The pro-agglomerative effect is, however, weakened as only the most productive firms with the largest product scope can locate in or migrate to the core region. Forslid and Okubo (2019) find the above theoretical postulates to be consistent with the data on location and product scope of manufacturing firms located in Japanese prefectures.

Brülhart (2011) in the conclusions of his survey of implications of trade liberalisation for intra-national geographies of individual economies (intra-national regional inequality) states that the results of both urban systems and NEG models are inconclusive. Everything depends on the modelling strategies and choices adopted. Empirical results are rather inconclusive as well; however, a majority of cross-country studies find no significant effect of openness on urban concentration or regional inequality. Whether trade liberalisation (or greater openness to trade) raises or lowers regional inequality depends on country-specific geography, which is to a large extent of exogenous character. The greatest benefits are likely to emerge in the case of regions, ceteris paribus, with inherently less costly access to foreign markets – border or port regions.

González Rivas (2007) postulates that an ability of a given region to capture the benefits related to greater trade openness depends primarily on critical endowments and thus the degree to which trade is likely to reduce regional inequality in a given country is mediated by the geographic distribution of its endowments. He tested the hypothesis for Mexico on a sub-national dataset from 1940. The results indicate that liberalisation benefits to a greater extent of regions with lower levels of education, thereby tending to reduce regional inequality. However, it also benefits more regions with higher levels of income and infrastructure, thereby tending to increase regional inequality. The second effect is stronger; thus, trade openness increases regional inequality.

Krugman (2010) states that recent developments in the regional evolution of China are in line with the postulates of the standard core-periphery model that predicts increasing regional specialisation as a result of economic integration (liberalisation).

Redding (2010) points to a major weakness of NEG theory in the empirical domain. Earlier Krugman (1998) noting the theoretical contribution of NEG by incorporating space into mainstream economics, fully inspecting the impact of increasing returns and identifying many non-linear aspects, stated that the weakness lied in lack of convincing empirical verifications. Nonetheless, some of the analyses – for instance by Davis and Weinstein (1996, 1998; 2002; 2008) – were very encouraging; however, they pointed to some important problems such as the assumption of homogeneity of preference (not in line with the rebuilding of Nagasaki or Hiroshima after the Second

World War). On the other hand, Davis and Weinstein (2003) proved the existence of the home market effects for a broad segment of the OECD manufacturing industry.

It is worth pointing out that economic geographers frequently question the basic assumptions, the structure, and logic of NEG models. Martin (1999a) considers it just like a reworking of traditional location theory and regional science using recent developments in formal (mathematical) mainstream economics. Therefore, they also question the policy relevance of this kind of modelling (e.g. Martin and Sunley, 2011).

Krugman (2010) on the other hand thinks that the possibilities of convergence between economic geography and NEG are rather dim by stating "Although both economists and geographers study these spatial processes, no fruitful exchange between the two is expected because of the use of different methodologies".

Garretsen and Martin (2010) point to two important weaknesses of NEG models: the oversimplified treatment of geography (pre-given, fixed and highly idealized abstract geometric space) and history (logical time and not real history). One of the first steps in this process is made in an empirical paper by Bosker et al. (2010) where the authors move from unidimensional NEG model and propose a strategy combining estimation and simulation accounting for heterogeneous and complex geographical structures. A combination of the estimation of structural NEG parameters with a simulation of the underlying multidimensional NEG model more accurately links the empirical results to the theory.

Storper (2011) postulates that only big changes in the openness to trade (for instance adjustments in the tariff levels or establishment or abolishment of trade barriers or trade liberalisation schemes) considered as major shocks to an economic system may result in significant structural adjustments in firms' decisions resulting in their reorganisation and potentially re-location as long as the shocks are big enough to overcome existing sunk costs and/or agglomeration economies and then readjustments in the location of labour.

Yu, Zhao, and Ming (2006) analysed the causes of industry agglomeration in China at the provincial level of spatial disaggregation over the period 1987-2001 using the NEG modelling framework. The authors conclude that liberalisation led to industry agglomeration. Furthermore, factors such as market size, the level of urbanisation, or investments in the infrastructure promoted industrial agglomeration. Coastal Chinese regions at the same time enjoy clear geographical advantages promoting their accelerated industrial growth.

Summing up, the bond between economic growth and openness of regions is complex and to some extent, an ambiguous issue. The relationship becomes even more blurred if we take into account the nonlinearity and heterogeneity of space. Nonetheless, overlooking the spatial interactions at the regional level of analysis, and thus of NEG or NNEG postulates, could lead to falsified conclusions and thus to wrong policy recommendations.

Part II: **State of Art**

Tomasz Brodzicki

3 Regions' trade openness

In this chapter, we will review the empirical literature on the complex nexus between trade and other aspects of openness of regions and their economic growth performance. We purposefully divide the review in discussing the two most important channels of impact – trade and FDI channel furthermore we present both the studies on the level of countries and then discuss the impact at the regional level.

3.1 Review of the empirical literature

In the empirical literature, two strands dominate – the macro approach with mostly cross-sectional or panel analysis of global or more homogeneous groups of countries and the micro approach – analysis for individual countries based on sectoral or firm-level data.

In both strands of literature, various variables are utilized as proxies for the overall extent of openness. These include openness ratio (trade/GDP), openness dummy – open/closed economy, rate of exports, the share of imports in GDP, real foreign exchange distortions, the average level of tariffs in general or the average level of US tariffs (Romalis, 2007), dummies for preferential and regional trade arrangements, the outward orientation index of the World Bank, the black market premium on foreign exchange, exports distortion index as well as various geographic variables (landlockedness, common border), etc. It is worth mentioning that even the openness dummy could have a rather complex structure. For instance, in Sachs and Warner (1995) an economy is referred to as open only if fulfils simultaneously the following set of conditions:

(a) average tariff rate on capital and intermediate goods below 40%;
(b) non-tariff barriers on less than 40% of import of capital and intermediate goods;
(c) black-market premium does not exceed 20% of official foreign exchange;
(d) non-socialist country;
(e) lack of state monopoly in exports of key branches.

Nonetheless, the openness ratio defined as the ratio of total trade to GDP seems to be the most popular.

In his famous cross-sectional regression analysis, Barro (1992) identified a positive and statistically significant impact of the level of openness on economic growth in a cross-section of countries. Dollar (1992) noting a potential bias utilized an index of exchange rate disturbances, finding it to affect economic growth adversely. The result was further confirmed by Easterly, Kremer, Pritchett, and Summers (1993) and Lee (1993) using similar approaches.

Sachs and Warner (1995) utilized a dichotomous index of openness conditional on meeting five criteria finding openness to matter for growth in a cross-section of countries. The index was also utilized by Gallup, Sachs, and Mellinger (2016), which led to analogous results even if deep-rooted geographical factors were considered. In his seminal study, Vamvakidis (1999) identified a positive and statistically significant effect of multilateral economic integration.

Wacziarg and Welch (2003) found the earlier studies applying the Sachs and Warner (1995) index to be sensitive to the period considered.

Edwards (1998) in his seminal study analysed the impact of nine different indices of openness /disturbances in the exchange rate on productivity as measured by TFP and thus indirectly on the real GDP per capita in a large cross-section of 93 countries. The impact was identified to be positive; however, its magnitude was found to be less significant in comparison to the traditional determinants of economic growth such as the initial level of GDP per capita (in line with the absolute/conditional convergence literature) or the initial level of human capital endowment (as postulated by the augmented Solow-Swan model of Mankiw et al. (1992) and some of the models of the new growth theory strand (Lucas, 1988, 1990). Human capital endowment directly affects the rate of domestic innovation (Romer, 1990) as well as the speed of adoption of technology from abroad or knowledge diffusion (Nelson and Phelps, 1966).

Due to a potential endogeneity, the instrumental variables (IV) approach is frequently utilized. For instance, Frankel and Romer (1996; 1999) propose an instrumental variable based on geographical factors that determine to a large extent the intensity of bilateral trade while being exogenous with respect to the level of income. The impact of openness proved surprisingly to be insignificant in two large cross-sectional datasets of countries considered by the authors.

Irwin and Terviö (2002) reiterated the test by Frankel and Romer (1999) in a slightly modified manner for a panel of countries. The results pointed to a positive relationship between the intensity of trade and the level of GDP per capita. Later on, Romalis (2007) found similar results using the IV approach in a large panel of countries (135) observed over 40 years (1960-2000).

In his comprehensive analysis, Vamvakidis (2002) tested six different measures of openness for an elongated period (1920-1999) finding that the positive relationship between openness and growth existed only after the 1970s. It could be related to a noticeable increase in the extent of openness with the beginning of the next phase of globalisation.

In contrast to aforementioned empirical studies, Wacziarg and Welch (2003) utilized a different approach to analysing the effects of cases of significant trade-policy liberalisations and finding that they were on average followed by an increase in the investment rate of 1.5 to 2%, and in the share of trade in GDP by 5% (increase in openness) while the ex-post growth rate was higher than ex-ante growth rate by a mean of 1.5%.

Using the extreme bounds analysis approach, Levine and Renelt (1992) found the index of openness to be one of the variables indirectly affecting the growth rate in a cross-section of countries through the impact on the process of accumulation of capital (investment rates). In the same study, they rejected the existence of the direct linkage.

In contrast, Doppelhofer, Miller, and Sala-i-Martin (2000) using the Bayesian averaging of classical estimates approach for a balanced panel of 88 countries and 68 significant determinants of economic growth found the time since the liberalisation of an economy to affect economic growth positively. It could mean that the benefits of liberalisation or openness accumulate in time and thus, short-run and the long-run impact could significantly differ. In the same study, the impact of the overall openness level was found to matter significantly less.

The quick review of the most important empirical studies on the nexus considered leads to the conclusion that the results obtained to a large extent depend on: dataset – scope and period (duration), the methodological approach adopted (cross-sectional vs panel), allowing for linear or non-linear impact, the choice of the openness proxy, taking care or not of potential endogeneity, the choice of the correct instrumental variable, taking care of outliers and other standard econometric problems (sample selection bias, heteroscedasticity, potential co-linearity).

3.2 Studies at the regional level

In comparison to the vast empirical literature on the nexus between openness and economic growth, the analyses conducted at the regional level are surprisingly rather scarce.

Soukiazis and Antunes (2011) conducted the analysis on the role of openness, export shares, or trade balances on the regional growth in Portugal at the NUTS 3 level over the period 1996-2005 further conditioning for the role of the human capital. The dynamic panel model estimated with the use of GMM proves that factors associated with external trade, including openness, human capital endowment, and sectoral labour shares (in particular in the industrial sector) are important determinants of regional growth affecting the conditional convergence processes as well. Furthermore, the interactions between the key variables also play an important role and to a large extent, explain different performances between regions of the Portuguese Littoral and Interior.

Boschma and Iammarino (2009) analysed the impact of trade linkages for Italian provinces at NUTS 3 levels and three-digit sectors over the period 1995-2003 looking for the impact of the so-called related variety. The hypothesis was positively verified – related variety contributed to regional economic growth. Well-endowed in complementary sectors Italian provinces showed superior performance. Boschma and Iammarino (2009) postulate furthermore that openness alone (more trade or more knowledge flows) does not affect growth, but this is due to the presence of related extra-regional knowledge which leads to intersectoral learning across regions.

Petrakos, Kallioras, and Anagnostou (2011) analysed the determinants of regional economic growth and convergence of 249 NUTS 2 regions of the EU in the period 1990-2003. Using the absolute β-convergence concept, the paper detected a mirror-image J-shaped relationship between regional growth and regional development levels. According to the authors, regional divergence factors are getting stronger, and, eventually, dominate at more advanced levels of development. Factors such as agglomeration economies, geography, economic integration, and economic structure create an overall unfavourable economic environment for lagging regions. More advanced regions of the EU tend to grow faster, as they are characterized by high levels of openness and high levels of structural similarity to the dominant economic paradigm.

Polasek and Sellner (2011) analysed the impact of three different types of globalisation variables, namely trade openness, EU integration (structural funds expenditures in the percentage of GDP) and technology transfer on the regional growth on GDP per capita in a panel of NUTS 2 EU-27 states in a period 2001-2006. Using the spatial Chow-Lin procedure they construct regional indicators, resulting in data predictions on a regional level for trade openness (referred to as a global indicator) and FDI inward stocks (referred to as a technology indicator). Using these, they analyse a cross-sectional spatial growth regression model. The results for the convergence model allowing for interactions (and thus GDP dependent convergence elasticities) show that higher openness to globalisation favours initially less developed regions. The convergence process in European regions follows a non-linear pattern and is furthermore exposed to heterogeneous influences. In addition, the authors have found the effects of trade openness to be higher than for the technology transfers (proxied by the inward FDI flows). An interdependence between FDI inward stocks and the human capital endowment of a region has also been detected.

In recent years several studies have been performed on Asian economies and their regions. Sun, Hone, and Doucouliago (1999) show in a study of Chinese regions at the manufacturing industries level that openness to trade (trade orientation and FDI) has a positive effect on technical efficiency.

Leong (2013) analysing the impact of SEZs as cases of liberalisation on regional economic growth in China and India found that both FDI and export positively affect growth. The presence of SEZs increases regional growth; however, an increase in the number of SEZs has a negligible effect on growth. Leong (2013) finds greater openness (wider liberalisation) as a precondition of further growth. Wei, Yao, and Aying (2007) in a panel of Chinese regions over the entire period 1979-2003 proved that FDI inflows were one of the forces behind the observed regional discrepancies in growth. The authors claim, however, that FDI cannot be blamed for the extent of regional inequality as it was due to the uneven distribution of FDI and not the FDI itself.

Anwar and Nguyen (2010) using a simultaneous equation model found in a panel of 61 Vietnamese provinces from 1996-2005, a mutually reinforcing two-way process between FDI and regional economic growth. The benefits of FDI inflow could be further strengthened by more investments into education and training, development of the financial market, and reducing the technology gap between foreign and local firms.

Shafiullah, Selvanathan, and Naranpanawa (2017) in a recent paper analysed in the export-led growth hypothesis in Australia taken as a whole and its regions at the sectoral level over the period 1990-2013 using quarterly data. The authors state in particular that the mining and fuel sector's exports played a crucial role in driving the economic growth of Australia and in three of its regions in the long run – namely New South Wales, Queensland, and Western Australia. Shafiullah et al. (2017) identify each Australian region's experience with ELG as region-specific. Traces of ELG in the short run were identified for South Australia, Tasmania, and Northern Territory. It, in turn, seems to depend on the composition of exports (product or sectoral-structure).

According to Kanbur and Venables (2005), rising spatial disparities in regional development in many developing states are mostly due to the uneven impact of increased trade openness and globalisation. It leads to efficiency gains mostly due to the concertation of economic activity in major cities and coastal districts adversely affecting inland regions. In a study on Latin America, Serra (2006) argue that regional disparities modestly increased, at least temporarily, in the wake of trade liberalisation. It was especially marked for Mexico.

Redding (2016) used a version of the quantitative spatial model to investigate the effects of a fall in trade costs between the US and Canada, leaving internal trade costs unchanged and allowing for heterogeneous worker preferences across locations. The analysis is conducted at the regional level. He states that given greater trade intensity with US states, Central Canada would gain more than Western Canada under population immobility. But in the case of a mobile population across regions, the improved market access of Central Canada would cause it to gain population. At the same time, Western Canada would see a decline in population. The reallocation of the population would continue until all Canadian regions gain equally from the fall in trade costs, in the absence of costs to mobility. In analysing counterfactuals, Redding (2016) states the welfare gains from trade (liberalisation) depend on changes in both domestic trade shares and reallocations of the population across locations. Furthermore, factor mobility introduces quantitatively relevant differences in the counterfactual predictions of the constant and increasing returns to scale models. Therefore, models excluding spatial interlinkages and factor mobility at the regional level of analysis can lead to falsified results. It is not the case for studies performed at the country-level were the estimates for welfare are correct.

When analysing the nexus between openness and economic growth at a regional level, we must note the direct or indirect impact of other accompanying variables or processes.

For instance, Sachs, Bajpai, and Ramiah (2002) studying σ-convergence, and ß-convergence show that more than 80% of the cross-state variation in growth rates among Indian states can be explained solely by an urbanisation variable. Agglomeration factors are also strongly postulated by NEG theories.

The role of human capital accumulation is clear on theoretical and empirical grounds; however, the scope of the definition of human capital differs. For example, in the study by Boschma and Fritsch (2009) point in line with Florida (2005) to an important contribution of the so-called creative class for regional growth in seven European countries. They are, however, not able to determine whether human capital as measured by the creative occupation, outperforms standard indicators based on formal education and whether formal education has a stronger impact. The creative class endowment is positively affected by the regional climate of tolerance and openness as well as regional job opportunities.

Other factors could matter as well, such as the economic structure or the size and the share of an industrial sector. For instance, the study by Hansen and Zhang (2010) points to the key role of the industrial sector in explaining the regional variation in growth among Chinese province. The result supports the Kaldorian approach to regional economic growth with cumulative causation between trade liberalisation, the rise in export demand, the growth of the industrial sector (industrialisation) and its impact on overall productivity and thus increases in international competitiveness.

One of the issues that cannot be overlooked is the issue of path-dependency in regional development. For instance, Felice and Vecchi (2015) indicate that the regional North-South variation in Italy was already present the moment the country was unified and then increased. The explanation of the present variation involves endogenous factors – natural resources, human capital endowment, and social capital.

Several studies have also been performed for Poland. Brodzicki (2015) attempted to identify shallow determinants of growth of Polish regions as well the sign and magnitude of macroeconomic education – externality and infrastructure externality. An augmented neoclassical growth model was constructed, incorporating a Mincerian approach to human capital accumulation, further assuming a direct impact of infrastructure on the overall productivity. The estimated panel model accounting for fixed region-specific effects was robust and explained approx. 90% of the observed variation in GDP per capita. The return to the accumulation of human capital through education and experience for Polish regions was found to be statistically significant, robust and positive. The macroeconomic infrastructure externality proved to be in turn positive however overall insignificant with the impact of the quality of railway.

In a recent article Ciołek and Brodzicki (2017) analysed the determinants of spatial variation and spatial spillovers of TFP at the level of local administrative districts. They utilized and tested an extended empirical version of the aforementioned Nelson and Phelps (1966) model accounting for potential spatial interactions among regions at a high level of spatial disaggregation. It required the use of dedicated spatial econometric methods. The authors stress that the TFP assumes the highest values in the metropolitan centres and spreads out on their nearest surroundings with the maximum value for the capital region – Warsaw. The secondary local hills in TFP are located in cities or towns with county rights. The range of TFP spillover is found to be roughly 175-200 km and is nonlinearly decreasing from the local productivity hills. Furthermore, the rate of growth of TFP showed spatial autocorrelation and was found to depend positively on the rate of increase in human capital endowment and on the gap from the leader under certain assumptions. The result is in line with the postulated of Nelson and Phelps. Furthermore, Ciołek and Brodzicki (2017) accounted for two channels of productivity diffusion related to international trade and factor flows, namely through imports and through the inflow of FDI. The authors found no evidence of the channel through imports (trade relations). However, the FDI channel was found to be robust and strong. It points to the need for broadening of the concept of openness to account for FDI inflows and outflows as well.

For comparative purposes, it is worth mentioning the results of similar studies. Bottazzi and Peri (2003) using R&D and patent data for European regions over the period 1977-1995 found knowledge spillovers to be relatively weak and localized within a distance of 300 km. Bronzini and Piselli (2009) analysed the relationship between TFP, R&D, human capital and public infrastructure on a panel of Italian regions over the period 1980-2001. The results indicated the existence of a long-run equilibrium between TFP levels and the three types of capital with human capital affecting the TFP the most. Moreno, Paci, and Usai (2016) investigated the spatial distribution of innovative activity and the role of technological spillovers in the process of knowledge creation across 138 regions of 17 countries in Europe over the period of 1978-1997 at sectoral level (3 digit ISIC sectors). The authors identified a strong initial central-periphery pattern of distribution of innovation activity with concentrations in Northern and Central regions with a tendency to decline (diffuse). They identified furthermore a robust and positive spatial autocorrelation in the innovative activity. External effects were also identified pointing to the role of technology diffusion within a distance of roughly 250 and 500 km. Sterlacchini (2008) adopted Fagerberg's technology gap model of economic growth (Fagerberg, 1988) and examined the relationship between the economic growth of 12 European regions over the period 1995-2002 and their knowledge and human capital endowments. Sterlacchini (2008) took into account foreign and domestic knowledge, the ability to utilize both sources, and the distance from the technology frontier. He controlled for potential agglomeration effects by including the log of population density. Gross domestic expenditure on research and development and the share of the population with tertiary education were found to be the most important determinants of growth in incomes per capita.

3.3 Empirical studies on the role of openness to FDI in economic growth

One of the important aspects of openness is the extent of openness to the inflow as well as an outflow of FDI. The theoretical channels have been discussed above.

In a seminal paper Borensztein, Gregorio, and Lee (1998) in a cross-country regression framework analysed the channels of the impact of FDI on growth, utilizing data on FDI flows from industrial countries to developing countries over two decades. The results obtained supported the notion that FDI is an important vehicle for international technology diffusion affecting the growth rate directly a bit stronger than indirectly through the impact on domestic investment. The authors noted, however, that the impact is conditional on the existence of a minimum endowment of human capital or in other words on a sufficient absorptive capability for advanced technologies. Growth process and knowledge acquisition could thus be, therefore said to be skilled-biased.

Balasubramanyam, Salisu, and Sapsford (1996) stress the significance of trade openness in the case of developing countries to acquire the beneficial effects of FDI inflow. In particular, export promotion policy proves to be more conducive to the nexus than the import substitution policy. In turn, Blomstrom, Lipsey, and Zejan (1992) argued that FDI had a positive growth effect only when a country was sufficiently prosperous in terms of the level of development. Alfaro, Chanda, Kalemli-Ozcan, and Sayek (2004) analysed the linkage between FDI and growth in a cross-country data set over the period 1975-1995 controlling for the level of development of the financial market. The role of FDI was identified as ambiguous as such; however, countries with more developed financial markets benefited significantly from FDI. The studies point to positive; however, the conditional impact of FDI on economic growth. The analysis by Lee and Chang (2009) using panel cointegration and panel error correction models for a panel of 37 countries over the period 1970-2002 proved the result showing a fairly strong, long-run relationship. The short-run relationship was, however, identified as weak.

Carkovic and Levine (2002), using a novel statistical method, postulated in contrast that FDI inflows did not exert an independent influence on economic growth. The authors controlled for potential biases in the estimation process due to endogeneity, the omission of country-specific effects, and the initial level of income. In the words of the authors ", while sound economic policies may spur both growth and FDI, the results are inconsistent with the view the FDI exerts a positive impact on growth that is independent of other growth determinants". Also, Mello (1999) in the non-OECD sample found no causation from FDI to growth based on fixed-effects regressions with country-specific intercepts, and even a negative short-run impact of FDI on GDP using the mean group estimator.

Mello (1997) stressed that the ultimate impact of FDI on output growth in the recipient economy depended on the scope for efficiency spillovers to domestic firms, by which FDI led to increasing returns in domestic production and increased in the value-added content of the FDI-related production. Tang, Selvanathan, and Selvanathan (2008) point to the complementarity between FDI and domestic investments in China. No crowding out of domestic investment has been observed.

In a recent paper, Iamsiraroj and Ulubaşoğlu (2015) scrutinized 108 published studies (meta-analysis) and tested the relationship in a global sample of 140 countries in the period 1970 to 2009, proving the positive impact of FDI on growth both in developed as well as developing countries. Iamsiraroj and Ulubaşoğlu (2015) stress the role of regional variation and contemporaneous FDI rather than past FDI, for growth. Furthermore, trade openness and financial development rather than schooling (human capital) were identified as appropriate absorptive capacity indicators for positive growth (please compare to results of previous studies).

Nair-Reichert and Weinhold (2001) emphasize that FDI, on average, had a positive impact on growth; however, the result proved to be highly heterogeneity across the group of developing countries. Furthermore, there was some evidence that the efficacy of FDI was higher in more open economies.

Similarly to trade openness, we must address the issue of causality between FDI and economic growth. Asheghian (2004) stressed that the US economic growth was mostly driven by TFP growth and the growth in domestic investment as well as FDI. Furthermore, the relationship between FDI and economic as well as TFP growth (and thus indirectly affecting growth) is uni-directional and going from FDI. Similarly, Hansen and Rand (2006) analysed the causality between FDI and growth in a sample of 31 developing countries covering three continents over the period 1970-2000. They identify a strong causal link from FDI to GDP in short and the long run. And interestingly they state the long-term impact is independent of the level of development of the recipient.

There are also studies pointing to the bi-directional relationship, for instance, Choe (2003), Jayachandran and Seilan (2010) for India or Malaysia, and Thailand (Chowdhury and Mavrotas, 2005). The bi-directional nature of the relationship is further postulated by Iamsiraroj (2016) using a simultaneous system of equations approach of 124 cross-country data for the period 1971-2010. Furthermore, trade openness alongside the labour force and economic freedom are identified as key determinants of FDI, which in turn accelerates the economic growth process. Basu, Chakraborty, and Reagle (2003) stressed the existence of a cointegrating relationship between FDI and economic growth using a panel of 23 countries. Interestingly, trade openness is stressed as a key determinant of the beneficial impact of FDI on growth. The authors namely identified two-way causality both in short and the long run only in open economies, whereas unidirectional long-run causality from growth to FDI in closed economies.

Fidrmuc and Martin (2011) analysed the role of FDI, trade, and growth in 11 CESEE countries at the country level over the period 1995-2009. They tested for the hypotheses of ELG and FDI-led growth in the region. The authors found the stock of FDI to be positively related to industrial production and economic growth. In nearly all CESEE countries exports and FDI had a significant impact on industrial growth performance, with exports playing a stronger role. The relationships between trade, FDI, and growth were identified as a complex with both variables identified as endogenous. Output growth for Poland, Romania, Slovakia, and Slovenia was found to profit from exports and FDI. The long-run industrial production was found at the same time not to be affected in Bulgaria, Croatia, Estonia, Hungary, and Lithuania, and as a result, the export-led/FDI-led growth hypothesis was rejected in these particular cases.

Summing up the empirical literature conducted at the level of countries brings rather mixed results on the nexus between FDI and growth in terms of existence, accompanying determinants, and direction of causality.

Chen and Fleisher (1996) identified the role of FDI in the process of conditional convergence of production per capita in Chinese provinces over the period of 1978-1993 alongside physical investment share, employment growth, human-capital investment, and coastal location of a region. The authors utilized an augmented Solow growth model framework. We can conclude that FDI could have a potential impact on the observed regional variation in the levels of productivity and thus, levels of development.

Sjöholm (1999) analysed productivity growth in Indonesian manufacturing companies across regions. He found that regional characteristics at the district level, rather than at the province level, seemed to explain productivity growth. This spatial scale seems to be more conducive to inter-industry knowledge spillovers. These, in turn, are positively affected by FDI as "domestic establishments benefit from a regional presence of foreign establishments in neighbouring industries". Sjöholm (1999) also identified intra-industry spillovers from FDI at the national level as domestic establishments in industries with a large foreign presence have shown high productivity growth.

Buckley, Clegg, Wang, and Cross (2002) analysed the impact of FDI inflow into 29 Chinese provinces over the period 1989-1999 trying to identify the impact of host country conditions on the nexus with growth. They proved to matter both at the national and regional levels. FDI concentrated in economically stronger regions, and the benefits related to FDI were a function of the strength of local competition.

Lessmann (2013) studied the impact of FDI inflow on regional variation in China, and a wider sample of 55 countries over 30 years, 1980-2009. Economic theory says that the level of economic development could have an impact on the FDI – regional inequality nexus. FDI could increase the extent of regional inequalities as they are usually spatially concentrated (FDI agglomeration effect). Lessmann (2013) found that FDI inflows increased regional inequality in low and middle-income countries, while there were no negative distributional consequences observed in the high-income economies. Furthermore, he stated that the higher mobility of individuals in developed countries, as well as government policies (linked to better institutional quality), were likely to at least partially mitigate the adverse negative impact on regional inequality.

Su and Liu (2016), in their econometric analysis, a panel of Chinese cities over the period 1991-2010, identified the positive role of FDI on the per capita GDP growth rate. The effect was intensified by the human capital endowment of the city, which authors interpret as human capital contributing to growth is to serve as a facilitator for technology transfers stemming from FDI.

The number of studies on the role of trade and FDI channels (globalisation) on the growth of regions is steadily increasing. The results are not uniform; nonetheless, openness affects the prosperity of individual regional economies. The effects of greater openness are, however, not always positive. They can be adverse, as well.

The access to larger and better datasets together with better analytical methodologies and tools allows for progress in our understanding of this complex issue. We are now better able to address the direction of causality or to account for spatial interactions and thus interdependencies in the economic growth of neighbouring regions. The next step is the utilisation of data on heterogeneous firms, their production as well as innovation activities and evolution in space and time. Only then will we be fully able to account for heterogenous regional economies with heterogenous firms and their reactions to greater openness due to trade liberalisation. The recent paper by Forslid and Okubo (2018), for instance, brings first interesting evidence in favour of NNEG models with multiproduct firms. The emergence of dynamic NNEG models is only a matter of time. On the empirical side, the multi-level approaches allowing for the linkages between national, regional, and local contexts could also bring interesting insights.

Stanisław Umiński

4 Dutch disease at regional level

Although Dutch disease (DD) is treated as a problem of "the whole" countries, it can also be used to reveal the strong nexus between regions' economic situation and foreign trade. The term itself relates to consequences of new, unexpected, large and growing foreign currency revenues from exports of natural resources. Once the huge layers of natural gas were discovered in the Netherlands' province of Groningen in the late 50s, growing revenues from exports soon translated into an appreciation of the Dutch currency, which resulted in deteriorated competitiveness of other than natural gas, exporting sectors. They were crowded out from the Dutch exports. The more natural gas was exported, the more other non-booming tradable sectors of the Dutch economy were in the worsened position (Lindert, 1986). The nature of DD was analysed by many authors (Corden, 1984; Corden and Neary, 1982; Fardmanesh, 1991; Kamas, 1986; Krugman, 1987; Neary, 1986; Usui, 1996) that studied several aspects of it. In brief, it is a change of relative productivity steady states between tradable and non-tradable sectors, due to foreign exchange rate appreciation. The question is, how strictly DD shall be associated only with the discovery and exports of natural resources. According to Orłowski (1996), DD syndrome may as well be the consequence of other sources of foreign currency revenues: improved terms of trade (rapid growth of prices of exported products, relative to imported ones), the inflow of FDI, the inflow of structural funds from the EU etc. Therefore, the term "generalised DD syndrome" shall be used, as DD can be a result of any other serious, stable, long-term sources of foreign currency.

One of the aspects of DD discussed in the literature is the responsible economic policy that could possibly neutralise its negative consequences. The question is how and at what level (country or region), the relevant policy shall be carried on, much depending on the model of economic or development policy and the way socio-economic governance system is organised (centralised vs decentralised). In a model of learning by doing related to DD, Torvik (2001) showed that economists have been treating the DD's syndromes in a far too pessimistic way. Through inter-sectoral productivity and knowledge spillovers, negative consequences of DD might be mitigated. Due to regional and sectoral idiosyncrasies, productivity and production levels might decrease or increase in both tradable and non-tradable sectors. Matsen and Torvik (2005) raise a question of wealth management, once DD syndrome occurs. The issue is how the optimum public expenditures path shall be formulated to reduce negative DD effects. Similar topics were the subject of research by other authors (Acosta, Lartey, and Mandelman, 2009; Athukorala and Rajapatirana, 2003) within Salter-Swan-Corden-Dornbusch model of the dependent, developing economy undergoing macroeconomic adjustments. According to Corden (1984), there are several reasons why the lagging sectors shall be protected: employment argument, infant industry argument, exchange rate protection (incl. sterilisation) and social welfare function.

Research on DD is predominantly conducted for countries. Foreign exchange policy, exchange rate volatility, the balance of payments adjustments as well as arguments for protectionism have been inquired in literature from a country perspective. However, DD has a strong regional dimension. DD has its origin in Groningen, the province of the Netherlands. The region which is at the same time a lucky one (as the discovery of natural resources is a blessing) and a troublemaker (as DD syndromes occur) is simply different from other regions. DD can, therefore, be analysed from a regional development policy or – precisely – a regional inequalities perspective.

Sometimes informal language is used to shed light on DD syndromes. For instance, Macmahon (1996) postulates that a gift horse has to be looked in the mouth while assessing federal transfers' impact on Canadian provinces. Such interpretation is close to the one described by Orłowski (1996), in which DD can be evoked by subsidies, that result in the increases of wages, which leads to deterioration of region's competitiveness and worsened ability to export. Wage increases have an equivalent effect to real exchange rate appreciation in models of DD.

Several studies of DD syndrome have been prepared for Australia. The western and northern Australian states have been growing rapidly, because of mining sector concentration and increases in demand for mining output. On the grounds of CGE models for regions, Giesecke (2007) concludes, however, that the relatively poor performance of south-eastern regions is a more complicated problem, which cannot be simply assigned only to DD. He points to more sophisticated causal relations, which embrace the character of regional policy, ability to compete with imports, productivity differences, development path dependency, the structure of the economy, and regional differences in propensity to consume. Mitchell and Bill (2006) use DD framework to interpret regional divergence in Australia. The problem of two-speed Australia is attributed to the mineral boom on the one hand and the shrinking of the manufacturing sector on the other hand. The serious regional differences in terms of trade of exporting products have been identified. Terms of trade have improved for commodities exported from resource-oriented regions, while deteriorated for regions in which agricultural exports are important.

Harilal and Joseph (2003) make interesting observations on a region's production structure shifts through resource movement effect and spending effect. The DD concept is used for interpretations of crisis in the goods-producing sector and the boom in the services-oriented sector. Due to differences in inflation rates among Indian regions, an effective exchange rate should be calculated. Coulombe (2013) within the core-periphery model for Canada, shows that particular regions (Quebec and Ontario) would be better served in terms of exchange rate if its volatility would not so much depend on prices of exported commodities. As other regions benefit directly from a boom in natural resources prices, Quebec's and Ontario's benefits stem rather from fiscal redistribution effects.

The research of Beine, Bos, and Coulombe (2009) proves how important the DD debate is for the Canadian economy. For the period 2002-2007, Beine, Bos, and Coulombe (2009) estimate that 42% of workplaces lost in Canada in manufacturing was due to DD. They treat DD as a problem that challenges economic policy. It is so because, what they observe, a boom for resources-based sectors does not last long, and manufacturing does not rebound after the resource boom is over. Papyrakis and Raveh (2014) pay special attention to the regional mechanism of DD, looking at spatial shifts of economic activity among Canadian provinces. They prove the usefulness of the DD concept for regional level analysis. With the use of panel data, Papyrakis and Raveh (2014) indicate two effects: spending effect and resource movement effect. They use Seemingly Unrelated Regressions (SUR) to model DD mechanism. Papyrakis and Raveh (2014) formulate an interesting conclusion: that DD syndrome is primarily generated by "point-source resources" (which relates to spatially concentrated mining activity); it is not by "diffuse-source resources" related activities (agriculture, forestry, hunting, and fishing). Regions' relative rich abundance in natural resources has been found to strongly correlate with variations in inflation rates and movements of factors of production. The paper is an inspiring piece of literature also in terms of the model estimated. Estimation of exports growth has been done with the use of the following independent variables for Canadian regions: exports as a time-lagged variable, resource abundance of a region, resource abundance of the rest of Canadian regions, inflation, capital movement, labour movement, prices, capital and labour (last three variables are time-lagged). Dubé and Polèse (2015) for 135 Canadian urban areas in the 35-year period perspective conclude that there is no evidence for a long-term DD effect on wages. The possible negative impact of a region's specialisation is very contextual and can hardly be generalised.

Zawalińska, Giesecke, and Horridge (2010) refer to DD in modelling spatial consequences of Poland's less favoured regions in terms of support from the EU Common Agricultural Policy (CAP) funds. The authors conclude that transfers increase farmers' income but are harmful to export-oriented sectors. CAP transfers discourage small farmers from transferring/selling land to the larger ones, which petrifies Poland's strongly fragmented, low productivity agriculture patterns. Tradable vs non-tradable sectors labour force transfers are mentioned in the research. CAP funds distributed to small farmers stop them from migrating towards high-growth sectors of the economy, which adversely affects economic growth.

Chao, Hazari, Laffargue, Sgro, and Yu (2006) show that DD not only can be a consequence of supply shock but also of a demand shock, for instance from the boom in the tourism sector, that might bring long-term immiserising welfare consequences. Zhang, Xing, Fan, and Luo (2008) analyse DD problem in China in the framework of regional development inequalities. They conclude that in per capita terms, economic trends in natural resource-poor areas are better than in resource-rich regions. The so-called resource curse helps explain regional inequalities in China, especially for the question of poverty in resource-rich regions of western China. The key to understanding this problem in China is property rights related to natural resources, which in China belong to the state. With reference to Ross (1999) and Stevens (2003), Zhang et al. (2008) indicate transmission channels of the so-called resource curse: worsening terms of trade, volatility in revenues, DD, weak linkages between economic sectors, rent-seeking and quality of institutions.

Barham, Bradford and Coomes (1994) have interpreted the consequences of the rubber boom in Amazonia, concluding that both public and private investments into the booming recourse-based sector in one region of the country resulted in the creation of an economic structure which is vulnerable and subject to harmful changes in terms of trade.

An example of the economy that has used rich natural resource endowment to generate economic growth is Chile (OECD, 2013) that managed to have strong exports growth combined with financial discipline and reduced the DD shock. However, Chilean regions that have large shares in a nation's exports (like the Antofagasta region) are at the same time very vulnerable to changes in the business cycles and in terms of trade.

Chile is a country for which analysis of a region's exports are done quite often, the reason being the detailed statistical data available. Rehner, Baeza, and Barton (2014) pay special attention to exports' uneven distribution in space and its consequences. They assess complex relationships between economic growth, export diversification, and dependency. The analyses are done in a long-term perspective in periods of both external shocks and strong Chilean currency. The high export specialisation of regional economies results in economic growth and export growth high volatility. Regions that are highly specialized in exports (especially exports of minerals) are strongly vulnerable to short-term demand crisis. In conclusion, Rehner et al. (2014) formulate strong recommendations to analyse specialisation patterns, export and economic growth at the regional level. They point to the issue of stability of the economic situation of regions that are heavily dependent on exports: stability is more important than dynamic growth.

Takatsuka, Zeng, and Zhao (2015) analyse DD within the context of NEG in a theoretical way for resource-based cities. Decreasing transport costs make firms move, which brings DD syndromes in terms of industry share and on welfare: the cost of deindustrialisation can be higher than gains from opening to trade.

4.1 Summary

DD represents an interesting exemplification of issues related to international economics, transposed to regions' economies. As a phenomenon traditionally assessed at country level, DD has its unquestioned regional dimension. Regional activity is unevenly distributed among regions – it is an obvious fact and a trivial statement. However, very often we forget that it brings several consequences for international economic relations of particular countries. Natural resources concentration in one region can cause DD – a regional issue can bring serious consequences for the whole economy.

Each region has its own balance of foreign trade. Thus the "national" exchange rate does not have to be the equilibrium one for all the regions within a country. Appreciation pressure "generated" by growing exports from one region – may not serve well other regions, especially when regions differ in terms of primary vs secondary sector in GDP or employment.

Detrimental consequences of DD can be mitigated. The question arises at what level it shall be done: central or regional. Central/national level policy issues might be used; for instance, tighter monetary policy can be applied, or a sort of sovereign wealth fund can be established, aimed at postponing the possible consumption boom effects from natural resources extraction. On the other hand, more emphasis can be put on regional redistribution policy. As regards regional policy, it can be managed from the central level or – according to subsidiarity principle – more decision can be attributed to regions themselves.

The source of DD syndromes can be not only exports of natural resources, but also other strongly regionally biased economic trends; for instance, the inflow of FDI, migrants' remittances, or inflow of EU structural funds. If they contribute to regional inflation rate increases, a country's foreign exchange rate held constant (ceteris paribus), they result in regions' foreign exchange rate real appreciation, finally causing competitiveness deterioration.

Stanisław Umiński

5 Overview of empirical research on regions' foreign trade activity

Foreign trade empirical analyses have predominantly been done for countries. For regions, the research is scarce. The following sections present selected, most important research focused on regional aspects of foreign trade (mostly exports). The author cannot guarantee that all the "traces" of foreign trade issues for regions have been effectively identified in the literature. But it is highly probable that the most interesting have been found.

5.1 Early works on regional exports

One of the first, interesting and worth mentioning inquiries into regional exports is Fieleke (1970), who analysed the consequences of tariff reductions within GATT Kennedy Round on New England manufacturing. For a regional level of analysis, research methods traditionally applied for countries have been used: nominal and effective tariff protection rates were calculated for major industries. In 1972, Golladay and Sandoval researched what is an optimal development policy for a region open to foreign trade: what policy instruments shall be used to reduce social costs and facilitate adjustments to exogenous economic shocks. Also, DeKaser and Sneddon Little (1994) examined exports of New England, searching for the reasons for its low competitiveness in the 80s and 90s of the previous century. The growing role of services in GDP and employment has been identified as the main structural reason, negatively affecting the export performance. Stabler and Howe (1988) divagated whether in the post-industrial area, exports of manufacturing products or – alternatively, of services – is more relevant for effective stimulation of regions' development. For the Canadian provinces, the dynamics of growth of services exports were higher than of manufacturing exports.

The research by Coughlin and Fabel (1988) as well as by Coughlin and Mandelbaum (1990) were related to factor endowments and the nature of US states' exports. The conclusion from the research is that the H-O model and its extensions can be used for a region's exports analysis; human and physical capital are sources of comparative advantage (unskilled labour is not).

Erickson (1989) examined the relation between US states' exports, industrial growth and employment. The research seems to be motivated by the growing funds spent on exports promotion. It was a time of US external trade deficit, and exports were perceived as an additional "engine" of industrial growth. However, the US domestic market was identified by Erickson (1989) as the most important target, which undoubtedly stems from the fact, that traditionally US economy is characterised by relatively low exports to GDP ratio. This fact relates to the important question: in which dimension (internal or external) shall competitiveness predominantly be assessed? Another early paper of Erickson (1978) is related to regional trade multipliers. However, trade is understood not necessarily as *foreign* trade but rather directed outside the region. The paper uses the Keynesian-type theoretical framework. The question arises, what precisely shall be treated as external trade – if looked at from a regional perspective. The American perspective is an exceptional one, as the country represents a big, relatively less open economy. Erickson and Hayward (1991) constructed a matrix of exports from US regions to foreign destinations. The research represents one of the first inquiries for the US on the role of foreign sales, combining data from different US Census Bureau records.

Lewandowski (1996) for US regions, looked for the sources of regions' export performance. Productivity, agglomeration economies and export performance were linked within a comparative advantage concept. Differences among regions (productivity of capital, the productivity of labour, R&D) are the source of their export performance.

Britton (2002) outlined the regional consequences of NAFTA trade integration for Canadian enterprises. He points out that in an opening business environment firms are stimulated to seek improvements in productivity and innovation. Trade liberalisation and the strengthened intensity of international relations result in relaxing/dismantling of economic links within the Canadian regions. Relations with regions of other countries gain in importance, and they result in the intensified transfer of knowledge, skills, competencies etc.

5.2 The role of foreign direct investment

As the research on the internationalisation of regions has proliferated, also the FDI question was raised, as the US economy has been more penetrated by foreign capital. Glickman and Woodward (1989) point to the complex influence of FDI on the US economy, saying that FDI is "neither nemesis decried by economic nationalists, nor the panacea its boosters claim .... It brings both good and bad, but crucially it brings a set of challenges to us all" (Glickman and Woodward, 1989, 1989, p. ix). Leichenko and Erickson (1997) assess the nexus between FDI and state export performance, suggesting that FDI positively contributes to states' long-term industrial competitiveness in foreign markets. This positive effect has been identified predominantly for durable goods industrial sectors (i.e. metals, machinery and electronics), in non-durables (as food products) FDI influence on export performance is weaker. According to Aitken, Hanson, and Harrison (1997) FOEs positively influence the export performance of the nearby domestic companies through the dissemination of information about foreign markets as well through technology and distribution channels that reduce foreign markets entry costs. Aitken et al. (1997) found that the probability that a domestic plant becomes an exporter, in a positive way is correlated with the proximity to a FOE.

There are several papers on the FOEs influence on regions' exports in China. For instance, Sun (2001) identified the strongest, positive influence on coastal Chinese provinces' exports and also a positive, but weaker one, for the central ones. For the western region, the influence has been found to be statistically insignificant. The strength of influence is dependent on regions' structural characteristics (level of development, industrial structure, openness). Similar "conditionality", as regards the nexus between regional exports, FDI and economic growth, was identified by Sun and Parikh (2010). In the research of Ma (2006), exporting activity (driven by FOEs) contributes to the inequalities among the Chinese provinces. Wu (2000), however, formulated different conclusions, after examination of trade and investment flows between the southern Chinese region and the rest of China: dynamically growing exports from coastal regions positively contribute to the development of inland regions. The positive effect of "advantages from backwardness" for midland China were identified, stemming from cooperation with the coastal, export-oriented provinces. Cooperation linkages that are initiated by the coastal regions' exporters evoke the catching-up effects in less developed Chinese regions.

5.3 Industrial vs export performance

Leichenko and Coulson (1999) examined the character of causality between US states' industrial performance and exports. The title of the paper needs some attention, as the term "foreign industrial exports" may be strange at first glance. However, from the US perspective, exports are often understood as sales external to the particular state – not necessarily being directed to other countries. Rather, on the contrary: in the US, there is a big domestic market and exports to GDP ratio is low (ca. 12). Thus, exports predominantly are understood as sales outside the state. Albeit strange for a non-US reader – the title of the paper precisely describes what the subject of the inquiry is. Leichenko and Coulson (1999) use the Granger causality method applied to VAR modelling. As a justification for doing so, they overview many different interpretations of the relation between economic growth and export performance. The first-round thought is that exports are the engine of economic growth, which not only stems from the so-called traditional export base theory, but also for the theory of endogenous growth. Growth external benefits arise from spillovers, associated with new product development. As the authors noticed, within H-O theorem, the direction of causality is reversed. Trade is a consequence of differences in factor endowments. A region or country specialises in the production and exporting of products, whose manufacturing requires more intensive use of a relatively more abundant (cheaper) factor(s) of production. Within the H-O theorem, factors' endowment is a source of economic growth. In new trade theory, the causal relationship between exports and (regional) growth is two-way. Exports positively contribute to regional economic growth because of economies of scale arising at the regional level. On the other hand, regional economic conditions, incl. agglomeration effects foster exports. As Leichenko and Coulson (1999, p. 483) point out, there is a situation of "strong regional economy promoting exports, and exports, in turn, promoting the regional economy". The main conclusion from the paper confirms the sophisticated relation between regional exports and growth and its bi-directional causality character.

5.4 Regional exports influence on economic development and employment

Another interesting strand of research is exports' influence on regional employment. Baldwin and Brown (2004) showed that the diversity of regions' economic structures and their higher export orientation result in decreased employment volatility in larger Canadian regions. In smaller regions, the effect was the opposite. Many offsetting effects were considered by the authors, reflecting the complexity of exports' influence on regional economies. For instance, engagement in international trade opens a region's economy for volatility and fluctuations that come from foreign markets – and it negatively influences the stability of employment. On the other hand, exporting enlarges the market in which a firm operates, and brings geographic diversification – these two effects positively influence employment. However, if firms export (as Baldwin and Brown, 2004 indicate) ceteris paribus they become bigger and therefore diversity decreases.

Similar research was carried on by Coulombe (2007), who focused on how globalisation influences regional differences in Canada. On the grounds of theoretical literature related to the nexus between international trade and regional growth, regions that are most vulnerable to volatilities in international trade have been identified. Between 1991 and 2000 for Canada, the share of foreign trade in GDP increased from 51% to 81%, which shows that the economy underwent serious changes, but the scope of internationalisation varied across regions. Contrary to other research results for Canada (based on sigma convergence), Coulombe (2007) who used conditional convergence models, did not identify the significant influence of a dynamic internationalisation process on the differences in regional development.

5.5 Regional exports promotion

Coughlin and Cartwright (1987) examined the relationship between export promotion, export performance and employment. The authors identified the positive and statistically significant influence of exports' promotion on employment, but for particular states, a big diversity of the export promotion elasticity of exports was revealed. There is a risk of detrimental competition between states, meaning that beggar-the-neighbour strategy would be used. This risk is associated with activities aimed at the attraction of FOEs. The efficiency of export promotion was also assessed by Cupitt and Reid (1991), who focused on a number of public funds allocated to the promotion, the number of states' foreign offices as well as personnel involved in promotional activity. The number of state offices was found to have no significant influence on export performance. State budget on international promotion had a negative influence on export performance – indicating that the ill-tailored promotional programs can lead to counterproductive results, negatively affecting regional competitiveness. The quality of the personnel involved in the promotional activity, as well as its quantity, turned out to be the most important factor.

The characteristics of comparative advantages of US states were examined by Clark, Sawyer, and Sprinkle (2005) with the use of RCA index. As the authors declare, they were inspired by the works of P.R. Krugman. The research was motivated by the willingness to check the effectiveness of exports promotion, performed at the state level. The comparisons were done for RCA indices calculated for exports and production, for which Clark et al. (2005) found 60% correlation. As the authors conclude, revealed comparative advantages shall be treated as guidance for distribution of public funds aimed at export promotion.

Within a similar venue, Cassey (2012) examined the consequences of overseas office closures of California, as a consequence of the state budgetary crisis in 2003. Cassey (2012) underlines the difficulty in estimating the effectiveness of exports promotion offices. Causality is a problem. It is hard to determine whether exports are large because a promotion office is efficient, or promotion office is established because a region already is a competitive exporter. Cassey (2012) treats the closure of the offices as a kind of natural experiment that helps to resolve the causality problem, using the difference-in-difference method. The author estimates a gravity type of model, with the dummy variable related to having an overseas office. Cassey (2012) concludes that estimation results are fragile, and different model specifications bring inconsistent conclusions.

Although a positive net gain calculated as the difference between exports increases and costs of offices operations has been identified, due to obtained low statistical significance, the office's effectiveness was doubtful. In another publication, Cassey (2011a) also asked a question related to causality and formulated the research question as follows: "Does the type of exports affect the odds that an overseas office exists?". In the estimated model, exports are supposed to be exogenous. Two types of goods are contrasted: relatively heterogeneous (food, beverages, processed agricultural exports) vs relatively differentiated (metal, computers, transportation equipment). The underlying idea is that the operation of an overseas office reduces exports' transaction costs. Using logit estimation, Cassey (2011a) concludes that increasing exports results in the increased odds ratio of the existence of a state overseas office in a particular country. However, no statistically important differences were identified for the two product groups in question. Cassey (2016) formulated the model that predicts a positive relationship between existing trade missions of US states' trade missions and exports by destinations. He treats trade missions as a form of public investment, aimed at increases in exports that are expected to reduce fixed costs associated with entering foreign markets. The approach proposed by Cassey is an extension of Melitz-Chaney monopolistic competition model (Chaney, 2008; Melitz, 2003) of firms' productivity differences, countries with asymmetric sizes and specific entry costs. Cassey's (2016) theoretical finding is that US states' governors' trade missions are established in those countries to which there are relatively large amounts of exports directed.

Regional activity in exports promotion was also assessed for other countries. For example, Gil et al. (2008) for Spain found that the efficiency of exports promotion is higher if done by regional agencies, than by national ones. The latter is more focused on relations between countries; the former has more precise knowledge of the needs of particular firms coming from concrete regions.

5.6 Regional trade measurement problems

Measuring state exports was an important aspect of discussion about a region's foreign trade in the US. Coughlin and Mandelbaum (1991) described and compared two ways in which manufacturing exports could be estimated. As those two sources provided conflicting information, the paper was a part of the discussion on the way the system of foreign exports data collection shall be organised. This historical discussion for the US, as perceived from today's perspective, is interesting because it shows important aspects, strengths and weaknesses of alternative methods of data collection. The two systems in question were: EME (Exports from Manufacturing Establishments) and OMC (Origin of Movement of Commodities). EME was based on the adjusted survey of manufacturing establishments. The data was relatively useful in estimating the number of jobs in manufacturing, dependent on foreign sales, registered at the state level. EME data has had the following shortcomings: it comprised only manufacturing exports, data was available with a delay of at least two years, the value of the shipment was reported, instead of value-added. An alternative system, OMC was intended to report "where merchandise begins its export journey" (Coughlin and Mandelbaum, 1991, p. 67). Data from OMC system did not so much inform about the place from which manufacturing production of a final good was coming from (as components may have come from various places), but rather the place from which the product export journey started, or the place in which shipped products were consolidated. The most important difference between EME and OMC is that EME's main task was to identify the location of production of exported products; in OMC identification of the location of production was not the primary goal.

Also, Cassey (2006) gives an extensive inquiry into the methodology of data collection on US states' exports. Pros and cons of different methods are presented, the main issue being the origin of movement vs origin of production. The detailed correspondence (or substitutability) between the two databases is analysed.

Our intention is not to describe the details of the US system of data collection on exports at the regional level. Those issues, however, are important as for instance in Poland within GUS (Poland's Main Statistical Office) the discussion was initiated on how the data on a region's exports shall be collected.[2]

5.7 Shift share and gravity

Cletus C. Coughlin's research deserves attention, as his inquiry on states' exports continued throughout the years. For instance, Coughlin and Pollard (2001), while looking into differences across US states in exports growth using shift-share analyses, distinguish an industry mix effect and a competitive effect. Industry mix effect means that a particular region's exports are more concentrated in those industries that witnessed exports' faster expansion, than for the whole nation. It has a positive sign, but it can also be negative if the expansion is slower, relative to the whole nation. The second one, the competitive effect, captures the deviations of a region's exports from what would be expected if it had grown due to the expansion of country exports. It enables to show the consequences of changes in such aspects, as regional factors endowment, export promotion etc. Coughlin and Pollard (2001) in fact, added the third component to the classical shift-share analysis: destination-country effect. The authors show big variations among states; however, the competitive effect turned out to be the most important determinant of exports growth relative to a nations' average – the reason maybe the importance of investment in human capital per worker.

Coughlin and Wall (2003) used a gravity model to assess changing patterns of exports from the US states. NAFTA agreement consequences have been assessed for particular states: their vulnerability to changes in trade liberalisation differs. The political dimension of trade liberalisation is also depicted, because the US House of Representatives members have expressed their opinion about the consequences of NAFTA, expecting jobs and wages increases in particular states. The authors apply standard international trade theory to regions' trade, including trade creation and trade diversion effects.

The study of Coughlin and Novy (2013) represents the usage of gravity models, which is aimed at the assessment of a border effect and comparison of international vs domestic border effect. Comparison of these two kinds of borders would also be

2 For more information on aspects of regional data collection on exports, see also in: Sneddon Little (1990); Ott (1988); Smith (1989).

interesting for other countries, including Poland. However, it is impossible because of a lack of statistical information on "domestic exports" geographical distribution. Interesting terminology has been worked out, as pointed out by Wolf (2000), who assessed domestic border effect or international home bias. Coughlin and Novy (2013) added an additional dimension to their study and built a database that consists of information on trade: within an individual state's trade (local trade), trade between states and trade between states and foreign destinations (countries). Their study brings rather surprising conclusions: the international border effect turned to be smaller than domestic border effect: the additional, marginal cost of exporting internationally compared to exporting to another US state (controlled for distance and trade partner size) is relatively smaller, compared to the cost associated with just "leaving" the state. There are three variants of distance calculation used in the paper, which shows the high quality (precision) of data available for US as well as the question of short ranges vs long-distance ranges in modelling trade flows. The efforts undertaken by Coughlin and Novy (2013), as well as by others (i.e. Nitsch, 2000; Wolf, 2000; Llano-Verduras, Minondo, and Requena-Silvente, 2011) show how important the method of distance calculation for gravity estimations is in trade models, especially in border effects assessments. This question shall be taken into consideration in research for Poland: region-country distance in gravity models shall be calculated not only with reference to location of capital of particular regions but also with reference to the other largest cities within the region.

In another paper, Coughlin (2004) also uses the concept of gravity to identify determinants of the changing geography of US states exports. The general conclusion is that proximity to markets or "distance of trade" matters. Coughlin concludes that although the "death of distance" has been proclaimed as a result of the globalisation and changes in communication, the importance of proximity as a determinant of trade intensity is increasing. The term (or concept) of "usual suspects" is used to identify the three most important determinants of the intensity of foreign trade links between US states and partner countries in foreign trade. These are trading partners' income growth, membership in NAFTA and changes in transportation costs. A new suspect is added, which is the fragmentation of international production.

Gravity framework has also been used by Cassey (2010a), who concludes that the gravity model cannot effectively explain why Texas' share in US trade to Mexico has been decreasing. The study proves how detailed and focused on particular region-country pairs research is in American literature. The way distance is measured strongly influences gravity model effectiveness. The general conclusion of Cassey (2010a) is that "talks about the death of distance" are exaggerated. Distance role is not decreasing in importance; however, the author identifies the decreasing role of the contiguity.

5.8 Exchange rate changes and regional trade

Cronovich and Gazel (1998) assessed the possible influence of exchange rates changes on regional exports. It seems a promising area of research also for other countries and their regions. Application of a lumpy country perspective (Courant and Deardorff, 1992), in which regions substantially differ as regards their export patterns (incl. export intensity as measured in per capita or per km^2 terms and exports structure by countries) drives the researcher's attention to the individual sensitivity to exchange rates volatility. This issue was initially mentioned in DD literature overview (section 4). Each region might have its own equilibrium exchange rate. Imagine, for instance, the situation of coal exporting regions of Poland during the period of low prices for coal on the international market. Their situation is not promising. Some competitive pressure on the coal mining sector could be reduced by exchange rate adjustments. Surely it is a controversial idea as the exchange rate is determined for the "whole country". However, if regions are treated as SOEs, exchange rate levels and their volatility seem to be on the list of determinants of regions' export performance. Cronovich and Gazel (1998) suggest that real exchange rates have a significant impact on regional exports if they are constructed/calculated in a proper way. It is necessary to use region-specific trade weights, instead of "standard", national trade weights. Research by Cronovich and Gazel (1998) is, in fact, an inspiration to pay more attention to region-specific factors that influence exports. So far, in the research of exports performance of Poland's regions, nor for regions of other countries, the issue of exchange rates has not been seriously treated. Consequences of exchange rate changes for Quebec's exports were also analysed by Dufort and Murray (2004), who also assessed the determinants of Quebec exports to the US. Their interpretation of possible consequences of exchange rate changes is based on classical rules, known from international economics, related to the short and long-run influence of appreciation and depreciation on export and import competitiveness. In 1988-1998, 80% of the growth of Quebec exports to the US was a consequence of the US GDP increase (demand effect), the remaining 20% came from trade liberalisation agreement and the Canadian dollar depreciation.

5.9 Andrew Cassey's comprehensive inquiry and stylised facts

A thorough study on regions' exports was presented by Cassey (2010b), who has formulated seventeen stylised facts on US states' exports. In another publication, Cassey (2011b) limits the number of these facts to nine. As proposed by the author, the proper level of analysis must be decided on. On the one hand, the "most local level" is recommended, in order to trace the foreign trade idiosyncrasy of particular local communities. On the other hand, the locality scale of the study shall be large enough to constitute a self-governed administrative unit, effective in economic policy implementation, capable of influencing foreign trade patterns. Publication by Cassey (2010b) is, in fact, inspiring research that could be done for regions of other countries if firm-level data is combined with regional data on exports. Each country is specific as far as its patterns of regions' exports are concerned, which stems from its political/ administrative framework (centralisation vs decentralisation being one of the most important questions from the point of view of exports analyses). Therefore, it is not possible to make the same array of research tasks for each country. The seventeen stylised facts identified in the quoted publication deserve attention and are inspiring for other countries' regions' exports research.

The US is a relatively less open economy, and it is not a surprise that for particular states exports represent a small fraction of total sales. This fraction, however, differs for each of the states, from a minimum of about 4-5% to a maximum of 31%. It sheds some light on the difference in states' vulnerability to shocks from external markets and the structure of their economies in terms of tradables vs non-tradables.[3] On the other hand, the percentage of exporting (vs non-exporting) firms is less diversified across states. It shows that although the heterogeneity concept holds (meaning that not all firms can become exporters), this heterogeneity is relatively evenly distributed regionally. Another stylised fact is that from each of the states, exports are only to a fraction of possible destinations. The same applies to imports. Some of the destinations that can be named "exotic" are served by a small number of exporters.

Using location quotients (LQ) that relate a state's share in US exports to its share in nations' value-added, Cassey (2010b) concludes that there exist specialised exporters. Specialisation shall not only by assessed as being to "any" destinations but also to particular ones (for instance state X has specialised in exports to country A). Next observation by Cassey (2010b) reminds us of a principle of comparative advantage: "nearly all states are relatively specialized in exporting something somewhere". That brings an important policy implication: even less developed regions – "weaker" in exports, as compared to the most competitive ones – always have the revealed specialisation in "something", sold "somewhere". Cassey (2010b) stipulates that regions' industrial mix does not necessarily have to be the primary determinant of export specialisation. Regions having access to the sea and possessing ports tend to export to

---

3 Also in other publications, the element of shock is used as a concept of research on regional aspects of foreign trade. For instance Todtling (1997) has identified the chances for the Austrian regions' exports, stemming from transformation process that started in the countries of Central and Eastern Europe. As he concludes, the consequences would be diversified, depending on the character of the Austrian regional economies, if they are central or peripheral, witness economies of scale effects and agglomeration tendencies, are endowed with proper transport infrastructure etc. Volpe Martincus and Blyde (2013) assessed the consequences of a shock, which was an earthquake in Chile, that negatively influenced exports. Earthquake consequences translated into changes in transport infrastructure, which resulted in transportation costs increases.

relatively more distant countries, which points to the role of infrastructure and the role of intermediaries in foreign trade.

5.10 Exports agglomeration

Exports are geographically concentrated. This observation shall not be a surprise, as a tendency to concentrate is a general phenomenon observed for economic activity. For the US (as well as for Poland) the concentration of exporting to specific destinations is observed. For instance, regions localised closer to Canada are relatively more specialised in exporting to this country (the same applies to northern regions of Poland specialised in exports to Scandinavian or Nordic countries).

As already mentioned, one of the factors embraced in the research on regions' exports is agglomeration. Empirical research on the nature of exports is advancing. It does not show "just" agglomeration but looks deeper into its nature. For instance, Cassey and Schmeiser (2013) show spillovers from the regional concentration of exports in Russia. Agglomeration happens "around" destination of exports. The authors underline the question of an informational trade barrier, which is a destination barrier. They use a monopolistic competition trade model with agglomeration component incorporated. Agglomeration leads to reductions in variable costs of exporting, due to economies of scale in shipment and transportation. As most shipments are small, benefits from containerisation are beyond individual exporters. If they agglomerate, they can overcome this barrier. Also, externalities from information spillovers are important, which reflects how-to export-related knowledge.

The research by Cassey and Schmeiser (2013) is an interesting contribution to the ongoing discussion in the literature on export spillovers. For example, Lovely, Rosenthal, and Sharma (2005) examined the role of specialised knowledge on foreign markets needed in exporting that contributes to the spatial concentration of exporters' headquarters. For France, Koenig (2009) showed a positive contribution of existing pools of exporters for decisions to start exports to particular countries (underlining destination-specific factors). Also, Aray (2015) proves that sunk costs associated with entering foreign markets are reduced if potential exporters can benefit from the experience of the nearby already exporting firms. Naudé and Matthee (Febr. 2007) as well as Ciżkowicz, Rzońca, and Umiński (2013) depicted the role of ports in regional exports performance, and Glejser, Jacquemin, and Petit (1980) identified clustering of exporters around GDP. Cassey, Schmeiser, and Waldkirch (2016), using spatial econometrics, looked even deeper into the nature of export externalities for Russia. They show that externalities, stemming from the neighbourhood of other exporters, are stronger if export sales are to the same country. In the case of exporting, generally, they are weaker.

The agglomeration issue is closely related to the role of metropolises in exports. Noponen, Markusen, and Driessen (1997) divagate over the international trade for lower than a state, level. They do it for metropolitan areas. Because metropolitan areas have relatively more diversified industrial structures, their positions in international trade substantially differ. The authors found that the existence of a harbour does not necessarily guarantee a superior position in trade, which brings the conclusion that a dummy variable related to a harbour shall be treated rather as a control, and not as a crucial explanatory variable.

Head, Mayer, and Ries (2004) used the HME concept to explain the industry concentration mechanism. Local spillovers and high demand that is an attribute of particular locations that witness home market effect, result in a disproportionate share of the industry. Therefore, the relatively small number of locations generate most of the export volumes. This phenomenon reflects the country's lumpiness, which is represented by the agglomeration of export potential around cities (Brakman and van Marrewijk, 2013). Exporting requires specialized knowledge that is agglomerated in cities (Lovely et al., 2005). As a small fraction of firms become exporters, this kind of knowledge is crucial. Exporting requires not only the possession of a manufactured product but rather a whole package of information and capabilities that make an international transaction possible. Simmie (2002) showed that clusters of innovative firms matter for exports. In a metropolitan, agglomerated, innovative area, an exporter has access to a pool of resources and competences, from which the ones needed for exports can be chosen. The author underlines the cumulative causation that self-perpetually reinforces metropolis' driving force in exports. Also, Thissen, Diodato, and van Ort (2013) proved the leading role of agglomerations in European regions' exports. Their conclusions, however, show convergence in export potential across the European regions, because central and eastern regions of Europe are catching up. In 2010 only two of Poland's metropolitan regions appeared on their map of trade flows above EUR 500 million threshold. By Berube and Parilla (2012), with reference to Krugman, metropolises are critical nodes of trade. These are cities, not nations, that were the original global commercial nodes. High productivity "concentrated" in metropolises positively influences exports (Melitz heterogeneity concept). Metropolitan areas shall not, however, be treated as a source of "only" international trade, but trade per se, which was shown by The Economist (2013).

5.11 Agricultural exports

Regions differ in their structural characteristics, which implies that the export base is diversified. Products offered by regions are not the same in terms of their tradability. Leichenko and Silva (2004) pay attention to the nexus between international trade, earnings and employment in US rural counties. Within the context of the NEG, in an open economy being subject to globalisation forces, an agglomeration brings far more spatial concentration for tradable sectors than for non-tradable ones. This implies the inferior capacity of rural areas to participate in international trade. Rural areas are relatively well endowed with unskilled labour and less endowed with physical and human capital.

Moreover, as Leichenko and Silva (2004) suggest, the type of existing agglomerations in rural areas (for instance in carpet or apparel manufacturing), instead of bringing positive spillovers, may, in fact, pose disadvantages. The authors stipulate that rural markets are therefore insulated from market signals and less probable to adopt more advanced technological solutions.[4] The authors conclude that export orientation harms employment and earnings in both urban and rural areas. This is because turbulences from international markets are transmitted into employment. Such conclusions raise doubts about the rationale of exports promotion. An important conclusion formulated by Leichenko and Silva (2004) is that relations between exports, imports, exchange rate changes and earnings and employment assessed at the regional level are very complex and "work" against conventional wisdom. Not only exports' but also imports' influence on regional economies shall be analysed.

Eff and Livingston (2007) asked if there is an export gap between rural and urban areas, which could negatively contribute to the economic prosperity of rural America. Three reasons why rural areas can be in a less favourable position in exporting that were identified by the authors are as follows: a rural character as such negatively influences the export capacity, the rural business environment is less competitive and rural regions are disadvantaged in terms of infrastructure. The probability that an establishment will export or not is modelled with the use of three sets of data: establishment (firm) characteristics (age, size, branch, industrial sector and its tradability) local business environment (information externalities, localisation economies, human capital and economic activity), infrastructural disadvantages (transportation and distance as well as infrastructure quality). The authors conclude that infrastructure slightly favours rural establishments. Human capital – on the contrary – has been identified as the most important component of the gap between rural and urban exporting. Also, information externalities (precisely saying: information externalities and the availability of educational and professional services) turned out to be a drawback for rural areas as far as their export potential is concerned. The size of the gaps between rural and urban areas concerning international trade has been smaller than expected. Demographic, sociological, human capital deficiencies, as well as poor access to information and professional services, were identified as the most important factors hindering propensity to export in rural areas. Similar conclusions, pointing low labour quality and poor skills, negatively affecting export potential and

4 For the role of technological potential and regional differences of exports see also in Johansson and Karlsson (2007) who found that investments in research and development increase Sweden's regions' exports divergence, by increases in the number export markets and of the exported products. Also for Sweden, Grasjo (2008) has identified statistically significant, positive influence of accessibility to R&D and university-educated labour on regional export performance.

competitiveness as of rural areas were formulated by Gale (1998) and Gale, McGranahan, Teixeira, and Greenberg (1999).

Ciżkowicz et al. (2013) estimated the model of agricultural exports that is particularly important for less developed Polish regions. The share of agricultural and food product exports in total regions exports was positively related to the agricultural employment share in the total labour force, access of the region to the sea and the share of people with secondary vocational education or post-secondary education in the population 15-64 years old. The share was negatively related to the location of the region at the border and population density. The authors conclude that agricultural and food products increasing share in total exports shall be treated a chance to improve the living standards of citizens living in Poland's underdeveloped regions.

5.12 Focus on particular regions

Another strand in the literature on regions' exports are publications devoted to each region, that represent rather more detailed analysis, that – depending on the purpose of the analysis and data availability – focus on: exports (and imports) trends, industrial structure of trade flows, country patterns, mode of transportation, etc. For the US, an example of such a short inquiry is Cassey and Lee (2015). They are strictly one region/state-oriented and do not include any more sophisticated models or calculation methods. They are rather informative, in nature. For Poland, Gawlikowska-Hueckel and Umiński prepared a series of publications and reports that have been focused on particular regions (Gawlikowska-Hueckel and Umiński, 2009; Gawlikowska-Hueckel and Umiński, 2011; Umiński, 2010).[5] Several publications were focused on particular Italian regions. For instance, Benedictis (2005) using comparative advantages indices, showed the positive contribution of industrial districts on the changing patterns of the Italian southern and northern regions' exports. Guerrieri and Iammarino (2006) examined the differences between southern Italian regions and showed their distinct export characteristics at NUTS 3 level. Attention has been paid to the growing regional export heterogeneity and the fact that "many Mezzogiorni" can be distinguished in southern Italy. For Mexican Yucatan, Biles (2004) made a critical appraisal of maquiladora export-oriented plants. He identified their positive impact on economic growth both for urban and rural areas. However, their activity does not contribute to long-term positive structural changes because of weak cooperative links between maquiladoras and Mexican domestic companies.[6]

5 See also in Ciżkowicz and Opala (2011).

6 Please notice that these conclusions are contrary to Aitken et al. (1997).

5.13 Border effect

An important part of the research is the examination of the border effect, the fundamental question being if borders between countries matter for trade. The intensive discussion was initiated by McCalum (1995), who has used the gravity model to compare the trade flows between Canadian provinces with trade flows between Canadian provinces and US states. McCalum made reference to Ohmae (1999), who declared that national borders have become less relevant than ever, and the world has become borderless. As McCalum (1995) showed, borders did matter. His publication evoked an intensive discussion on the meaning of national borders. Helliwell (1996) for Quebec identified a very strong border effect, while Anderson and Smith (1999b) after incorporation of the wider data set, found the border effect still to be significant, but weaker. In another publication, Anderson and Smith (1999a) postulate that in trade between Canada and the US, a strong border effect exists. Still, due to important differences between the provinces, their individual border effects shall be analysed. Brown and Anderson (2002) recommended that in estimations of the border effect, a region's industrial structure shall also be taken into account because the border effect strength in particular industries differs.

Border effect assessments were also done for other countries, for which it is possible to compare intranational (interregional) trade with international trade. A very strong border effect was identified by Gil-Pareja, Llorca-Vivero, Martinez-Serrano, and Oliver-Alonso (2005). Trade between the Spanish regions (in the period 1995-1998) turned out to be 21 times higher than the Spanish regions' international trade (controlled for market size and distance in the gravity model). The authors conclude that the strengths of the border effect turned out to be different for each of the Spanish regions. Relatively less intensive border effect (12-16 times) was identified by Gil-Pareja, Llorca-Vivero, and Martínez-Serrano (2006) for the Basque country, its intensity being higher for imports than for exports. The introduction of the euro did not decrease the tendency of the Basque country to trade more with other Spanish regions than with other countries. Consequences of the euro introduction were also examined by Costa-i-Font and Tremosa-i-Balcells (2003), who found the biggest Spanish regions to be best prepared to participate in the European currency area. The authors also identified important differences in the volatility of regional, real exchange rates.[7]

5.14 Main research on Poland's regional exports

As regards Poland, Cieślik (2005) analysed regions' exports as a part of the research focused on the geography of FDI in Poland. The author found that the geographical

7 For the consequences of euro introduction see: Duque, Ramos, and Suriñach (2005)

concentration of FOEs is accompanied by higher exports of domestic enterprises. However, due to highly aggregated statistical data, it was not possible to identify the character of the externalities between those two groups of firms. Gawlikowska-Hueckel and Umiński (2013b) presented the assessment of Poland's regions competitiveness with a focus on exports. The authors conclude that much more attention shall be put in order to promote exports at the regional level. FDI inflow has been identified as a factor contributing to the emergence of the so-called hot spots – areas of the dynamic exports changes. Umiński (2012) made a comprehensive assessment of Poland's regions' exports also with reference to theoretical aspects of international trade, FDI, competitiveness and location aspects – reviewed within a regional perspective. A gravity, panel model, was estimated for Poland's regions, revealing the significant influence of distance, regions' and countries' GDP and openness on bilateral region-country trade flows. Umiński (2016) underlines the principle of subsidiarity as a justification of export promotion policy performed at the regional level. Majkowska-Szulc (2016), while presenting aspects of the EU commercial policy, concludes that although the EU commercial policy is a common policy with the EU's exclusive competences, within the development of the EU law, it is possible to preclude actions aimed at exports promotion at a regional level aimed at regional cohesion. Komornicki and Szejgiec (2015) presented the participation of local Polish units in the global economy and areas of exports concentration. The authors found overall exports concentration to be higher in western Poland. The number and the extent of export centres have increased, as compared to the situation at the beginning of the twenty-first century. Export tends to concentrate predominantly around industrial production centres and around the capital city, in which FOEs' headquarters are established.

Gajewski and Tchorek (2017), using firm-level survey dataset, unveiled differences in determinants of export performance in Poland's structurally different areas. Firms from Poland's less developed regions in the East in their export strategies benefit from family ties in business and from product innovation and non-price competitiveness. In the western part of the country, export success predominantly stems from economies of scale and foreign ownership.

Nazarczuk and Umiński (2018a) showed the geography of openness to foreign trade in Poland. High regional dissimilarities were identified, as well as the crucial role of foreign ownership. The role of SEZs has grown. The role of foreign ownership was also inquired by Nazarczuk et al. (2019). The detailed analysis of foreign trade in SEZs was presented by Nazarczuk and Umiński (2019) and in Nazarczuk and Umiński (2018b). Nazarczuk, Umiński, and Márquez-Ramos (2020) present the vulnerability of Polish and Spanish regions in the sphere of foreign trade to the consequences of Brexit. Brodzicki and Umiński (2017) unveiled the role of metropolises and path dependency for exports of Poland's regions. Brodzicki et al. (2019) identified the patterns and determinants of IIT and its vertical and horizontal components for regions of Spain and Poland.

5.15 Conclusions

International trade constitutes an important part of international economics as such. Empirical research on international trade of countries is enormous. For regions, one can find a relatively limited number of publications, although it is on the rise.

Empirical research can be performed if relevant statistical data is available. This is why the US and Canada are the two countries for which the first, leading research was done. It also explains why for these two countries, related research is most abundant. One may consider it a paradox because the US does not represent a type of economy with higher openness (as measured by exports to GDP ratio). Rather, on the contrary – exports to GDP for the US are one of the lowest, which reflects the situation of a big economy with a large home/domestic market. As Umiński (2012) noticed, the Americans pioneered in many areas of economic research; therefore, one shall not be surprised that their interest in regional aspects of exporting was revealed relatively early. The second reason was already mentioned, which is statistical data availability at a highly disaggregated level.

Elimination of trade barriers between countries and thereof globalisation resulted in the increased exposition of regions' economies to impulses (and shocks) coming from foreign markets. Parallelly, the competitiveness debate has been initiated. It increased countries' and consequently their regions', willingness to evaluate their positions among others. External economic relations (predominantly trade) have become the area at which the so-called ability to compete is judged.

The US system of data collection for exports (and imports) exemplifies how detailed/precise statistics for regions can be available. Canada or Chile are other good examples, in Europe, Spain shall be mentioned in this respect. Review of the American literature shows how long and how consequently the methodological issues of data collection and dissemination have been discussed. A scientific debate resulted in a series of publications showing the pros and cons of various statistical solutions, which shall be treated as a guide or benchmark for countries that are improving their public statistics systems. The corresponding research for Poland can only be done with the use of data depicting the place in which an exporter has its seat. As the availability of precise and reliable statistics on exports and imports for Poland's regions is becoming more important, the system of data collection and dissemination shall be seriously improved. The US, Canadian or Spanish systems can be treated as benchmarks; however, France shall also be considered. For France, researchers have access to individual firm's statistical data, including precise information on exports. Shall the system of public statistics in Poland be improved, it also ought to embrace information on domestic sales vs exports. This would enable us to assess the strength of the border effect for Poland's regions.

As the US example shows, promotion efficiency is an important aspect of an inquiry on the region's exports. In the EU, commercial policy lies within the exclusive competences of its institutions. Regions of the MS are not directly involved in the promotion of exports. Nevertheless, it is done indirectly, for instance through financial assistance for participation in foreign fairs, provision of information on foreign markets or establishment, and operation of regions' foreign representative offices. As stems from other countries' experience, for Poland, an attempt to measure the efficiency of promotion shall also be done. For instance, a relevant binary variable in the gravity model shall be included, informing if a region has its foreign representative office established in a certain country.

Regions are SOEs, whose export and import links are diversified. A promising area of research would be to analyse the consequences of trade agreements that the EU is negotiating (for instance with the EU or Canada) for particular regions, at least with attention to the intensity of their relations with countries in question or the number of firms involved. It could shed interesting light on the consequences for regions' labour markets.

In the export analysis performed for regions with the predominant use of gravity models, frequently the lagged variables are used. It reflects the long-term perspective required to capture, for instance, FDI influence on exports, indigenous capital investments, or exports – done previously. The inclusion of the time-lagged exports on the list of independent variables in the model would enable to capture the persistence of trade links and the entry costs borne so far by exporting firms.

Regions' prosperity depends not only on exports but also on import-related issues. The ability to compete with imports shall also be a subject of research, as well as imports influence on regional economies in a long-term perspective.

The overview of literature brings inconclusive results as far as how the existence of harbours influences regions' exports. It can bring a superior position; however, it rather shall be treated as a control, and not as a crucial explanatory variable. Due to containerisation, many benefits and advantages of harbours were transferred to inland regions or cities. The quality of transport infrastructure, linking inland regions to harbours, gains in importance.

Agglomeration of exporters and concentration of exports has drawn some attention in the research for Poland. However, more emphasis should be put on the identification of factors that make exporters localise close one to another. The character of externalities between them shall be inquired.

The Spanish literature underlined the consequences of euro introduction for regional economies and their trade links' patterns and intensity. This issue for Poland did not draw serious attention of researchers, with few exceptions (Gajewski, Gawlikowska-Hueckel, and Umiński, 2009). Poland's membership in the eurozone is not expected from a short-term perspective. However, in the long-term, it is more likely, and the relevant research on the euro introduction consequences for regions ought to be performed, at least tracing the intensities of trade relations with the eurozone member countries.

The nexus between trends in regional trade (exports, imports and trade balance) and exchange rate changes seems to be another promising subject to be assessed.

Poland is not yet a member of the eurozone, exchange rate changes thus affect external trade far more than, for instance, in most of the eurozone regions. The consequences of exchange rate alterations are usually measured at the country level. However, it's very likely, that in particular regions, the sensitivity of exports, imports and trade balance to exchange rate changes are diversified. Two aspects shall be distinguished. The first one is the sensitivity of a region's external trade to exchange rate volatility, which is usually included in the gravity-type modelling. The second one is the elasticity of regions' trade flows to appreciation or depreciation of the national currency. As suggested by the literature for the US regions, the trade-weighted, region-specific exchange rates shall be used.

The export base concept was referred to in the early literature on regional exporting activity for the US. This seems to be especially interesting with reference to the smart specialisation concept. The question how regional industrial base translates into the character of exporting activity shall be a subject of through research (Cordes et al., 2016). It would also shed light on the intermediary function performed by some exporting regions (see more in Komornicki and Szejgiec, 2017).

The assessment of FOEs' role in a region's export performance deserves special attention. As FOEs are the providers of external economies to the regions, their influence on exports is expected to be significant (Nazarczuk, Umiński, and Jurkiewicz, 2020). The following topics (nexus between FDI and exports and FOEs vs domestic firms comparisons) are recommended to be analysed: (i) FDI influence on export intensity (exports per capita) and exports dynamics, (ii) FDI and the strengths of exports revealed comparative advantages, (iii) FDI and quality of exports (unit exports value, technological advancement), (iv) nexus between FDI and exports intensive and extensive margins, (v) FDI and intensity of IIT trade.

Within the general assessment of regions' exports, the question of agricultural and food products can be distinguished. For instance, the question arises if exports from agriculture-oriented regions are mediocre as a consequence of agricultural products being less competitive by their nature, or the regions are lacking human capital and informational capacities – much required in exporting activity.

Cities and metropolises seem to become more important in exports (as they become trade nodes of the globalising world), the relevant variables reflecting metropolisation shall be used in modelling. As suggested by Sassen (2009), cities and metropolises serve different functions in the globalised economy. Therefore, their special functions shall be distinguished in the research. For instance, Functional Urban Areas delimitations can be used.

The publication edited by Batabyal and Nijkamp (2015) shall be mentioned in the trade-related literature on regional aspects of the trade. Within the book, one finds the overview of theoretical concepts, originating from the international trade literature, which can be used for interpretations of trade between regions. The chapters of the book are focused on such particular questions as analysis of trade flows between the US regions, consequences of openness to trade for cities in 84 countries and application of the gravity principle to the analysis of the developing transport infrastructure in Turkey. The main message of the book is the necessity to shift the attention of researchers from trade between countries to trade between regions.

Part III: **Empirical Analyses of Regions' Foreign Trade**

Tomasz Brodzicki

6 Trade openness of Polish and Spanish regions

The principal aim of this chapter is to present the level of openness of analysed Polish and Spanish NUTS 2 regions and changes in it and to identify the potential relationship between the extent of openness of regions and their economic growth.

The extent of economic openness is not easy to define, and many definitions coexist. An open economy is defined, for instance by www.businessdictionary.com as "a market-economy mostly free from trade barriers where exports and imports form a large percentage of the GDP. No economy is open or closed in terms of trade restrictions, and all governments have varying degrees of control over movements of capital and labour. The degree of openness of an economy determines a government's freedom to pursue economic policies of its choice and the susceptibility of the country to international economic cycles".

The above definition stresses the extent of liberalisation of flows of both goods as well as of flows of major production factors such as labour and capital. Nonetheless, the most widely utilized matric of openness – the openness index – is calculated as a ratio of a country's/region's total trade to its GDP. According to the World Bank national accounts database, the global openness index in 2015 was 58%, and it reached its maximum level in 2008 (60.34%). In comparison, it was only 24.21% in 1960, 38.78 in 1980, and 51.37% in 2000. Except for recent years, in relation to the global financial crisis, the overall level of openness has significantly and visibly increased. At the same time, the extent of openness varies greatly between countries, and to an even larger extent, between regions within individual countries.

As an illustration of the above, in the present study we are dealing with NUTS 2 regions of Poland, and Spain observed over the period 2005 to 2014. Over the period the openness, the ratio increased in most of the regions (on average by 9%). The openness ratio dropped only in the case of Mazowieckie, Balearic Islands, Canary Islands, and Madrid (please refer to Fig. 6.1). At the other extreme, the highest increases have been reported in Andalusía, Łódzkie, Dolnośląskie and Opolskie (by more than 15%), Lubuskie by approx. 25%, Region of Murcia by 33%, and Pomorskie by 34.3%. The lowest openness ratio in 2014 was observed in the Canary Islands (island region of Spain) and the highest for the Pomorskie – the seaside region of Poland with two significant seaports located in Gdańsk and Gdynia with the biggest container terminal in the Baltic Sea Region located in Gdańsk (Deepwater Container Terminal).

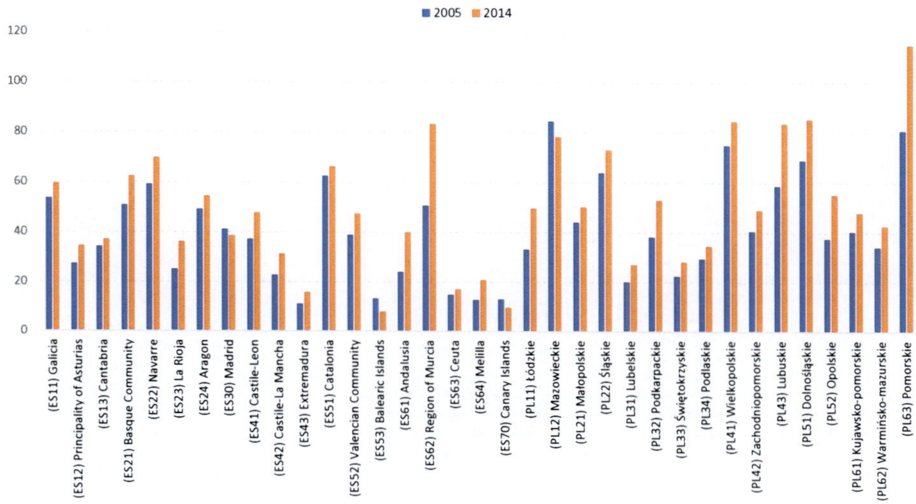

Figure 6.1: Openness ratios of Polish and Spanish NUTS 2 regions in 2005-2014

Source: Own elaboration based on Polish and Spanish regional trade datasets.

In Figure 6.2 we observe the level of GDP per capita in EUR per capita in Spanish and Polish NUTS 2 regions in 2005 and 2014. One can note that GDP per capita is significantly higher in Spanish regions than in Polish regions. The highest GDP per capita in 2014 was observed in Madrid, the Basque Community, Navarre, and Catalonia. The highest GDP per capita in Poland in 2014 was observed in the capital region of Mazowieckie. It, however, exceeded at the same time the level of GDP per capita of only three Spanish NUTS 2 regions – Melilla, Andalusia, and Extremadura. The distance between Polish and Spanish regions in terms of the overall level of development is nonetheless shrinking. It can be seen in Figure 6.3. It shows the average growth rate of GDP per capita (left-hand side) and the change in GDP per capita in EUR between 2005-2014 (right-hand side) in Spanish and Polish NUTS 2 regions. Polish regions are growing (on average) faster than Spanish regions. The fastest growth rates are observed in the Basque Community and Madrid. In Poland, this applies to Mazowieckie and Dolnośląskie. GDP per capita in EUR terms decreased in the observed period in the case of Balearic Islands (ES53), Melilla (ES64), and Canary Islands (ES70).

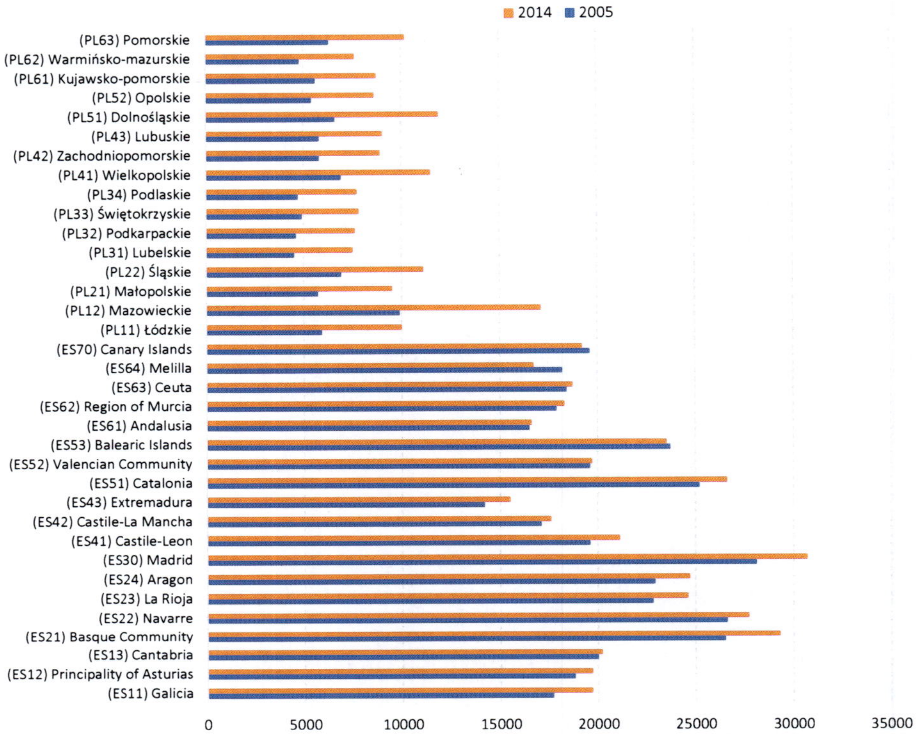

Figure 6.2: GDP per capita in EUR per capita in Spanish and Polish NUTS 2 regions
Source: Own elaboration.

Investigating the issue further, we can state that within the joined group of regions, we observe a clear beta-absolute (please refer to Figure 6.4) and sigma-convergence in GDP per capita. Within countries, the evidence points, however, to sigma-divergence (please refer to Figure 6.5). The standard deviation of GDP per capita is non-decreasing, taking all the periods considered into account. It holds in particular for Spain, after the financial and eurozone crises.

Greater openness seems overall to affect regional economic growth in our sample positively. The relationship between the initial level of openness in 2005 and the average growth rate of GDP per capita in the analysed period is positive (please refer to Figure 6.6). It also seems to hold with the GDP per capita when we compare the initial and final year of our analysis (please refer to Figure 6.7). Of course, drawing more robust conclusions requires the use of more formal econometric techniques. The

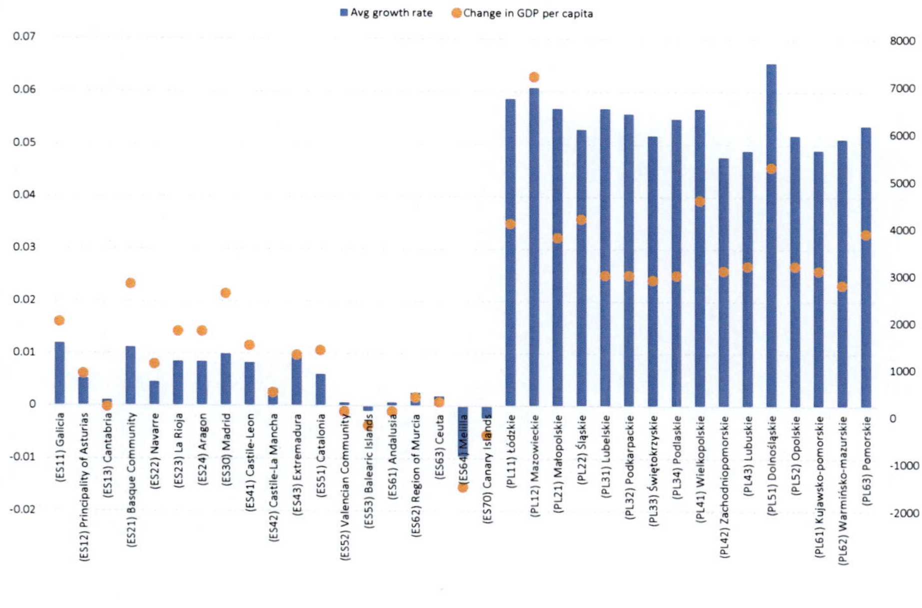

Figure 6.3: The average growth rate of GDP per capita (left-hand side) and the change in GDP per capita in EUR between 2005-2014 (right-hand side) in Spanish and Polish NUTS 2 regions

Source: Own elaboration.

main empirical analysis in the area was published in the journal article by Brodzicki (2017b).

The main conclusions from the analysis mentioned above are the following. Using a dynamic panel data model estimated with the two-step GMM, an empirical growth model for Polish and Spanish NUTS 2 regions was estimated over the period 2000-2014 to identify the dependence of regional growth on the extent of openness. Greater openness seems overall to affect regional economic growth in our sample positively. The results of the Granger non-causality test point, however, to the existence of a bidirectional relationship between the variables.

Its impact on the dependent variable (real GDP per capita) is positive and statistically significant. A greater degree of trade openness thus boosts the economic growth of Polish and Spanish regions, ceteris paribus. In an extension of the base specification of the model, we accounted for the potential joint effect of openness and human capital endowment on the level of GDP per capita by an introduction of an interaction term. The magnitude of the impact of openness when we accounted for the interaction was significantly stronger; however, the coefficient on the interaction term was negative and statistically significant which meant that it decreased in the level of the human capital endowment. An increase in the extent of openness brought stronger effects on GDP per capita of regions with initially lower levels of the human capital endowment. In the last two specifications of the model, it was controlled for regional

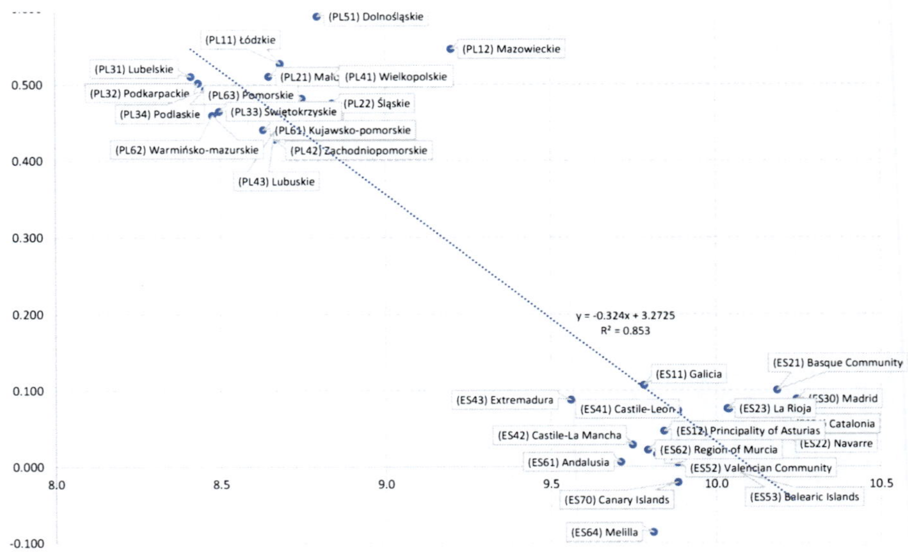

Figure 6.4: Beta-absolute convergence in the sample of Polish and Spanish regions
Source: Own elaboration.

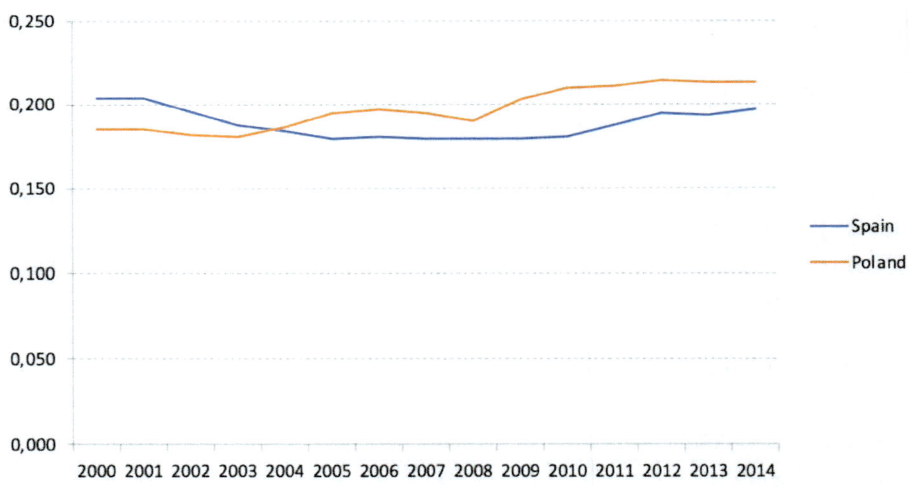

Figure 6.5: Sigma-convergence of GDP per capita in the sample of Polish and Spanish regions
Source: Own elaboration.

infrastructure endowment and its quality. The impact was statistically significant and positive in line with the results by Cieślik and Rokicki (2010) for Poland or the results of Crescenzi and Rodríguez-Pose (2008) for the whole of Europe.

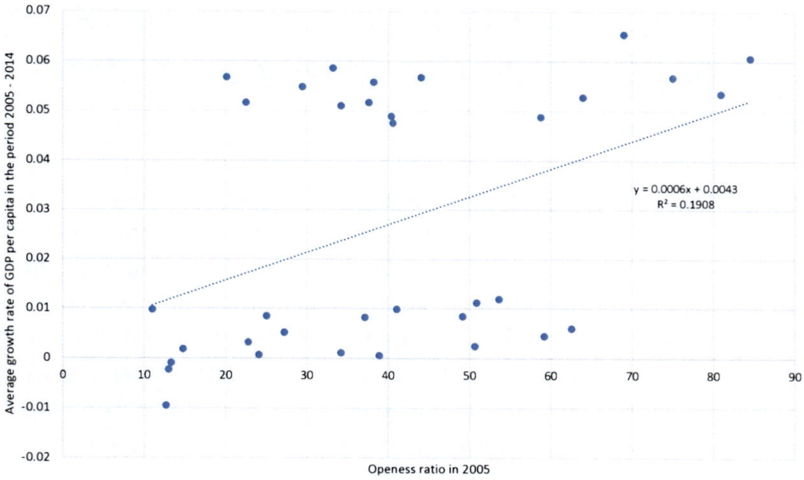

Figure 6.6: Sigma-convergence of GDP per capita in the sample of Polish and Spanish regions
Source: Own elaboration.

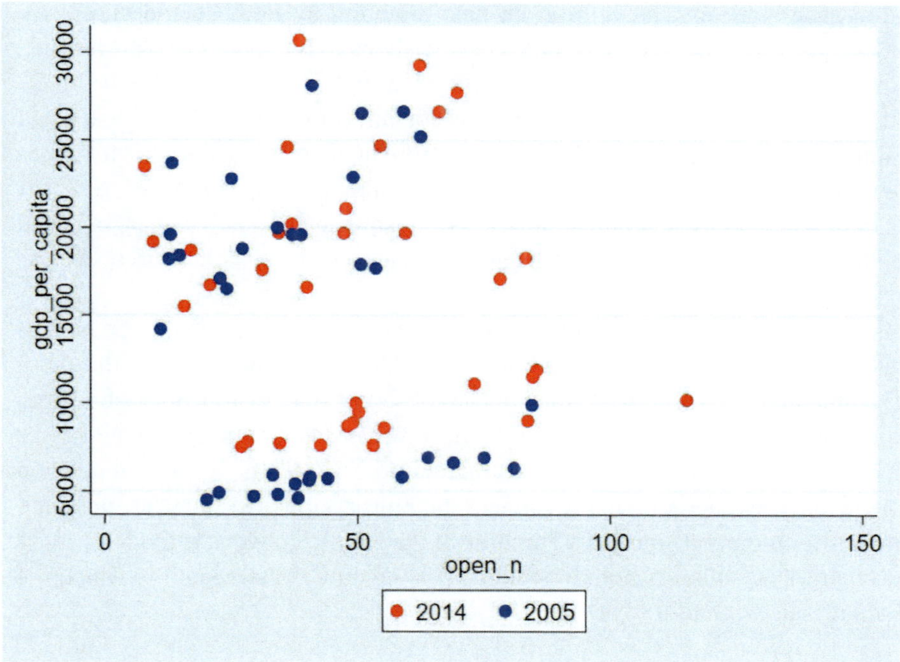

Figure 6.7: Relationship between the extent of openness and the level of GDP per capita in the sample of Polish and Spanish regions in 2005 and 2014

Source: Own elaboration.

Stanisław Umiński, Jarosław M. Nazarczuk, Tomasz Jurkiewicz

7 Basic taxonomy of exporting activity parameters for Poland and Spain

In the following chapter, various parameters of regions' exporting activity are presented. The diagnosis bears important benefits. It is the sine qua non condition for an effective exports promotion and shows the character of regions' vulnerability. Exports characteristics will constitute a base for taxonomies or regions. Similar regions will be identified. Promotion tools could then be used for those regions, depending on which group they are in. For instance, other tools of promotion are relevant for regions with a high share of FDIs, high-tech industries and high exports per capita; and others for regions with a high share of agricultural products, low-tech products oriented and low exports per capita.

7.1 Geographical structure

As exports are usually analysed at country level, many interesting regional differences in geographical structure are not paid attention to. Both Poland and Spain belong to the largest EU members, with a relatively large number of NUTS 2 regions, having different structural characteristics. Both countries are peripheral in the EU and border a "big" MS (France for Spain and Germany for Poland), which is expected to result in regions' specific geographical structure of exports because gravity forces come to play. For instance, western regions of Poland are expected to have a higher share of Germany in their exports than eastern regions, which shall also be reflected in the overall EU share in exports thereof. The same regularity shall occur for the Spanish regions.

As regards the relations with the EU28 or in fact, with 27 MS of the EU, the highest shares (exceeding 80%) are observed predominantly for Poland's regions (for 9 out of 16) (Table 7.1). The level higher than 80% is observed only for one Spanish region, Extramadura. As for relations with the NMS, regions of Poland show higher shares (than Spanish ones), which reflects the gravity forces as well as the special position of Poland and the other NMS in the cooperation links established by MNEs, predominantly in the automobile industry. For none of the Spanish regions is the NMS share higher than 10%, while Zachodniopomorskie is the only Polish region in which the NMS share is lower than 10% (5.5).

Table 7.1: Regional exports by destinations in 2015

Code	Region name	Share of exports directed in 2015 to						LQ*	
		EU 27	EU 15	NMS	BRU	FAR	REST	EU 27	NMS
PL11	Łódzkie	74.1	54.5	19.6	8.0	4.7	13.1	0.938	1.064
PL12	Mazowieckie	77.1	55.3	21.8	7.2	2.7	13.0	0.976	1.187
PL21	Małopolskie	84.6	60.2	24.3	4.3	2.8	8.4	1.070	1.323
PL22	Śląskie	86.6	64.0	22.6	2.9	2.1	8.4	1.096	1.229
PL31	Lubelskie	81.0	63.7	17.2	6.6	3.7	8.7	1.025	0.937
PL32	Podkarpackie	62.9	50.8	12.1	6.5	4.2	26.3	0.796	0.660
PL33	Świętokrzyskie	80.5	57.1	23.4	5.7	0.8	12.9	1.019	1.274
PL34	Podlaskie	76.2	52.5	23.7	9.8	4.2	9.9	0.964	1.287
PL41	Wielkopolskie	83.9	69.2	14.6	3.5	1.7	11.0	1.061	0.795
PL42	Zachodniopomorskie	65.5	60.1	5.5	2.4	2.4	29.7	0.829	0.298
PL43	Lubuskie	87.8	73.4	14.4	4.3	1.7	6.3	1.111	0.785
PL51	Dolnośląskie	83.2	63.0	20.2	2.4	5.1	9.3	1.052	1.096
PL52	Opolskie	86.4	63.6	22.8	3.7	1.4	8.6	1.093	1.239
PL61	Kujawsko-pomorskie	83.1	69.7	13.3	5.7	2.3	9.0	1.051	0.724
PL62	Warmińsko-mazurskie	77.8	63.7	14.1	4.9	3.9	13.5	0.984	0.765
PL63	Pomorskie	60.4	47.7	12.7	4.1	4.3	31.1	0.764	0.692
ES11	Galicia	75.2	68.8	6.4	0.7	3.2	20.9	1.143	1.091
ES12	Principality of Asturias	53.7	50.1	3.6	0.6	4.2	41.5	0.817	0.617
ES13	Cantabria	70.4	65.1	5.2	0.4	3.1	26.1	1.070	0.898
ES21	Basque Community	64.0	57.7	6.3	0.9	5.6	29.6	0.973	1.077
ES22	Navarre	72.1	63.9	8.2	0.6	3.0	24.3	1.096	1.404
ES23	La Rioja	73.2	68.8	4.4	0.5	2.9	23.4	1.113	0.758
ES24	Aragon	73.0	67.8	5.2	1.0	5.4	20.6	1.111	0.899
ES30	Madrid	57.7	53.8	3.9	0.7	7.0	34.7	0.877	0.664
ES41	Castile-Leon	76.4	66.9	9.5	0.6	5.2	17.8	1.161	1.631
ES42	Castile-La Mancha	74.7	69.8	4.9	1.6	5.0	18.7	1.136	0.845
ES43	Extremadura	80.5	77.5	3.0	1.9	2.5	15.2	1.224	0.518
ES51	Catalonia	65.5	59.6	5.8	0.8	5.7	28.0	0.996	1.001
ES52	Valencian Community	61.3	55.7	5.7	1.3	4.4	32.9	0.933	0.976
ES53	Balearic Islands	79.2	76.2	3.0	0.2	3.7	16.9	1.205	0.516

continued Table 7.1: Regional exports by destinations in 2015

Code	Region name	Share of exports directed in 2015 to						LQ*	
		EU 27	EU 15	NMS	BRU	FAR	REST	EU 27	NMS
ES61	Andalusia	61.2	55.0	6.2	0.5	7.4	30.9	0.931	1.062
ES62	Region of Murcia	65.6	61.1	4.6	0.5	9.3	24.5	0.998	0.784
ES63	Ceuta	3.1	3.1	0.0	0.0	58.5	38.4	0.047	0.000
ES64	Melilla	17.9	17.7	0.1	0.0	0.1	82.0	0.272	0.023
ES70	Canary Islands	31.1	30.5	0.6	0.1	8.7	60.1	0.473	0.109

Source: own calculations based on the data obtained from Customs Chamber in Warsaw and Spanish DataComex database (http://datacomex.comercio.es).

Notes: Shares are presented in percentages. NMS – new member states of the EU, BRU – Belarus, Russia, Ukraine, FAR – Far East countries, REST – rest of the world. We refer to EU 27 as the country of export's origin is located in the EU.

Relations with BRU are far more important for Poland's regions, which again reflects the gravity forces (proximity and adjacency). Only for four Spanish regions (Aragon, Castile-La Mancha, Extramadura and Valencian Community) is BRU share 1% or more, while for Poland's regions the corresponding shares are much higher, for Podlaskie (situated at the eastern border of Poland), reaching almost 10%. Shares of FAR countries are relatively lower for Polish regions than for Spanish ones. In Spain, Ceuta is an evident outlier, while in Poland the highest FAR share is observed for Dolnośląskie.

Substantial regional differences are identified as regards the importance of REST countries in exports. In Poland, the highest REST shares in exports are for those regions in which the shipbuilding or metal constructions industries are located (Pomorskie, Zachodniopomorskie), and the production is directed towards non-EU countries, such as Norway and flags of convenience countries. Also, for Podkarpackie the REST share is high, as in this region there is an aircraft industry cluster located, which implies strong production/cooperative and trade relations with the US. For Spanish regions, the REST shares are higher, the outlier being Melilla (82%).

Regions' different positions in their relative intensity of geographical trade links can better be captured when the LQ concept is used.

$$LQ_i = \frac{EX_i}{EXj}$$

Where:

LQ_i – *location quotient in region i, representing the role of EU27 or NMS in exports,*

EX_i – *the share of a region's exports directed to EU27 or NMS in total region's exports,*

EXj – *the share of a country's exports directed to EU27 or NMS in total national exports.*

Higher dispersion of LQ indices for EU27 is observed for Spanish regions than Polish ones. In the Spanish and Polish regions treated jointly, the lowest LQ is for the EU27 are for Ceuta, Melilla and Canary Islands (which obviously reflects their idiosyncratic character), while the highest is for Extramadura and Balearic Islands. In trade relations with NMS, Poland's regions show higher LQ indices, which again reflects their proximity to the countries forming the NMS group. Much depends, however, on the specific character of the region's exports profile; as, for instance, for Zachodniopomorskie the lowest LQ is observed (0.298), if we do not consider Spanish outliers, such as Balearic and Canary Islands and Ceuta and Melilla.

The above-presented differences in a region's geographic export profile bring important information showing the region's vulnerability for economic and trade shocks if they occur in the MS or outside the EU. They may also be considered if changes in the EU commercial policy are implemented or planned, such as new trade agreements. Also, any potential trade conflicts or disputes between the EU and its trading partners can be analysed in terms of regions' export intensity and the vulnerability thereof.

Regions' export profiles in terms of their geographical links are changing. Firms are searching for new partners and exports markets, market niches are discovered, regional authorities and promotion agencies are using advanced tools to boost exports and direct them to the new destinations. Table 7.2 presents these alterations, expressed in shares and in changes in LQ. The changes shall be monitored. They reflect the changing vulnerability as well as indicate the assistance possibly required by exporting firms in retaining their position in the markets already served or in entering new ones.

Regions' exports geographical profiles can also be described and interpreted in a more detailed way, with the use of information showing the shares of the particular countries in a region's exports. Such a detailed analysis is beyond the scope of the presented inquiry. Only the overall concentration of exports is presented (Fig. 7.1). As can be seen, regions significantly differ in the presented ranking. The lowest share of the three most important countries in exports is observed for the Principality of Asturias and Andalusia, while the highest is for Opolskie, Lubuskie and Extramadura (if outliers such as Ceuta and Melilla are not considered). The above-presented analysis showing the geographical concentration of exports need further, much more detailed analysis at regions' level. Generally, it is difficult to unequivocally judge what better suits regional exports: geographical concentration or diversification. The related discussion showing the pros and cons of concentration is presented for product structure of exports in the next paragraphs.

Table 7.2: Change in the share of regional exports directed to particular destinations in 2005-2015

Code	Region name	Change in the share of exports directed to						Change in LQ*	
		EU 27	EU 15	NMS	BRU	FAR	REST	EU 27	NMS
PL11	Łódzkie	-2.1	-6.5	4.5	-6.1	3.4	4.7	-0.02	-0.02
PL12	Mazowieckie	4.9	2.6	2.4	-7.8	-0.2	3.0	0.06	-0.21
PL21	Małopolskie	2.6	0.3	2.3	-3.9	0.5	0.8	0.03	-0.25
PL22	Śląskie	0.1	-8.0	8.1	0.0	1.1	-1.1	0.00	0.19
PL31	Lubelskie	11.2	6.9	4.2	-8.8	-2.9	0.5	0.14	0.01
PL32	Podkarpackie	-7.3	-2.9	-4.3	-8.5	2.5	13.3	-0.09	-0.52
PL33	Świętokrzyskie	5.3	-3.0	8.3	-5.5	-2.5	2.7	0.07	0.19
PL34	Podlaskie	4.1	-5.6	9.7	-10.5	2.3	4.2	0.05	0.28
PL41	Wielkopolskie	1.0	-2.7	3.7	-2.4	0.6	0.8	0.01	0.01
PL42	Zachodniopomorskie	-11.3	-13.6	2.3	-1.5	0.8	12.0	-0.14	0.07
PL43	Lubuskie	3.7	-1.5	5.2	-4.4	0.5	0.2	0.05	0.12
PL51	Dolnośląskie	-6.2	-12.4	6.2	-0.4	2.2	4.5	-0.08	0.09
PL52	Opolskie	-0.4	-7.6	7.1	-0.8	-0.3	1.5	0.00	0.12
PL61	Kujawsko-pomorskie	5.4	1.1	4.3	-4.8	-1.2	0.6	0.07	0.08
PL62	Warmińsko-mazurskie	-3.7	-7.9	4.2	-1.9	2.8	2.8	-0.05	0.06
PL63	Pomorskie	-1.9	-7.9	6.0	-0.2	1.3	0.8	-0.02	0.21
ES11	Galicia	1.5	-2.1	3.6	0.4	-0.3	-1.6	0.15	0.36
ES12	Principality of Asturias	-20.3	-22.3	1.9	0.4	2.2	17.7	-0.18	0.18
ES13	Cantabria	-3.3	-5.4	2.0	0.1	-0.4	3.6	0.07	0.04
ES21	Basque Community	-7.5	-9.6	2.2	0.4	2.0	5.1	0.01	-0.02
ES22	Navarre	-8.6	-13.4	4.8	-0.1	0.1	8.5	0.00	0.49
ES23	La Rioja	-7.7	-9.4	1.8	-1.5	1.6	7.5	0.02	0.05
ES24	Aragon	-12.1	-14.1	2.0	0.3	4.1	7.7	-0.04	0.02
ES30	Madrid	-12.8	-14.4	1.5	0.1	3.4	9.4	-0.08	0.04
ES41	Castile-Leon	-11.8	-15.5	3.7	0.1	3.8	7.9	-0.03	0.07
ES42	Castile-La Mancha	-7.2	-8.0	0.8	0.4	2.9	3.9	0.03	-0.26
ES43	Extremadura	-9.9	-11.5	1.6	-0.4	1.4	8.9	0.00	0.15
ES51	Catalonia	-9.2	-10.8	1.6	-0.2	2.2	7.2	-0.02	-0.13

continued **Table 7.2:** Change in the share of regional exports directed to particular destinations in 2005-2015

Code	Region name	Change in the share of exports directed to						Change in LQ*	
		EU 27	EU 15	NMS	BRU	FAR	REST	EU 27	NMS
ES52	Valencian Community	-8.8	-9.8	1.0	-0.7	0.7	8.8	-0.02	-0.28
ES53	Balearic Islands	26.8	24.7	2.2	-0.1	-2.6	-24.1	0.50	0.29
ES61	Andalusia	-4.4	-7.7	3.3	0.0	2.8	1.6	0.04	0.28
ES62	Region of Murcia	-2.5	-2.9	0.4	-0.1	1.4	1.1	0.08	-0.34
ES63	Ceuta	-11.8	-11.2	-0.5	0.0	58.5	-46.8	-0.15	-0.15
ES64	Melilla	7.6	14.8	-7.2	-4.2	0.1	-3.5	0.13	-1.95
ES70	Canary Islands	-20.2	-20.1	-0.1	-0.2	4.3	16.1	-0.22	-0.08

Source: own calculations based on the data obtained from Customs Chamber in Warsaw and Spanish DataComex database (http://datacomex.comercio.es).

Notes: Changes in shares are presented in pp. NMS – new member states, BRU – Belarus, Russia, Ukraine, FAR – Far East countries, REST – rest of the world.

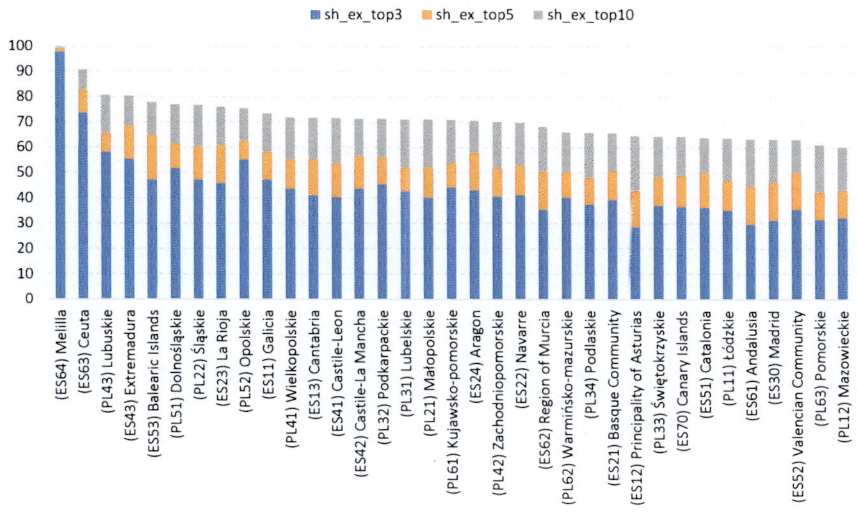

Figure 7.1: Share of exports to 3-5-10 most important partners

Source: own elaboration.

Information: Shares are presented in percentages. Sh_ex_top3 depicts the share of 3 most important destination countries in total regions' exports. Sh_ex_top5 and sh_ex_top10 denote the share of 5 and 10 most important trade partners respectively.

7.2 Product structure, concentration and revealed comparative advantages

One of the criteria by which to assess regions' exports relates to the product structure. To an extent, it reflects regional production capabilities; however, a region can also perform an intermediary function, which is usually the case in coastal regions or the ones in which transport and logistics hubs are located. Table 7.3 shows the structure of exports by CN sections, which provides a rough view of the characteristics of exports. 21 CN sections were grouped into 11 sections to improve the data visibility and to capture the main structural characteristics and the changes thereof. The highest (above 20%) shares of s1 (live animals, animal and vegetable product, animal and vegetable fats and oils) are observed in exports of Extramadura, Andalusia, Region of Murcia, and Podlaskie, while the lowest (below 5%) for Principality of Asturias, Cantabria, Basque Community, La Rioja, Madrid, Ceuta, Małopolskie, Śląskie, Podkarpackie, Dolnośląskie and Opolskie. The highest shares of particular sections are a characteristic feature of small territories, such as Ceuta and Melilla. However, also for other regions that cannot be treated as outliers, high shares occur. The examples are 50.8% for base metals and articles of base metal in the Principality of Asturias; 39.5% in Podkarpackie, 37.3% in Dolnośląskie, 30.5% in Mazowieckie for electromechanical and precision industry products; 43.8% for vehicles, aircrafts in Navarre and 38.4% in Aragon 36.7% in Castile-Leon and 34.1% in Śląskie.

Table 7.3: Share of exports by CN sections in regions of Poland and Spain in 2015

Region	s1	s2	s3	s4	s5	s6	s7	s8	s9	s10	s11	Bray-Curtis 2005-2015
(ES11) Galicia	10.0	3.9	9.2	2.5	3.6	26.0	2.1	6.6	7.2	27.9	1.2	0.192
(ES12) Principality of Asturias	3.4	1.4	15.8	1.4	4.9	0.7	2.1	50.8	12.7	5.8	1.0	0.111
(ES13) Cantabria	3.8	11.3	10.8	13.3	1.3	5.0	0.9	23.1	19.5	10.7	0.3	0.216
(ES21) Basque Community	1.5	2.8	13.7	7.1	2.9	0.5	1.5	23.7	21.6	23.7	1.1	0.058
(ES22) Navarre	5.4	6.3	1.7	3.5	3.4	0.3	0.7	8.6	25.5	43.8	0.7	0.076
(ES23) La Rioja	2.1	35.4	4.1	7.9	7.1	15.6	2.0	12.9	5.1	6.1	1.7	0.112
(ES24) Aragon	8.5	2.5	4.5	3.9	3.3	12.6	0.7	4.5	18.2	38.4	3.0	0.181
(ES30) Madrid	3.0	2.1	28.4	5.7	2.2	4.4	5.0	4.2	21.5	21.2	2.2	0.131

continued Table 7.3: Share of exports by CN sections in regions of Poland and Spain in 2015

Region	s1	s2	s3	s4	s5	s6	s7	s8	s9	s10	s11	Bray-Curtis 2005-2015
(ES41) Castile-Leon	7.1	5.6	11.3	5.3	2.1	0.4	1.6	5.2	23.5	36.7	1.2	0.131
(ES42) Castile-La Mancha	17.1	18.0	7.7	9.6	1.8	10.9	4.0	7.6	17.6	2.9	2.7	0.154
(ES43) Extremadura	24.8	33.7	3.8	4.8	7.7	2.2	4.0	11.8	5.7	1.2	0.3	0.163
(ES51) Catalonia	9.1	5.3	22.3	9.2	3.3	8.2	1.6	6.1	15.0	17.5	2.4	0.096
(ES52) Valencian Community	17.2	3.9	11.7	5.0	1.3	7.2	10.5	4.1	10.2	25.9	3.0	0.106
(ES53) Balearic Islands	6.9	1.9	21.6	20.5	0.5	11.6	2.2	1.0	11.4	21.6	0.9	0.452
(ES61) Andalusia	33.9	5.5	20.2	2.5	1.1	1.8	2.6	13.1	10.0	8.4	0.9	0.089
(ES62) Region of Murcia	35.8	11.1	31.8	8.5	0.4	1.6	0.3	4.6	4.1	0.3	1.4	0.237
(ES63) Ceuta	0.0	1.1	20.1	2.1	0.3	10.0	0.8	58.3	6.3	0.2	0.9	0.820
(ES64) Melilla	13.3	0.1	0.5	1.8	0.5	1.7	0.6	1.2	80.2	0.1	0.0	0.564
(ES70) Canary Islands	15.0	2.9	24.4	0.9	2.5	1.6	4.2	2.9	17.2	27.8	0.6	0.466
(PL11) Łódzkie	12.2	6.6	7.8	8.3	4.0	9.3	2.2	13.4	25.3	6.2	4.9	0.212
(PL12) Mazowieckie	12.4	9.0	18.2	6.3	3.3	2.1	1.3	6.3	30.5	4.6	6.0	0.072
(PL21) Małopolskie	4.9	7.4	6.9	11.6	5.1	1.4	2.3	15.4	27.5	14.5	3.0	0.124
(PL22) Śląskie	1.8	2.0	9.0	7.4	1.1	1.5	4.8	16.4	17.7	34.1	4.2	0.158
(PL31) Lubelskie	17.9	7.7	20.2	3.3	3.5	2.3	0.5	7.4	13.0	17.2	7.1	0.152
(PL32) Podkarpackie	2.1	2.1	4.7	9.7	6.9	1.2	2.2	10.5	39.5	16.4	4.5	0.229
(PL33) Świętokrzyskie	5.5	4.9	5.5	3.1	10.8	5.0	19.2	21.3	18.1	3.8	2.9	0.110
(PL34) Podlaskie	34.2	7.0	2.9	7.3	11.3	2.7	1.9	4.7	16.2	4.8	7.1	0.201
(PL41) Wielkopolskie	11.5	5.1	10.6	6.2	4.1	1.9	3.0	5.4	20.5	17.9	13.9	0.172

continued **Table 7.3:** Share of exports by CN sections in regions of Poland and Spain in 2015

Region	s1	s2	s3	s4	s5	s6	s7	s8	s9	s10	s11	Bray-Curtis 2005-2015
(PL42) Zachodniopomorskie	11.5	6.3	10.3	6.2	10.4	2.3	2.2	8.3	10.3	19.0	13.1	0.117
(PL43) Lubuskie	6.6	1.8	1.5	6.1	14.2	4.4	2.3	12.3	24.5	10.8	15.6	0.235
(PL51) Dolnośląskie	2.0	1.5	3.3	8.4	1.4	2.1	4.9	18.9	37.3	12.5	7.8	0.075
(PL52) Opolskie	3.1	10.9	17.9	8.7	7.3	4.3	1.2	11.9	21.1	10.1	3.4	0.160
(PL61) Kujawsko-pomorskie	6.0	7.4	6.0	13.6	14.6	4.2	0.4	14.7	15.7	5.3	12.0	0.073
(PL62) Warmińsko-mazurskie	10.3	3.9	1.5	29.7	7.3	4.7	2.5	4.9	12.5	4.7	17.9	0.179
(PL63) Pomorskie	11.6	2.9	15.7	3.4	4.9	2.6	0.5	4.9	16.8	33.3	3.4	0.123

Source: own elaboration.

Notes: 21 CN sections were grouped into 11: (s1) live animals, animal and vegetable products, animal and vegetable fats and oils; (s2) food, beverages, spirit and tobacco products; (s3) mineral and chemical products; (s4) plastic, rubber, skins and leather products; (s5) wood and paper products; (s6) textiles and footwear products; (s7) articles of stone, plaster, cement; glass and ceramics, precious metals and articles; (s8) base metals and articles of base metal; (s9) electromechanical and precision industry products; (s10) vehicles, aircrafts, etc.; (s11) miscellaneous manufactured articles. Detailed table of the above classification is available in the annex in the Table A1.

The last column in the table and figure 7.2 present Bray-Curtis index, informing about the intensity of changes in the composition of regional exports between 2005 and 2015. Ceuta, Melilla and the Spanish islands are outliers, being small territorial units, thus witnessing intensive changes. Other regions, which were also between 2005 and 2015 subject to strong structural changes are Podkarpackie, Łódzkie, Lubuskie and Podlaskie. On the other hand, the most stable structures of exports are in Navarre, Andalusia and Dolnośląskie.

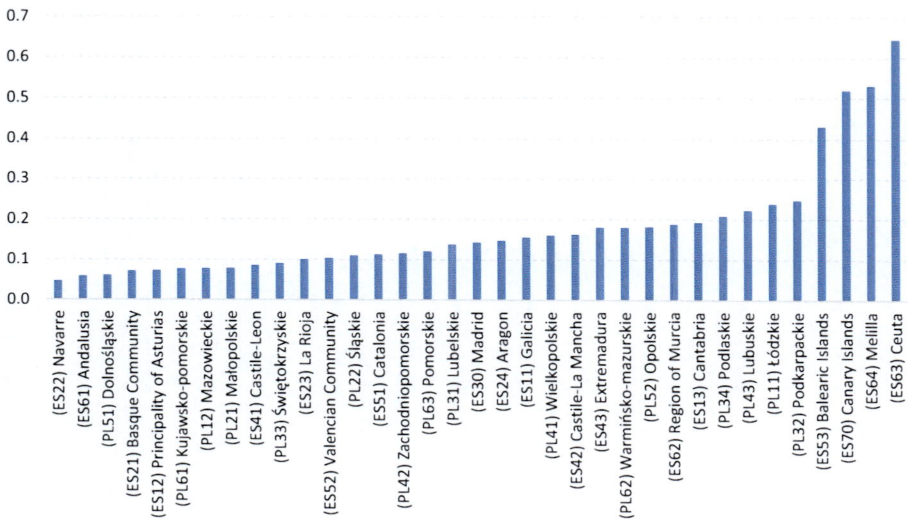

Figure 7.2: Intensity of changes in the composition of regional exports between 2005 and 2015

Source: own elaboration.

Notes: Higher Bray-Curtis values indicate more intense amendments in the composition of regional exports at CN section level (1-digit). The value of the index ranges from 0 to 1.

Another aspect of regions' structural differences in exports is the share of agricultural products. The highest shares of agricultural products (above 15% in 2015) are observed in the regions of Murcia, Podlaskie, Andalusia, Extramadura, Lubelskie and Valencian Community (Fig. 7.3). A high share of agricultural products reflects the structure of a region's economy – a high share of agriculture in GDP or employment usually corresponds to a high share of agricultural products in overall exports. It also reflects the character of comparative advantages that a region reveals in exports. The tariffs for agricultural products are higher than for industrial ones, which makes exports from these regions directed outside of the EU face higher protectionism. In regions with a strong industrial base, agricultural products share in exports is usually very low. However – as the example of Mazowieckie shows – in the case of regions which are leaders in exports and represent the strong industrial base, agricultural products' share can be relatively high. It may stem from the role played by the region, having a strong position as an export intermediary platform to BRU countries. In the case of small regions, such as the Canary Islands, high volatility in the agricultural products' share in exports is a result of the possible influence of individual transactions on exports' overall value.

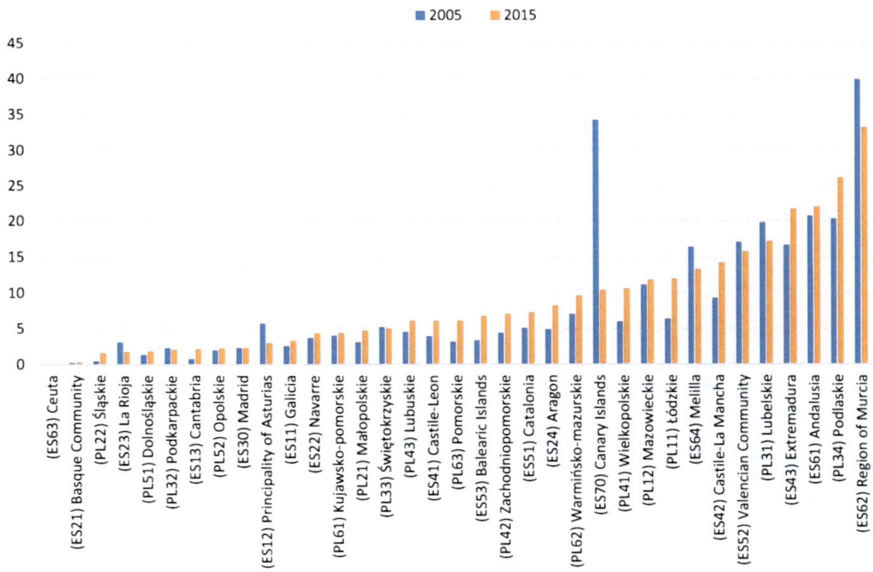

Figure 7.3: Share of agricultural products in total regions' exports (%)
Source: own elaboration.

The concentration of exports depicts specialisation but also vulnerability to the consequences of economic shocks. The fundamental question is what "pays off", what better contributes to the long-term development of the regional economy: specialisation or diversification of exports? The problem can be interpreted with reference to several theoretical strands: international trade theory, regional economics and investment portfolio (risk diversification). The specialisation is an issue deeply embodied in the international trade literature, corresponding to the division of labour and focusing on the activities in which absolute or comparative advantages are revealed. In the literature (Armstrong and Taylor, 2000; Behrens and Thisse, 2007; Dixon, 1973) the concept of comparative advantages and the related specialisation is discussed in the debate on regional competitiveness. According to Davis, Weinstein, Bradford, and Shimpo (1997), predictions of the H-O model (which is a flagship international trade theory) on the character of regional specialisation can be misleading. The problem is the equalisation of regions' factor abundance, stemming from production factors' mobility. On the other hand, Courant and Deardorff (1992) encourage to focus research on a region's exports because regional export specialisation patterns significantly differ from the overall country patterns. Also, NEG brings an interesting insight into the relations between agglomeration, specialisation and exports. When, however, the "old, good" theory of portfolio diversification is applied, regions with the diversified export structure are in a better position, as they are less exposed to structural shocks.

The literature presenting the consequences of regional exports specialisation (vs diversification) is not abundant. Nazarczuk et al. (2018) for Poland's counties conclude that specialisation (concentration) positively contributes to the value of exports per capita. However, if concentration embraces primary commodities, regions can be more exposed to economic shocks (Herzer and Nowak-Lehnmann D., 2006). According to Nazarczuk, Umiński and Gawlikowska-Hueckel (2018), smart specialisation programmes ought to search for new export industries and products, instead of exclusively concentrating on the already existing revealed specialisations. Choosing the former option may increase a regional economy's vulnerability to economic shocks.

Various measures have been used to assess the concentration of exports of Spanish and Polish regions. They are based on 4-digit CN classification. Table 7.4 presents the number of products with RCA indices higher than the chosen thresholds (from 2, 5, 10, 20). The analysis has revealed significant differences among regions thereof.

Table 7.4: The no. of 4-digit CN product groups with high RCA in exports

	No. of product groups with RCA higher than								**Difference**			
Region	**2**	**5**	**10**	**20**	**2**	**5**	**10**	**20**	**2**	**5**	**10**	**20**
	2005				**2015**				**2015-2005**			
(ES11) Galicia	115	53	22	9	131	76	39	13	16	23	17	4
(ES12) Principality of Asturias	81	51	35	22	94	63	43	27	13	12	8	5
(ES13) Cantabria	90	52	33	23	99	61	36	23	9	9	3	0
(ES21) Basque Community	159	61	23	4	152	64	27	9	-7	3	4	5
(ES22) Navarre	91	48	20	8	98	46	22	13	7	-2	2	5
(ES23) La Rioja	80	51	33	17	100	62	43	24	20	11	10	7
(ES24) Aragon	91	37	16	6	122	51	18	10	31	14	2	4
(ES30) Madrid	135	36	15	4	116	35	10	6	-19	-1	-5	2
(ES41) Castile-Leon	102	40	12	8	102	43	19	8	0	3	7	0
(ES42) Castile-La Mancha	146	75	35	14	167	80	39	20	21	5	4	6
(ES43) Extremadura	110	69	45	28	118	74	47	27	8	5	2	-1
(ES51) Catalonia	208	65	13	4	212	63	15	2	4	-2	2	-2
(ES52) Valencian Community	180	92	47	15	170	83	42	15	-10	-9	-5	0
(ES53) Balearic Islands	40	25	15	10	58	30	15	9	18	5	0	-1
(ES61) Andalusia	123	70	37	23	132	65	47	25	9	-5	10	2
(ES62) Region of Murcia	113	67	45	27	110	70	45	24	-3	3	0	-3
(ES63) Ceuta	2	2	2	2	29	21	11	5	27	19	9	3

continued **Table 7.4:** The no. of 4-digit CN product groups with high RCA in exports

Region	No. of product groups with RCA higher than								Difference			
	2	5	10	20	2	5	10	20	2	5	10	20
	2005				2015				2015-2005			
(ES64) Melilla	25	16	13	7	25	18	14	7	0	2	1	0
(ES70) Canary Islands	44	26	21	9	75	38	27	15	31	12	6	6
(PL11) Łódzkie	193	106	62	25	155	76	33	13	-38	-30	-29	-12
(PL12) Mazowieckie	178	80	30	13	151	55	19	3	-27	-25	-11	-10
(PL21) Małopolskie	139	71	36	15	131	70	28	12	-8	-1	-8	-3
(PL22) Śląskie	90	45	22	9	113	47	22	10	23	2	0	1
(PL31) Lubelskie	122	66	36	18	136	57	29	12	14	-9	-7	-6
(PL32) Podkarpackie	124	62	34	15	111	45	20	5	-13	-17	-14	-10
(PL33) Świętokrzyskie	94	57	39	28	100	61	46	29	6	4	7	1
(PL34) Podlaskie	96	54	32	16	131	66	38	14	35	12	6	-2
(PL41) Wielkopolskie	131	54	31	10	144	65	32	10	13	11	1	0
(PL42) Zachodniopomorskie	126	73	42	20	127	68	40	19	1	-5	-2	-1
(PL43) Lubuskie	120	61	39	22	112	63	36	12	-8	2	-3	-10
(PL51) Dolnośląskie	110	46	23	8	108	40	14	7	-2	-6	-9	-1
(PL52) Opolskie	129	66	36	18	132	68	31	12	3	2	-5	-6
(PL61) Kujawsko-pomorskie	146	83	41	16	129	74	42	16	-17	-9	1	0
(PL62) Warmińsko-mazurskie	88	49	30	16	77	46	29	18	-11	-3	-1	2
(PL63) Pomorskie	82	39	24	11	80	41	17	6	-2	2	-7	-5

Source: own elaboration.

For instance, in 2015, the number of product groups with RCA higher than 2 ranged from 25 for Melilla, to 212 for Catalonia. The number is affected by the region size. However, it differs among regions with similar sizes. If RCA=20 threshold is considered, the number of product groups ranges from 2 (for Catalonia) to 29 (for Świętokrzyskie). The RCA matrix reminds us of the logic of comparative advantages. Even though the region does not belong to the most competitive regions, still it has products in which comparative advantages are revealed. Another question is what percentage of the region's exports (in terms of value) is covered by the product groups in which comparative advantages exist. Estimation of it could be an interesting further research direction.

The export profiles of regions are determined by their structural characteristics and industrial base. Thus, they do not fluctuate much, are rather stable. However, it does mean they are constant in time. Their changes are shown in the table as “difference”. For instance, between 2005 and 2015 in Madrid, the number of 4-digit product CN product groups with RCA higher than 2 decreased by 19. These changes shall be subject to an inquiry of the authorities engaged in exports promotion and monitoring of regions’ competitiveness, as well as taken into account while regional smart specialisations are formulated and implemented.

Gini index is often used as a measure of concentration (Fig. 7.4). Its values over 0.5 indicate over-representation of several product groups in total regions’ exports, compared to benchmark distribution in all other regions. Excluding outliers, the highest concentration of exports structure in 2015 was for La Rioja, Warmińsko-Mazurskie, Navarre and Castile-Leon, while the lowest was for Madrid, Mazowieckie and Catalonia. High concentration may stem from several factors, with an idiosyncratic character. Warmińsko-Mazurskie is an interesting case on which to be commented. It belongs to the group of Poland’s less developed regions, with mediocre overall competitiveness. However, the region attracted a big foreign direct investor that operates in the tyre industry, and the related products dominate in exports.

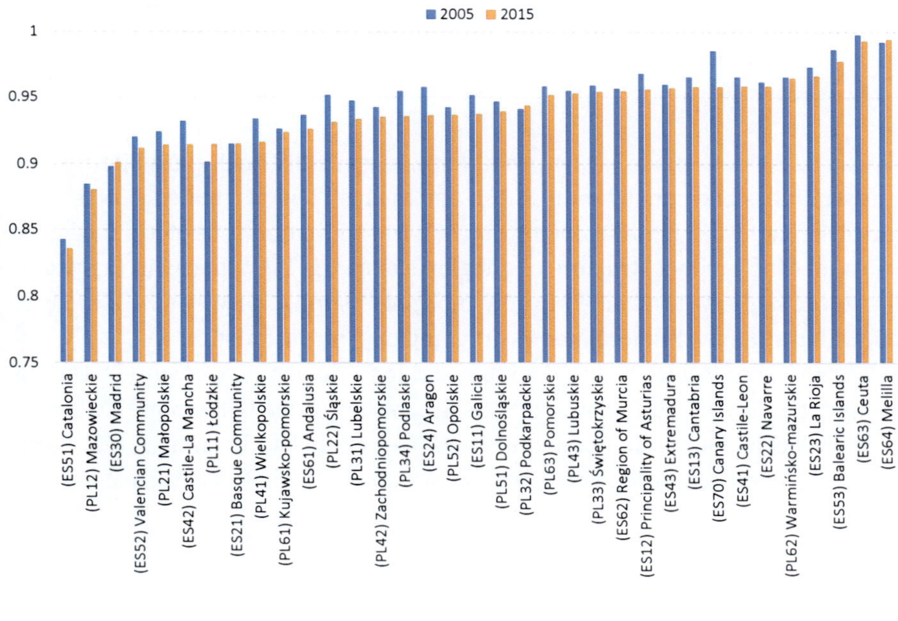

Figure 7.4: Gini index of 4-digit CN groups product concentration

Source: own elaboration.

Notes: Calculations based on 4-digit level CN data for regional exports.

Several alternative measures can be utilised for the assessment of regional exports concentration. HHI index, for instance, shows a slightly different ranking of regions (Fig. 7.5).

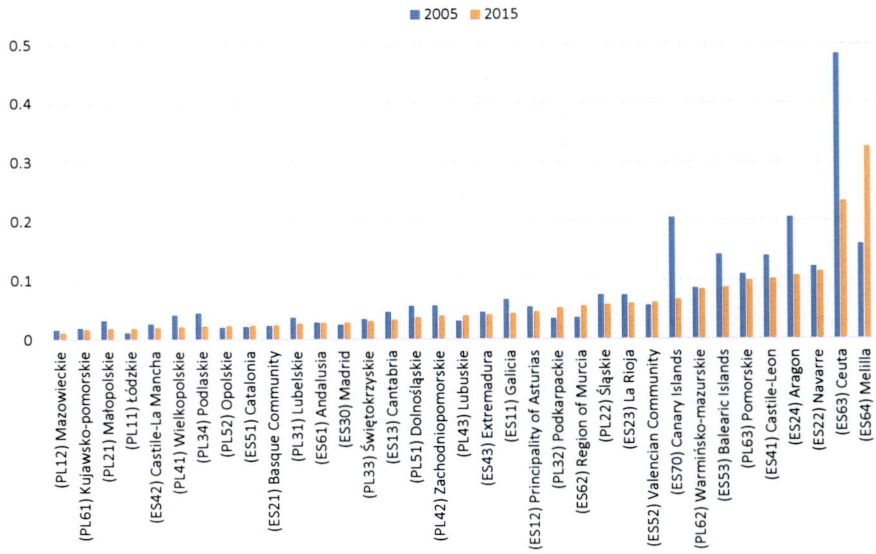

Figure 7.5: HHI of product concentration in regions' exports
Source: own elaboration.

As indicated, regions' export structures differ. Consequently, their dissimilarity can be assessed. It has been done for the Polish and Spanish regions treated jointly, with the use of the Hallet dissimilarity index (Fig. 7.6). The minimum value of 0 of the index indicates that the product structure of a region's export is the same as in the whole population of regions. The value of unity represents strong, usually single-product concentration strongly differentiated vs other regions' characteristics.

It is the case of Melilla, Ceuta, La Rioja and the Principality of Asturias. On the other hand, the lowest dissimilarity indices are in the case of Catalonia, Wielkopolskie, Mazowieckie, Valencian Community and Madrid. It shall be noticed that these are the largest contributors to overall exports, which affects their relative smaller dissimilarity.

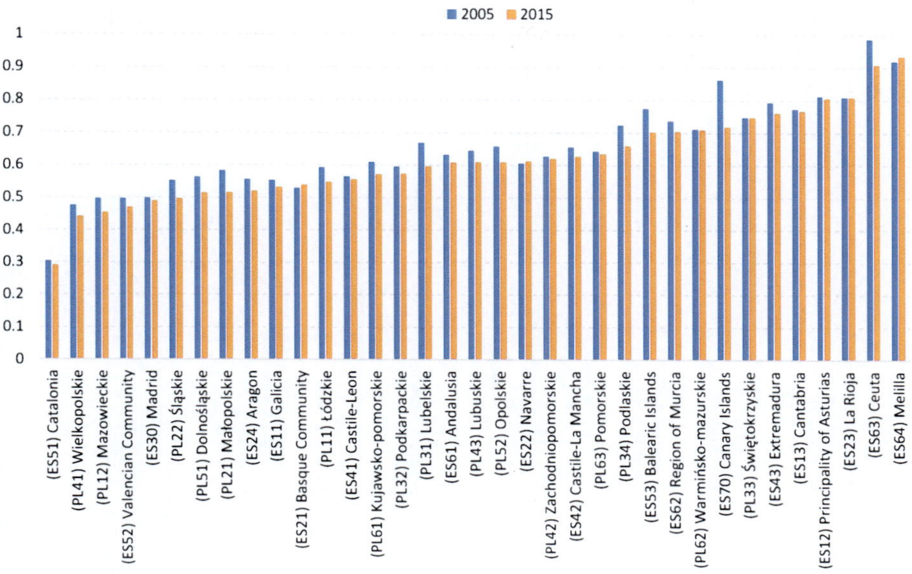

Figure 7.6: Hallet index of 4-digit product dissimilarity in exports
Source: own elaboration.

7.3 The quality of exports

The role of high-tech products in regions' exports deserves particular attention. High-tech products are often used in competitiveness assessments; however, solid success in exports can also be based on medium high-tech commodities. Building the economic capacity, generating high-tech products capable of competing on the international markets was a challenge both for the Spanish and the Polish economy. For the economy of Poland, it has been a bigger challenge, after decades of the centrally planned economy, isolation from international markets as well as almost non-existing competition. The economic effectiveness in the "economy of shortages" was verified not through confrontation with other enterprises operating on the free market, but rather through checking if the centrally defined production plans were achieved. International trade was carried within the Council of the Mutual Economic Assistance (Comecon), isolated from the economic system in which the most industrialised and competitive nations functioned. The transition to a market economy in Poland was initiated when the preparations to the establishment of the competitive single European market were already proceeding in the EU.

Figure 7.7 shows the share of the high-tech products in the regions' exports of Spain and Poland. The leader in the ranking is Madrid, while Podkarpackie takes the second position. Madrid represents the capital region of Spain, while Podkarpackie position stems from the aircraft industry heavily represented in this region. Also, in

Ceuta and Melilla, the high-tech products share in exports is relatively high. These two small territories are followed by the capital region of Mazowieckie in Poland and Catalonia in Spain.

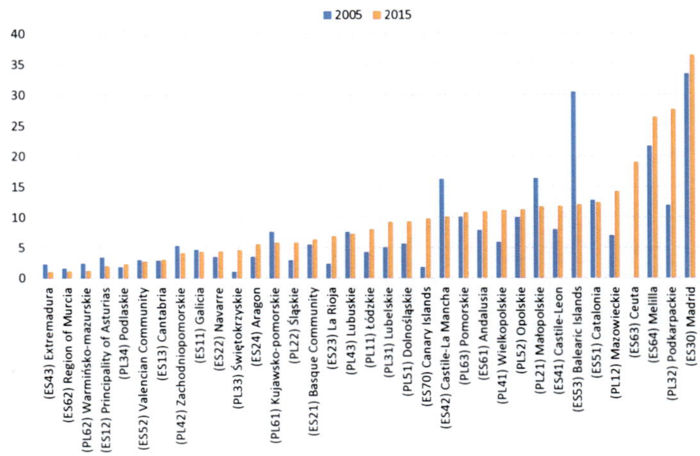

Figure 7.7: Share of high-tech products in total regional exports

Source: own estimation.

Alternatively, to the share of high-tech products in exports, its quality can be assessed by showing the mean value of 1kg of exports. This approach is used, for instance, in the IIT analysis, broken into its horizontal and vertical components. The mean value of 1kg of exports shows regions' positions in the quality ladder (Fig. 7.8). The leaders in this ranking are Melilla, Dolnośląskie, Podkarpackie, Madrid and Castile-Leon. The lowest values are registered for the Principality of Asturias, Świętokrzyskie, Region of Murcia, Zachodniopomorskie and Andalusia.

7.4 Export intensity

The value of exports per capita is the most frequently utilised measure of openness. As a rule, it is used for countries; however, when applied to regions, it shows interesting regional lumpiness. As mentioned in the literature overview, high openness can be interpreted as proof of high competitiveness; on the other hand, an open economy is vulnerable to economic shocks, which may negatively affect the regional labour market. Among Polish and Spanish regions analysed jointly, the highest per capita exports (above 6k EUR) are in Navarre, Basque Community, Catalonia, Aragon, Galicia and Region of Murcia (Fig. 7.9). The most open of Poland's regions (exports per capita) are Dolnośląskie, Pomorskie, Lubuskie, Wielkopolskie, Śląskie and Mazowieckie. In the vast majority of regions, between 2005 and 2015, exports per capita increased. It shall be noticed that the differences between regions in their exports per capita are significant, which should be taken into account in the analysis of regional economies' various aspects of vulnerability. Openness needs further, detailed inquiry for particular regions. A regional economy can have extraordinary openness to trade relations with the UK, which makes it highly vulnerable to the consequences of Brexit (Nazarczuk, Umiński and Márquez-Ramos, 2020). Exporters in such a region might need assistance in adjustments to the new circumstances, information about the new rules applicable to trade between the EU and the UK and the new markets alternative to the UK.

In regional analysis, various variables are calculated per km^2 (Bradley et al., 2017, p. 153; Zaucha and Ciołek, 2014, p. 144). Exports per 1 km^2 can be interpreted as a proxy showing the "capacity of space" to generate sales demanded by demanding foreign customers. Figure 7.10 shows significant differences between the regions of Poland and Spain. Changes in the values of exports per 1 km^2 in small territories such as Melilla shall be treated with due caution, as they probably show the effects of individual high-value transactions. If Melilla, as an outlier is excluded, the higher values of exports per km^2 are in Madrid, Basque Community, Catalonia, Śląskie, Valencian Community, Dolnośląskie, Region of Murcia and Navarre.

7.5 The role of FDI in exports

Poland's transition from centrally planned to a market economy has been facilitated by FDI. Incoming FDI positively affected Poland's competitiveness due to technology transfer, investments in machinery and equipment, and incorporating Poland's firms into international value chain networks. FOEs perform the coordination role in the global value chains (Forsgren, 2008). The literature, however, does not give the simple answer on the nexus between FDI and export performance (Brodzicki, Jurkiewicz, Márquez-Ramos, and Umiński 2019). Much depends on the character of FDI (vertical vs horizontal), the motivation of investors in particular regions and regions' characteristics (proximity to big, absorptive markets, transport infrastructure, accessibility, institutional quality, metropolitan status). As pointed by Nazarczuk and Umiński (2018a), FOEs play a crucial role in determining the spatial distribution of exports in Poland. According to Nazarczuk, Umiński and Brodzicki (2019), FOEs compared to domestic (Polish) owned exporters, in their locational preferences pay special attention to proximity to infrastructure, agglomeration externalities and the vicinity of metropolises.

As the data for Spain is not available, the share of FOEs in the value of exports is presented only for Poland (Fig. 7.11). In six regions (Śląskie, Lubuskie, Dolnośląskie, Łódzkie, Podkarpackie and Wielkopolskie) the share is higher than 60%, the lowest

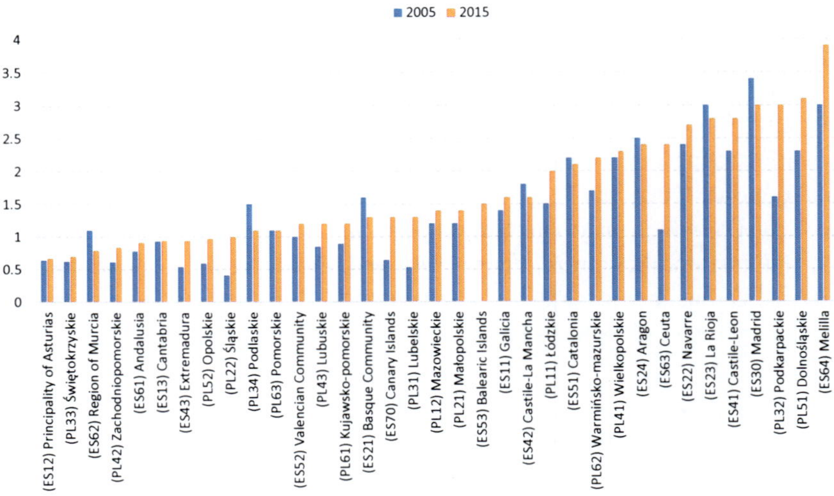

Figure 7.8: Mean value of 1kg of exports (in EUR)

Source: own estimation.

Notes: Data for the Balearic Islands were excluded in 2005 due to credibility concerns.

(below 40%) is in Podlaskie and Pomorskie. Pomorskie is an interesting case, showing that low participation of FOEs is accompanied by high exports per capita and high exports share in GDP. Thus, export success results from the activity and competitiveness of domestic-owned enterprises. Part of this success probably also stems from an intermediary function of the region. Its harbours and logistic facilities link other regions' exporters with foreign markets. The regional level analysis enables us to capture interesting changes that often are hard to notice. An example is a decrease in FOEs' share in exports in the Podlaskie region between 2005 and 2015. The reasons for this kind of changes shall be subject to thorough inquiry by regional authorities; they may indicate serious structural problems and changes as well as competitiveness deterioration. Please bear in mind that in Poland, FOEs – generally – positively contribute to exports of regions (Brodzicki et al., 2018; Komornicki and Szejgiec, 2015; Nazarczuk and Umiński, 2018a).

7.6 Intensity of IIT

The regional heterogeneity presented so far encourages us to refer to a region as an SOE concept and assess the IIT intensity. The reasons why IIT intensity of regions' foreign trade deserves attention have been described by Brodzicki, Jurkiewicz, Márquez-Ramos, and Umiński (2019). High IIT intensity proves strong economic integration of trading partners and participation in the global value chains. This is particularly important because IIT assessed at a regional level not only stems from a love for variety, which traditionally in the literature has been treated as a determinant of IIT,

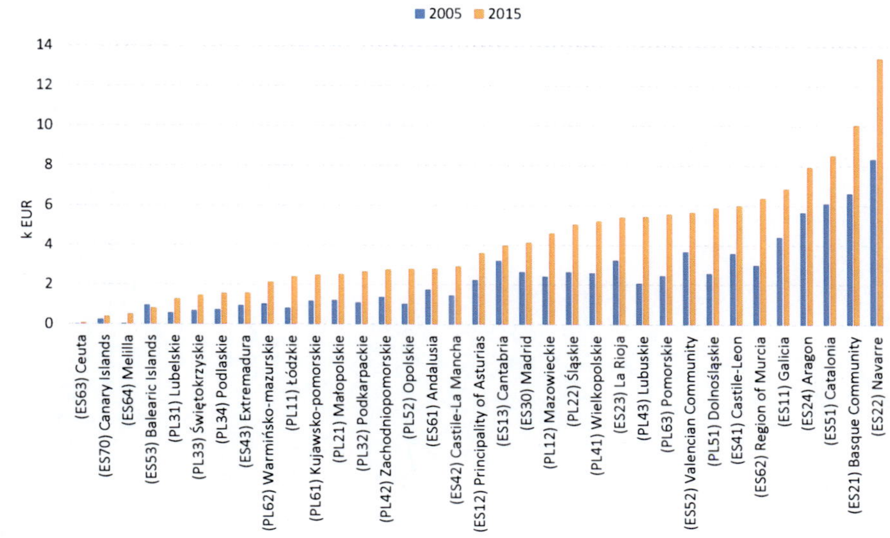

Figure 7.9: Exports per capita (in k EUR)
Source: own estimation.

but also from the fragmentation of production (Yoshida, 2008). One of the main arguments to analyse IIT intensity it that, compared to H-O type of trade, it has less effect on the distribution of income of trading partners. Before IIT index for regions will be presented and interpreted, it shall be mentioned that IIT intensity for regions is lower than for the whole country. The reason is that the probability that an exporter and importer are located in the same region is lower than them being located in the same country. For instance, if an exporter and an importer of product A or its variants are in Pomorskie, exports and imports do overlap – thus IIT is registered. If, however, an exporter is in Pomorskie and an importer in Dolnośląskie, export and import overlap is registered for Poland, but neither for Pomorskie nor Dolnośląskie.

The highest intensity of IIT is observed for three of Poland's regions: Podkarpackie, Pomorskie and Zachodniopomorskie (Fig. 7.12). Their foreign trade is specific, compared to other regions of Poland. EU countries' share in their exports is low, compared to other regions. Also, the structure of exports is specific. Aviation-related products have a high share in the foreign trade of the Podkarpackie region, while in Pomorskie and Zachodniopomorskie trade, maritime vessels and metal constructions are important. Among regions of Spain, the highest IIT intensity is registered for Madrid and Catalonia, and slightly lower for Aragon, Basque Community and Navarre.

IIT characteristics for regions of Poland and Spain were analysed thoroughly by Brodzicki, Jurkiewicz, Márquez-Ramos and Umiński (2019) in a paper presenting the results of the same research project. Attention has been paid to the determinants not

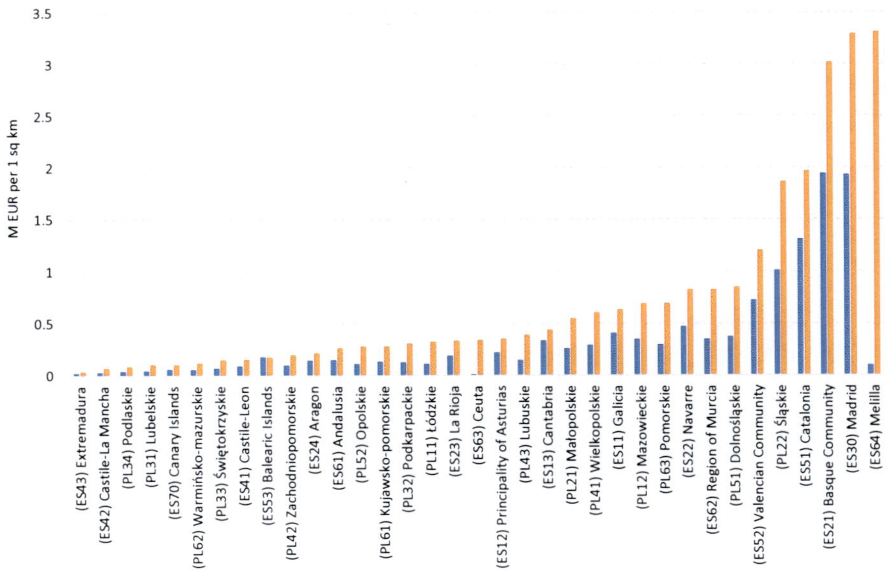

Figure 7.10: Exports per 1 sq. km

Source: own estimation.

only of IIT itself but to its vertical and horizontal components. Several hypotheses were tested by the authors. The main conclusions are that IIT intensity is determined by the size and the distance of trading partners. Smaller distance positively contributes to the intensity of IIT, so does symmetry in partner size. Differences in GDP per capita have a negative effect on IIT. Contrary to expectations, differences in institutional quality have a positive impact on IIT. Metropolitan status of a region, as well as FDI, have a positive impact. IIT was split into horizontal and vertical dimensions, for the differences in determinants of both types of IIT, please refer to Brodzicki et al. (2019).

7.7 Cluster analysis of Spanish and Polish regions' exports

As shown above, on the grounds of the available statistical information, many detailed analyses can be performed. Undoubtedly, they are important for regional or national authorities involved in regional policy, assessments and monitoring of competitiveness as well as exports promotion. The high detailedness however, also has drawbacks, because it makes synthetic, comparative analysis difficult to be carried on. A solution is a cluster analysis, which enables classification of objects (regions) into homogenous groups. One possible variant of this method is the hierarchical agglomerative approach, in which objects are presented in a dendrogram graph. The vertical axis presents the regions; each region is unique. Moving to the right makes the

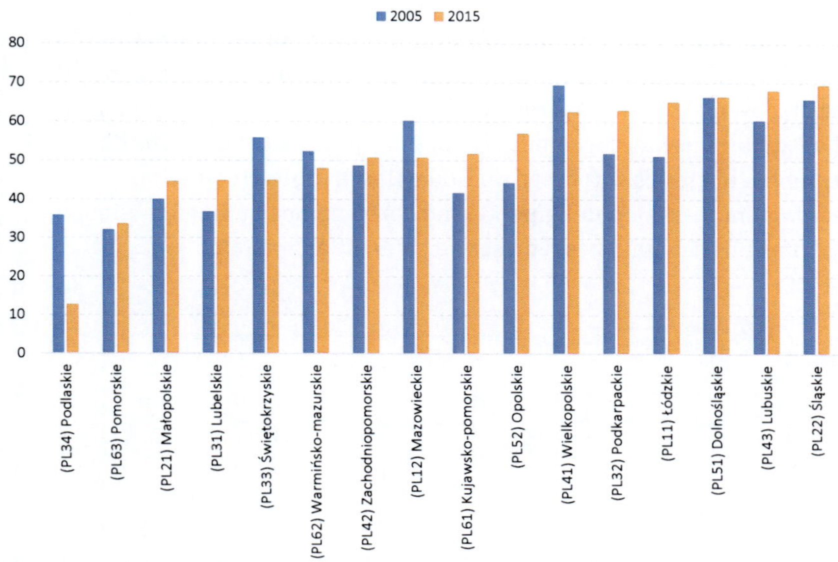

Figure 7.11: Share of FOEs in the value of exports of Polish regions (%)
Source: own estimation.

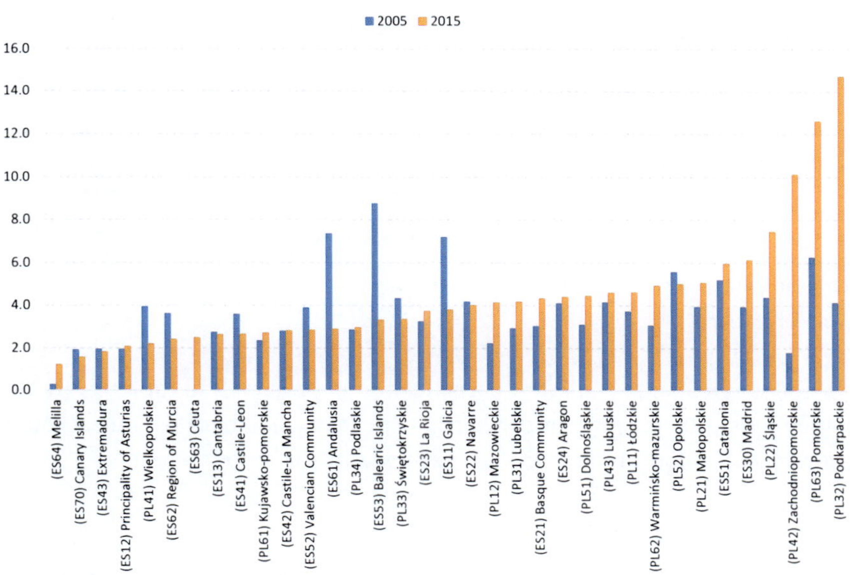

Figure 7.12: Intra-industry trade at regional level
Source: own elaboration.

decision threshold lower; therefore, it is possible to decide when regions are joined into clusters. Finally, all the regions can be combined into one.

In the analysis performed, several agglomeration methods and measures of distance were used. Ward's method of classification together with the Euclidean distance approach have proven to be the most effective in the identification of the homogenous clusters. The variables used were standardised, prior to classification. The choice of an optimal number of groups was based on Duda/Hart Je(2)/Je(1) statistics.

The dendrogram presented in figure 7.13 indicates regions grouped by similarity differences. Longer horizontal lines represent greater differentiation.

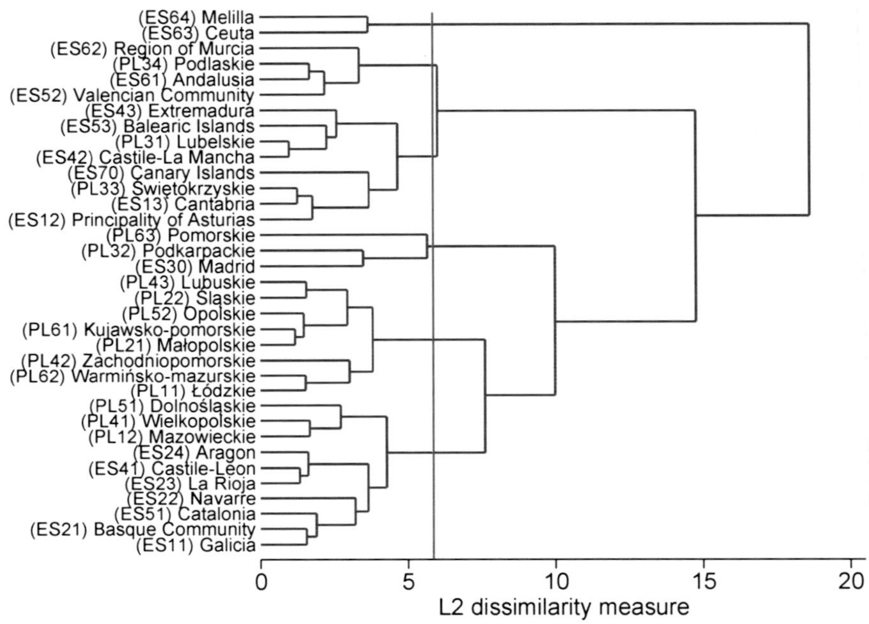

Figure 7.13: Dendrogram
Source: own elaboration.

The list of the variables used in Ward classification is presented in table 7.5. In our opinion, they constitute the most important statistics that shall be taken into account in the taxonomy of regions, related to their participation in exports.

Table 7.5: Descriptive statistics used in taxonomy

Variable	Description	Mean	Std. Dev.	Min	Max
ex_value	Value of 1 kilo of exports [in EUR]	1.710477	.8438793	.6657239	3.91442
hhi_ex	HHI of exports	.0599396	.0625377	.0112648	.3251462
sh_ht	Share of high-tech products in exports	9.475217	7.785948	1.047045	36.45537

continued **Table 7.5:** Descriptive statistics used in taxonomy

Variable	Description	Mean	Std. Dev.	Min	Max
sh_eu	Share of exports sent to EU countries	68.76857	18.61278	3.1	87.8
iit	Intra industry trade index	4.420286	2.905831	1.22	14.76
sh_c_top3	Share of exports sent to 3 most important export destinations	43.80514	13.00303	28.6	97.86
sh_agri	Share of agricultural products in exports	8.7	7.788566	0	33.2
ex_pc	Exports per capita [in EUR]	4140.194	2919.076	81.0544	13416.63
tr_open	Trade openness index = (exports+imports)/GDP *100	49.62117	24.40064	7.903726	115.1515
Standardised values					
z_ex_cost	Value of 1 kilo of exports [in EUR]	9.15e-09	1	-1.238036	2.611681
z_hhi_ex	HHI of exports	-1.27e-09	1	-.7783279	4.240748
z_sh_ht	Share of high-tech products in exports	-8.62e-09	1	-1.082485	3.465237
z_sh_eu	Share of exports sent to EU countries	2.77e-09	1	-3.528143	1.022493
z_iit	Intra industry trade index	2.59e-09	1	-1.101332	3.558264
z_sh_c_top3	Share of exports sent to 3 most important export destinations	-3.46e-09	1	-1.169354	4.157097
z_sh_agri	Share of agricultural products in exports	6.81e-09	1	-1.117022	3.145637
z_ex_pc	Exports per capita [in EUR]	-7.43e-09	1	-1.390556	3.177867
z_tr_open	Trade openness index = (exports+imports)/GDP *100	-6.54e-09	1	-1.709686	2.685599

Source: own elaboration.

With reference to Duda/Hart Je(2)/Je(1) statistics, six clusters of regions were established. Their detailed statistics are available in tables A.2 and A.3 in the appendix.

Cluster 1 consists of 10 Polish and Spanish regions: (ES11) Galicia, (ES21) Basque Community, (ES22) Navarre, (ES23) La Rioja, (ES24) Aragon, (ES41) Castile-Leon, (ES51) Catalonia, (PL12) Mazowieckie, (PL41) Wielkopolskie and (PL51) Dolnośląskie. Compared to other clusters, its characteristics are high value of 1 kilogram of exports, high product concentration of exports (measured by HHI), the moderate share of high-tech products, the high share of EU in exports, low IIT intensity, the medium share of exports sent to the three most important destinations, low share of agricultural products in exports, very high exports per capita and high trade openness index.

Cluster 2 consists of Polish regions only: (PL11) Łódzkie, (PL21) Małopolskie, (PL22) Śląskie, (PL42) Zachodniopomorskie, (PL43) Lubuskie, (PL52) Opolskie, (PL61) Kujawsko-pomorskie, (PL62) Warmińsko-mazurskie. Its characteristics can be described as follows: the low value of 1 kilogram of exports, low product concentration of exports (HHI), low share of high-tech products, the highest share of EU in exports, high IIT intensity, the medium share of exports sent to the three most important destinations, low share of agricultural products in exports, moderate level of exports per capita and moderate trade openness index.

Cluster 3 is composed of three regions: (ES30) Madrid, (PL32) Podkarpackie and (PL63) Pomorskie. Its features are high value of 1 kilogram of exports, the highest product concentration of exports (HHI), the highest share of high-tech products, relatively low share of EU in exports, very high IIT intensity, low share of exports sent to the three most important destinations, very low share of agricultural products in exports, moderate level of exports per capita and very high trade openness index.

Cluster 4 includes: (ES13) Cantabria, (ES42) Castile-La Mancha, (ES43) Extremadura, (ES53) the Balearic Islands, (ES70) the Canary Islands, (PL31) Lubelskie and (PL33) Świętokrzyskie. Its characteristics are the low value of 1 kilogram of exports, low product concentration of exports (HHI), low share of high-tech products, moderate share of EU in exports, low IIT intensity, medium share of exports sent to the three most important destinations, relatively high share of agricultural products in exports, low exports per capita and low trade openness index.

Cluster 5 is composed of: (ES52) Valencian Community, (ES61) Andalusia, (ES62) Region of Murcia, (PL34) Podlaskie. Its characteristics are very low value of 1 kilogram of exports, low product concentration of exports, very low share of high-tech products, moderate share of EU in exports, low IIT intensity, low share of exports sent to the three most important destinations, very high share of agricultural products in exports, moderate exports per capita and moderate trade openness index.

In cluster 6 there are two Spanish regions: (ES63) Ceuta and (ES64) Melilla. Their features are as follows: very high value of 1 kilogram of exports, very low product concentration of exports, the high share of high-tech products, very low share of EU in exports, very low IIT intensity, the very high share of exports sent to the three most important destinations, moderate share of agricultural products in exports, very low exports per capita and very low trade openness index.

While interpreting the results obtained in the cluster analysis, one must remember that grouping of objects is done according to an algorithm. Accordingly, individual regions were jointed/classified into six clusters. The particular clusters are more or less consistent, which means that the distances of particular regions to the centre of each cluster differ. If in one cluster there are regions that differ in terms of one of the features, it means that the similarity of other features was decisive in classification.

As proved in the above cluster analysis, similar regions' exports characteristics go across countries, as in the case of 4 out of 6 clusters, Spanish and Polish regions are mixed. In cluster 6 there are two Spanish regions, which represent specific cities (administrative units). Particular cluster features shall be useful in addressing the economic policy instruments aimed at exports promotion. They can be a starting point in profiling regions in terms of their export SWOTs.

Appendix

Table A.1: Detailed classification of sectors used in chapter 7

No.	Industry	Sections
1	Live animals, animal and vegetable product, animal and vegetable fats and oils	SECTION I - LIVE ANIMALS; ANIMAL PRODUCTS SECTION II - VEGETABLE PRODUCTS SECTION III - ANIMAL OR VEGETABLE FATS AND OILS AND THEIR CLEAVAGE PRODUCTS; PREPARED EDIBLE FATS; ANIMAL OR VEGETABLE WAXES
2	Food, beverages, spirit and tobacco products	SECTION IV - PREPARED FOODSTUFFS; BEVERAGES, SPIRITS AND VINEGAR; TOBACCO AND MANUFACTURED TOBACCO SUBSTITUTES
3	Mineral and chemical products	SECTION V - MINERAL PRODUCTS SECTION VI - PRODUCTS OF THE CHEMICAL OR ALLIED INDUSTRIES
4	Plastic, rubber, skins and leather products	SECTION VII - PLASTICS AND ARTICLES THEREOF; RUBBER AND ARTICLES THEREOF SECTION VIII - RAW HIDES AND SKINS, LEATHER, FURSKINS AND ARTICLES THEREOF; SADDLERY AND HARNESS; TRAVEL GOODS, HANDBAGS AND SIMILAR CONTAINERS; ARTICLES OF ANIMAL GUT (OTHER THAN SILKWORM GUT)
5	Wood and paper products	SECTION IX - WOOD AND ARTICLES OF WOOD; WOOD CHARCOAL; CORK AND ARTICLES OF CORK; MANUFACTURES OF STRAW, OF ESPARTO OR OF OTHER PLAITING MATERIALS; BASKETWARE AND WICKERWORK SECTION X - PULP OF WOOD OR OF OTHER FIBROUS CELLULOSIC MATERIAL; RECOVERED (WASTE AND SCRAP) PAPER OR PAPERBOARD; PAPER AND PAPERBOARD AND ARTICLES THEREOF
6	Textiles and footwear products	SECTION XI - TEXTILES AND TEXTILE ARTICLES SECTION XII - FOOTWEAR, HEADGEAR, UMBRELLAS, SUN UMBRELLAS, WALKING STICKS, SEAT-STICKS, WHIPS, RIDING-CROPS AND PARTS THEREOF; PREPARED FEATHERS AND ARTICLES MADE THEREWITH; ARTIFICIAL FLOWERS; ARTICLES OF HUMAN HAIR

No.	Industry	Sections
7	Articles of stone, plaster, cement; glass and ceramics, precious metals and articles	SECTION XIII - ARTICLES OF STONE, PLASTER, CEMENT, ASBESTOS, MICA OR SIMILAR MATERIALS; CERAMIC PRODUCTS; GLASS AND GLASSWARE SECTION XIV - NATURAL OR CULTURED PEARLS, PRECIOUS OR SEMI-PRECIOUS STONES, PRECIOUS METALS, METALS CLAD WITH PRECIOUS METAL, AND ARTICLES THEREOF; IMITATION JEWELLERY; COIN
8	Base metals and articles of base metal	SECTION XV - BASE METALS AND ARTICLES OF BASE METAL
9	Electromechanical and precision industry products	SECTION XVI - MACHINERY AND MECHANICAL APPLIANCES; ELECTRICAL EQUIPMENT; PARTS THEREOF; SOUND RECORDERS AND REPRODUCERS, TELEVISION IMAGE AND SOUND RECORDERS AND REPRODUCERS, AND PARTS AND ACCESSORIES OF SUCH ARTICLES SECTION XVIII - OPTICAL, PHOTOGRAPHIC, CINEMATOGRAPHIC, MEASURING, CHECKING, PRECISION, MEDICAL OR SURGICAL INSTRUMENTS AND APPARATUS; CLOCKS AND WATCHES; MUSICAL INSTRUMENTS; PARTS AND ACCESSORIES THEREOF
10	Vehicles, aircraft, etc.	SECTION XVII - VEHICLES, AIRCRAFT, VESSELS AND ASSOCIATED TRANSPORT EQUIPMENT
11	Miscellaneous manufactured articles	SECTION XIX - ARMS AND AMMUNITION; PARTS AND ACCESSORIES THEREOF SECTION XX - MISCELLANEOUS MANUFACTURED ARTICLES SECTION XXI - WORKS OF ART, COLLECTORS' PIECES AND ANTIQUES

Source: own elaboration.

Table A.2: Mean groups' values of standardised variables

Group	z_ex_ value	z_hhi_ex	z_sh_ht	z_sh_ eu28	z_iit	z_sh_c_ top3	z_sh_agri	z_ex_pc	z_tr_open
1	0.641	-0.092	-0.103	0.300	-0.152	-0.131	-0.403	1.116	0.608
2	-0.412	-0.363	-0.328	0.643	0.399	0.104	-0.353	-0.325	0.279
3	0.778	0.002	1.988	-0.453	2.323	-0.592	-0.668	-0.004	0.790
4	-0.696	-0.255	-0.382	0.006	-0.580	-0.173	0.175	-0.733	-1.055
5	-0.831	-0.289	-0.666	-0.145	-0.559	-0.706	1.997	-0.014	0.068
6	1.721	3.503	1.700	-3.131	-0.881	3.230	-0.263	-1.317	-1.259

Source: own elaboration.

Table A.3: Mean groups' values of unstandardised variables

Group	ex_value	hhi_ex	sh_ht	sh_eu28	iit	sh_c_t~3	sh_agri	ex_pc	tr_open
1	2.252	0.054	8.676	74.360	3.980	42.107	5.560	7399.024	64.453
2	1.363	0.037	6.924	80.738	5.579	45.158	5.950	3192.795	56.433
3	2.367	0.060	24.952	60.333	11.170	36.107	3.500	4127.798	68.896
4	1.123	0.044	6.504	68.887	2.734	41.551	10.063	2000.968	23.888
5	1.009	0.042	4.293	66.075	2.795	34.628	24.250	4098.310	51.291
6	3.163	0.279	22.711	10.500	1.860	85.805	6.650	294.901	18.896

Source: own elaboration.

Tomasz Brodzicki, Stanisław Umiński, Laura Márquez-Ramos

8 Modelling orthodox and non-orthodox determinants of foreign trade

The number of studies devoted to the foreign trade of regions (that is, subnational spatial units) is increasing (Batabyal and Nijkamp, 2015; Bentivogli et al., 2018; Cassey et al., 2016; Cassey and Schmeiser, 2013; Dühr, 2005; Koenig, Mayneris, and Poncet, 2010; Kounetas and Napolitano, 2018; Nazarczuk and Umiński, 2018a). It, in particular, applies to medium and large-sized countries, where the extent of regional heterogeneity is large. One could give several reasons that drive attention to the regional level of analysis. They have recently been exemplified by Brodzicki and Umiński (2017) as treatment of a region as an SOE, increasing interdependence of regional economies due to the persistence of globalisation processes and an increasing role of the subsidiarity principle, transferring more power and responsibilities in governance to regional authorities. In related disciplines such as international business, researchers have begun to recognize the weakness of using country border-based data, as they may contain systematic biases and because important benefits and costs may be overlooked (Mudambi et al., 2018). In international trade studies, we consider as an additional reason in favour of using regional trade statistics – the accuracy of country bilateral trade data (Bhagwati, 1974; Makhoul and Otterstrom, 1998).

This is particularly important for the analysis of the determinants of trade flows. Between the causes of discrepancies in international trade statistics, there are structural differences in the compilation and statistical criteria. This is important because, as pointed out by Makhoul and Otterstrom (1998, p. 1604), "structural problems may reveal themselves as inconsistencies among countries with regard to trade coverage, recording of values, an indication of trading partners, time lags, variations in exchange rates, and changes in data collection systems". In this research, focusing on (subnational) regions for two specific EU countries, we avoid structural differences, and we improve the accuracy of the data.

Our main contribution to the body of regional economics literature is that we go beyond standard determinants of trade intensity and aim at the identification of the impact of several new variables to explain regional trade, which we refer to as non-orthodox factors. To do so, we focus on regional trade statistics from regions in Poland and Spain to analyse their determinants of bilateral trade flows. In contrast to previous studies that construct the regional trade statistics for analysis,[8] we focus on the regional trade statistics sourced from customs agencies.

8 For example Thissen, Lankhuizen, and Jonkeren (2015) construct a simulated trade matrix for trade between European regions.

Two countries are the subjects of the analysis, which is justified for several reasons. Poland and Spain are MS of the EU, represent similar levels of development, can be regarded as peripheral countries of the EU, having similar numbers and sizes of NUTS 2 regions. Spain has been a member of the EU since 1986 and represents old MS, while Poland entered the EU in 2004 and belongs to the group of new MS. Poland enjoys derogation from participation in the eurozone, Spain introduced the euro. Several differences between Poland and Spain can be identified. They relate to institutional quality and to historical factors that may still influence the patterns of regions' trade (Brodzicki, Jurkiewicz, Márquez-Ramos and Umiński, 2019).

We identify the determinants of the intensity of foreign trade of the Spanish and Polish NUTS 2 regions with all existing trade partners on a bilateral basis over the period 2005-2014. We do so within the framework of an augmented panel gravity model. Recently, Márquez-Ramos (2016b, 2016c) stated that the regional (subnational) context interacts with the national and the supranational context in a gravity model approach. In this research, we consider (orthodox and non-orthodox) factors determining bilateral trade flows at three geographic levels: regional, national, and supranational.

We estimate a gravity model and utilize a solid method of estimation to obtain unbiased estimates, that is, the Poisson Pseudo Maximum Likelihood (PPML) estimator (Santos Silva and Tenreyro, 2006) applied to a semi-mixed effects model. Methodologically speaking, in this approach, the pair effects are random to control for unobserved cross-sectional heterogeneity, and following Lombardía and Sperlich (2012), an extra fixed clustering variable is introduced. This furthermore applies that the gravity equation does not have to be log-linearized; thus there is no need for elimination of zero trade flows or the so-called zero-adjustment.

The application of the gravity approach in the regional analysis is driven by two main reasons. On the one hand, the regional perspective allows the capture of new determinants of trade flows, which cannot be assessed at the country level. These are, for instance, historical circumstances and the nature of the border effect, as shown by Brodzicki (2017b), infrastructural issues (Alamá-Sabater, Márquez-Ramos, Navarro-Azorín, and Suárez-Burguet, 2015) or the role of metropolises. On the other hand, an inquiry into the nature, performance, and competitiveness of regions' exports – possible with the use of a gravity approach – bears important information for regional authorities or any other agents engaged in regional development issues, e.g., related to export promotion at the regional level (Gil-Pareja, Llorca-Vivero, Martínez-Serrano, and Requena-Silvente, 2015).

We contribute to the body of empirical trade literature by bringing the analysis of trade in the regional context beyond a single country and verifying the hypotheses related to determinants of trade for Spain and Poland in order to check their universal nature.

8.1 Hypotheses

The research sets, as a principal aim, the identification of the role of relevant orthodox and non-orthodox determinants in the region's foreign trade. They are presented in Table 8.1.

Table 8.1: The set of the testable hypotheses

Hypothesis	Description	Justification
1	The similarity in trading partners' level of development (GDP per capita or TFP) positively contributes to the intensity of trade relations	According to the Linder hypothesis (Linder, 1961), we expect partners to trade more intensively, the more similar their level of development is. The similarity in TFP reflects correspondence in the supply side, particularly in the levels of technological sophistication and overall productivity. Similarity measured by GDP per capita reflects the proximity at the demand side.
2	Direct geographical neighbourhood (adjacency) has a positive impact on bilateral trade	The justification for this hypothesis is in the gravity model itself (adjacency is the closest kind of proximity). Also, as exporting is a risky and difficult activity for a happy few (Mayer and Ottaviano, 2008; Melitz and Redding, 2014), the adjacency reflects the presence of common land borders and the likelihood of the greater number of border crossings, facilitating trade. Also, the information gap about the partners in trade is lower, which reduces the overall risk and entry costs associated with exporting. A thorough interpretation of the adjacency role was provided by Hummels (1999), who associates the adjacency with lower direct trade costs.
3	Metropolitan character of a region positively contributes to the export intensity	Metropolises are perceived as nodes of the globalized economy. They contribute to foreign market risk reduction due to agglomeration externalities, associated with information spillovers. According to NEG and new trade theory, metropolises are characterised by a greater scale of economic activity, more diversified economic structure, and concentration of tradable sectors (Behrens, 2005) – home market effect. For Poland, Brodzicki and Umiński (2017) find that metropolises have a statistically significant and positive influence on foreign trade flows. However, if entrepreneurs' (corporations) preferences are strongly focused on cost reduction (costs in metropolises are usually higher than elsewhere), exporters may prefer non-metropolitan locations.

continued **Table 8.1:** The set of the testable hypotheses

Hypothesis	Description	Justification
4	Quality of institutions positively affects bilateral trade	Institutions matter for regional development (Rodríguez-Pose et al., 2013). Their impact in the European context is more important than the first-nature geographic factors (Ketterer and Rodríguez-Pose, 2018). Álvarez, Rodríguez-Pose, and Zofío (2018) show their significance for shaping international trade flows between countries. Thus, we can postulate that greater institutional quality of both the region and its trade partner intensifies commercial links through the reduction of risk of business contracts. As shown by Do and Levchenko (2006), better contract enforcement, superior property rights, and better investors' protections enable agents to overcome frictions. Better institutions also reduce vulnerability to shocks, allowing for greater adaptive capacity (Bradley et al., 2017; Davoudi, Zaucha, and Brooks, 2016).
5	Historical path-dependency affects the existing trade relations in the region-country framework	According to Eichengreen and Irwin (1998), persistence in trade relations stems from historical bonds between trading partners. Persistence reflects longstanding ties, i.e., for former Spanish (Martinez-Galarraga, 2014), Portuguese or French colonies (Head and Mayer, 2014) or former partitions of Poland (Brodzicki and Umiński, 2017). The persistence does not always have to facilitate trade – adverse effects due to past animosities can persist over prolonged periods as well.
6	FDI inflows have an impact on the intensity of bilateral trade	FDI can exert a substitution or complementary effect on trade, depending on the character of FDI. The substitutive relation between FDI and exports is expected if the main aim of FDI is tariff jumping (Blomström et al., 2002). In case of substantial differences in factor endowments between countries, Helpman (1984) and Helpman and Krugman (1985) predict that FDI flows create complementary trade. According to Jensen (2002), the positive effect of FDI can unambiguously be expected only in case of resource-seeking, vertical FDI. Estrin et al. (2008) point out that the nexus between FDI and trade is strongly dependent on the relative position of the subsidiaries within the MNE, which influences the probability of exporting and its intensity.

Source: Own elaboration.

8.2 Empirical strategy

It seems to be a consensus that a gravity model "works well" in its baseline specification, including distance and market size of trading partners. A thorough overview of the evolution of the gravity concept, the theoretical underpinnings of the gravity equation, and its usage were presented by Head and Mayer (2014). Looking from this perspective, our approach corresponds with the supply-side derivation of the gravity model, which rests on the Ricardian comparative advantages, perceiving regions as parts of the global economy. Furthermore, as shown by Kepaptsoglou et al. (2010), the selection of other (non-orthodox) independent variables varies with the character of the research. In most empirical studies, the gravity approach is used to estimate, for instance, the consequence of monetary integration, customs unions implemented, export promotion carried on, etc., and the estimation strategy envisages the use of relatively few explanatory variables. This is due, basically, to the extended use of a strategy that consists of including several sets of fixed effects to avoid endogeneity in the gravity model at the country-level (Márquez-Ramos, 2016b).

Unfortunately, with this strategy, the identification of a number of key variables is not possible. Although there have been some methodological advances that allow identifying variables that by using a full battery of fixed effects could not be identified (Baier and Bergstrand, 2009; Heid, Larch, and Yotov, 2017), the approach we propose here is different. We aim at the identification of non-orthodox factors that influence trade with the purpose to help regions and actors responsible for export promotion at the regional level to increase export (or total trade) capabilities. This approach is consistent with the idea of using a region-to-country dataset to take into account the full structure of the gravity model. It can be treated as an alternative to the wide use of country-to-country statistics and several sets of fixed effects to control for potential omitted variable biases (Márquez-Ramos, 2016b). At the same time, this approach allows not only considering supranational factors (e.g., trade agreements), but also the region and country characteristics.

Our empirical strategy is the following. We construct a basic specification of an augmented gravity model and, in steps, add additional orthodox and non-orthodox variables to test the hypotheses. The analysis is conducted separately for total trade and exports of regions. Furthermore, we estimate the model jointly for all Spanish and Polish regions and then disjointedly, in a comparative manner, to identify discrepancies of reaction to various orthodox and non-orthodox factors investigated.

The factors included in the empirical analysis represent standard (or orthodox) determinants, such as the role of distance and size; and non-orthodox determinants, such as the differences in the level of development and technological sophistication, as measured by TFP, exchange rate variability and factors of structural character: metropolitan nature of some regions, cultural and institutional variation or trade-persistence (long-term nature historical factors, such as former colonies or partitions), quality of institutions or the impact of FDI.

To obtain unbiased results and to avoid heteroskedasticity and the zero trade flows adjustment, we utilize novel empirical approaches. An important problem in modelling gravity and in particular in the case of regions' trade is the phenomenon of zero trade flows. The distribution of zero-trade flows is not random. They occur predominantly in relations with small, remote trade partners and are more likely when the analysis is applied to the region-to-country framework. The typical log-linearized model in the case of zero trade flows requires the necessary adjustments or treatments as missing data[9].

Specifically, we use the estimation of a semi-mixed effect model with the PPML estimator. The estimator can be applied to a nonlinear multiplicative model (Santos Silva and Tenreyro, 2011; Westerlund and Wilhelmsson, 2011).

The functional form of the gravity model is based on the PPML approach. Time fixed effects are included. Trade-partners specific effects η_{ij} are estimated as random effects. We account for the importance of multilateral trade resistance by the inclusion of pair-specific effects, which enables us to capture the overall level of trade protection (Anderson and van Wincoop, 2003).

The PPML approach in a gravity context was extended by Savasci (2011), who suggested the use of PPML, where the pair effects were introduced as random, to control for unobserved cross-sectional heterogeneity. The problem in the estimation of the proposed version of the model is potential misspecification, due to the assumption of independence with the random effects. As a solution to the problem, Proença, Sperlich, and Savaşcı (2015) proposed a method which relaxes the strict assumption of the random effects model but entails more restrictions than the standard fixed-effects model, that is through the introduction of a fixed clustering variable (a semi-mixed effects model, SMEM). SMEM includes a nonparametric proxy in a parametric multilevel model to filter out potential mean dependency between the random effects and covariates (Lombardía and Sperlich, 2012). The inclusion of a nonparametric filter does not degrade the estimation of the effects of time-invariant variables – that is time, and other fixed effects can be included in the specification of the model. The resulting model is a semi mixed-effects model, in the sense that it still has a residual random effects component. The SMEM approach has recently been applied by Brodzicki and Umiński (2017) for the case of foreign trade of Polish regions.
The SMEM model has the following form (Proença et al., 2015):

$$T_{ijt} = exp\left[ln\alpha_0 + \beta_1 \log(Y_{it}) + \beta_2 \log(Y_{jt}) + \gamma \log(Z_{ij}) + \alpha_t + \eta_{ij}\right]\varepsilon_{ijt}$$

where Z_{ij} is the distance between the trade partners and η_{ij} are random effects.

9 The solution could be the application of PPML estimators. Santos Silva and Tenreyro (2006) argued that the standard logarithmic transformation in the gravity model might not be an appropriate approach to estimate elasticities. It is because trade models containing multiplicative errors do not satisfy the assumption of the homoskedasticity of the error term due to the dependency between the error term of the transformed log-linear model and the regressors.

The dependent variables in our empirical model are the value of total trade (*ttrade*) in thousands of EUR between a given region i and a given trade partner j in a year t and the value of exports (*exports*) in thousands of EUR from a given region i to a given trade partner j in a year t.

In the baseline specification, we control for the physical distance between trade partners, as measured by the log of distance in kilometres (*ln_distance*) and their sizes, as measured by the log of real GDP (*ln_rGDP_r; ln_rGDP_c*) in million USD. We control for the similarity in the levels of economic development, as measured by the log of absolute difference in real GDP per capita between a given region, and a given trade partner (*diff_y*). Because Hypothesis 1 states that trading partners trade more intensively the more similar their level of development is; thus, the coefficient on the variable is expected to be negative.

The data for regional institutional quality from the University of Gothenburg is available for two years only. To obtain a panel, we acknowledged their regional variation within Poland and Spain and took into account their evolution for both countries from the Global Governance Indicators database (*r_inst_quality*). Furthermore, we performed principal component analysis on the spectrum of institutional quality variable[10], provided in the Global Governance Indicators dataset to obtain a single institutional proxy for countries (*c_inst_quality*).

In the calculation of TFP for regions, we utilized the following approach. We took the data for TFP for Poland and Spain from PWT 9.0. Acknowledging that TFP is a prime source of variation in real GDP per capita, we took information on the value of real GDP per capita in a region, relative to country mean as a rough approximation of a region's TFP. Using the information on regions TFP and trade partners TFP we calculated the difference in TFP measure (*diff_tfp*) as the log of the absolute difference between the two values. In order to address potential collinearity with the log of GDP per capita, we drop the difference in GDP per capita in model specifications incorporating differences in TFP levels.

To account for the metropolitan status of a region we consulted the ESPON (Dühr, 2005) study on metropolitan areas in the EU, constructing a dummy variable for metropolitan areas (*metro*) and in addition, we took into account the Metropolitan European Growth Areas (MEGA) classification thus creating dummy variables for MEGA 1, 2, 3 and 4 regions (*mega1, mega2, mega3, mega4*, respectively). MEGA 1 currently have a global impact, while MEGA 4 are potential metropolises with European significance. Table 8.2. describes the variables used together with the character of the variable (orthodox versus non-orthodox) as well as the geographical scale of spatial variation (regional, national, or supranational) and the expected direction of impact.

10 These included: voice and accountability, political stability and absence of violence, government effectiveness, regulatory quality, rule of law as well as control of corruption.

Table 8.2: Description of the key variables

Variable	Description	Character of the variable	Geographic scale of spatial variation	Presumed impact on the dependent variable	Hypothesis number
ln_distance	Log of distance in km between region's and trade partner's capital cities	orthodox	regional and national	negative	*
ln_rgdp_c	log of real GDP of the partner country	orthodox	national	positive	*
ln_rgdp_r	Log of real GDP of a region	orthodox	regional	positive	*
diff_y	Difference in the level of development as measured by the log of absolute difference in real GDP per capita	orthodox	regional and national	negative	H1
diff_tfp	Difference in the level of technological sophistication as measured by the log of absolute difference in the TFP levels	non-orthodox	regional and national	negative	H3
adjacency	Adjacency between a region and a partner country	orthodox	regional	positive	H2
access_2_sea	Access to sea by a region	orthodox	regional	positive	*
c_landlocked	Landlockedness of the partner country – CEPII	orthodox	national	negative	*
mega1	Region having MEGA 1 status in accordance with the ESPON MEGA classification	non-orthodox	regional	positive	H3
mega3	Region having MEGA 3 status in accordance with the ESPON MEGA classification	non-orthodox	regional	positive	H3
mega4	Region having MEGA 4 status in accordance with the ESPON MEGA classification	non-orthodox	regional	positive	H3
metro	Metropolitan status of the region in accordance with the ESPON MEGA classification (MEGA 1, 2, 3 or 4)	non-orthodox	regional	positive	H3
eu28	Dummy variable for partner country in the EU	orthodox	national and supranational	positive	*
r_inst_qual	Regional institutional quality – QoG	non-orthodox	regional	positive	H4

continued **Table 8.2:** Description of the key variables

Variable	Description	Character of the variable	Geographic scale of spatial variation	Presumed impact on the dependent variable	Hypothesis number
c_inst_quality	Partner country institutional quality – result of principal component analysis on World Bank governance indicators	non-orthodox	national	positive	H4
history	Dummy variable for common historical ties between a region and a given trade partner (including partitions and colonies)	non-orthodox	regional and national	positive/negative	H5
pl_p_common	Dummy for a region in a common partition with a foreign country	non-orthodox	regional	positive/negative	H5
pl_p_deu	Dummy for Polish region in the former Prussian partition	non-orthodox	regional	positive/negative	H5
pl_p_rus	Dummy for Polish region in the former Russian partition	non-orthodox	regional	positive/negative	H5
pl_p_aus	Dummy for Polish region in the former Austro-Hungarian partition	non-orthodox	regional	positive/negative	H5
ln_no_fdi_cum_za	Log of the cumulated number of FDI in the region from a trade partner – zero adjusted (FDI inflow)	non-orthodox	regional and national	positive/negative	H6
ln_no_fdi_area_za	Log of the cumulated number of FDI in the region from a trade partner per square km – zero adjusted (FDI inflow)	non-orthodox	regional and national	positive/negative	H6
ln_value_esp_reg_fdi_abroad_za	Log of the value of Spanish regions FDI in foreign trade partners – zero adjusted (FDI outflow)	non-orthodox	regional and national	positive/negative	H6

Source: Own elaboration based on a review of the theoretical and empirical literature. * denotes variables of a baseline gravity equation, including distance, market size, and trade costs.

Regarding the data panel, it has been constructed for the trade of 16 NUTS 2 level regions of Poland (voivodships) and 19 NUTS 2 (autonomous regions) level regions of Spain with all possible trade partners (countries). The panel covers the period from 2005 to 2014 and is unbalanced due to missing observations. The dataset has been acquired from a number of sources. The trade data for Polish and Spanish regions have been obtained from the Polish Customs Chamber (Izba Celna) and retrieved from the Spanish DataComex database (http://datacomex.comercio.es), according to the headquarters of exporters companies.

The main source of auxiliary data for countries is the Penn World Tables PWT 9.0. (Feenstra, Inklaar, and Timmer, 2015). The main source of auxiliary data for regions is the Quality of Government EU Regional Dataset (Charron et al., 2016). The information on the institutional quality of countries has been obtained from the 2016 version of the Worldwide Governance Indicators of the World Bank (Kaufmann, Kraay, and Mastruzzi, 2011). The data on FDI inflows by trade partner into regions has been obtained from PAIiIZ for Poland and from http://datainvex.comercio.es, and from the Spanish Ministry of Economy and Competitiveness. The distance between trade partners has been calculated in kilometres, between the capital cities of the regions and the partner countries, with the use of "as the crow flies" method, using the information on their longitude and latitude. Additional geographical information has been acquired from CEPII (Mayer and Zignago, 2011; Melitz and Toubal, 2014).

8.3 Empirical results

Our empirical results for Polish and Spanish regions, taken jointly, are presented in Tables 8.3 and 8.4.

Tables 8.5 and 8.6 provide separate estimates for Polish and Spanish regions' exports. We have to stress that the general fit of the augmented gravity model is high. The model explains approx. 75 to 80% of the variation in the observed variables. The dummy for EU28 is the clustering variable used in the semi-mixed effect method of estimation.

According to our results, the impact of distance is negative and above one (in absolute terms). In addition, the impact of the size of the region and the size of trade partners is statistically significant and positive. The magnitude of the impact is generally higher for the size of the region than the size of the trade partner. The negative impact of distance is more pronounced for exports than for total trade (compare Table 8.4 to 8.3). The magnitude for exports is higher for more peripheral Polish regions than more central Spanish regions (Tables 8.5 and 8.6).

In all estimated models, the impact of dissimilarity in the levels of economic development is statistically significant and negative (except for several specifications for Polish regions, not accounting for the institutional quality). Thus, partners of a similar level of development (as measured by GDP per capita), in accordance with the Linder hypotheses, trade more. Also, the impact of the difference in TFP levels between the region and its trade partner is statistically significant and negative. It is worth noting that the magnitude of the impact is several times higher for Polish regions' than Spanish regions' exports, depicting significantly higher elasticity of reaction. Thus, hypothesis H1 has been positively verified.

The adjacency, as expected (H2), has a positive impact on bilateral trade flows. Its impact is visibly more important for Spanish regions. This could be due to the importance that France represents for Spanish exports. Trade flows originating from Spain go mainly to European destinations, and the trade is principally done using road transport. Therefore, the frontier with France is highly important, as is the main way to cross the Pyrenees Mountains (Márquez-Ramos, 2015). Gallego and Llano (2017), commenting on the limited number of road crossings with France in the Pyrenees, speak of dam-like effects on trade. Poland borders seven countries and has numerous border crossings. This, in turn, is in line with the result of Martincus (2010) for Brazilian regions, which suggest that trade openness favours location in regions closer to the largest neighbour trading partner.

In the joined sample of Polish and Spanish regions, the impact of access to a sea by a region is positive and statistically significant. It also holds for Spanish regions taken separately. The impact on Poland's regions exports is positive, however, not statistically significant. It could be related to the more pronounced role of the maritime transport for Spanish trade flows. In Q1 of 2017, the gross weight of seaborne goods amounted to 113.4 M tonnes in Spain and only 18.3 M tonnes in the case of Poland (according to the mar_go database of EUROSTAT). It should be stressed, however, that the impact of landlockedness of the trade partner is negative and statistically significant in all specifications considered.

The metropolitan status of a region in accordance with the ESPON classification boosts its total trade and exports in the joined sample of Polish and Spanish regions, even if we control for historical factors. If we control for the variation in the significance in the metropolitan area (a division of MEGA 1 to 4), the elasticities differ. They are positive for total trade (with the highest magnitude of the impact for MEGA3 – or weak European metropolitan areas: Mazowieckie (Warsaw), Pais Vasco (Bilbao) and Valencia, and positive and robust for exports of MEGA3 and MEGA4 (potential metropolitan areas with the European significance) regions. On the other hand, if the analysis is conducted for Polish and Spanish exports disjointedly, the coefficient on the metro variable is not statistically significant for Poland and is negative for Spain. At the same time, the impact of MEGAs is generally negative, ceteris paribus. From the country-level perspective, the nexus between the metropolitan status and exports requires further investigation.

In each model, from the sixth specification onwards, we control for regional governance quality and partners' institutional quality. The results are robust with the positive impact of institutional quality of the trade partner only. The lack of statistical significance of the coefficient on the regions' institutional quality could stem from the lower dispersion of the variable, compared to the one observed for countries. Further research on this relationship is recommended. H4, therefore, has been only partially verified.

In the next specifications, we test for the impact of historical ties, ceteris paribus. It includes former colonies of Spain and the relatively recent impact of partitions of

Poland. The impact of history is generally positive in the joined sample, supporting the notion of trade persistence. It is further analysed in separate models for Poland and Spain and indicates a distinct difference. Spanish regions, in general, export more to former Spanish colonies (Table 8.6). However, due to the data character that we use, we cannot observe regional variation in this case. For Poland, the impact varies between regions and the former empire that a given region had belonged to, before 1918. The impact differs clearly between former Prussian, Russian and Austro-Hungarian regions of Poland (Table 8.5). The findings are in line with the results reported by Brodzicki and Umiński (2017).

In the final set of specifications, we control for the impact of FDI inflows and outflows from regions. We introduce the information on a cumulated number of FDI (zero-adjusted) and the relative number of FDI per km^2, for a given trade partner in a given region. The impact of both on total trade in the joined sample is negative; however, statistically significant only in the first case. The impact on exports is positive, however not statistically significant for the first variable, and negative, for the second variable.

The impact for exports of Polish regions (Table 8.5) of both variables is positive, although not statistically significant. In the case of exports of Spanish regions (Table 8.6), it is positive for a cumulated number of investors and negative for the area-adjusted variable. In the case of Spain, due to data availability, we can additionally account for the value of FDI outflows by Spanish regions that have a positive impact. It is in line with the notion that FDI flows are complementary with regional trade flows and in line with results obtained for other countries (see, for example, Leichenko and Erickson (1997) for the US).

8.4 Conclusions

Although the gravity approach has been intensively used in international economics, the determinants of regional export activity still require thorough investigation. Both international and regional aspects are involved. The studies of a similar kind have been conducted in some countries and their regions; however, our objective is to verify both orthodox and non-orthodox determinants for regions in two EU member states.

The empirical results have proven most of the theoretical postulates related to factors potentially determining trade relations in a “region-to-country” framework. In particular, the paper has identified the determinants of the intensity of foreign trade of the Spanish and Polish NUTS 2 regions with all existing trade partners on a bilateral basis over the period 2005-2014. The augmented gravity panel model has been estimated with the use of a novel and superior method of estimation, namely the semi-mixed effects by PPML.

Table 8.3: Estimates for the value of total trade of Polish and Spanish regions

VARIABLES	(1)	(2)	(3)	(4)	(5)	(6)	(7)	(8)	(9)
ln_distance	-1.085***	-1.094***	-1.102***	-1.069***	-1.065***	-1.052***	-1.010***	-1.025***	-1.011***
	(0.0132)	(0.0139)	(0.0137)	(0.0144)	(0.0146)	(0.0142)	(0.0133)	(0.0149)	(0.0133)
ln_rgdp_c	0.856***	0.834***	0.837***	0.830***	0.830***	0.820***	0.816***	0.831***	0.819***
	(0.00725)	(0.00769)	(0.007)	(0.00766)	(0.00751)	(0.00819)	(0.00816)	(0.0104)	(0.00862)
ln_rgdp_r	1.091***	1.075***	1.079***	1.011***	0.979***	1.021***	1.039***	1.083***	1.047***
	(0.0105)	(0.0110)	(0.0106)	(0.0151)	(0.0241)	(0.0153)	(0.0159)	(0.0216)	(0.0180)
diff_y	-0.142***	-0.142***		-0.162***	-0.156***	-0.153***	-0.172***	-0.183***	-0.177***
	(0.0204)	(0.0209)		(0.0208)	(0.0200)	(0.0220)	(0.0229)	(0.0237)	(0.0234)
adjacency	0.241***	0.207***	0.171***	0.208***	0.233***	0.214***	0.176***	0.193***	0.182***
	(0.0455)	(0.0466)	(0.048)	(0.0467)	(0.0470)	(0.0470)	(0.0477)	(0.0479)	(0.0476)
access_2_sea		0.0706***	0.072***	0.0582**	0.0689***	0.0658***	0.0721***	0.0774***	0.0604**
		(0.0236)	(0.0234)	(0.0239)	(0.0248)	(0.0243)	(0.0253)	(0.0252)	(0.0266)
c_landlocked		-0.266***	-0.287***	-0.283***	-0.282***	-0.305***	-0.242***	-0.258***	-0.246***
		(0.0255)	(0.0253)	(0.0253)	(0.0250)	(0.0257)	(0.0272)	(0.0274)	(0.0271)
mega1					0.263***				
					(0.0649)				
mega3					0.347***				
					(0.0497)				
mega4					0.170***				
					(0.0355)				
eu28	0.262***	0.266***	0.297***	0.301***	0.308***	0.255***	0.321***	0.331***	0.325***
	(0.0262)	(0.0272)	(0.0260)	(0.0260)	(0.0253)	(0.0259)	(0.0260)	(0.0261)	(0.0263)
diff_tfp			-0.067***						
			(0.009)						

continued **Table 8.3:** Estimates for the value of total trade of Polish and Spanish regions

VARIABLES	(1)	(2)	(3)	(4)	(5)	(6)	(7)	(8)	(9)
metro				0.199***		0.177***	0.158***	0.143***	0.159***
				(0.0342)		(0.0351)	(0.0364)	(0.0368)	(0.0361)
r_inst_quality						-0.114**	-0.121**	-0.119**	-0.115**
						(0.0501)	(0.0507)	(0.0500)	(0.0504)
c_inst_quality						0.0332***	0.0307***	0.0368***	0.0315***
						(0.00641)	(0.00633)	(0.00587)	(0.00626)
history							0.387***	0.382***	0.384***
							(0.0427)	(0.0418)	(0.0425)
ln_no_fdi_cum_za								-0.0248***	
								(0.00844)	
ln_no_fdi_area_za									-4.066
									(3.101)
Constant	4.498***	5.056***	4.797***	5.507***	5.803***	5.366***	4.863***	4.321***	4.758***
	(0.174)	(0.192)	(0.176)	(0.204)	(0.261)	(0.213)	(0.217)	(0.277)	(0.241)
Observations	39,118	38,377	38,377	38,377	38,377	38,098	36,321	36,321	36,321
R-squared	0.781	0.777	0.778	0.777	0.780	0.778	0.780	0.782	0.780
No of parameters	7	9	10	10	12	12	13	14	14
Log likelihood	5.260e+12	5.160e+12	5.140e+12	5.130e+12	5.110e+12	5.050e+12	4.830e+12	4.820e+12	4.830e+12

Source: Own estimation in STATA 15. Semi-mixed effects model estimated with PPML. Robust standard errors in parentheses. *** p<0.01, ** p<0.05, * p<0.
Dependent variable – the value of total trade in USD.

Table 8.4: Estimates for exports of Polish and Spanish regions

VARIABLES	(1)	(2)	(3)	(4)	(5)	(6)	(7)	(8)	(9)
ln_distance	-1.237***	-1.259***	-1.262***	-1.242***	-1.247***	-1.190***	-1.161***	-1.152***	-1.167***
	(0.0133)	(0.0154)	(0.0150)	(0.0161)	(0.0159)	(0.0151)	(0.0148)	(0.0168)	(0.0150)
ln_rgdp_c	0.821***	0.790***	0.794***	0.787***	0.790***	0.748***	0.739***	0.731***	0.751***
	(0.00728)	(0.00784)	(0.00767)	(0.00784)	(0.00795)	(0.00744)	(0.00737)	(0.00992)	(0.00771)
ln_rgdp_r	0.988***	0.948***	0.957***	0.907***	0.966***	0.929***	0.944***	0.921***	0.982***
	(0.0102)	(0.0111)	(0.0113)	(0.0162)	(0.0241)	(0.0161)	(0.0166)	(0.0231)	(0.0183)
diff_y	-0.164***	-0.157***		-0.173***	-0.167***	-0.174***	-0.190***	-0.183***	-0.214***
	(0.0168)	(0.0174)		(0.0162)	(0.0161)	(0.0167)	(0.0170)	(0.0174)	(0.0176)
adjacency	0.277***	0.203***	0.180***	0.204***	0.208***	0.231***	0.211***	0.202***	0.238***
	(0.0436)	(0.0478)	(0.0480)	(0.0483)	(0.0504)	(0.0483)	(0.0484)	(0.0482)	(0.0508)
access_2_sea		0.222***	0.224***	0.213***	0.196***	0.226***	0.227***	0.224***	0.176***
		(0.0262)	(0.0263)	(0.0270)	(0.0276)	(0.0273)	(0.0284)	(0.0289)	(0.0292)
c_landlocked		-0.346***	-0.369***	-0.360***	-0.359***	-0.420***	-0.377***	-0.368***	-0.393***
		(0.0318)	(0.0311)	(0.0317)	(0.0321)	(0.0314)	(0.0322)	(0.0322)	(0.0321)
mega1					-0.0511				
					(0.0675)				
mega3					0.0823*				
					(0.0493)				
mega4					0.113***				
					(0.0388)				
eu28	0.415***	0.414***	0.456***	0.434***	0.437***	0.272***	0.312***	0.309***	0.331***
	(0.0247)	(0.0273)	(0.0281)	(0.0264)	(0.0261)	(0.0284)	(0.0277)	(0.0278)	(0.0277)
diff_tfp			-0.0562***						
			(0.00878)						
metro				0.124***		0.0787**	0.0594	0.0678	0.0647

continued **Table 8.4:** Estimates for exports of Polish and Spanish regions

VARIABLES	(1)	(2)	(3)	(4)	(5)	(6)	(7)	(8)	(9)
				(0.0389)		(0.0396)	(0.0407)	(0.0427)	(0.0396)
r_inst_quality						-0.121**	-0.128**	-0.129**	-0.104*
						(0.0595)	(0.0609)	(0.0611)	(0.0595)
c_inst_quality						0.105***	0.104***	0.101***	0.107***
						(0.00480)	(0.00478)	(0.00511)	(0.00469)
history							0.226***	0.232***	0.211***
							(0.0454)	(0.0458)	(0.0451)
ln_no_fdi_cum_za								0.0135	
								(0.00909)	
ln_no_fdi_area_za									-21.89***
									(3.570)
Constant	6.378***	7.352***	6.989***	7.649***	7.035***	7.446***	7.178***	7.459***	6.686***
	(0.133)	(0.156)	(0.158)	(0.175)	(0.249)	(0.180)	(0.185)	(0.261)	(0.205)
Observations	47,378	46,373	46,373	46,373	46,373	45,875	43,456	43,456	43,456
R-squared	0.774	0.766	0.765	0.764	0.765	0.772	0.769	0.770	0.771
No of parameters	7	9	10	10	12	12	13	14	14
Log likelihood	2.360e+12	2.250e+12	-1.129e+12	2.250e+12	2.240e+12	2.130e+12	2.070e+12	2.070e+12	2.050e+12

Source: Own estimation in STATA 15. Semi-mixed effects model estimated with PPML. Robust standard errors in parentheses. *** p<0.01, ** p<0.05, * p<0.1. Dependent variable – the value of exports in USD.

Table 8.5: Estimates for exports of Polish NUTS 2 regions

VARIABLES	(1)	(2)	(3)	(4)	(5)	(6)	(7)	(8)	(9)	(10)	(11)	(12)	(13)
ln_distance	-1.298***	-1.320***	-1.333***	-1.320***	-1.313***	-1.216***	-1.242***	-1.247***	-1.240***	-1.253***	-1.214***	-1.234***	-1.240***
	(0.0149)	(0.0154)	(0.0156)	(0.0154)	(0.0151)	(0.0173)	(0.0242)	(0.0241)	(0.0248)	(0.0239)	(0.0176)	(0.0238)	(0.0240)
ln_rgdp_c	0.793***	0.751***	0.762***	0.751***	0.752***	0.738***	0.749***	0.749***	0.744***	0.749***	0.734***	0.743***	0.747***
	(0.00974)	(0.00969)	(0.00951)	(0.00965)	(0.00918)	(0.0104)	(0.0129)	(0.0127)	(0.0129)	(0.0123)	(0.0107)	(0.0133)	(0.0128)
ln_rgdp_r	1.252***	1.270***	1.218***	1.249***	1.716***	1.127***	1.137***	1.126***	1.120***	1.118***	1.115***	1.119***	1.129***
	(0.0189)	(0.0211)	(0.0202)	(0.0314)	(0.0511)	(0.0353)	(0.0370)	(0.0366)	(0.0369)	(0.0366)	(0.0355)	(0.0374)	(0.0366)
diff_y	0.172***	0.164***		0.161***	0.142***	-0.189***	-0.168***	-0.175***	-0.173***	-0.167***	-0.183***	-0.160***	-0.163***
	(0.0269)	(0.0280)		(0.0277)	(0.0280)	(0.0473)	(0.0510)	(0.0488)	(0.0495)	(0.0489)	(0.0475)	(0.0550)	(0.0515)
adjacency	0.0821	0.0880	0.0638	0.0828	0.114*	0.158**	0.188***	0.183**	0.199***	0.182**	0.150**	0.182**	0.185***
	(0.0727)	(0.0750)	(0.0747)	(0.0743)	(0.0644)	(0.0705)	(0.0713)	(0.0718)	(0.0732)	(0.0728)	(0.0704)	(0.0718)	(0.0711)
access_2_sea		0.0506	0.0489	0.0330	0.264***	0.000161	0.0105	0.00177	0.00421	-0.00344	-0.00785	0.00608	0.0103
		(0.0701)	(0.0696)	(0.0699)	(0.0629)	(0.0681)	(0.0700)	(0.0685)	(0.0688)	(0.0688)	(0.0679)	(0.0703)	(0.0699)
c_landlocked		-0.359***	-0.370***	-0.359***	-0.424***	-0.345***	-0.342***	0.364***	-0.373***	-0.346***	-0.313***	-0.337***	-0.339***
		(0.0346)	(0.0323)	(0.0346)	(0.0334)	(0.0354)	(0.0381)	(0.0373)	(0.0397)	(0.0396)	(0.0357)	(0.0374)	(0.0379)
eu28	0.345***	0.404***	0.412***	0.402***	0.479***	0.357***	0.343***	0.344***	0.345***	0.339***	0.355***	0.361***	0.348***
	(0.0372)	(0.0372)	(0.0379)	(0.0376)	(0.0355)	(0.0394)	(0.0407)	(0.0397)	(0.0397)	(0.0399)	(0.0391)	(0.0521)	(0.0420)
diff_tfp			-0.0106***										
			(0.0117)										

continued **Table 8.5:** Estimates for exports of Polish NUTS 2 regions

VARIABLES	(1)	(2)	(3)	(4)	(5)	(6)	(7)	(8)	(9)	(10)	(11)	(12)	(13)
metro				0.0446		0.0817*	0.0787*	0.0844*	0.0941**	0.0947**	0.0978**	0.0914**	0.0854*
				(0.0420)		(0.0421)	(0.0440)	(0.0433)	(0.0434)	(0.0434)	(0.0421)	(0.0451)	(0.0442)
mega3					-1.031***								
					(0.102)								
mega4					-0.352***								
					(0.0522)								
r_inst_ quality						-0.0898	-0.0863	-0.0868	-0.0894	-0.0863	-0.0905	-0.0850	-0.0962
						(0.0629)	(0.0661)	(0.0650)	(0.0651)	(0.0652)	(0.0625)	(0.0665)	(0.0653)
c_inst_ quality						0.123***	0.117***	0.119***	0.127***	0.120***	0.129***	0.111***	0.115***
						(0.0107)	(0.0113)	(0.0112)	(0.0116)	(0.0108)	(0.0114)	(0.0160)	(0.0118)
history							-0.113*					-0.110*	-0.115*
							(0.0606)					(0.0601)	(0.0611)
pl_p_ common								-0.127**					
								(0.0606)					
pl_p_deu									-0.139**	-0.154**			
									(0.0703)	(0.0692)			
pl_p_rus									0.230***		0.262***		
									(0.0757)		(0.0713)		
pl_p_aus										-0.637***	-0.627***		

continued **Table 8.5:** Estimates for exports of Polish NUTS 2 regions

VARIABLES	(1)	(2)	(3)	(4)	(5)	(6)	(7)	(8)	(9)	(10)	(11)	(12)	(13)
										(0.0644)	(0.0642)		
ln_no_fdi_cum_za												0.0203	
												(0.0309)	
ln_no_fdi_area_za													109.4
													(168.6)
Observations	21,566	20,930	20,930	20,930	20,930	20,768	19,776	20,768	20,768	20,768	20,768	19,776	19,776
R-squared	0.786	0.776	0.776	0.777	0.820	0.781	0.770	0.769	0.768	0.767	0.783	0.769	0.770

Source: Own estimation in STATA 15. Semi-mixed effects model estimated with PPML. Robust standard errors in parentheses. *** p<0.01, ** p<0.05, * p<0.1. Dependent variable – the value of exports in USD. The constant term always positive and statistically significant removed from the presentation for clarity.

Table 8.6: Estimates for exports of Spanish NUTS 2 regions

VARIABLES	(1)	(2)	(3)	(4)	(5)	(6)	(7)	(8)	(9)	(10)
ln_distance	-1.085***	-1.060***	-1.085***	-1.063***	-1.057***	-1.108***	-1.214***	-1.161***	-1.219***	-1.153***
	(0.0224)	(0.0242)	(0.0238)	(0.0244)	(0.0247)	(0.0238)	(0.0240)	(0.0282)	(0.0246)	(0.0252)
ln_rgdp_c	0.795***	0.758***	0.784***	0.759***	0.756***	0.748***	0.779***	0.738***	0.784***	0.735***
	(0.00985)	(0.00990)	(0.00969)	(0.00984)	(0.00989)	(0.00940)	(0.0104)	(0.0154)	(0.0108)	(0.0130)
ln_rgdp_r	0.950***	0.887***	0.890***	1.002***	0.942***	1.020***	1.032***	0.955***	1.042***	0.958***
	(0.0139)	(0.0143)	(0.0143)	(0.0340)	(0.0429)	(0.0348)	(0.0355)	(0.0422)	(0.0364)	(0.0340)
diff_y	-0.312***	-0.349***		-0.351***	-0.342***	-0.230***	-0.159***	-0.163***	-0.166***	-0.153***
	(0.0240)	(0.0232)		(0.0233)	(0.0231)	(0.0240)	(0.0259)	(0.0257)	(0.0267)	(0.0260)
adjacency	0.488***	0.378***	0.370***	0.375***	0.392***	0.367***	0.304***	0.269***	0.312***	0.309***
	(0.0473)	(0.0490)	(0.0491)	(0.0475)	(0.0460)	(0.0474)	(0.0487)	(0.0474)	(0.0508)	(0.0470)
access_2_sea		0.475***	0.468***	0.527***	0.550***	0.531***	0.529***	0.549***	0.502***	0.540***
		(0.0298)	(0.0299)	(0.0355)	(0.0361)	(0.0351)	(0.0355)	(0.0347)	(0.0376)	(0.0347)
c_landlocked		-0.556***	-0.534***	-0.553***	-0.558***	-0.637***	-0.567***	-0.548***	-0.571***	-0.550***
		(0.0599)	(0.0620)	(0.0593)	(0.0586)	(0.0490)	(0.0468)	(0.0455)	(0.0472)	(0.0461)
eu28	0.509***	0.530***	0.684***	0.525***	0.533***	0.323***	0.295***	0.270***	0.297***	0.297***
	(0.0347)	(0.0375)	(0.0355)	(0.0372)	(0.0372)	(0.0391)	(0.0370)	(0.0359)	(0.0371)	(0.0375)
mega1					-0.125					
					(0.104)					
mega3					-0.166**					
					(0.0818)					
mega4					-0.277***					
					(0.0836)					
diff_tfp			-0.0554*							

continued **Table 8.6:** Estimates for exports of Spanish NUTS 2 regions

VARIABLES	(1)	(2)	(3)	(4)	(5)	(6)	(7)	(8)	(9)	(10)
			(0.0114)							
metro				-0.259***		-0.276***	-0.291***	-0.317***	-0.279***	-0.319***
				(0.0770)		(0.0770)	(0.0778)	(0.0775)	(0.0772)	(0.0746)
r_inst_quality						0.152*	0.152	0.159*	0.155*	0.134
						(0.0901)	(0.0926)	(0.0913)	(0.0930)	(0.0917)
c_inst_quality						0.0868***	0.113***	0.0984***	0.114***	0.103***
						(0.00683)	(0.00668)	(0.00740)	(0.00673)	(0.00692)
history							1.257***	1.141***	1.266***	1.081***
							(0.0448)	(0.0555)	(0.0453)	(0.0515)
ln_no_fdi_cum_za								0.0514***		
								(0.0115)		
ln_no_fdi_area_za									-6.009*	
									(3.618)	
ln_value_esp_reg_fdi_abroad_za										0.0196***
Observations	25,812	25,443	25,443	25,443	25,443	25,107	23,680	23,680	23,680	23,680
R-squared	0.794	0.811	0.810	0.815	0.818	0.820	0.821	0.825	0.820	0.824

Source: Own estimation in STATA 15. Semi-mixed effects model estimated with PPML. Robust standard errors in parentheses. *** p<0.01, ** p<0.05, * p<0.1. The constant term always positive and statistically significant removed from the presentation for clarity. Full results available upon request.

As the gravity model has been proven to be a useful and robust tool to estimate the nature of the region-to-country trade – it should be more intensively used by regional authorities to assess the impact of various policy scenarios and predict their consequences.

The model has been jointly estimated for all Spanish and Polish regions and then in the second step disjointedly, in a comparative manner. The orthodox or standard determinants of trade flows, such as distance and market size, prove the robustness of the application of the gravity approach to the "region-to-country" trade framework. The impact of other standard variables such as adjacency is in line with theoretical postulates. Polish and Spanish regions trade more with partners at a similar level of development in line with the Linder hypothesis. As regards non-orthodox factors, the similarity in productivity levels as measured by TFP, the institutional quality of trading partner, the metropolitan status of the region, and historical linkages influence the bilateral trade flows. Therefore, we agree with Linders, Burger, and van Oort (2008), that more elaborate variety of tangible and intangible dimensions of transactional distance are crucial to correctly interpret differences between trade partners.

The export potential of a region can be boosted by the attraction of FDI, thus proving the importance of effective regional promotional activity and raising high investment attractiveness. As we have shown, the similarity in the level of development boosts bilateral trade. It paradoxically could direct export promotion policies towards more dissimilar partners. However, it could be highly region-specific and requires further investigation, also embracing the structural factors. Having shown that adjacency matters, promotional activity should be more pronounced on non-border regions.

Tony Cavoli, Dandan Lin, Laura Márquez-Ramos

9 Insights for Australia – regions in foreign trade

Advances in international trade literature have shown that, overall, trade is good; however, gains from foreign trade are not the same for everyone. Foreign trade may generate adverse welfare and labour impacts in local markets, increasing economic inequality. Therefore, a better understanding of foreign trade patterns and trends in territories at a higher disaggregation level than the traditional country-unit is desirable. This chapter focuses on Australian regions.[11]

Australia is an interesting case study due to its geographical and economic conditions: it is the world's sixth-largest country in geographical terms and one of the least densely populated, where the population is concentrated in a few cities. In addition, Australia is highly dependent on a few large "neighbouring" countries, especially China, and it is highly specialised in a few sectors, particularly primary industries and services. In other words, the diversification of Australian exports in terms of both markets and products, or as commonly known in the international trade literature, the extensive margin of trade, is low.[12] Consequently, Australia is vulnerable to external shocks.

Australia's vulnerability to external shocks is of considerable policy relevance. For example, policymakers in Australia fear that the ongoing trade war between China and the US has significant negative consequences for the Australian economy.[13] Motivated by the high dependency of Australia on a few sectors and trading partners, we focus on the relationship between foreign trade and regional inequality. Although Australia is an interesting and relevant case to study in a globalised world, foreign

---

11 In this chapter, Australian regions refer to eight Australian states. This is different to the concept of "regional Australia", which refers to the non-metropolitan parts of the country and includes towns, small cities, and areas that lie beyond the major capital cities (Sydney, Melbourne, Brisbane, Perth, Adelaide, and Canberra).

12 At country level, the international trade literature has explored the evolution of the extensive margin of trade in different economic areas. For example, using two different methodologies to compute the margins of trade (for products), Bensassi, Márquez-Ramos, and Martínez-Zarzoso (2012) focus on exports from North Africa, while Márquez-Ramos, Florensa, and Recalde (2015) focus on Latin America. To the best of our knowledge, there is not previous research focusing on the evolution of trade margins in Australian regions.

13 See, e.g., the article *'Wrong place at the wrong time': how the US-China trade war is putting the squeeze on Australia"* (The Guardian, 21 September 2019, available at https://www.theguardian.com/business/2019/sep/21/wrong-place-at-the-wrong-time-how-the-us-china-trade-war-is-putting-the-squeeze-on-australia). Other example is the Chinese economic slowdown. However, consequences of "China trade shocks" for Australia are unclear (see, e.g., the article in The Conversation, 2 August 2019, "*Australia depends less on Chinese trade than some might think*", available at http://theconversation.com/australia-depends-less-on-chinese-trade-than-some-might-think-120423).

trade in Australian regions, as well as its relationship to trade policy and economic inequality, is understudied.

Our contribution to the literature is threefold. First, we identify "hot issues" in the Australian context regarding foreign trade in regions. To do so, we review the existent related literature for Australia at both country and regional level. Second, we provide a comprehensive collection of stylised facts about foreign trade (exports) in Australian regions. Finally, we interact trade policy and economic inequality with trade patterns and trends in Australian regions. More specifically, we focus on the co-movements of Australian foreign trade (exports/openness) with trade liberalisation and unemployment. Crucially, in our analysis, we focus on both trade in goods and trade in services.

A brand of the literature closely related to our research is that of smart specialisation. Conceived within the reformed Cohesion Policy of the European Commission, smart specialisation is a policy approach that aims to boost jobs and growth by enabling the identification and development of competitive advantages. A key characteristic of smart specialisation is the place-based dimension, which relates to a strong anchorage in territories (Gómez Prieto, Demblans, and Palazuelos Martínez, 2019). Smart specialisation in Australia has been locally driven; that is, existent initiatives have not been driven by policy interventions. The Australian experience shows that, although the interest in the smart specialisation can increase and take shape, a wider policy framework support from other levels of government is needed to take it forward. In addition, more emphasis on coherence and collaboration, against a history of fragmentation and competition, is required (Gómez Prieto et al., 2019; Wilson, 2018). Place-based innovation becomes shaped by emerging global opportunities, such as those related to foreign trade because regions can analyse their core assets and seek new market opportunities.

The rest of the chapter is structured as follows. Sections 9.1 and 9.2 review the literature on Australian foreign trade. Then, we present our main analysis: firstly, we describe the characteristics of Australian exports at country-level; secondly, we describe Australian foreign trade (exports) by region and, thirdly, we analyse how regional exports interact with trade liberalisation. In section 9.6, we analyse the relationship between regional unemployment and foreign trade (openness). The final section concludes and provides a number of relevant insights on the relationship between trade policy, foreign trade, and economic inequality in Australian regions.

9.1 Review of country-level studies

Australian foreign trade (and foreign trade by Australian regions in particular) has been scarcely studied. To better understand the context of Australia's foreign trade, we survey, as a first step, related studies at country-level (subsection 9.1). In a second step, we survey the most related literature that relies on Australian subnational units (regions) (subsection 9.2).

For Australia, country-level studies have focused on geographical disadvantages and its "remoteness" in the world economy, the DD, trade policy (trade liberalisation and trade protectionism), the bilateral trade relationship of Australia with its trade partners, as well as its participation in value chains. Regional-level studies identify "hot issues" such as DD consequences associated with the mining boom. In addition, employment inequality and asymmetric regional urban development policies have been analysed. These factors contribute to shape regional economic patterns in Australia and validate the importance of considering the heterogeneity of Australian states (that is, regional heterogeneity). Tables 9.1 and 9.2 summarise the studies reviewed in this section.

Australian foreign trade with neighbouring countries has been studied using the gravity model. This brand of the literature finds that Australia's trade openness is relatively low compared to the rest of the world. This is partially due to the large geographic size of Australia and its remoteness with the rest of the world (Guttmann and Richards, 2006).

Australia shares similar trade patterns with other economic regions in the world, such as Latin America (Cortes, 2007). In addition to geographical factors and trade openness, political influence is a relevant factor shaping Australian trade patterns. Previous literature finds that Australian foreign trade is positively associated with trading partners' economic size, GDP per capita, openness, and common language, and negatively associated with distance (Rahman, 2009). There are several countries that have the potential to increase trade with Australia. It is particularly relevant for a low diversified economy (in terms of both destination markets and products exported), as Australia is.

Geographical distance is a clear disadvantage for Australian participation in foreign trade. However, relative distance also matters (Baldwin, 2006). For example, New Zealand and Australia are quite far in terms of absolute distance, but their relative distance is low when compared to their distance with the rest of the world. In the international trade literature, the concept "multilateral resistance" has emerged and should be controlled in gravity models to obtain unbiased estimators (Anderson and Wincoop, 2003; Head and Mayer, 2014).

Besides New Zealand, Australia is the most remote country in a number of reviewed studies (Battersby and Ewing, 2005). However, the importance of remoteness may have fallen over time, together with decreasing trade cost. Indeed, even with the disadvantage of its remote location, Australia has achieved higher trade levels than those expected from gravity estimations. It may be due to its unique geostrategic context, as Australia is relatively close to large countries such as China and India. Therefore, the geographical isolation of Australia interacts with the importance of its (neighbouring) trading partners. In this regard, trade between Australia and China has increased dramatically in recent years. One of the reasons behind this increasing

Table 9.1: Literature review: country-level studies about the Australian context (ordered by year of publication and authors' surname)

Author/s	Research question /Hypothesis analysed	Data source	Data sample	Methodology	Main results
(Battersby and Ewing, 2005)	How do distance and economic size influence trade?	IMF Data from (Maddison, 1995) and (Maddison, 2001)	Annual data 1980-2001 1950-1998 73-222 countries	Gravity model	Location and economic size are associated with Australia's aggregate trade.
(Baldwin, 2006)	How does the Euro affect trade?	Multiple data source such as from (Rose, 2000)	Annual data 1980, 2000, 1980-2002 Euro countries	Gravity model	The research question is not answerable at the aggregate level.
(Guttmann and Richards, 2006)	What are the determinants of trade openness?	IMF DOTS data World Economic Forum's Global Competitiveness Report	Annual data 1971–2000 120 countries	Gravity model	Australia's low trade openness is due to its large geographic size and the remoteness of its geographic location.
(Cortes, 2007)	How do economic distance, openness, population, and political influence shape trade between Australia and Latin America?	Department of Foreign Affairs and Trade Australian Bureau of Statistics (ABS) (Heston, Summers, and Aten, 2006); (Central Intelligence Agency, 2007)	Annual data 1998 to 2004, 9 Latin American countries	Gravity model	A similar trade pattern than Australia was found in Latin American countries. Political influence, Australia's trade openness, and economic distance play an important role in trade.
(Sheng and Song, 2008)	Comparative advantage and Australia-China bilateral trade	ABS China Bureau of Statistics United Nations UNCTAD	Annual data 1997-2006 Australia China	Gravity model	Demand factors, comparative advantages, and reduced trade barriers foster bilateral trade. Australian exports to China are associated with Chinese exports to the world.

continued **Table 9.1:** Literature review: country-level studies about the Australian context (ordered by year of publication and authors' surname)

Author/s	Research question /Hypothesis analysed	Data source	Data sample	Methodology	Main results
(Rahman, 2009)	Who has the potential to be an Australian trading partner?	World Bank International Monetary Fund (IMF)	Annual data 2001,2005 50 countries	Gravity model	Australian trade is positively associated with trading partners' economic size, GDP per capita, openness, and common language; but negatively associated with distance. Singapore, Argentina, and other countries are identified as potential trading partners for Australia.
(Koitsiwe and Adachi, 2015)	DD hypothesis	ABS	Annual data 1975-2013 Australia	Vector autoregressive approach	The mining boom stimulates the service sector but harms the manufacturing sector.
(Turnbull, Sun, and Anwar, 2016)	How does trade liberalisation and FDI influence Australian productivity?	ABS Productivity Commission OECD	Annual data 1988-2012 Australia	Simultaneous equations model	Trade liberalisation, and not inward FDI, has a positive impact on Australian manufacturing productivity.
(Productivity Commission, 2017)	What is the effect of increasing protectionism for Australia?	World Bank United Nations WTO	Annual data 1982-2016 US, Mexico, China	Computable general equilibrium models	US trade protection policy is likely to reduce Australia's main export (iron ore and steel) but increase the exports of other sectors.
(Dungey, Fry-Mckibbin, and Volkov, 2020)	DD hypothesis	Reserve Bank of Australia	Quarterly data 1988-2016	Structural vector autoregression	The DD affects non-tradable sectors through macroeconomic tunnels such as the appreciation of the exchange rate, investment in the mining sector, and the reallocation of resources to the mining sector.

Source: own elaboration.

(Australia-China) bilateral trade is that Australia presents comparative advantages in products that complement China's comparative advantages (Sheng and Song, 2008).

A shortcoming of the strong complementarity between Australia and China trade is that Australian exports depend on Chinese exports. Consequently, restrictions from the rest of the world on Chinese exports may have important consequences for Australian exports. For instance, the increase in US trade barriers to Chinese imports affects Chinese exports of final goods. Because China has a comparative advantage in labour-intensive assembly, which positions China at the end of global production chains (David, Dorn and Hanson, 2013) it is expected that Australia will be negatively affected, as Australia is located in an early stage of value chains with China. In an *ex-ante* quantification for Australia about the effects of increasing protectionism in the US, tariff increases in products from China lead to a restructuration of global trade patterns, including markets in Australian main export products (Productivity Commission, 2017).

Regarding particular sectors, a key pillar of the Australian economy is mining. Therefore, researchers in Australia have focused on testing the DD hypothesis. This literature has provided evidence on how the mining sector boom affected other sectors (i.e., manufacturing and services). The mining boom stimulated the sector of services but harmed the sector of manufactures (Koitsiwe and Adachi, 2015). In addition, the DD affects non-tradable sectors through macroeconomic factors such as the appreciation of the exchange rate, investment in mining, and reallocation of resources (Dungey, Fry-Mckibbin, and Volkov, 2020). Crucially, the manufacturing sector in Australia has experienced a decline in recent years due to factors such as rising production costs, increased consumer demand for services, and the strength of the Australian dollar. However, trade liberalisation presents a positive impact on Australian manufacturing productivity (Turnbull, Sun, and Anwar, 2016).

9.2 Review of trade-related studies for Australian regions/cities

Results on the impact of the DD vary from country level to the regional level (Shafiullah, Selvanathan, Naranpanawa, and Chai, 2019). While the DD from the mining boom at national level negatively affects the manufacturing sector, only some Australian states are affected. Regional-level evidence also shows that the mineral-rich states (i.e., Western Australia, Queensland, and the Northern Territory) suffer from the DD in the tourism (Dwyer, Pham, Jago, Bailey, and Marshall, 2014).

Because in our empirical analysis, we will analyse the relationship between trade policy, foreign trade, and regional inequality (see Figure 9.1), we pay attention to these magnitudes in this regional-level review. In this regard, Australia has experienced increasing regional inequality in the past 30 years due to the rise of knowledge-intensive services, differentials in government policy and investment, the resources boom, and the declining competitiveness of the manufacturing sector (SGS Economics and Planning, 2018).

Figure 9.1: Analysis of foreign trade in Australian regions and relationships of interest
Source: Own elaboration.

Australia's biggest city (i.e., Sydney) has experienced labour market declines in the last decade due to the ineffective application of urban policy such as poor housing, and transport capacity. In addition, the structural change in Sydney's labour market is associated with the mining boom from the mining regions (Mitchell and Bill, 2006). The housing boom in Sydney, the increase of inflation and interest rate, and the fiscal drag, also contribute to the trends of the so-called two-speed Australian economy, which refers to sectoral and regional imbalances. Otherwise, Melbourne's economy has been restructured from the manufacturing sector to the professional, and financial & insurance sector in the last two decades, due to successful investment and road projects (SGS Economics and Planning, 2018). With the end of mining in Perth, the government is seeking alternative sources of economic growth. For example, the Government of Western Australia provides a regional development plan for population growth, infrastructure priorities, and land use planning over the next 20 years (Western Australian Planning Commission, 2015). For Queensland, researchers are also "keen to help" to avoid the DD impact on other sectors from the coal boom (Wade, 2007).

9.3 Characteristics of Australian exports and interaction with trade liberalisation

Australia specialises and trades goods and services of a few sectors, mainly primary industries and services (see Table 9.3). The top 10 goods and services exports in 2017 are from the industry "Mining & quarrying" (45.6%), followed by "Education & training" (7.8%), "Administrative & support services" (5.5%), and "Agriculture, forestry & fishing" (3.5%).

We list Australia's top 20 trading partners (both imports and exports) in Table 9.4. The order is based on the percentage share of trade in goods and services in 2018. For example, 24.4% of Australia's foreign trade activities is with China, followed by 9.7% with Japan, and 8.8% with the US.

Australia has been at the forefront of multilateral trade liberalisation since it became a founding member of the World Trade Organisation (WTO, 2018). Currently,

Table 9.2: Literature review: trade-related studies about the Australian context at regional level (ordered by year of publication and authors' surname)

Author/s	Research question /Hypothesis analysed	Data source	Data sample	Methodology	Main results
(Mitchell and Bill, 2006)	What changes the employment pattern of Sydney?	ABS	Quarterly data 1989-1990 2000-2006 National and Sydney	Descriptive statistical method	Changes in employment patterns are associated with the mining boom, the housing boom, an increase of inflation, and interest rate.
(Wade, 2007)	DD prevention	Australian Mining news	Queensland	2007 News	Researchers keen to avoid the DD in Queensland.
(Dwyer, Pham, Jago, Bailey, and Marshall, 2014).	DD hypothesis	Tourism Research Australia ABS	Quarterly data 2005-2012 National and States level	The computable general equilibrium model	DD effects were found in the tourism sector at the national level and in the mineral-rich states. Business tourism benefits, but leisure tourism loses out.
(Western Australian Planning Commission, 2015)	Regional policy	State agencies, utilities and departments such as Department of Premier and Cabinet, Department of Health, Western Power	Plans for the next 20 years Western Australia	2015 Government report	Identification of Western Australia's Great Southern regional development plans on economic development, physical and social infrastructure, environment and security.
(SGS Economics and Planning, 2018).	Urban policy	ABS	Annual data 1998-2018 National and Major cities	SGS method focuses on the Production measure of GDP	Information on Australian regional urban planning on infrastructure, investment, and economic development challenges.

continued **Table 9.2:** Literature review: trade-related studies about the Australian context at regional level (ordered by year of publication and authors' surname)

Author/s	Research question /Hypothesis analysed	Data source	Data sample	Methodology	Main results
(Shafiullah, Selvanathan, Naranpanawa, and Chai, 2019).	DD hypothesis	ABS, IMF, DFAT, Reserve Bank of Australia	Quarterly data 1974-2013 National and States level	Augmented Dickey–Fuller test Arai–Kurozumi test	DD effects were found in the manufacturing sector at the national level. The DD effect was found only in Victoria, Queensland, South Australia, and Tasmania.

Source: own elaboration.

Australia is at a relatively high level of trade liberalisation by positively implementing the reforms and reducing trade barriers. These reforms include the floating of the dollar, the deregulation of financial markets, the decentralisation of the industrial relations system, the introduction of competition policy, broadening the tax base, and corporatisation of government businesses (The Centre for International Economics, 2017). The reforms of economic deregulation and trade liberalisation started around the mid-1970s in Australia.

Because regional trade integration and regional trade liberalisation are the focus of this section, Table 9.4 lists existing, and those that are being negotiated, FTAs with the major Australian trading partners. There are 14 FTAs with Australia in force. Importantly, a trade agreement with the European Union is currently in the process of being negotiated.

Figure 9.2 shows the historical export flows in millions of Australian dollars (AUDm) with Australia' top 20 trading partners. The solid blue line shows average exports with FTA trading partners; the orange dotted line shows average exports with non-FTA trading partners.

There are two key intersections (in 2009 and in 2015) of these two lines. Regarding the first intersection, during the 2009-2010 global financial crisis, Australian exports declined, particularly with FTA partners. In 2010, however, exports with non-FTAs (a group that included the largest Australian trading partner, i.e., China) increased significantly.

Interestingly, from 2009 to 2014, average trade with FTA partners is lower than that with non-FTA partners. Although many trade agreements (i.e., AANZFTA, MAFTA, and KAFTA) came into force during this period, this situation did not reverse until 2015 (i.e., the year in which we observe the second intersection of the blue and orange lines). In that year (2015), the two FTAs with the largest Australian trading partners (i.e., China and Japan) entered into force. In 2018, Australian exports to FTA partners are significantly higher than exports to non-FTA partners.[14]

From this analysis at country-level, we learn that trade liberalisation (i.e., more FTAs with Australia entered into force) and Australian exports are positively correlated. It is worth mentioning, however, that a substantial number of FTAs partners are also the top exporting countries for Australia. This points towards the existence of endogeneity concerns, which prevent us from any causal interpretation.[15]

14 As there was an export decline to Japan in 2016, this change mostly depends on exports to China.

15 See, for example, Márquez-Ramos, Martínez-Zarzoso, & Suárez-Burguet (2011).

9.4 Regional analysis

We start with the identification of export variation across Australian regions (Figure 9.3). Specifically, we illustrate the geographic variation both in exports in goods and export in services for the eight Australian states.[16]

Figure 9.4 displays exports in goods, while Figure 9.5 displays exports in services in two years: 2011 and 2017. The dark blue colour in the figures denotes higher export flows in regions. This analysis provides a visual illustration of the regional heterogeneity of exports within Australia. With the comparison of exports in 2011 and 2017, we observe that, although overall exports have largely increased from 2011 to 2017, the origins of the exports remain the same, both in exports of goods and of services.

Figure 9.4 shows that exports of goods are concentrated in WA and QLD, followed by NSW. In 2017, top goods exported in WA were iron ores and concentrates, gold, natural gas, and crude petroleum (DFAT, 2018). QLD top goods exported are coal, natural gas, beef, copper, and vegetables. NSW top goods exported include coal, copper ores and concentrates, aluminium, beef, and refined petroleum. In short, most of the top goods exported in Australian regions are mining products and agricultural products, as found in the aggregate analysis (Table 9.3).

Table 9.3: Australia's top 10 goods and services exports in 2017

Rank	Goods and Services	AUD mln	% Share	Industry (ANZIC)
1	Iron ores & concentrates	36,092	16.3%	Mining & quarrying
2	Coal	57,129	14.8 %	Mining & quarrying
3	Education-related travel services	30,263	7.8%	Education & training
4	Natural gas	25, 620	6.6 %	Mining & quarrying
5	Personal travel (excl. education) services	21,281	5.5 %	Administrative & support services
6	Gold	17, 632	4.6 %	Mining & quarrying
7	Aluminium ores & conc (incl. alumina)	8,426	2.2%	Mining & quarrying
8	Beef	7,451	1.9%	Agriculture, forestry & fishing
9	Wheat	6,062	1.6%	Agriculture, forestry & fishing
10	Crude petroleum	5,246	1.4%	Mining & quarrying

Source: Own elaboration with data from (DFAT, 2019b) and (ABS, 2018a).

16 The sources of the regional data used in this study are the Australia Bureau of Statistics (ABS), and Australian Government, Department of Foreign Affairs and Trade (DFAT).

Table 9.4: Top 20 goods and services trading partners in 2018

Rank	Goods and Services	% Share	FTA	Year in Force
1	China	24.4	ChAFTA	2015
2	Japan	9.7	JAEPA, CPTPP	2015, 2018
3	US	8.8	AUSFTA	2005
4	Republic of Korea	6.6	KAFTA	2014
5	India	3.6		Under Negotiation
6	New Zealand	3.5	AANZFTA, CPTPP	1983, 2018
7	UK	3.5		Prospective FTA Negotiation
8	Singapore	3.5	SAFTA, CPTPP	2003, 2018
9	Thailand	3.1	TAFTA	2005
10	Germany	2.8		Under Negotiation-EU
11	Malaysia	2.7	MAFTA, CPTPP	2013, 2018
12	Hong Kong (SAR of China)	2.4	A-HKFTA	2020
13	Indonesia	2.1	IA-CEPA	2020
14	Taiwan	2.0		
15	Vietnam	1.6	AANZFTA, CPTPP	2010,2018
16	Italy	1.3		Under Negotiation-EU
17	France	1.2		Under Negotiation-EU
18	United Arab Emirates	1.2		
19	Netherlands	1.0		Under Negotiation-EU
20	Canada	0.9	CPTPP	2018

Source: Own elaboration with data from (DFAT, 2019a; DFAT 2019b).

Figure 9.5 shows regional exports in services in 2011 and 2017. Exports of services are concentrated in NSW and VIC, followed by QLD. NSW and VIC top exporting services include education-related travel, personal travel, and professional and management consulting services in 2017 (DFAT, 2018). QLD top exports in services include personal travel (excluding education), education-related travel, and financial services. As in trade in goods, exports in services are concentrated in a few sectors.

Table 9.5 shows the major exports for the eight Australian regions. The top 5 major exports for each state are listed at product and industry level. Although there are important variations across Australian regions on the export volumes and export types, the major exports in goods in Australia are concentrated in two industries: “Mining & Quarrying” and “Manufacturing”. Most of the Australian states rely on exporting mining commodities, except VIC and ACT. Manufacturing appeared as a relevant (top exported) industry in almost all states (excluding NSW and NT), and it

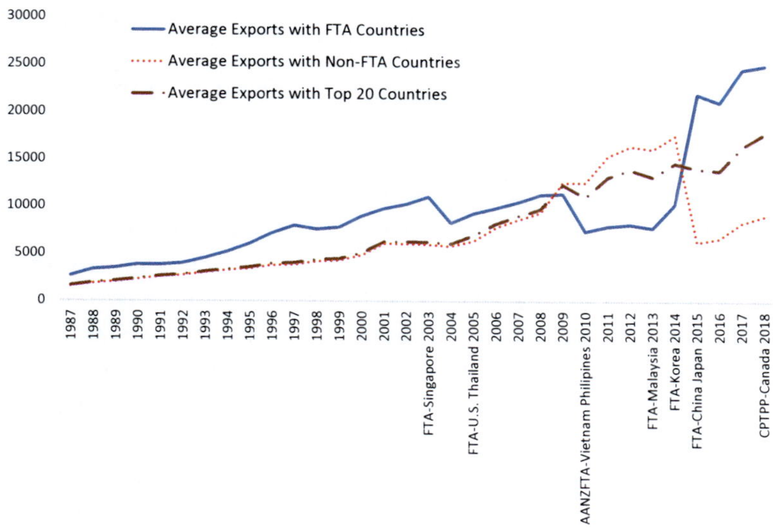

Figure 9.2: Australia's exports with top 20 trading partners 1987-2018
Source: Own elaboration with data from (DFAT, 2019b).

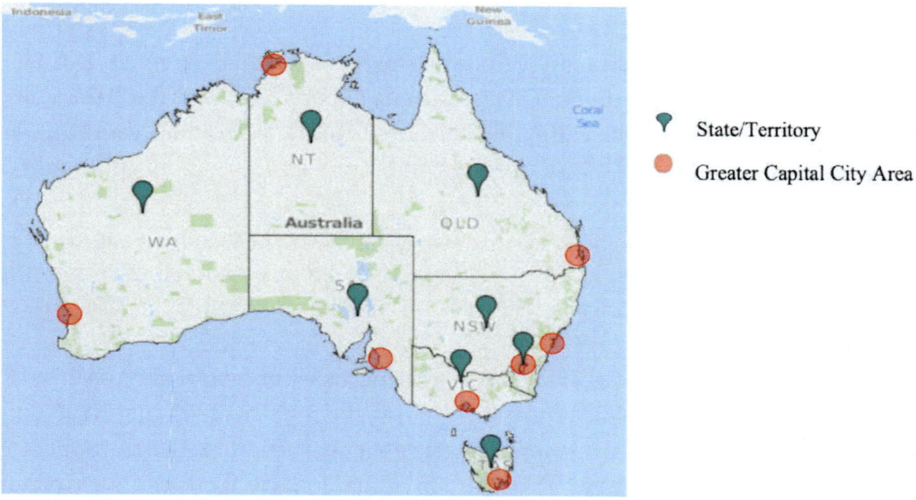

Figure 9.3: Australian State/Territory

Notes: Australia has eight states that are: New South Wales (NSW), Victoria (VIC), Queensland (QLD), South Australia (SA), Western Australia (WA), Tasmania (TAS), Northern Territory (NT), and Australian Capital Territory (ACT).

is strongly related to agriculture and farming. The major services exports are concentrated in three industries: "Education & Training"; "Transport, Postal & Warehousing"; and "Professional, Scientific & Technical Services". NSW, VIC, QLD, SA and ACT export "Education & Training" services. NSW, VIC, QLD, SA, NT and ACT export

"Transport, Postal & Warehousing" services. NSW and VIC export "Professional, Scientific & Technical Services".

Regarding specialisation, WA and QLD specialise in goods exports. NSW and VIC specialise in services exports. These findings are consistent with patterns observed in Figures 9.4 and 9.5.

For a better understanding of trade patterns in Australian regions, we focus on the analysis of the main exporting destinations for the eight Australian regions (see Table 9.6). Interestingly, main export destinations for Australian regions are FTA partners (marked with "*"). It suggests that lower trade barriers under trade agreements are associated with higher Australian regional exports. The geographical isolation of Australia limits its foreign trade to only a few (large) trading partners. In line with the analysis at country-level, the regional analysis finds that large trading partners (China, Japan, and the US) frequently appear as top destinations of Australian exports in regions. Overall, the Asia-Pacific economic area and the US appear as key destinations for Australian regions foreign trade, excluding the case of ACT (the region that includes the capital of the country).

9.5 Regional exports and trade liberalisation

To extend the analysis to Australian regions, we rely on a regional openness to trade index, which is calculated as the sum of imports and exports relative to the gross state product for each region. In line with previous literature (Márquez-Ramos, 2016b), we analyse the evolution of the regional openness index and its association with exports and trade liberalisation (FTAs).

In Figure 9.6, the solid blue line ("——") represents average regional exports with FTA countries. The red dotted line ("······") represents average regional exports with non-FTA countries. The black dashed line ("- - - -") represents the regional openness to trade index.[17]

In most Australian regions trade openness increases and co-moves positively with average exports with FTA countries, excluding the regions of WA and NT. From 2013 to 2015, four FTAs entered into force. Because average exports with FTA countries increased over this period, trade liberalisation seems to have increased Australian regions' openness to trade. Otherwise, for the regions of WA and NT, trade openness is decreasing and co-moves with average exports with non-FTA countries, which have also decreased over time. Overall, our results provide evidence that trade liberalisation is positively correlated with regional openness to trade.

17 In order to facilitate the interpretation of potential correlations, we use the openness index value ten times for illustration.

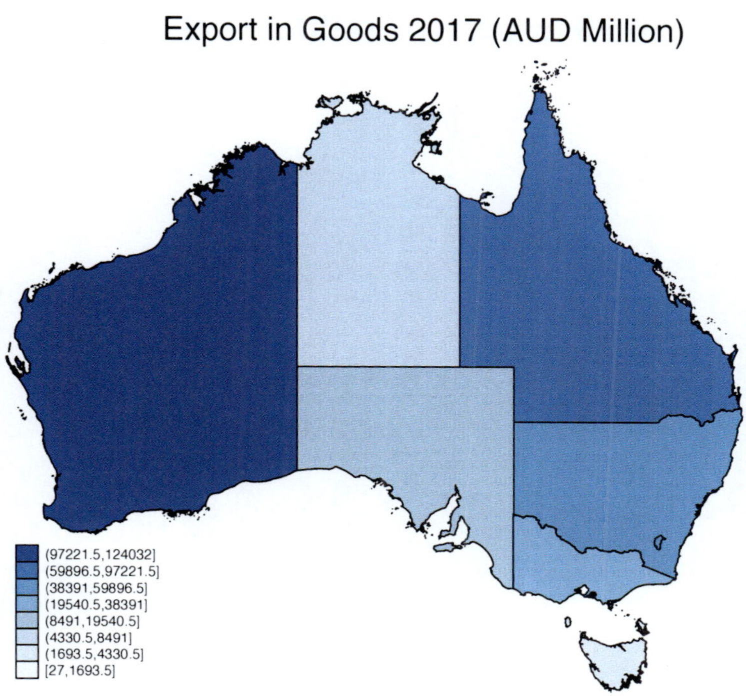

Figure 9.4: Australian state/territory exports in goods 2011 & 2017

Source: Own elaboration with data from (ABS, 2019c).

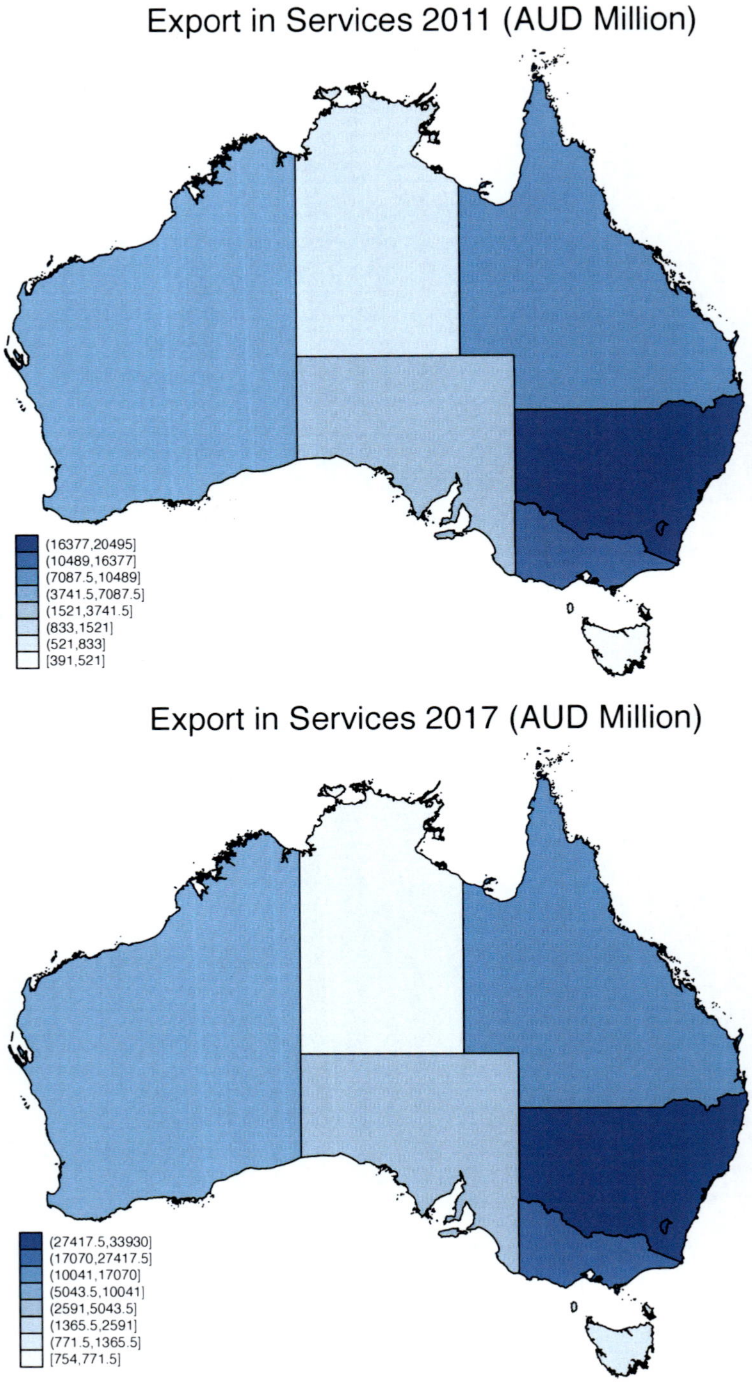

Figure 9.5: Australian state/territory export in services 2011 & 2017

Source: Own elaboration with data from (ABS, 2019c).

Table 9.5: Australian state/territory top 5 exports in 2017

Rank	NSW's major exports in 2017	AUDm	Industry (ANZSIC 2006)	Types
1	Coal	15,232	Mining & Quarrying	Goods
2	Education-related travel	10,284	Education & Training	Services
3	Personal travel (excl education)	7,246	Transport, Postal & Warehousing	Services
4	Professional & management consulting	3,234	Professional, Scientific & Technical Services	Services
5	Copper ores & concentrates	2,121	Mining & Quarrying	Goods
Rank	VIC's major exports in 2017	AUdm	Industry	Note
1	Education-related travel	9,089	Education & Training	Services
2	Personal travel (excl education)	5,172	Transport, Postal & Warehousing	Services
3	Wool & other animal hair (incl tops)	1,792	Manufacturing	Goods
4	Professional & management consulting	1,324	Professional, Scientific & Technical Services	Services
5	Meat (excl beef)	1,355	Manufacturing	Goods
Rank	QLD's major exports in 2017	AUDm	Industry	Note
1	Coal	29,187	Mining & Quarrying	Goods
2	Natural gas	Np	Mining & Quarrying	Goods
3	Personal travel (excl education)	5,046	Transport, Postal & Warehousing	Services
4	Beef	4,152	Manufacturing	Goods
5	Education-related travel	4,135	Education & Training	Services
Rank	SA's major exports in 2017	AUDm	Industry	Note
1	Alcoholic beverages	1,502	Manufacturing	Goods
2	Education-related travel	1,468	Education & Training	Services
3	Wheat	1,250	Manufacturing	Goods
4	Copper	1,157	Mining & Quarrying	Goods
5	Personal travel (excl education)	802	Transport, Postal & Warehousing	Services
Rank	WA's major exports in 2017	AUDm	Industry	Note
1	Iron ores & concentrates	62,093	Mining & Quarrying	Goods
2	Gold	17,741	Mining & Quarrying	Goods
3	Natural gas	Np	Mining & Quarrying	Goods
4	Crude petroleum	4,470	Mining & Quarrying	Goods

continued **Table 9.5:** Australian state/territory top 5 exports in 2017

Rank	NSW's major exports in 2017	AUDm	Industry (ANZSIC 2006)	Types
5	Wheat	2,532	Manufacturing	Goods
Rank	TAS's major exports in 2017	AUDm	Industry	Note
1	Zinc	639	Mining & Quarrying	Goods
2	Aluminium	450	Mining & Quarrying	Goods
3	Iron ores & concentrates	218	Mining & Quarrying	Goods
4	Other ores & concentrates	157	Mining & Quarrying	Goods
5	Beef	152	Manufacturing	Goods
Rank	NT's major exports in 2017	AUDm	Industry	Note
1	Natural gas	np	Mining & Quarrying	Goods
2	Live animals (excl seafood)	420	Agriculture, Forestry & Fishing	Goods
3	Other ores & concentrates	417	Mining & Quarrying	Goods
4	Personal travel (excl education)	386	Transport, Postal & Warehousing	Services
5	Aluminium ores & conc (incl alumina)	345	Mining & Quarrying	Goods
Rank	ACT's major exports in 2017	AUDm	Industry	Note
1	Gold coin & legal tender coin	20,361	Manufacturing	Goods
2	Education-related travel	786	Education & Training	Services
3	Government goods & services	452	Public Administration & Safety	Services
4	Personal travel (excl education)	246	Transport, Postal & Warehousing	Services
5	Plastic articles	6	Manufacturing	Goods

Source: Own elaboration with data from (DFAT, 2018). "np" denotes not published.

9.6 Regional openness to trade and unemployment

The relationship between foreign trade and regional inequality has been studied previously: foreign trade may increase regional inequality (Bakker, 2018). Import competition increased unemployment and reduced wages in the US trade-exposed labour market (David, Dorn and Hanson, 2013). In Austria, trade openness has a mixed impact on employment and wages across heterogeneous regions (Brülhart, Carrère, and Robert-Nicoud, 2018). However, to the best of our knowledge, the relationship between foreign trade and regional inequality has not been explored in Australian regions. We provide insights on how employment and foreign trade interact in

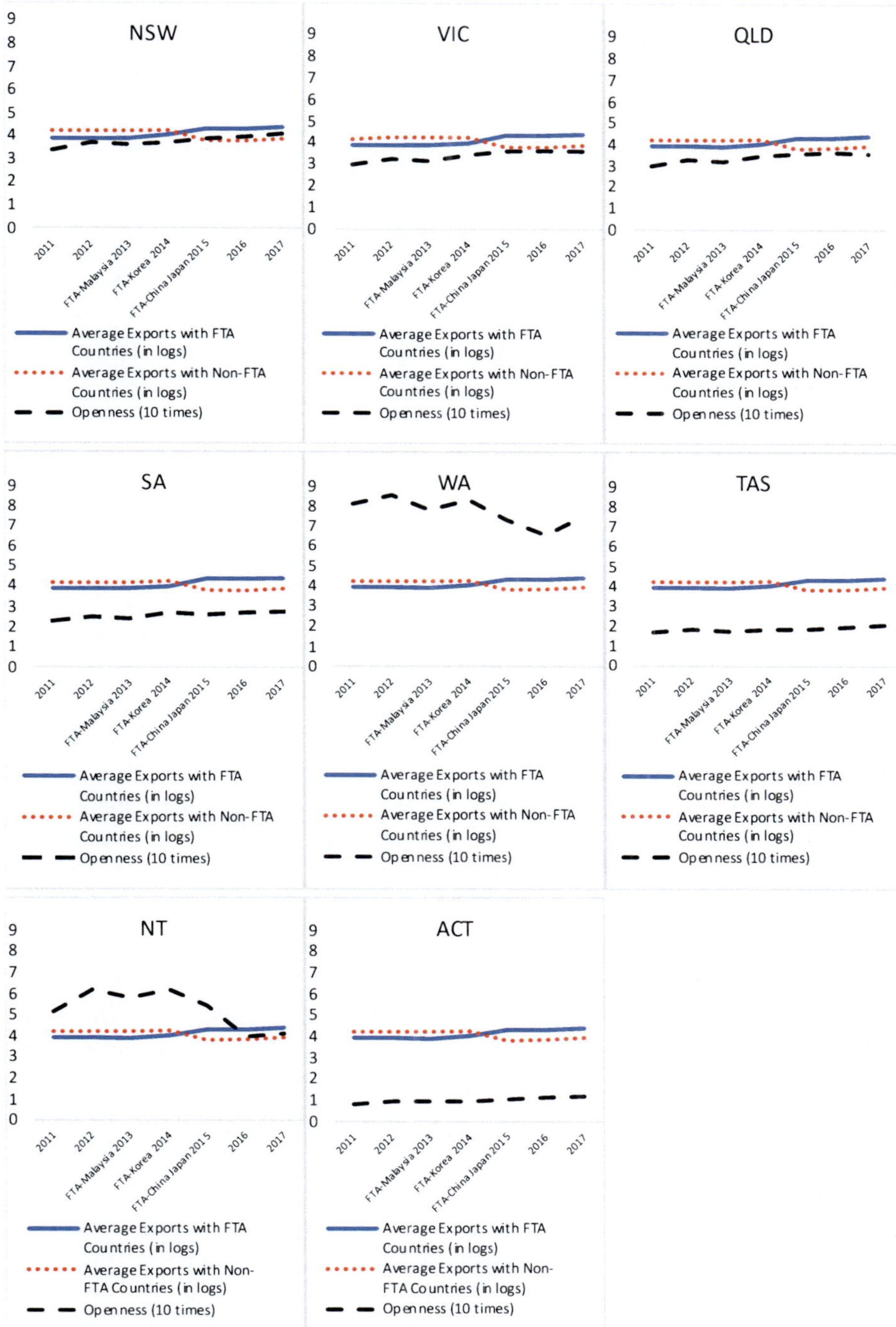

Figure 9.6: Regional openness to trade, national exports, and trade agreements
Source: Own elaboration with data from (DFAT, 2019b, DFAT, 2018).

Table 9.6: Australian state/territory export destinations and share of total exports in 2017

Rank	NSW (22.2%)	VIC (12.8%)	QLD (22.4%)	SA (3.9%)	WA (34.7%)	TAS (1.3%)	NT (1.7%)	ACT (0.6%)
1	Japan*	China*	China*	China*	China*	China*	China*	Switzer-land
2	China*	US*	Japan*	US*	Japan*	Malaysia*	Japan*	Hong Kong (SAR of China) *
3	Republic of Korea*	New Zealand*	India	Malaysia*	Hong Kong (SAR of China)*	Taiwan	Indonesia	Belgium
4	Taiwan	Japan*	Republic of Korea*	India	Republic of Korea*	Japan*	Thailand*	
5	US*	Singa-pore*	Taiwan	Japan*	UK	Indonesia	Republic of Korea*	

Source: Own elaboration with data from (DFAT, 2018). Australia's FTA partners are marked with "*". The percentages are the states' export of Australia's total export.

Australia by using regional unemployment rates and the regional openness to trade index.

Figure 9.7 shows that, from 2011 to 2017, the unemployment rate has increased in five regions: VIC (from 5.2 to 6.1), QLD (from 5.6 to 6.1), SA (from 5.0 to 6.1), WA (from 3.9 to 5.5), and TAS (from 5.2 to 6.1). Two regions, NSW (from 5.2 to 4.9) and ACT (from 4.1 to 4.0), have experienced a decrease in the unemployment rate. In NT, the unemployment rate remained the same (at 3.6).

For the most part, the changes in the regional unemployment rate over the six-year period analysed (2011-2017) are modest – WA being an exception here. The same can be observed from the trade openness data – again WA being an exception, and also NT exhibiting more pronounced variation slightly over the sample period. We note that there seems to be a positive association between trade openness and unemployment for most regions (yet again WA is the exception here), indicating a possible impact on unemployment through import competition, though this association is not emphatic. Such gentle movements in each series make deciphering any meaning relationship between the two variables based on possible regional resource re-allocation difficult.

That said, we can observe interesting patterns by looking individually at WA and NT. For WA, there has been a reduction in trade openness and a corresponding rise in the unemployment rate between 2011 and 2017 – to the point where the two series intersected in 2016. As trade openness diminishes, fewer resources are likely to be devoted to domestic production in the export sector. But since the export sector is relatively large in WA, there appears to be less of substitution in terms of employment to the non-export sector, which might thereby offset the effect on unemployment. Equally, there does not appear to be any corresponding reallocation of labour from WA to other states in a way that might correspond to the reduction in trade openness in WA.

The story is different for NT. NT has experienced a reduction in trade openness as well as in the unemployment rate (especially from a peak in 2013). Here, a reduction in trade openness may be associated with by a reduction of resources in the export sector, but such a decrease in resource allocation in this sector can be accommodated in the non-export sector. The result may well be a reduction in unemployment.

9.7 Conclusions

We contribute to the literature by analysing foreign trade patterns and trends in Australian regions, as well as their co-movement with other factors that are relevant for Australia (i.e., trade policy and economic inequality). To do so, considering regional heterogeneity in Australian foreign trade is important: Australia is the sixth-largest country in the world in geographic terms, but the population is much smaller than in other industrialised countries analysed in this book. Interestingly, the population in Australia is highly concentrated in a few Eastern and South-Eastern cities. In addition, the geostrategic position of Australia is different from any other developed country in the world. “Neighbouring” countries include large international partners such as China, Japan, and India.

In a review of the existing country-level literature, we find that Australia’s foreign trade issues analysed include trade policy, openness to trade, geographic factors and remoteness, comparative advantages, and industrial structure changes such as a declining manufacturing sector. At the regional level, we observed evidence of the production matrix diversification in Australian regions (due to the rise of services), as well as the analysis of issues such as government policy, investment, and the mining boom.

Australia’s exports are highly concentrated in terms of both trading partners and sectors. Australian exports are mainly centred around mining and agriculture with exports also relatively high in the education and tourism areas. The largest export sector, mining, is not concentrated in the same manner as to how Australia’s population is concentrated, with most mining taking place in the western and northern parts of the country. Education and tourism exports are concentrated in closer alignment with population concentrations.

Australia’s trading partners are drawn predominantly from Asia – with seven of the country’s top ten trading partners from the Asia-Pacific economic area. It is due to some extent to natural complementarities through comparative advantages, and in

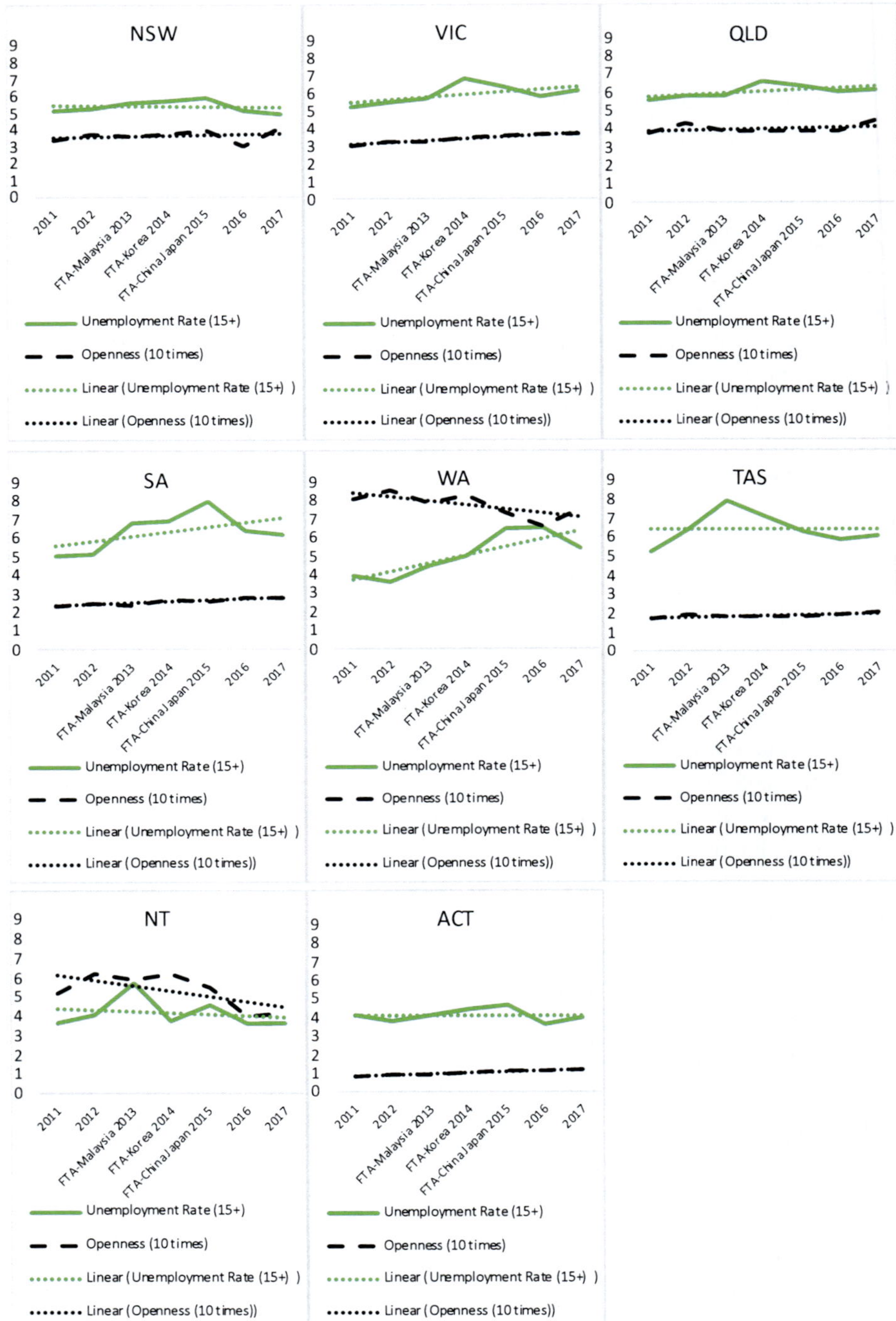

Figure 9.7: Regional openness to trade and unemployment

Source: Own elaboration with data from (Australian Government, 2019; DFAT, 2018).

the involvement in global value chains made possible by Australia's exports of raw materials.

Given this, Australia has a strong incentive to engage in free trade, and, as such, is active in the negotiation of policies of trade liberalisation. Australia has engaged in early trade negotiations with ASEAN nations such as Singapore and Thailand and has recently enacted trade agreements with 3 of the top 4 trading partners – China, Japan, and Korea. The analysis above suggests that trade activity and trade liberalisation appear to be positively correlated at both a national and regional level, suggesting that investment in trade liberalisation policies in Australia are in many respects justified.

A possible consequence of trade openness is the emergence of DD that might result in increased trade in mining and other export sectors. Our analysis above examines this from a regional perspective; are there shifts in employment that might occur as a result of an expansion of trade in Australia's export industries? The evidence for this is not persuasive, possibly due to the way in which export industries are concentrated in this country. We do however, find that regional trade openness is associated with unemployment rates, though not in a way that might suggest a reallocation of resources across regions.

Our results relate to recent research for Australia's regions recognising that diversification (resilience to economic shocks) and specialisation (efficiency of production) can co-exist (Murphy, Hicks, Morrison, Basu, Ranshaw, 2019). It is worth noting that existing innovative policy approaches, such as smart specialisation, can enhance regional employment. For implementing such an approach effectively in Australia, not only is an increasing emphasis on coherence and collaboration needed, and the support of an Australian policy framework that considers the different levels of government in the country (federal, state, and local), as highlighted in Wilson (2018) and Gómez Prieto et al. (2019); but also a better understanding of the interaction of smart specialisation initiatives with unemployment and foreign trade.

Clinton Uzobor

10 Insights for Canada – regions in foreign trade

Canada is the country for which one of the first documented regional exports analysis was made (DeKaser and Sneddon Little, 1994; Fieleke, 1970; Golladay and Sandoval, 1972; Stabler and Howe, 1988), which was due to data availability. Since then, the literature on Canadian provinces' exports has flourished, and many interesting research threads have evolved, showing the changing nature of the inquiry into the nexus between regional and international issues. Canada has always relied on exports as its major source of income, especially during the era of the expansion of global trade. Before the financial and economic crisis (2008+), Canada witnessed sustained and relatively high economic growth rates. It came as a result of large inflows of foreign capital, which subsequently led to a boom in domestic investment and consumption. However, as in the case of many other economies, the question is asked about the consequences of the growing intensity of trade links of the Canadian provinces with foreign markets, as well as about their changing patterns. Trade is often perceived to create winners and losers; trade can as well enhance or hinder welfare, and lead to regional inequalities. Trade is highly localized. Thus, to deeply understand the dynamics characterising foreign trade relationship, it is crucial not to limit the analyses of trade performance at the national level, but more importantly, to also examine trade at a disaggregated provincial level. Export performance varies significantly across provinces. As a large economy, Canada represents an interesting case study of regional heterogeneity with distinct international trade profiles. The focus of this study is on the Canadian provinces' exports.[18]

Canada represents an interesting case, due to its geographical location,[19] close to its major trading partner (US), current position as one of the top 10 leading economies

---

18 Canada is made up of 10 provinces and 3 territories – Western Canada Provinces: (Alberta-AB, Saskatchewan -SK, Manitoba - MB, and British Columbia -BC); Atlantic Provinces: (Newfoundland and Labrador -NFLD&L, Prince Edward Island -PEI, New Brunswick -NB, and Nova Scotia - NS); Central Canada Provinces: (Ontario -ON and Quebec -QB); Territories: (Northwest Territories - NWT, Yukon, - YKT and Nunavut - NVT). But most studies only consider the provinces, since activities in the territories are mostly considered inconsequential.

19 Canada maintains the world's longest *undefended border with the US*. In terms of geography (9,985,000 km^2), it is the second largest country in the world after Russia (Government of Canada, 2018). Canada has a population of 37 million, with a GDP of CAD2.22 trillion in 2018 (Statistics Canada, 2019a). The big chunk of Canadian population lives in the cities and big metropolitan provinces. The central provinces of Ontario (39% of the total) and Quebec (23% of the total) are more populated, other provinces are either moderately or sparsely populated.

in the world and advances made so far towards quick recovery[20] from the impact of the global financial crisis.

Canadian exports' characteristic feature is a strong orientation towards its southern neighbour (US) on the one hand, and its sectoral diversification,[21/22] but diversified by products.[23] Overall, the Canadian economy has gained immensely from export activities in several ways, with an increase in exports linked to higher incomes and living standards (Foreign Affairs and International Trade Canada, 2012). However, the large share of export in the Canadian economy also increases Canada's exposure to external shocks. The response of Canada to changes in the foreign markets has very important policy implications. For example, most trade analysts are of the view that the recent NAFTA renegotiation will impact greatly on Canada, given that more than 75% of its export activity is destined for NAFTA partners. In the same manner, to mitigate this exposure, Canada would have to pursue a wider export diversification, both at the product and geographical (market) levels.

Generally, the study focuses on the main characteristics of Canadian exports by provinces. First, we provided analysis on the nature of shifts in the frontier of provincial exports, in relation to the influence of border and external relations. Second, we looked at the structure of Canadian exports and provided important facts about the international trade (exports) of the Canadian provinces. Finally, we also presented the relationship between trade (exports) openness and the prosperity of the province, by analysing the correlation between exports per capita and GDP per capita. In the same manner, we also analysed the provincial labour market as it relates to trade openness.

The remainder of the paper is structured as follows: section 10.1 presents the main, selected publications on the Canadian foreign trade. Section 10.2 and 10.3 present a brief analysis of the dynamics in exports, at country and provincial levels. Section 10.4 and 10.5 identifies the nature of co-movement in the export dynamics

---

20 The quick recovery can be attributed to sound pre-crisis fiscal policy, a solid financial system, a relatively robust external sector and the economic strength of its resource-rich western provinces.

21 Canada's top 10 export sectors in 2018 are: mineral fuels including oil: USD99.3 billion (22% of total exports); vehicles: USD60.5 billion (13.4%); machinery including computers: USD34.5 billion (7.7%); gems, precious metals: USD18.3 billion (4.1%); wood: USD14.3 billion (3.2%); plastics, plastic articles: USD13.6 billion (3%); electrical machinery, equipment: USD13.4 billion (3%); aircraft, spacecraft: USD10.6 billion (2.4%); aluminium: USD10 billion (2.2%); paper, paper items: USD8 billion (1.8%).

22 The concentration of Canadian exports to the US is in line with what economic theory predicts. The gravity model of trade tells us that economic size and geographic proximity are the most important determinants of bilateral trade patterns.

23 The exports diversification by product may not have been the *ex-ante* expectation since Canada is known for its energy and automobile exports. The Canadian product concentration ratio (HHI score) is 0.09 in 2018. This concentration ratio has changed little over the past 28 years, hovering around 0.07 and 0.12 since 1990, but always remaining under the 0.15 benchmark.

(exports per capita versus GDP per capita) by provinces. The final section gives a brief conclusion on some interesting peculiarities of the Canadian provinces' exports, the reorientation of some provinces towards the foreign markets and their weakening links with the other Canadian provinces, and a few policy implications regarding the influence of globalisation on provincial economies.

10.1 Review of Literature

The review of the literature on the Canadian provinces' exports shows that the research was predominantly focused on the border effect problem; however, also other problems were the subject of research (consequences for welfare, resource course, fluctuating global oil prices). Recent research has moved from the simple exploration of border effects and trade policies to the examination of the likely resultant variation in the provincial export dynamics. A handful of previous studies has been summarised in Table 10.1.

Table 10.1: Literature review on the border effect and external relations for the Canadian provinces

Author(s)	Topic Addressed	Data	Methodology	Main results
McCallum (1995)	National borders matter: Canada-US regional trade patterns	Cross-sectional, 1988	Gravity model	Trade between the two Canadian provinces was 22 times larger than trade between a Canadian province and a US state.
Helliwell (2000)	How much do national borders matter?	Panel, 1990–96	Gravity model	Showed that Quebec trades more than 20 times as much with other provinces than it does with U.S states of comparable size and distance. Border effect dropped between 1990 and 1996 due to ratification in Canada-US FTA in 1988 and improvement in the gravity model.
Anderson and van Wincoop (2003)	Gravity with gravitas: A solution to the border puzzle	Cross -sectional, 1993	Gravity model	National borders reduce trade between the US and Canada by about 40%, while reducing trade among other industrialized countries by about 30%.

continued **Table 10.1:** Literature review on the border effect and external relations for the Canadian provinces

Author(s)	Topic Addressed	Data	Methodology	Main results
Hillberry (1998)	The national border effect in US commodity flow data	Panel, 1994	Gravity model	Showed that the border effect between 1990 and 1996 declined from 19.5 to 11.9. The paper attributes the decrease to the Canada-US Free Trade Agreement.
Helliwell, Lee, and Messinger (1999)	Effects of the Canada-US FTA on interprovincial trade	Panel, 1988 -96	Gravity model	First, the results show clearly that the FTA increased province-state trade relative to interprovincial trade. The second results suggest that the FTA-related reductions in Canadian tariffs led to increases in imports from the US and to reductions in interprovincial trade.
Knox (2001)	Canada's agree-ment on (AIT) internal trade: it can work if we want it to	Exten-sive data analysis on Canadian trade policy	Descriptive/ analytical research	Author claimed no real effectiveness of the AIT and argued that AIT failed on many fronts leaving many interprovincial barriers still in place.
Coulombe (2003)	International trade, interpro-vincial trade and Canadian provin-cial growth	Trend analysis: 1981 and 2000	L-curve and conditional convergence-growth model	There is an 'L' curve that characterises the compara-tive evolution of interprovin-cial and international trade shares in GDP between 1981 and 2000.
Kukucha (2009)	The provinces and Canadian foreign trade policy	Time-series Data: 1997 – 2006	Descriptive/ analytical method	The author analysed the role of provinces in the global political economy and argued that states and provinces still can formulate independent policy.
Obstfeld and Rogoff (2000)	The six major puzzles in interna-tional macroeco-nomics. Is there a common cause?	Periods consistent with all the puzzles addressed	Constant elasticity of substitution model	Found enough ground to acknowledge findings of McCallum on border effect as one the trade puzzles and also showed the essential role of trade costs.

continued **Table 10.1:** Literature review on the border effect and external relations for the Canadian provinces

Author(s)	Topic Addressed	Data	Methodology	Main results
Zestos and Tao (2002)	Trade and GDP growth: causal relations in the US and Canada	Time-series data (1948-1996)	Vector error correction (VEC) model	Found a bidirectional causality for Canada from the foreign sector to GDP, but a weaker relationship between the foreign sector and GDP for the US. The Granger causality tests suggest that Canada is a more open economy than the US and more trade-dependent.
Frankel and Romer (1999)	Does trade cause growth?	Cross-sectional, 1985 for 63 countries	Gravity model	Found that trade appears to raise income by spurring the accumulation of physical and human capital and by increasing output for given levels of capital.
Gaston and Trefler (1997)	The labour market consequences of the Canada-US free trade agreement	Panel, 1989-1993	Descriptive/analytical method	The authors found contractions in employment across all industries caused by the FTA. The authors showed that FTA was not primarily responsible for Canadian job loss, and only account for about 15% of such losses. They further found that other factors (including the quest to curb inflation) account for more than 80% of job losses in Canada.
Townsend (2007)	Do tariff reductions affect the wages of workers in protected industries?	Micro-data on individual workers, 2007	Descriptive statistical method	The author showed that relative wages fell in the industries that faced the deepest tariff cuts. This effect was experienced regardless of whether workers belonged to a union, suggesting that CUSFTA reduced the returns to industry-specific human capital for those workers in the most heavily affected industries.

continued Table 10.1: Literature review on the border effect and external relations for the Canadian provinces

Author(s)	Topic Addressed	Data	Methodology	Main results
Beaulieu (2000)	The Canada-US Free Trade Agreement and Labour Market Adjustment in Canada	Improvement covering the 1997 empirical investigation up to 2000 period	Descriptive/ analytical method	The author provided evidence suggesting that the Canada-US FTA (CUSFTA) had almost no effect on earnings and had a small negative effect on manufacturing employment. The author further suggested that a change in trade policy may affect skilled and less-skilled workers differently and claimed that the tariff reductions lowered employment predominantly among less-skilled workers but did not affect the earnings of either skilled or less-skilled workers.

Source: own elaboration.

The implicit framework of the structural gravity model of trade by Anderson and van Wincoop (2003) was meant to explore the extent of trade diversion between interprovincial trade and province-US states trade, in an attempt to revisit the standard border effect literature of McCallum (1995) on Canada and the US. One of the key anchors of the model is Armington's assumption that goods have a place of origin characteristics. The goods can either be traded intra-nationally or/and internationally. Thus, diverting international trade in favour of the national market is one of the resultant effects of trade barriers. Anderson and van Wincoop (2003) proved the non-similarity in the estimates from the standard McCallum-type border effect. Through the gravity framework, McCallum (1995) studied the effect of barriers to trade on Canada-US regional trade patterns. Particularly for the 1988 period, McCallum proved that trade between two Canadian provinces was 22 times larger than trade between a Canadian province and a US state. This same conclusion was also reached by Helliwell (2000), who observed the existence of huge trade between Quebec and other Canadian provinces than with US states of the same size and distance. Obstfeld and Rogoff (2000) acknowledged and referred to this finding as one of the trade puzzles. As has already been acknowledged, an increase in the structure of Canadian tariff would artificially encourage interprovincial trade and results in trade diversion at the expense of the international channels. A reduction or total removal of the same tariff would lead to an increase in international trade, thereby causing a decrease in interprovincial trade channels. The institution of FTA brought notable changes to the patterns of provincial trade in Canada. The agreement between Canada and US was effective from January 1, 1989, to January 1, 1998, the content of FTA eliminated or reduced tariffs and non-tariff trade barriers for both countries (Hillberry, 1998). On January 1, 1994, the agreement was extended to Mexico, with the adoption of the NAFTA as the new name. Following this agreement, trade between Canada and its agreement neighbours have continued to expand. Helliwell et al. (1999) have extensively documented and analysed the fall in the relative importance of interprovincial trade vis-à-vis international trade. Using industry-level data on merchandise trade and tariffs, the authors revealed a possible link between FTA and a relative decrease in interprovincial trade.

Other studies on provincial trade have shown numerous other ways in which external relation and border can influence exports, and how these effects can manifest at different levels, including at the sectoral and specific good levels. It is the anchor point of the analysis, well documented in Kukucha (2009), where it was argued that barriers to trade erected by the government are the sources of sectoral variances through which national borders display its relevance or effect. He finds that government regulations are (in most cases) extreme when it comes to food and textile products when compared to other sectors where such government presence is almost completely absent, such as transportation equipment. Some analysts have also considered the importance of export autonomy characterising provincial trade.

10.2 Trade policy and the evolution of Canadian exports

Prior to the shocks of 1980s, the entire world was blessed with a rise in international trade. Even more in 1990, after the demise of the former Soviet Union, and the rise of the emerging economy of China (Coulombe, 2003). This period also witnessed a reduction in international trade barriers. For Canada, the reduction in international barriers was stretched further in 1989, after accenting to FTA with the US. Some interprovincial level trade barriers were also raised, and this resulted in major setbacks to Canada until 1995, following the birth of AIT (Coulombe, 2003). Knox (2001) insisted that the real effectiveness of AIT is still riddled with uncertainty. Thus, the questions often raised are those that ask what role adjacency and trade policy played in shaping Canadian trade patterns? Detailed answers to these questions would require the availability of sectoral data and empirical testing through econometric modelling and analysis. However, such deeper econometric pursuit is beyond the scope of this paper.

In this section, we focused on the empirical analysis of the evolution of exports in relation to liberalisation policy, using the latest available data. The comparative evolution of provincial exports is provided by 1981-2017 annual data on goods and services, which is also useful in identifying some important structural changes that took place in the provincial export patterns. The questions often raised relate to the nature of the economics of export patterns. A handful of these questions are: why was the share of intra-national exports declining in the 1980s, and remained constant in the 1990s (a period when the international export share was rising), but fluctuated in 2000s? What role did adjacency and external relations such as the CUSFTA and now NAFTA play in shaping Canadian trade patterns? Clearly, we approached the questions by first unravelling the nature of diversion in the international and interprovincial export patterns, as a result of the gravity forces.

The two measures of openness are captured by the shares of interprovincial and international exports in the overall GDP.

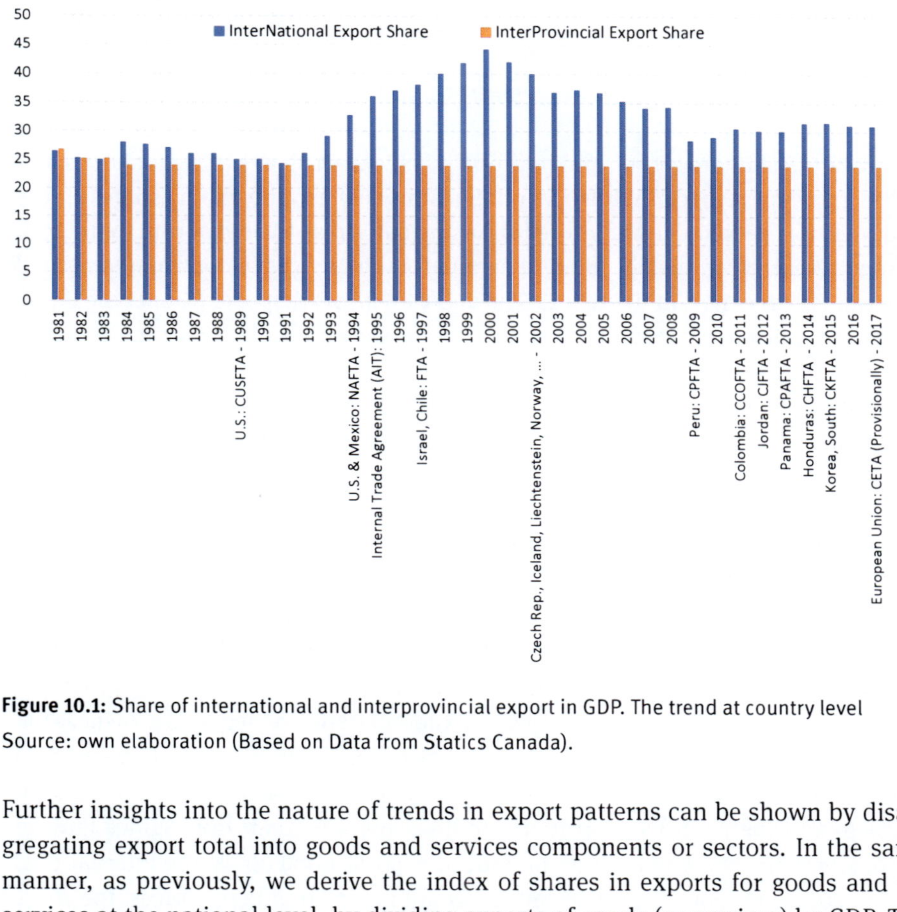

Figure 10.1: Share of international and interprovincial export in GDP. The trend at country level Source: own elaboration (Based on Data from Statics Canada).

Further insights into the nature of trends in export patterns can be shown by disaggregating export total into goods and services components or sectors. In the same manner, as previously, we derive the index of shares in exports for goods and for services at the national level, by dividing exports of goods (or services) by GDP. The result is shown in figure 10.2.

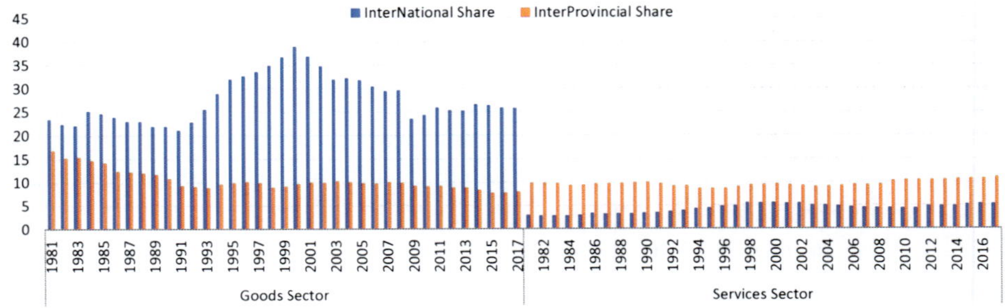

Figure 10.2: Share of international and interprovincial exports in GDP (showing the composition of goods vs services exports) – at the country level

Source: own elaboration (Based on Data from Statics Canada).

The indicators of international and interprovincial export shares differ for goods and services in many respects. While the relationship between the export shares in the two outlets (for goods sector) followed the same pattern as total export in figure 10.1, the trend reveals a completely different pattern for the services sector when compared to the same total export in figure 10.1. The analysis shows that over 80% of the Canadian merchandise export made its way to the foreign markets, indicating the high level of Canada's involvement and share in international trade in goods. In terms of services exports, the trend shows a continuous decline over the years for the international market but sluggishly stayed on the path of growth interprovincially.

10.3 Evolution of exports by province

For the provinces, we studied the evolution of exports using the 2005 pre-recession and 2017 annual data. A look at the frontiers of the aggregate relationship between interprovincial and international export shares reveals the two large central provinces of Ontario and Quebec as the major drivers. Export patterns in these two provinces followed a similar trend as the overall Canadian pattern. The international openness of both provinces decreased in 2017 when compared to 2005 pre-recession level. Atlantic provinces experienced similar trends in the evolution, apart from Prince Edward Island, where the share of the interprovincial exports stood above the international share in 2017, and more than 2005 levels. For all other Atlantic provinces, the share of international export decreased substantially compared to those of interprovincial export shares when compared to 2005 pre-recession levels. The four western provinces exhibit little similarity in the evolution of export links. The two Canadian provinces of British Columbia and Saskatchewan did not witness a substantial fall in the share of interprovincial exports throughout the period under emphasis. Manitoba's interprovincial export shares increased at the same rate as the 2005 pre-recession level in 2017 over the international share.

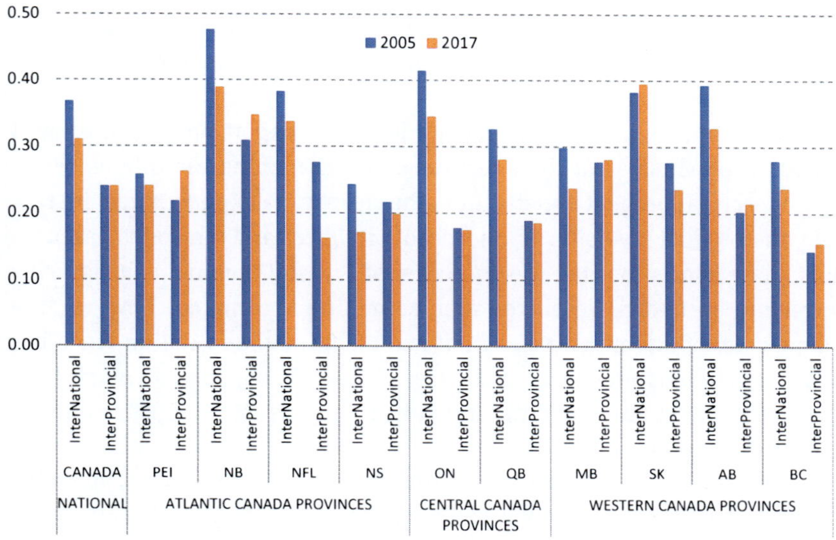

Figure 10.3: Share of provincial international and interprovincial exports in GDP, 2005 and 2017
Source: own elaboration (Based on Data from Statics Canada).

Canadian trade patterns and their drivers have transformed dramatically in response to the global economic environment. Canada's openness has continued to expand. The economy is yet to recover fully from the impact of the global financial crisis, coupled with the recent NAFTA renegotiation. The contents of the new terms are expected to have a huge impact on Canada, as approximately more than 75% of its export activity is destined for NAFTA partners – especially its southern neighbour, which also is the source of about one-third of foreign direct investment inflows.

10.4 The provinces' exports dynamics and characteristics

In this part, we mainly focus on international trade (exports of goods and services); export data is defined as the total business shipments (goods and services) from respective Canadian provinces to other countries. Statistics Canada and Industry Canada (Trade Data online) are the two main sources of our data on exports. For Canada, two main classifications of databases are available: (i) by products, (ii) by industry (economic activity). Both data classifications are relevant and were utilised in our study. Our export dynamics measures are captured by different ratios and indices, which includes percentage growth in exports, provincial share in total national export, trade openness (export to GDP ratio and export per capita), shares of sectoral products, export destinations, concentration ratios (HHI), the share of high-tech products in total exports. However, one of the limitations encountered relates to data suppression for confidentiality reasons.

In this subsection, we identify the peculiarity in the export profiles of each of the ten Canadian provinces and three territories, by examining the differences in their dominant sectoral product exports and other respective export characteristics. For example, the product diversification levels of provinces and territories based on 2018 Customs data shows that the western coast of British Columbia is historically known for relying on natural resources such as mining and timber. However, the economy is now benefiting much more from manufacturing, and the province has also recorded tremendous growth from services. Alberta has gained so much from natural resources, including oil and natural gas. It also has an abundance of zinc, silver, nickel, and uranium.

On the other hand, the provinces of Manitoba and Saskatchewan supply over 20% of the world's wheat. These two provinces, including Alberta, also engage in some notable forms of farming that contribute to the national economy. Manitoba has also expanded tremendously in manufacturing in the recent period. Interestingly, today Canada is on record as the highest producer of potash in the world all because of the province of Saskatchewan.

Importantly, the central Canada provinces of Ontario and Quebec form the industrial hub of Canada. They are leaders in a variety of manufactured goods. Ontario is also widely known for its orchard and wine production. The Atlantic provinces of New Brunswick, Nova Scotia, Newfoundland, and Prince Edward Island have benefited immensely from fishing and natural resources such as timber, and potatoes in Prince Edward Island. PEI and Nova Scotia have gained more from services when compared to their counterparts in the Atlantic. Lastly, the three Canadian territories are purely driven by natural resources, such as minerals, precious metal and stones. The Northwest territory has continued to make a fortune from diamonds; the Yukon territory has advanced with copper, the territory of Nunavut has made progress with iron ores. The three territories also benefited immensely from gold.

Table 10.2: Export dynamics and GDP by provinces and territories, 2005 and 2018

EXPORTS DYNAMICS	GOODS AND SERVICES EXPORTS		Growth in Exports	EXPORT SHARES*		EXPORT PER CAPITA		EXPORT - GDP RATIO		PER CAPITA GDP	
Value	**Value in (CA$Millions)**		**Value in %**	**Value in %**		**Value in (CA$)**		**Value in %**		**Value in (CA$)**	
Georaphy/Year	**2005**	**2018**	**2005 - 2018**	**2005**	**2018**	**2005**	**2018**	**2005**	**2018**	**2005**	**2018**
Canada	523 945	713 351	36,1	100	100	16 250	19 250	36,86	32,08	44 089	60 011
Provinces											
Newfoundland & Labrador	8 536	15 010	75,8	1,63	2,10	16 596	28 558	38,29	45,16	43 342	63 243
Prince Edward Island	1 096	1 587	44,8	0,21	0,22	7 938	10 333	25,67	22,69	30 928	45 539
Nova Scotia	7 838	7 944	1,4	1,50	1,11	8 357	8 279	24,33	17,91	34 345	46 226
New Brunswick	12 200	14 464	18,6	2,33	2,03	16 309	18 762	47,58	39,13	34 279	47 950
Quebec	91 691	129 922	41,7	17,50	18,21	12 094	15 490	32,62	29,57	37 079	52 384
Ontario	231 347	292 534	26,4	44,15	41,01	18 465	20 430	41,51	34,12	44 486	59 879
Manitoba	12 901	17 890	38,7	2,46	2,51	10 949	13 219	29,90	24,61	36 613	53 708
Saskatchewan	17 197	32 938	91,5	3,28	4,62	17 310	28 322	38,28	40,83	45 221	69 373
Alberta	88 750	123 377	39,0	16,94	17,30	26 718	29 074	39,33	35,78	67 929	81 256
British Columbia	50 242	74 624	48,5	9,59	10,46	11 974	14 921	28,35	25,26	42 229	59 066
Territories											
Yukon	170	216	27,1	0,03	0,03	5 329	5 319	10,81	4,93	49 307	75 002
NorthWest Territories	1 940	2 296	18,4	0,37	0,32	44 700	51 072	43,62	10,25	102 465	105 214
Nunavut	35	544	1 454,3	0,07	0,08	11 536	14 264	30,09	3,83	38 333	89 698

Source: Own Analysis Based on the Data Obtained from Statistics Canada and Industry Canada, Note: * in national exports.

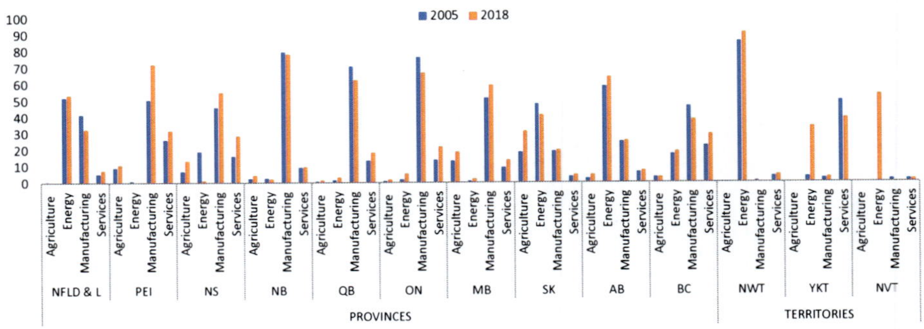

Figure 10.4: Percentage share of sectors in total provinces and territories' exports, 2005 and 2018
Source: own elaboration (Based on Data from Industry Canada-Trade Data Online).

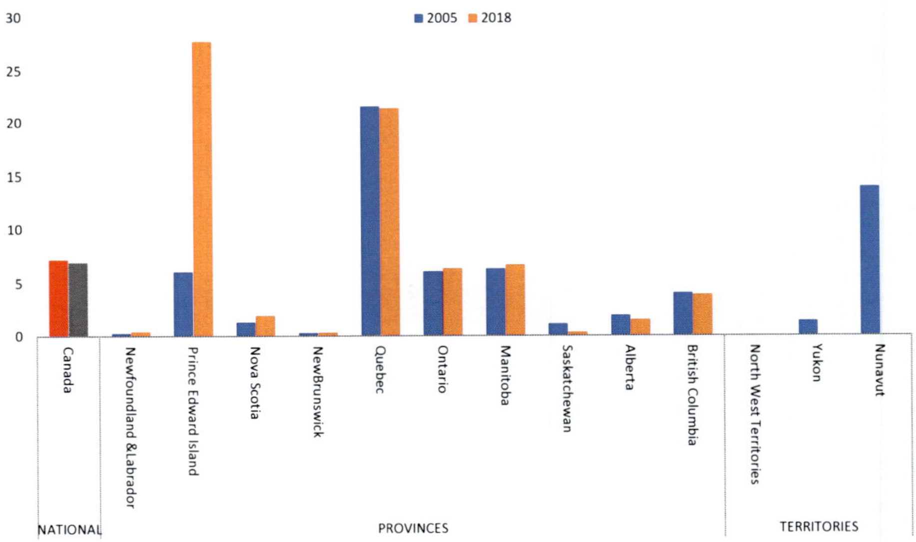

Figure 10.5: The percentage share of high-tech products in total provincial and territorial exports 2005 and 2018

Source: own elaboration (Based on Data from Industry Canada – Trade Data Online).

High-tech are products with a high intensity of expenditures on R&D, such as in aerospace, computers, pharmaceuticals, scientific instruments, and electrical machinery. Performance in high-tech exports was led by provinces where the manufacturing sector is the key component of the total exports. Among all the Canadian provinces and territories, the strongest exports performance in high-tech stems from aircrafts and unwrought aluminium exports from Quebec; motor vehicles and unwrought gold exports from Ontario; pharmaceutical sales from Manitoba; and turbo propellers shipment from Prince Edward Island. They constitute the leading provinces in the Canadian manufacturing exports and, by extension, the shipment of high-tech products to the global markets. The metropolitan provinces of Quebec and Ontario stand out more in high-tech shipment. Overall, the average value for Canada of high-tech exports as a percentage of total manufactured exports was 15.6% in 2018.

Table 10.3 outlines the share in percentages of exports directed to top destinations and the rest of the world. Among the top export destinations are the US, the EU, China, Japan, India, South Korea, Mexico and the rest of the world (Rest W). The LQ index was calculated as the ratio of exports (directed to particular destination) to the total province or territorial exports divided by the ratio of total exports shipment to a particular destination, at the national level.

The US is a very important destination for all the Canadian provinces and the territory of Yukon (the outlier 94.57%) among all the provinces and territories. The huge share evidence recorded in the US market reflects the importance of adjacency, the role of trade policy (especially the NAFTA), and other key forces within the framework of the gravity. All the provinces recorded export share of more than 1% from China, EU and Rest of W – which has shown substantial differences among the provinces and territories. The territories of Northwest and Nunavut are the main exporter for Canada to both the European Arctic States and rest of the world. While the mineral export of Alberta and Yukon went to the US, those of the Northwest and Nunavut territories headed to the European Arctic States and rest of the world in 2018.

The LQ accounts for the differences in relative intensity of trade links attributed to each of the provinces and territories in geographical terms. The index revealed substantial comparative advantage for the provinces in many markets. For example, British Columbia was found comparably better in South Korea, Japan, India, China and other parts of the world. Saskatchewan also gained an advantage in China, India, Mexico, Japan and the rest of the world. Among all the provinces and territories, Newfoundland and Labrador, Nunavut and Northwest territory are comparatively strong in the EU markets. Interestingly, no strong comparative advantage was revealed for all the provinces and territories in the US market – only New Brunswick, Alberta, and Ontario showed a weak advantage with the key partner of Canadian trade.

Concentration index was derived using the HHI.[24] It has been utilised in this work as an inverse measure of export diversification. Export diversification refers to the

24 The three categories and thresholds jointly approved in 2010 by the Federal Trade Commission and the US Department of Justice are as follows: Diversified (unconcentrated) exports or markets: HHI < 0.15, Moderately concentrated Exports or markets: $0.15 \le$ HHI < 0.25, and Highly concentrated exports or markets: HHI ≥ 0.25.

extent to which provincial and territorial export base is broad, in terms of products, trading partner countries or provinces of production.[25] For the sake of interpretation of the HHI, this paper followed the Horizontal Merger Guidelines jointly approved in 2010 by the Federal Trade Commission and the US Department of Justice, to differentiate between levels of diversified and concentrated exports or markets.

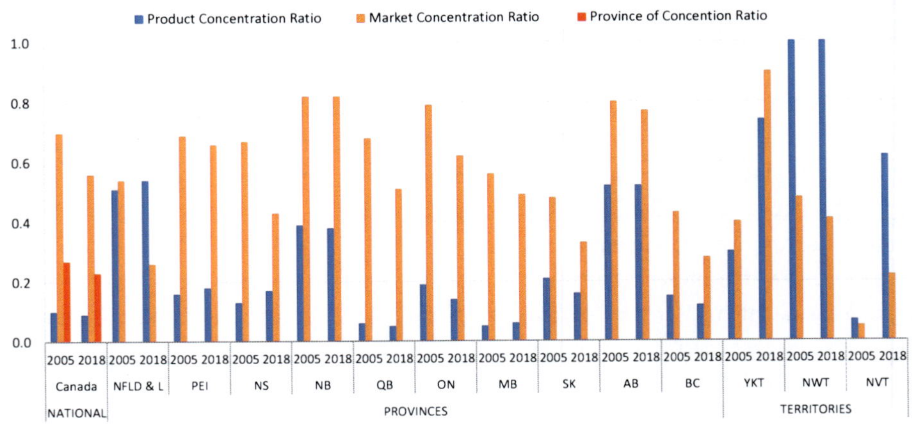

Figure 10.6: HHI of product and market concentration in provinces' exports
Source: own elaboration (Based on Data from Statistics Canada).

Canada has a highly concentrated destination market, with the majority of its exports going to its neighbour and principal trading partner, the US. Provincially, Ontario's exports were deemed moderately diversified product-wise, but highly concentrated marketwise, mainly due to motor vehicles and parts (representing on average 21% of Ontario's exports in 2018). With a concentration ratio of less than 0.15, Quebec, Manitoba, and British Columbia had a diversified basket of export goods, at the considered level of product aggregation. Product export from Saskatchewan, Nova Scotia, and Prince Edward Island was moderately concentrated since the concentration ratio was such that $0.15 \leq HHI < 0.25$. Exports from Newfoundland and Labrador and New Brunswick, including all the three territories were deemed highly concentrated, as given by a Herfindahl-Hirschman index greater than 0.25 in the period. All the provinces and territories apart from Nunavut were considered highly concentrated geographically. While the province and other territories reached HHI greater than 0.25, Nunavut was deemed moderately concentrated given that the territory maintained an HHI of < 0.25.

25 Data on province of production at the provincial level is supressed for confidentiality reasons, the concentration index for province of production is only available at the country level: https://www150.statcan.gc.ca/t1/tbl1/en/tv.action?pid=1210012901

Table 10.3: Provincial and territorial exports by destinations in 2018

	% SHARE OF EXPORT IN 2018 DIRECTED TO:								Location Quotiens (LQ)*							
Geography	**China**	**EU 28**	**India**	**Japan**	**S. Korea**	**Mexico**	**USA**	**Rest of W.**	**China**	**EU 28**	**India**	**Japan**	**S. Korea**	**Mexico**	**USA**	**Rest of W.**
Canada	4,74	7,62	0,74	2,22	1,00	1,41	75,00	7,27								
Provinces																
NFLD and Labrador	5,54	33,23	0,43	2,25	0,17	0,02	48,60	9,76	1,17	4,36	0,58	1,01	0,17	0,01	0,65	1,34
Prince Edward Island	1,64	9,57	0,12	1,26	0,99	0,30	73,97	12,13	0,35	1,26	0,17	0,57	0,99	0,22	0,99	1,67
Nova Scotia	13,70	9,47	0,49	1,62	1,87	1,20	62,78	8,87	2,89	1,24	0,66	0,73	1,86	0,85	0,84	1,22
New Brunswick	1,00	2,01	1,02	0,51	0,19	0,12	90,18	4,98	0,21	0,26	1,39	0,23	0,19	0,08	1,20	0,69
Quebec	3,91	11,61	0,72	1,72	1,27	2,27	69,65	8,85	0,83	1,52	0,97	0,78	1,27	1,61	0,93	1,22
Ontario	1,76	8,74	0,15	0,74	0,33	1,37	80,97	5,93	0,37	1,15	0,21	0,34	0,33	0,98	1,08	0,82
Manitoba	7,85	3,58	0,28	5,34	0,56	2,67	69,68	10,03	1,66	0,47	0,38	2,41	0,56	1,90	0,93	1,38
Saskatchewan	14,99	2,51	2,05	3,66	0,38	2,67	54,94	18,79	3,16	0,33	2,79	1,65	0,38	1,90	0,73	2,58
Alberta	4,47	1,23	0,08	1,66	0,47	1,04	87,27	3,77	0,94	0,16	0,12	0,75	0,47	0,74	1,16	0,52
British Columbia	14,74	5,94	3,36	10,82	6,22	0,45	47,98	10,49	3,11	0,78	4,57	4,88	6,20	0,32	0,64	1,44
Territories																
NorthWest	0,02	53,67	32,79	0,00	0,00	0,00	0,07	13,46	0,00	7,04	44,53	0,00	0,00	0,00	0,00	1,85
Nunavut.	0,01	70,02	0,00	3,96	0,00	0,00	0,11	25,90	0,00	9,18	0,00	1,79	0,00	0,00	0,00	3,56
YuKon	0,00	0,56	0,01	0,07	0,00	2,22	94,57	2,56	0,00	0,07	0,02	0,03	0,00	1,58	1,26	0,35

Source: Own Analysis Based on the Data Obtained from Statistics Canada - Industry Canada (Trade Data Online).

Generally, Canada, through the provinces and territories, has continued to show strong performance in trade. However, the country is still facing a relatively less diversified export market, with about 75% of foreign sales destined for the US alone. As can be expected, the obtained HHI calculations were in line with expectations, showing a high correlation with the US share in exports.

Although, in recent years, Canadian exporters have enjoyed remarkable success in penetrating other international markets, with much of the additional growth coming from shipments to Asia and Europe. Sales to China have increased, as have exports to the UK, and a number of other countries in recent years. Overall, the US is far more important to Canada than any other destinations, and the reflections are all over the entire Canadian provinces and territories, though the story is different for Newfoundland and British Columbia, which seemed to be more geographically diversified, as well as the territories of Northwest and Nunavut, which are geographically concentrated to the EU market. There is not much evidence pointing to the impact of NAFTA for many of the provinces and territories in terms of trade relationship with Mexico.

10.5 Trade openness and provinces' prosperity

As mentioned earlier, all the Canadian provinces and territories have relied on export revenues as a contributor to their economic growth, and many studies have been carried out to unravel the nature of the relationship. Interestingly, many authors in the past have studied the relationship between trade openness and economic growth – particularly exports, since it constitutes a large component of aggregate demand, such that an increase in exports leads to an increase in aggregate demand and results in higher economic growth (Frankel and Romer (1996) expanded on the similar issue). As expected, Zestos and Tao (2002) found a causal relationship between trade and economic growth for Canada and the US.

In our case, we extend the analysis to Canadian provinces and territories by examining the correlation between export per capita and per capita GDP. Export per capita is defined as the ratio of total exports to the province's population, and per capita GDP is defined as the ratio of the province's income level to their respective population. In our analysis, we provided insight regarding the specific directions of the GDP per capita in response to changes in the values of the export variable, for the period of 2010-2018. To further strengthen the results from our correlation coefficients, we have also analysed how well trade openness explains or predicts the future prosperity of the provinces and territories, by considering the coefficient of determination (R^2) measures. An R^2 of 50% and above denotes a strong explanatory power, while an R^2 of less than 50% denotes weak explanatory power.

Table 10.4: Correlations of provincial and territorial export per capita and GDP per capita, 2010 -2018

PROVINCES/ TERRITORIES	*VARIABLE*	Canada EXP. Per Cap.	NFLD&L EXP. Per Cap.	PEI EXP. Per Cap.	NS EXP. Per Cap.	NB EXP. Per Cap.	QB EXP. Per Cap.	ON EXP. Per Cap.	MB EXP. Per Cap.	SK EXP. Per Cap.	AB EXP. Per Cap.	BC EXP. Per Cap.	YKT EXP. Per Cap.	NWT EXP. Per Cap.	NVT EXP. Per Cap.
Canada	GDP Per Cap.	0,98901 $R^2 = 0.99$													
NFLD&L	GDP Per Cap.		0,72414 $R^2 = 0.85$												
PEI	GDP Per Cap.			0,93914 $R^2 = 0.97$											
NS	GDP Per Cap.				0,64068 $R^2 = 0.80$										
NB	GDP Per Cap.					-0,2106 $R^2 = 0.45$									
QB	GDP Per Cap.						0,98379 $R^2 = 0.99$								
ON	GDP Per Cap.							0,95514 $R^2 = 0.98$							
MB	GDP Per Cap.								0,82865 $R^2 = 0.91$						
SK	GDP Per Cap.									0,76653 $R^2 = 0.88$					
AB	GDP Per Cap.										0,95603 $R^2 = 0.98$				
BC	GDP Per Cap.											0,9944 $R^2 = 0.99$			
YKT	GDP Per Cap.												-0,3383 $R^2 = 0.58$		
NWT	GDP Per Cap.													0,689 $R^2 = 0.83$	
NVT	GDP Per Cap.														0,95431 $R^2 = 0.98$

Trade openness (international export) increases and correlates positively with the economic prosperity of most of the provinces and territories, apart from New Brunswick and Yukon, where the relationship is negative. Thus, strong results at the country level and from most of the provinces and territories combined, show that provincial openness to trade (in particular, international export) correlates with the provincial prosperity (proxied by per capita GDP). It is supported by a high coefficient of determinations at the country level and for many of the provinces and territories.

10.6 Provincial openness to trade and the labour market fundamentals

The relationship between trade liberalisation and the labour market situation has generated a lot of controversy among researchers. For example, in the 1980s, there was an extensive deliberation regarding the effects of CUSFTA. During this period, there were widespread fears, especially those harboured by the labour unions and those opposed to the idea of external agreements, that trade liberalisation with the US would adversely impact wages and employment of workers in domestic industries. In fact, the 1990-1992 recession was perceived by some trade analysts (opposed to free trade) as evidence of the negative influence of trade on the labour market. Some studies likewise have measured the impact of the reduction in industry-related tariffs on wages and employment. A close example is Gaston and Trefler (1997), who aggregated establishment data, and provided some evidence of the negative impact of

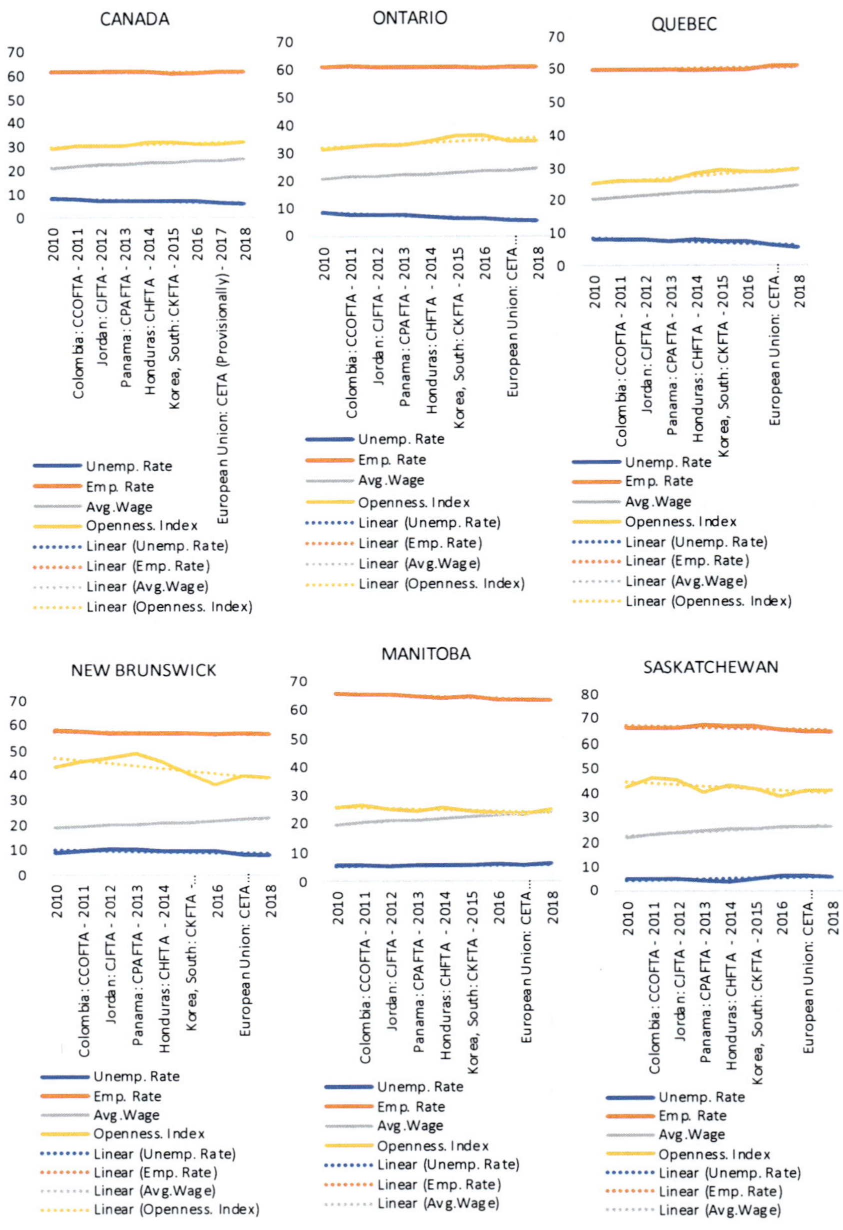

Figure 10.7: Provincial trade openness and key labour market indicators

Source: own elaboration.

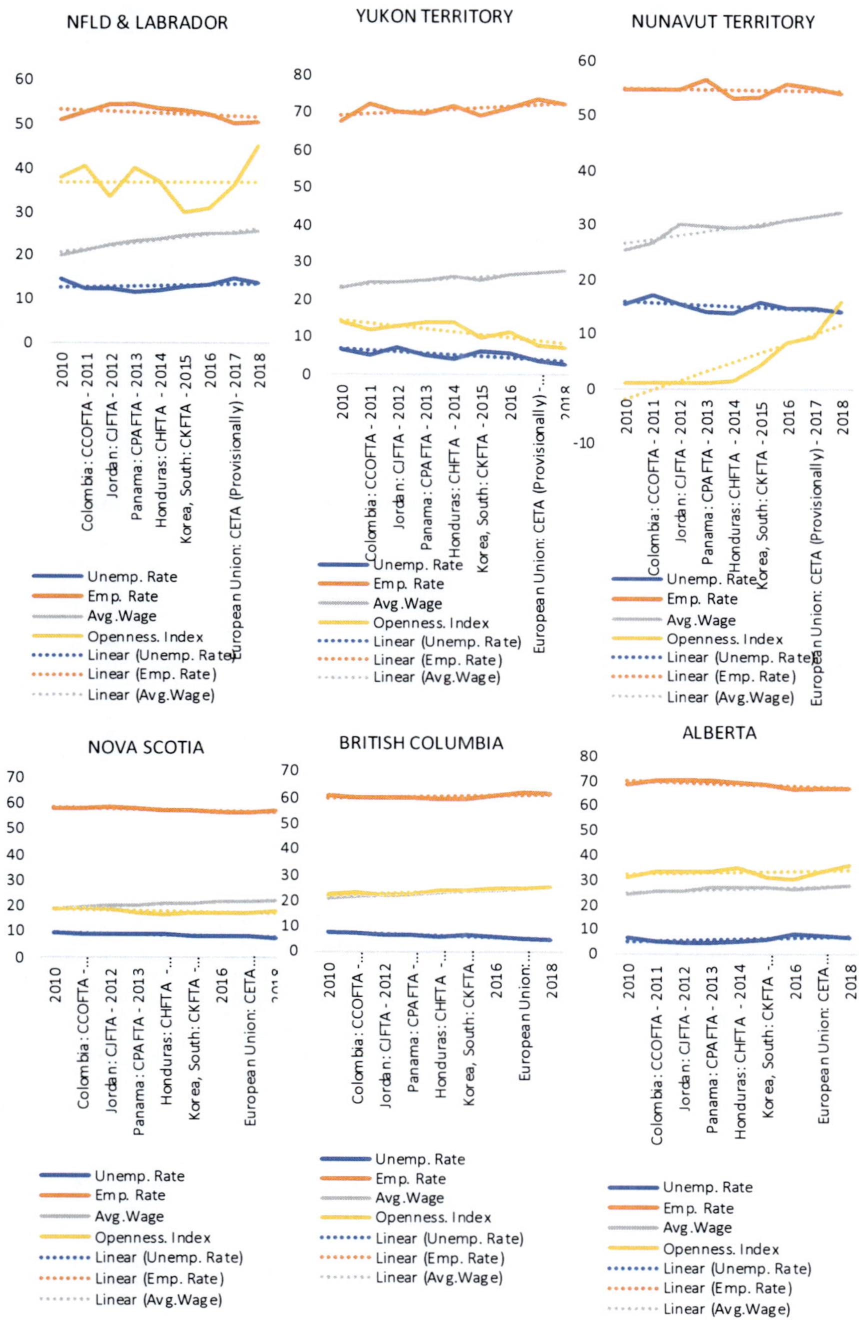

continued **Figure 10.7:** Provincial trade openness and key labour market indicators

Source: own elaboration.

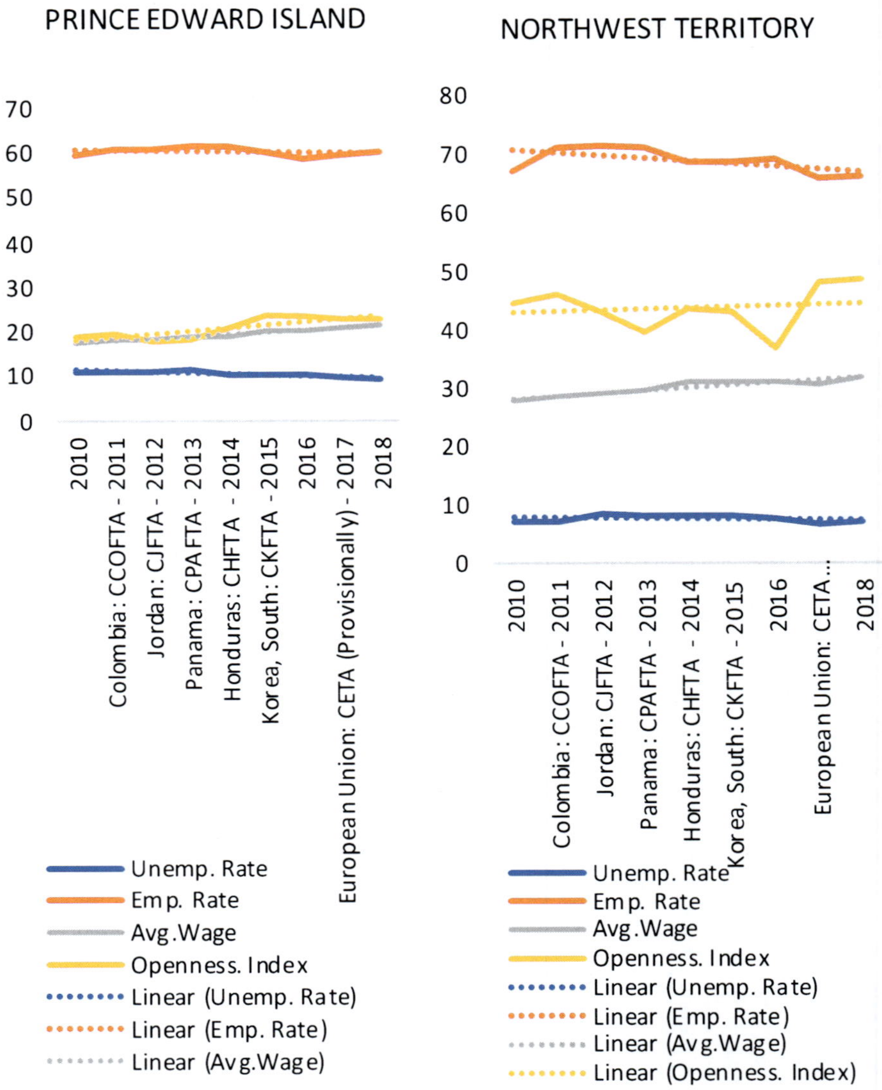

continued **Figure 10.7:** Provincial trade openness and key labour market indicators

Source: own elaboration.

tariffs' reductions on employment, but found minimal of such effect on wages (further proof of sticky downward wage theory), this is also in line with the findings of Beaulieu (2000). However, through the application of household data (with the leverage to control for individual workers' characteristics such as gender, education experience etc.), Townsend (2007) revealed some significant negative influence of tariffs reduction on wages. As the actual relationship remains uncertain and the debate keeps on stretching, the labour market consequences of trade openness are analysed in this section for the Canadian sub-regions. Specifically, we provide insights on the relationship by interacting provincial and territorial employment rates, unemployment rates, average hourly wage and the index of provincial trade openness.

The sample period 2010 to 2018 reveals wage and employment growth were spread across many of the provinces, with a corresponding fall in the rate of unemployment in many of the provinces and territories. The unemployment rate increased only in the province of Manitoba (5.4 to 6.0), and the Northwest territory (6.6 to 7.3). Other provinces and territories saw a reduction in the rate of unemployment viz: QB (6.1 to 5.5), ON (6.0 to 5.6), NFLD&L (14.8 to 13.8), PEI (9.8 to 9.4) NS (8.4 to 7.5), NB (8.1 to 8.0), SK (6.3 to 6.1), and (7.8 to 6.6), BC (5.1 to 4.7), YKT (3.6 to 2.7) and NVT (14.6 to 14.1). In BC, QB, ON, and YKT unemployment rate decreased below the national average (5.8). The sample period showed expansion of many of the provinces in trade openness. The expansion in openness seems to have worked to bring down the level of unemployment in these provinces and territories. Average hourly wages also rose in many of the provinces and territories, but not at the same pace with openness expansion, except in BC and PEI where they both grew at the same rate and MB where they both increased at similar pace towards the end of the sample period. Although the result is not the same for Nova Scotia, Yukon and Nunavut, where openness to trade is still lower than would be expected to take into consideration their respective average hourly wage levels. Nunavut is a special case with trade openness that seems to have staggered below unemployment and average wage levels until 2018 when openness rose to tame the unemployment level. Still, the average wage remained high, waiting to be fully utilised. A closer look at figure 10.7 confirms the Central Canada provinces of ON and QB as the key drivers of the changes (in the labour market) we noticed at the national level.

10.7 Conclusions

Our contribution is mainly on the characteristics of Canadian international trade (exports) by provinces and territories. In doing so, we first looked at the comparative evolution of the Canadian trade patterns both at the country and provincial levels, in order to identify changes in export structure. We showed how trade at the national level has diverted towards the international frontier in response to adjacency and changes in external relations, while the interprovincial outlet has remained constant over time. More importantly, we analysed the export dynamics of the Canadian provinces and territories, reflecting the heterogeneity of their export profiles. In Canada, we do not make the economic comparison between the provinces and the territories, the territories are scarcely populated, and cannot compare with the provinces in terms of economic engagements, the activities of Canadian territories do not impact much on the overall Country level.

Canada, being the world second-largest country in terms of geography, has a population of over 37 million people, with more than half of the number concentrated in the central provinces of Ontario and Quebec, the two largest metropolitan provinces in Canada. As the 10th in the global ranking of the world largest economies, Canada is blessed – being geo-positioned close to the world's largest economy – the US. Thus, our analysis at country level reveals a remarkable shift in the evolution of trade patterns, which seem to have favoured international trade over interprovincial trade as a result of the interplays of some key gravity forces. A closer look at the recent years (pre-recession 2005 and post-recession 2018) produced similar results for most of the provinces and territories, who also are not immune from border effects and are inevitably controlled by the whims and caprices of national trade policies. Overall, while Canadian exports were found to be diversified by product and were discovered to be concentrated by the geographic market – hugely to its southern neighbour (US). It is the propelling the idea behind Canada's goal of increasing overseas exports by over 50% if possible, by 2025.

Provincially, we analysed dynamics in exports, which identified the peculiarity of individual provinces and territories in terms of export product-mix and their respective level of international engagement and export performance. The range of goods and services exported by Canadian provinces are wide, with sufficient distribution among commodity groupings that are considered diversified in the portfolio of Canadian exports. The largest sectors are manufacturing and energy. Agriculture and services have also performed remarkably in some of the provinces. All Canadian provinces and territories have relied on export revenues as their source of growth. With high export concentration, provincial export earnings may suffer from commodity price fluctuations driven by unexpected changes in the global economic environment and subsequently lead to significant trade shocks. As a result, Canada has continued to engage in policy negotiations that will aid the increase of overseas exports. Although some experts have considered the FTA with Canada's second-largest trading partner. The conclusion of the Canada-EU FTA beyond the provisional level will be a good step in the right direction to increase export.

Concerning the state of the labour market, one visible experience is that the Canadian labour market has continued to stay resilient in recent years, despite the challenges posed by the global economic environment. For all the Canadian provinces, the emerging signals across key labour market indicators point to a tightening of the labour market, with several of the indicators showing positive trends for the provinces in the most recent years, which includes total employment growth and a decreasing trend in the provincial unemployment rate. Also, the average earnings saw a notable increase in all the provinces. All of these performances came in the same period with stronger economic growth in many of the provinces.

Some of the provinces and territories are driven by natural resource abundance. Thus, export exposure can result in DD or the so-called resource curse, which are susceptible to an increase in mining, and oil and gas exports. Our analysis that tended to expose this phenomenon was carried out at the provincial and territorial levels. In our efforts, we tried to answer the question of whether there is a correlation between the degree of international export exposure and the provinces' prosperity. Our findings answered the above question in an affirmative way and conceded to the fact that increased openness to international exports enhances the provinces' prosperity. Evidence from the resourced based provinces of Albert, Saskatchewan, and Newfoundland and Labrador, as well as Northwest territory, are a good case in point.

Part IV: **Policy Implications and Possibilities**

Krystyna Gawlikowska-Hueckel

11 Possibilities of supporting exports at regional level

One of the effects of globalisation is the growing openness of an economy and its consequences. The progressing liberalisation eliminates traditional tools of protecting manufacturers, including protective tariffs, quota systems, direct support for exports (taking the form of subventions or subsidies) or several quality standards the diversification of which has been hampering international trade.

When the application of these instruments is limited or impossible, there is more competition currently faced by countries, regions and companies, the development of which is to a large extent related to the ability to export.

In this context, the following questions arise:

- How can entrepreneurs be encouraged to take the risk of internationalisation when the economy is open and strongly competitive?
- What are the possible tools (compatible with the EU laws) of supporting exporters at the regional level?
- Do NUTS 2 European regions (for example in Poland and Spain) use these instruments and which of them are most frequently applied?

An attempt to answer these questions is the aim of this paper.

Most topical publications have been used for this analysis: books, articles, publications and documents of the EU. A detailed preliminary survey of the information referring to regional systems of innovation, available at the European Commission website (https://s3platform.jrc.ec.europa.eu/) has been carried out. Provisions referring to the support of exports in the development strategies and regional operational programmes of Polish and Spanish NUTS2 units have also been analysed.

Referring to the first issue, it is good to notice Melitz and Redding (2014), who state that companies operating within the same sector are not homogenous, and only some of them will try to expand to foreign markets. Two fundamental questions emerge in this context:

- if there is a demand from abroad for the products of a given sector, why do some of the companies fail to join "the internationalisation game"?
- the question mentioned in the introduction, i.e. how to encourage the passive ones to start exporting?

The answer to the first question is provided by the results of numerous studies, such as Gawlikowska-Hueckel and Umiński (2016), Brodzicki et al. (2018) and Cieślik (2017).

On the basis of those studies, it can be noted that exporting companies are, as a rule, the larger ones; in Poland, they are mainly export-oriented FOEs which are at the same time importers. Without too much simplification, it may be said that they are more familiar with foreign markets (foreign capital involvement), more likely to take the risk (larger own resources) and have a better chance of participation in IIT.

The replies to the questionnaires distributed among non-exporters show their reluctance to start exporting connected with four types of barriers: (i) strictly export-related, perceived as external factors such as customs formalities, complicated procedures, the need to respect specific standards, etc., (ii) related to insufficient resources (dearth of capital, finance and human resources), (iii) marketing-related (logistic problems, lack of information, lack of efficient advertising, poor knowledge of foreign market essentials) and (iv) obstacles of a personal nature resulting from attitudes (aversion to taking the risk, insufficient knowledge, reluctance to cooperate) (PWC, 2017).

A survey carried out on a sample of 700 enterprises in Poland (Gawlikowska-Hueckel and Umiński, 2016) shows that the obstacles most frequently mentioned by non-exporters, discouraging them from going international, are a lot of competition, foreign exchange risk, insufficient information on foreign markets and the absence of good cooperation with other companies.

These entrepreneurs expect national and regional institutions to help them with market research, clarification of procedures, search for business partners or better, more transparent information.

The context of the second question presented in the introduction is more complex. The curbs on the possible use of all export-support tools by the EU member states are connected with respecting the Community laws concerning trade and competition policies (Majkowska-Szulc, 2016).

Trade policy is one of the cornerstones of European integration which has created the framework of ‘a level playing field’ for the member states in both internal and external trade of the EU and resulted in trade creation and shifting (Gawlikowska-Hueckel and Zielińska-Głębocka, 2004; Kawecka-Wyrzykowska, 2009; Zielińska-Głębocka, 2012).

This policy is a sole competence of the EU; therefore, the application of export-supporting tools is strictly limited by the provisions of the European treaties. Regulations concerning trade policy are included under Title II “Common Commercial Policy” of part five “External Action by the Union” of the Treaty on the Functioning of the EU. For the present discussion, the most significant are the provisions that it is not possible to infringe on "equal rights for all the entrepreneurs without the EU consent".[26]

The EU position concerning the elimination of barriers limiting free trade is strict, which does not mean that the European Commission fails to notice changes taking place in the world trade (Nacewska-Twardowska, 2013). The process of these changes was discussed in the communication from the External Relations Section of the European Commission to the European Parliament, the Council, the European Economic and Social Committee Council, and the Committee of the Regions (European Commission, 2010a). Potential effects of ongoing transformations have also been identified:

- competition is intensifying due to new IT and transport technologies, coupled with the future "green" technologies. They transform not only the way in which added value is generated and distributed, but also contribute to increase in the mobility of goods, services and factors of production, capital in particular (CESE, 2011). This results in the exposure of a greater number of social and economic sectors to foreign competition;
- the role of knowledge and innovation, which have become the engines of growth, has changed. This has had a revolutionary impact on the classical division of labour, consistent with comparative advantages. Countries specialise in "tasks" performed by employees with special skills, thanks to which they gain a competitive edge, also making use of differences in social and tax regulations;
- competition contributes to more innovation, which may result in pay inequalities between unskilled and skilled workers, between people who possess capital and those who do not, between those who work in sectors exporting goods and services, and those who work for internal market-oriented industry;
- this requires synchronisation of activities within the framework of trade policy and other activities, particularly these concerning "transformation and adjustment in the labour market, limiting the emission of greenhouse gases, social and economic cohesion, the single market, as well as cooperation and development";
- competition for natural, energy and food resources is on the increase, with an impact on terms of delivery; therefore attention must be paid to the security of supplies (European Commission, 2011).

---

26 Equal rights for all the enterprises related to Treaty provisions which stipulate that within the EU it is impossible (without the EU consent) to: take any action with regard to changes in tariff rates, the conclusion of tariff and trade agreements relating to trade in goods and services, and the commercial aspects of intellectual property, foreign direct investment, the achievement of uniformity in measures of liberalisation, export policy and measures to protect trade such as those to be taken in the event of dumping or subsidies.

The awareness of these tendencies bore an impact on the preparation by the EC of the new approach to commercial policy. The document stresses that "better economic results are achieved when markets are open to trade" and that the debate and negotiations held within the EU and WTO should focus on the EU trade policy to be of "more strategic and long-term nature" (European Commission, 2011).

The "new approach" also assumes that the efficiency of EC actions will provide a new, deregulated partnership between the Commission, the member states and entrepreneurs operating in third countries, where thanks to the knowledge of the local conditions it is easier to identify barriers to trade and overcome them". The scope and scale of the Commission's activities should be adequate to the importance of various markets.

The other policy limiting the possibility of direct support for enterprises is the competition policy. This policy is regulated by the Treaty on the Functioning of the European Union (Art. 101, 102, 103).

The goal of the competition policy (like of the trade policy) is to eliminate activities infringing on free competition or free trade through unlawful practices and agreements.[27] It is worth mentioning that "the state aid used for achieving allocation goals, thus substituting economic mechanisms of specialisation, particularly if designed to fix the existing inefficient structures of production, employment and exports, is particularly harmful" (Gawlikowska-Hueckel and Zielińska-Głębocka, 2004, p. 136).

Art. 101 of TFEU says that there are exceptions to these rigorous provisions. They may not be applied to enterprises which contribute to "improving the production or distribution of goods or to promoting technical or economic progress".

The EU laws concerning trade and competition policies clearly define aid rules (Korbutowicz, 2016). The EU policies, however, create a logical matrix which practically means that within trade and competition regulations there are exceptions which can switch on tools of support, within the policies of cohesion, agriculture, industry and innovation.

The most important of them (in terms of the volume of expenditure) is the cohesion (regional) policy, which has also undergone a significant evolution as far as goals, scope, and priorities of actions are concerned.

The growth of its importance is usually associated with the establishment (1973) and the operability (1975) of the European Regional Development Fund (the first tool for financing regional policy was created 1958, i.e. the Social Fund, which focused its intervention on the labour market; in 1964 the Guarantee Section of the European Agricultural Guidance and Guarantee Fund (EAGGF) was created. The Section

---

27 The following shall be prohibited as incompatible with the internal market: all agreements between undertakings, decisions by associations of undertakings and concerted practices which may affect trade between Member States and which have as their object or effect the prevention, restriction or distortion of competition within the internal market (TFUE, 2004).

financed projects related to the restructuring of rural areas).[28] The 45-year-long experience with the ERDF resulted in numerous publications on the theory of cohesion, convergence, and catch up process, and to a genuine evaluation of the effectiveness of the policy (which should result in a better standard of living in the regions of the lower level of social and economic development).

Of the monographs focusing on the efficiency of the policy, we ought to mention the studies of Bachtler and Mendez (2007). The macroeconomic results of the policy have been presented by Bradley (2009), Bradley and Zaleski (2003), and Bradley, Morgenroth, and Untiedt (2003). At EU level, cyclic reports are produced on the development of socio-economic cohesion (the most recent was published in 2017). This type of research was conducted in Poland by Szlachta (1992, 2010), Zaucha et al. (2015), Churski (2008), Gorzelak (2014), Łaźniewska, Gorynia, and Chmielewski (2012). Numerous studies criticise the efficiency of regional policy. These include Sapir's report (Sapir, 2003) and papers of Ederveen, Gorter, Mooij, and Nahuis (2002) and Boldrin and Canova (2001). These publications underline the waste of resources, lack of efficient control, corruption, the increase in debt due to the necessity of co-financing European projects.

The goal of cohesion policy (regional, structural) is defined by the provision of the Treaty: Member States are "ANXIOUS to strengthen the unity of their economies and to ensure their harmonious development by reducing the differences existing between the various regions and the backwardness of the less-favoured regions." The legal foundations of the regional policy were formulated in the Single European Act.

Radical changes in cohesion policy started with the reforms adopted within the so-called Delors Package (Gerbet, 2016). Legal foundations of the reformed policy were formed under the Treaty on European Union (TEU) where Art. 130A contains the following provision: "In order to promote its overall harmonious development, the Community shall develop and pursue its actions leading to the strengthening of its economic and social cohesion. In particular, the Community shall aim at reducing disparities between the various regions and the backwardness of the least-favoured regions".

The new solutions consisted in increasing inputs for the regional development, integrated programming, multi-year financing, focusing recourses on precisely defined goals, defining the rules and the directions of operations at the Community level, and comprehensive monitoring.

---

28 Under the Treaty of Maastricht (1992), the Cohesion Fund was established which was and is earmarked for the countries where the Gross National Income was lower than 90% then EU average. The Fund supported the development of particularly capital-intensive structural investments. In 1967, within the structures of the European Commission, Directorate Regional for Regional Policy (earlier called DG XVI, afterwards DG REGIO) was established.

Further changes in legal foundations concerning the cohesion policy were introduced under the Treaty of Lisbon, wherein Art. 3 and Arts. 174-178 previous provisions were expanded.

The evolution of cohesion policy was connected with two processes: the broadening of the integration, which resulted in the formulation of new goals of regional policy, or significant extension of the area of intervention[29] and the deepening of integration, which resulted in higher exposure to competition (which affected most of all poorer regions).

Therefore, the instruments of regional policy were supposed, first of all, to neutralise the adverse effects of the deepening integration on the regions which – due to their low standard of living – were particularly severely hit by the growing competition.

Cohesion policy includes the six-year programming and financing framework, which guarantees the reception of funds in the long run. At present, the sources of funding include the European Regional Development Fund, the European Social Fund and, although not a structural fund, the Cohesion Fund supporting the two. Legal foundations for more activity of the European Investment Bank have been established; the Bank is deeply involved in money lending activities, thus supporting the financing of European projects.

The new approach to cohesion policy in the period of 2014-2020 was related to the changes in the paradigm of that policy; these amendments were related to the studies carried out by international organisations, first of all by The World Bank (2010) and the OECD (2009).

The attention of the World Bank was focused on the importance of metropolitan areas, which – because of high innovation potential, human capital included – guarantee that funds are invested more effectively.

The 7th Report on economic, social, and territorial cohesion (Dijkstra, 2017) says that the Regional Competitiveness Index (RCI) is the highest in strong capitals and other metropolitan regions. It results from the fact that the existing environment favours new ideas, products, and processes, thanks to which there is an inflow of creative and qualified employees. The activity increases the tendency to undertake the business activity and results in creating clusters. Thus, it makes the areas more innovative, the enterprises stronger, more ready to take the risk, and more open to internalisation.

29 As an example of the problems of different nature the regional policy had to face together with expanding the Union by well-off countries (Sweden, Finland, Austria) in 1995 were occurring in some northern reaches of Finland and Sweden depopulation tendencies (due to adverse climatic conditions). The highest challenge was the 2004 EU enlargement, when the population of the EU increased by 20% due to the accession of 10 countries, while the GDP increased by 5% Gawlikowska-Hueckel (2005); Pietrzyk (2004).

On the other hand, the OECD studies (2009) stress the role of endogenous resources and qualitatively new ideas, such as information society, knowledge-based economy, communication and information technologies, learning regions. The rationality of allocating resources to well-developed regions results from the fact that their potential facilitates the creation of innovative solutions, the beneficiaries of which (sooner or later) will become the less developed ones. It is supported by the diffusion of knowledge and development processes. The approach of this type undermines the sense of carrying out the compensatory regional policy.

The results of the research of international institutions and the debate at EU level was reflected in the decisions concerning the cohesion policy in the programming period of 2014-2020. At the same time, the improvement of the competitiveness level was stressed, simultaneously limiting the pool of resources earmarked for cohesion. Scientific research and innovations, implementation of digital agenda, support for SMEs and low-carbon economy were regarded as priorities (Gawlikowska-Hueckel and Szlachta, 2014).

These priorities are consistent with the Europe 2020 strategy (European Commission, 2010c), which assumes that development should be smart (based on knowledge and innovation), sustainable (using the resources in an efficient way), and more competitive.

The strategy emphasises the impact of exports on growth: "The EU prospects thanks to trade – it exports all over the world and imports both raw materials and finished products. Under high competitive pressure on the export markets (...) we must become more competitive in relation to our major trade partners by increasing our efficiency".

This also refers to the advancement of the regions and particularly to those whose productivity is lower than the EU regional average.

The special role of the cohesion policy is demonstrated by the fact that in 2014-2020 the largest pool of funds, EUR 351.8 billion was allocated to it, which makes it the main investment tool. It should, however, be noted that the share of the less developed regions and of the Cohesion Fund in the allocation went down from ca. 80% to 70% (Szlachta, 2012).

Another policy which makes it possible to use exporter support instruments at the regional level is the industrial policy, within which 'the new approach' was devised. In the initial period of the changes, it was decided that it should provide a more unequivocal response to globalisation-related problems. The challenges are important enough for sectoral instruments (previously discarded by the policy) to be engaged. The European Commission stresses the need for the introduction of key enabling technologies, flagship initiatives and priority lines.

In addition to "the challenges of globalisation and adjusting production processes and products to a low-carbon economy" (European Commission, 2010b), re-industrialisation of EU member states has become an issue. "Europe needs to reverse the declining role of industry in Europe for the 21st century. ... To achieve this, a comprehensive vision is needed, focusing on investment and on innovation, but also mobilising all the levers available at EU level, notably the single market, trade policy, SME policy, competition policy, environmental and research policy in favour of European companies' competitiveness" (European Commission, 2012).

Two flagship initiatives concerning industry have been formulated in the Europe 2020 paper:

- An industrial policy for the globalisation era, which is supposed to engage tools that will improve the business environment for SMEs and "to support the development of a strong, sustainable industrial base able to compete globally";
- "Innovation Union", which is to improve access to finance for research and innovation so as to ensure that innovative ideas can be turned into products and services which create growth and jobs.

The new approach to industrial policy in the EU (European Commission, 2012) is based on the assumption that competitiveness and sustainable EU industrial development are a priority. If this goal is to be achieved, the industrial policy must be understood more broadly and cover the areas directly related to costs, prices and innovation-based competitiveness of the industry and its individual sectors, but also to account for the impact of all other political initiatives on competitiveness.

Industry plays a key role, in view of the fact that one in four new jobs is in industry and results in one job in the service sector. Some 75% of the export volume is from industry, which is also responsible for 80% of private R&D expenditure.[30]

From the perspective of export support instruments, it is important that industrial policy accepts the use of selective tools (the choice of industries and priorities). Vertical measures (taken within the industrial policy) can be coupled with support for the industries decided to be of key importance for smart specialisations.

The approach of various policies and the set of tools they have at their disposal, together with limitations resulting from the EU legal provisions point to the relatively narrow margin of the authorities' freedom as far as the internationalisation support at the regional level is concerned. As has already been mentioned, this results mainly from rigorous provisions of the policy of competition, which hinder a broader use of aid.

The 7th Report on Economic, Social, and Territorial Cohesion (Dijkstra, 2017, p. 189) says that the fundamental source of support for the SMEs was the aid granted "to mitigate the effects of the crisis through loans (when no other sources of funding are available)". Direct support (in 2007-2013) was granted to 2% SMEs in the EU (400,000 out of 23 million).

30 A change in industrial policy and industry revival attempts are also linked with the loss of 3 million industrial jobs in EU member states in the wake of the 2008 crisis European Commission (2012).

The analysis discussing the kind of applied tools is the answer to the third question asked in the introductory part of the chapter.

The survey of the possibility of supporting the expansion to foreign markets opens the presentation of the institutions created in support of exporters in Poland.

Table 11.1 shows that Polish institutions of export support offer mainly activities of horizontal nature, which are in conformity with trade and competition policies. These activities must not be disregarded. As the research of the International Trade Centre shows, the role of the organisations promoting trade is very important, and their activities stimulate growth (International Trade Centre, 2016).

Some of the activities of the institutions mentioned above are financially supported. For example, costs of participation in fairs and exhibitions abroad, participation in outgoing trade missions, costs of international certification, implementation of sectoral promotional projects or the organisation of conferences and shows are subsidised.

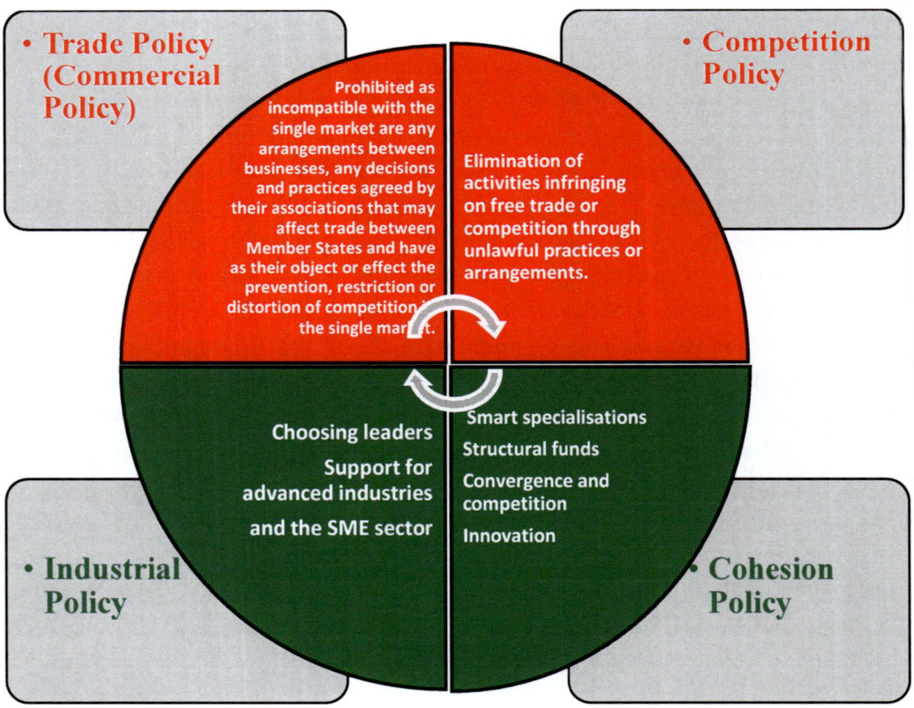

Figure 11.1: Limitations and opportunities of internationalisation support under EU policies

Source: own elaboration.

Regional chambers of commerce are interested in creating "groups of interest" composed of a couple or a dozen of companies interested in a common project (such as standardisation of services or financing a common laboratory).

It should be mentioned that membership in chambers of commerce in Poland is not mandatory (like in the UK, unlike in Germany, where the system requires membership of all businesses, which translates into greater advantages of being a member). The limited participation of businesses is a curb on the effectiveness of the Agency.

Export financing is based on an OECD document Arrangement on Officially Supported Export Credits, which was incorporated into the acquis in April 1978.

In Poland, the allowed instruments include government loans (including *tied aid*), export credits granted by the Bank Gospodarstwa Krajowego (BGK), refunds of part of the interest on fixed-rate export credits granted by the BGK and the premiums on credit insurance by KUKE SA.

Internationalisation support instruments within the cohesion policy are reflected in regional operational programmes (RPOs) – see tables 11.2 and 11.3. As seen in the RPOs of most voivodships, problems of internationalisation of businesses are included. This shows that regional authorities are aware of export-related growth opportunities.

It should be added that regional operational programmes are financed under the cohesion policy, so the support funding comes from the EU budget.

Noteworthy is the fact that support opportunities for the voivodships of eastern Poland were created within Activity 1.2 SME Internationalisation by a dedicated programme *Polska Wschodnia* (Eastern Poland) and national operational programmes. Nevertheless, two of the voivodeships concerned, Warmińsko-mazurskie and Lubelskie, included internationalisation efforts in their regional programmes. The RPO of the former includes Measure 3b: Preparation and Implementation of New Business Models for SMEs with a View of Their Internationalisation, while the programme of Lubelskie includes Measure 3.6. Business Marketing.

It is interesting that relatively the greatest support is offered by the voivodeships considered to be internationalisation leaders: Mazowieckie, Wielkopolskie, Dolnośląskie and Małopolskie.

It is interesting to identify support tools used in the Spanish regions and compare them with those used in Poland.

Summarizing, the EU's common commercial policy and especially competition policy are a curb on the use of many direct tools to support exporters at the regional level. Taking into account these restrictions, regions of Poland and Spain use instruments that are horizontal in nature or are allowed by the EU regulations, regarding, e.g. the SME sector (as not threatening competition). That is why the tools used in both countries are similar.

The support of the SME sector is most often used; this support takes various forms such as: creating new SMEs business models to increase international expansion, improving the competitiveness of the business sector, development of SMEs'

Table 11.1: Various types of institutions and kinds of support for exports at the regional level

Institutions of support at the national level	Institutions of support at the regional level	Kinds of support offered
Polish Investment and Trade Agency Polish Agency for Enterprise Development	Regional chambers of commerce Agencies of regional development Special economic zones Regional clusters (brand promotion) Regional exporters' associations	Promotion Organisation of fairs and exhibitions Networking activities Information on markets Organisation of economic missions Aid in obtaining product certificates Internet export promotion websites
Foreign Trade Offices		Market information (analyses, reports, guidelines), Co-networking with local companies and institutions, Organisation of trainings for Polish and foreign companies, Status reports on business partners

Source: own elaboration.

innovation potential and their entrepreneurship to allow them to access new markets in the globalized economy, promotion of an entrepreneurial culture, facilitation for exporters to improve export diversification, and increase of the number of sales markets. Four Polish and ten Spanish regions declare such form.
Assistance in participating in fairs and exhibitions is included in operational programmes of eight Polish regions and four Spanish regions. Other forms of support include programmes promoting exports and internationalisation, guidance for companies embarking on the process of internationalisation, advisory services in the field of the undertaking and developing export activities in strategies, export development plans, and legal advice.

Promoting partnerships, collaborations, creating cooperation networks, and joint projects are also very important.

It should also be emphasized that certain tools are related to the specificity of the region, e.g. in the Baleares Programme, it is mentioned that the traditional "sea, sun and sand" business model has to be transformed at regional and firm levels. Diversification is necessary to escape low-cost competition.

The Canary Islands also want to "support companies with export potential in the field of renewable energy and water treatment, activities related to the maritime sector". It should be added that only in one Polish region (Zachodniopomorskie) is the support earmarked only for enterprises operating in the area of smart specialisations of West Pomerania.

Table 11.2: Types of internationalisation support at the regional level in Poland

Actions	(PL11) Łódzkie	(PL12) Mazowieckie	(PL21) Małopolskie	(PL22) Śląskie	(PL31) Lubelskie	(PL32) Podkarpackie	(PL33) Świętokrzyskie	(PL34) Podlaskie	(PL41) Wielkopolskie	(PL42) Zachodniopomorskie	(PL43) Lubuskie	(PL51) Dolnośląskie	(PL52) Opolskie	(PL61) Kujawsko-pomorskie	(PL62) Warmińsko-mazurskie	(PL63) Pomorskie*
■ Creating new SMEs business models to increase international expansion	x		x									x			x	
■ Supporting participation in national and international fairs, organisation of exhibitions and study visits	x	x	x		x						x	x	x	x		
■ Support for investor service centres and exporters			x		x											
■ Support for the investment processes in the region			x						x		x				x	
■ Economic promotion of the region		x	x		x				x		x				x	
■ Advisory services in the field of the undertaking and developing export activities in strategies, export development plans, legal advice									x					x		
■ Preparation of cooperation offers and trade negotiations, search and selection of partners on selected foreign markets, search and selection of business partners on the target market									x							

continued **Table 11.2:** Types of internationalisation support at the regional level in Poland

Actions	(PL11) Łódzkie	(PL12) Mazowieckie	(PL21) Małopolskie	(PL22) Śląskie	(PL31) Lubelskie	(PL32) Podkarpackie	(PL33) Świętokrzyskie	(PL34) Podlaskie	(PL41) Wielkopolskie	(PL42) Zachodniopomorskie	(PL43) Lubuskie	(PL51) Dolnośląskie	(PL52) Opolskie	(PL61) Kujawsko-pomorskie	(PL62) Warmińsko-mazurskie	(PL63) Pomorskie*
■ Advisory services related to the development and preparation for the implementation of a new business model; services directly related to the implementation of the new business model, including costs of advertising materials, training, translations, tests participation in international fairs, exhibitions or business missions					x	x	x	x							x	
■ Purchase of fixed assets, excluding real estate or intangible assets in connection with preparation for internationalisation of the business.					x	x	x	x							x	
■ Comprehensive support for individual enterprises in expanding to foreign markets										x						

Source: own elaboration on the basis of a critical review of regional strategies/operational programmes.

Notes: * Internationalisation activities were not included in the Pomorskie Regional Operational Programme. However, the National Operational Programme may be used.

Table 11.3: Types of internationalisation support at regional level in Spain

Actions	(ES11) Galicia	(ES12) Principality of Asturias	(ES13) Cantabria	(ES21) Basque Community	(ES22) Navarre	(ES23) La Rioja	(ES24) Aragon	(ES30) Madrid	(ES41) Castile-Leon	(ES42) Castile-La Mancha	(ES43) Extremadura	(ES51) Catalonia	(ES52) Valencian Community	(ES53) Balearic Islands	(ES61) Andalusia	(ES62) Region of Murcia	(ES63) Ceuta	(ES64) Melilla	(ES70) Canary Islands
■ Improving the competitiveness of the business sector, development of SME-s innovation potential and their entrepreneurship to allow them to access new markets in the globalized economy	×	×	×			×	×		×	×	×		×		×				
■ Facilitation for exporters to improve export diversification and increase the number of sales markets. Institutional support for Spanish exporting companies								×	×				×		×				
■ Supporting participation in national and international fairs, organisation of exhibitions and study visits					×	×		×					×						
■ Programmes promoting exports and internationalisation									×		×	×				×			
■ Support and guidance for companies embarking on the process of internationalisation									×			×							
■ Promotion of the region, regional brand and business activity					×	×			×										×

continued **Table 11.3:** Types of internationalisation support at regional level in Spain

Actions	(ES11) Galicia	(ES12) Principality of Asturias	(ES13) Cantabria	(ES21) Basque Community	(ES22) Navarre	(ES23) La Rioja	(ES24) Aragon	(ES30) Madrid	(ES41) Castile-Leon	(ES42) Castile-La Mancha	(ES43) Extremadura	(ES51) Catalonia	(ES52) Valencian Community	(ES53) Balearic Islands	(ES61) Andalusia	(ES62) Region of Murcia	(ES63) Ceuta	(ES64) Melilla	(ES70) Canary Islands
■ Training programmes for exporters									x							x			
■ Promote partnerships, collaborations, joint projects and increase participation in international networks					x		x	x		x		x				x			

Source: own elaboration on the basis of a critical review of strategies/operational programmes.

Jarosław M. Nazarczuk, Krystyna Gawlikowska-Hueckel, Tomasz Jurkiewicz

12 Increasing regional competitiveness in exports through smart specialisations: the case of Spanish and Polish regions

The problem of competitiveness has been broadly discussed in the literature. All participants of the debate agree that competitiveness as a category is not precise, which leaves it open to various interpretations. The existing literature identifies new characteristics of competitiveness. This is probably the reason why there is no single definition of the concept.

Given the abundance of different theoretical and empirical approaches to competitiveness and recent deliberations on the smart specialisation strategy towards its application in regional strategic documents, the chapter depicts how the smart specialisation concept can be used in order to raise regional competitiveness. By analysing different regional strategies of Polish and Spanish regions and relating them to real trade flows, we not only depict the importance of smart specialisation exports thereof but also formulate important policy implications regarding the inclusion of foreign trade activity in regional strategic documents.

12.1 Defining competitiveness

The first theorist to tackle the problem of competitiveness comprehensively at the country level was Porter. He believed that competitive advantage is rooted in "the results achieved by firms in competitive markets." If their advantage is a lasting one, it becomes a sustainable competitive advantage. At its source are lower costs, diversification and concentration on specific products or markets (Porter, 2010).

It should be noted that according to Porter (1998), competitive advantage results from a connection between the unique environment of a country and its competitive benefits, created by various industries (firms). Ultimately, it is the effectiveness of enterprises that is behind the economic strengths of countries or regions. The fact is stressed by Huggins et al. (2013), who say that in identifying the premises for national competitiveness, Porter pointed to the role of firms, their strength and "capacity to innovate". Competitiveness changes with time and does not depend only on the strengths and strategies of the firm, but also on how the rivals behave. "Competitiveness is not driven by static efficiency, but competitiveness is a function of dynamic progressiveness, innovation and an ability to change and improve" (Porter, 2010).

The concept of competitiveness is not, in Porter's view, unequivocal. The category of productivity is more precise. A high standard of living is now definitely less dependent on the abundance of factors of production, low cost of capital and labour or low currency prices than on productivity and the ability to improve it. It is also stressed by Krugman (1990, p. 9), who resolutely argues that "Productivity isn't everything, but in the long run it is almost everything", while Begg (1999, p. 795) maintains that productivity and competitiveness are identical concepts "at the full employment level of national income".

OECD (1992) defines competitiveness as "the degree, to which a state may produce goods and services that should pass the test of international competition and in the same time to maintain and develop its incomes at the national level, in the condition of market liberalisation".

In the Sixth Periodic Report of the European Commission (1999), competition is defined as "the ability to produce goods and services which meet the test of international markets, while at the same time maintaining high and sustainable levels of income or, more generally, the ability of (regions) to generate, while being exposed to external competition, relatively high income and employment levels," and "in other words, for a region to be competitive, it is important to ensure both quality and quantity of jobs".

Ciampi (1995, pp. 2–3) highlights the fact that competitiveness can be verified by the development of international specialisation. "Competitiveness implies elements of productivity, efficiency, profitability. But it is not an end in itself or a target. It is a powerful means to achieve rising standards of living and increasing social welfare – a tool for achieving targets. Globally, by increasing productivity and efficiency in the context of international specialisation, competitiveness provides the basis for raising people's earnings in a noninflationary way. It increases the value-added and growth potential, stimulating not only resource-saving innovation but the investment to expand capacity and to create jobs as well".

In many of the studies devoted to the issue of competitiveness, three levels of analysis may be identified; the first one deals with countries, the second with regions and the third one with firms. It should be noted that the competitiveness of firms, unlike that of nations or regions, is mercilessly verified by the market – the enterprises unable to stand the pressure of competition are eliminated from the market.[31]

By contrast, regions are perceived as deadlocked in space, and their existence continues irrespective of the condition and strength of their economies. Another important difference is that regional competition is not a zero-sum game; a rise in the competitiveness of one region does not occur at the expense of reducing the output of its rival or eliminating it altogether – as is often the case with firms.

Although factors affecting the sustainability or increased market share are different in the case of firms, regions and nations, many characteristics of competitiveness

31 With the possible exception of state-owned companies, which may be assisted through various forms of public aid.

are the same at all levels of analysis. While studying the competitiveness of firms or regions, it is impossible to ignore the macroeconomic conditions of the country or the quality of its institutions. Furthermore, as it has already been mentioned, the competitiveness of regions or nations is rooted in the power of the firms operating in their territory. This is because "competitive advantage is created and sustained through a highly localized process" (Porter, 1990, p. 19). For this reason, the levels of analysis tend to overlap, as competitiveness studies identify a host of hierarchically structured factors, which give a comprehensive description of competitiveness.

12.2 Concepts related to competitiveness

In the discussion of competitiveness, many other categories emerge, like competitive position, competitive capacity, competitive advantage. The concept of competitive advantage and competitiveness are equivalent to the perfect competition model. However, competition is now distorted by market prices, production factor prices, marketing costs and currency rates (Kannapiran and Fleming, 1999, p. 10).

Competitive position is determined by static advantages, which identify the scale of the differences (in absolute or relative terms) in the productivity of labour and capital. As the level of competitiveness and competitive advantages apply to different "competitiveness players", the advantages are not permanent and tend to fluctuate.

Bossak (2000, p. 47) defines competitive capacity as "the ability to fight, compete for the benefits connected with the nation's participation in the international division of labour". The ability to fight successfully occurs when the competitive position is sufficiently strong.

The ability is shaped during a process of constant change (so it is dynamic) and may result in improvement or deterioration of the competitive position. If less-developed regions manage to raise productivity vis-à-vis their competitors, the process of catching up occurs.

An improvement or a deterioration in the competitive position does not automatically cause changes in the competitive capacity. If a higher share in global export trade is used as a measure of the change in competitive capacity, it may not necessarily be an outcome of a better competitive position, as it may result from a better market for low-processed goods or materials, changes in terms of trade or exchange rate fluctuations.

A competitive position (and consequently, a competitive capacity) is sustainable in the long run if the pattern of exports matches the trends of global demand. It should be added, however, that these are high-tech goods that should prevail; otherwise, the advantages will not last long (e.g. a high share of oil in exports in a period of great global demand does not create such an advantage).

Hausner (2013) points out that absolute advantages are static, while the relative (comparative) advantages are dynamic. Once Ricardo's definition has been accepted, the authors claim, it means that "some of the resources in a given economy are used less effectively than in the economies with which it has to compete, but at the same time there are periods in which they are used more effectively, narrowing the absolute productivity gap between the resources. This means that the comparative advantages may lead to absolute advantages".

The common element in all these definitions is that competitiveness or the related concepts must *per se* involve the need to be compared with others (other entities, regions or nations). Martin (2003, pp. 2–4) confirms that competitiveness must be based on the test of international markets. Such a test should contain two parts: (a) the ability to sell one's goods abroad and (b) to face strong competition from foreign competitors in an open economy.

For a region to improve its competitive position, it is necessary that the firms located there conduct high-value-added activities. "To be competitive...means to be able to employ national resources, notably the nation's workforce, in such a way as to earn a rising level of real income through specialisation and trade in the world economy" (Scott, 1985). This corroborates the previously mentioned claim by Porter that enterprises are the leverage of competitiveness, securing competitive advantages for a region. Budd and Hirmis (2004, p. 1018) reiterate that there are "two parts to achieve a competitive advantage. First, the ways in which firms organize and undertake distinct activities is the basis for the growth and competitive advantage. Second, the process of discovering novel and enhanced ways of competing in the market. This constitutes innovation that includes not only technical progress but also improved working and managerial methods".

12.3 The smart approach in regions' development path and competitiveness

A discussion of a policy to enhance the competitive potential must not ignore smart specialisation, which has recently become a very prominent concept, aiming at boosting regional innovativeness, as well as their competitiveness and eventually economic growth. Through this concept, the EU tries to decrease the productivity difference of its regions with global leaders (Foray, David, and Hall, 2009) by implementing a novel approach towards innovation policy, where development of regional competitive advantage at the international scale is a crucial aspect (Dziemianowicz and Peszat, 2014). The concept is based on the place-based and evidence-based approach to building regional policy (Tödtling and Trippl, 2005), abandoning the prior top-down attitude in favour of bottom-up policies, with significant input of non-governmental entities in the process of policy prioritisation (Gianelle, Kyriakou, Cohen, and Przeor, 2016).

According to Foray (2014) smart specialisations refer to capacity an economic system has (i.e. region), in order to find/create new specialities through the discovery of new opportunity domains (activities), thanks to the existing concentration of competences, resources, capital in those domains. This capacity should have the proper strength to initiate structural transformations, diversification of economic activity, modernisation or emergence of new services/industries. Therefore, to some extent, it is usually adjacent to the existing regional strengths/advantages.

The rationale of smart specialisations relies on the effective use of locally available resources[32]/structures, subsequently transformed with the support of new (but related) research activities (Hassink and Gong, 2019) that focus on finding R&D and innovation in the existing economic structures across sectors (Foray, 2014). These new innovative domains may emerge as projects that are a complement to the existing economic structures/capabilities. Thus, the concept is more about "smart diversification" or "diversified specialisation" or "related variety" than on preserving the existing industry structures/sectoral composition of regional economies, with which it is commonly mistaken.

Within the concept, regions have to identify their key areas of competences, assets, potential or existing comparative advantages, thanks to which they may differ from other regions. These specialisations should rely on the innovative (in comparison to other regions) creation of capabilities (Asheim, 2019), which will eventually lead to incremental structural shifts, which opens more dynamic growth trajectories, even for regions whose advantages tend to fade. Actually, regional economic transformation is one of the key goals of the smart specialisation strategy, which with the use of "punctual and targeted government intervention supports the most promising new activities in terms of discovery, experimentation, potential spillover and structural changes" (Foray, 2014) tries to raise regions' competitiveness. Thus, it leads to new specialities developments, which are somehow related to the existing production assets.

In the policy, the attention is put to (Foray et al., 2009): (i) concentration of priorities, (ii) concentration on the transformation of structures (not structures itself), (iii) favouring the development discovery logic. This may be concisely summarized as the creation of such a development path for the region, in which growth factors are adequate to the endogenous potential (strengths, prospects and advantages are properly used), where a region can identify areas in which it will be able to generate innovations/comparative advantages (Trippl, Zukauskaite, and Healy, 2019). Thus, the approach means the rejection of the one-size-fits-all approach, in exchange for tailored-made policy, maximising region's growth prospects, through

32 Inputs can be also attracted from other regions, especially in the times of growing importance of intangible assets and remote working.

the transformation of available or creating new activities/domains, preferably with the intensive use R&D.

Since exports may be treated as a platform for international competitiveness (Krammer, 2017), that gives an opportunity of verifying regional comparative advantages (at international level) and knowing that exports *per se* provide a significant development chance, thus regional programs could promote the expansion of export-led activity in particular domains (i.e. high-tech or in line with regional SS).

However, Iacobucci and Guzzini (2016) point out that the analysis of strategic documents within the area of smart specialisations brings insufficient inter-regional connections between the selected domains. Furthermore, Radosevic and Ciampi Stancova (2018) imply that trans-regional cooperation, including foreign trade, is a neglected aspect of SS operation, which offers many opportunities. One of the reasons responsible for the situation might be poor understanding or insufficient knowledge on the international competitiveness of local/regional activities by the authorities (Hassink and Gong, 2019).

12.4 The role of smart specialisation-related exports in regional exports

Generally, the number of empirical papers evaluating the international aspect of smart specialisations (SS) is very limited, especially within the level of regions. That is why the following analysis presented in the chapter describes the extent to which regional exports conform to SS. The data utilised in the chapter was obtained from the Customs Chamber in Poland and Spanish DataComex (http://datacomex.comercio.es) at 4-digit CN. Owing to the database Eye@RIS, it was possible to grasp SS formulated in particular regions of Poland and Spain. Since SS are characterised by particular NACE rev. 2 activities, there was a need to precisely recode the branch/sector codes to particular product groups in exports at 4-digit CN. However, due to imprecisely formulated SS in agriculture in the Eye@RIS database, one has to bear in mind that estimates for the role of SS in agriculture-related exports may be slightly overestimated. Thus, the authors present the data on exports conforming to SS separately for agricultural and manufacturing goods. Unavailability of data on regional exports in services has restricted the analysis to the first and second sector only. One should remember that in the case of metropolitan regions or border regions, this kind of exports may play an important role in total regions' exports. Two regions of Spain (ES63) Ceuta and (ES64) Melilla, which are city-regions located in Africa were excluded from the analysis, due to the lack of SS priorities.

The approach towards data analysis in the chapter rests on the assumption that regions are analysed without national-wide division. Thus, we present (in most of the cases) regions of two countries jointly, to see if the regional-heterogeneity or national-heterogeneity better depicts the existing differences among regions. Most of the charts and tables present data for the year 2015 only. Since the data till 2005 is also available, one may hypothetically verify regional trajectories towards the importance of SS in exports. These are only potential trajectories showing rather the directions to which regional economies direct to, knowing that SS were introduced at the end of the study period.

Coming back to the analysis, the share of exports compliant with regional SS in 2015 was on average higher in Poland (48.1%) than in Spain (38.3%). In this respect, well-developed and industrialised regions of Poland (Dolnośląskie, Łódzkie, Wielkopolskie), together with Spanish Galicia and Aragon (mid-ranged in terms of GDP with a significant role of agriculture in the latter) had the highest share (Fig. 12.1). On the other side of the distribution, one may notice Balearic Islands, Catalonia, Region of Murcia (Spain), and Śląskie, Zachodniopomorskie (Poland). The group consisted of highly differentiated regions, indicating the role of the sectoral structure as well as their border/remote location.

In particular regions, like Extremadura, Valencian Community (Spain) and Podlaskie, Lubelskie (Poland), the contribution of agricultural products in exports compliant with SS was significant and exceeded 15% in all of the above-mentioned cases. Yet, the highest was in Podlaskie (ca. 26%). The contributions were representing the agriculturally-based type of the economy, in which the first sector played an important role.

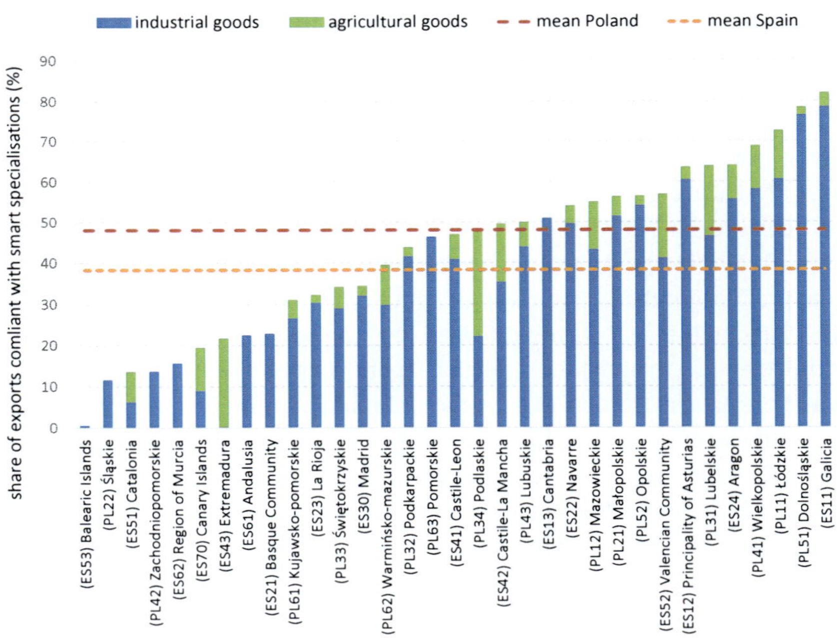

Figure 12.1: Share of exports compliant with regional smart specialisations in 2015 in total exports (%)

Source: own elaboration. Notes: (ES63) Ceuta and (ES64) Melilla were excluded from the analysis.

To reveal the importance of SS-related exports in relative terms, we calculate modified location quotient, in which regional shares of SS-compliant exports are related to national shares thereof. Thus, the distinction between regions with a relatively low and high share of exports in line with SS is based on the value of the LQ index (Table 12.1). Lower mean share of SS-compliant exports in regions of Spain has probably affected the final results, as regions of this country dominate among regions having the highest values of the index (above 1.3). Only three Polish regions – Dolnośląskie, Łódzkie, Wielkopolskie anticipated higher than 1.3 values of the location quotient.

As far as hypothetical changes of the LQ index are concerned, the highest was observed in the case of Canary Islands (-0.871), Podkarpackie (0.373) and Castile-La Mancha (0.331). In the first case, they might be the result of relatively small economy of the Canary Islands and prior high importance of agriculture, to which a few new big firms starting their operation might affect the results significantly. In the case of Podkarpackie, it was due to almost twice as high export share of manufacturing products in line with SS, at least to some extent thanks to the expanding aviation sector. Castile-La Mancha contrary to the previous cases, anticipated an increase in the role of agricultural (4.0 pp.) and manufacturing (4.6 pp.) products as well. Thus it generated a high increase in total SS-related exports contribution.

Another dimension diversifying regional export characteristics is product concentration. Since regions have different compositions of sectors and their importance for the whole regional economy, we have decided to present values of the export product analysis divided into those (i) compliant with SS and (ii) non-SS compliant – with the use of HHI (Fig. 12.2).

The resulting image clearly differentiates variation among the two, indicating higher in the case of SS-related exports. In regions of Pomorskie, Podkarpackie (Poland), and the Balearic Islands, Castile-Leon, Navarre, Aragon (Spain) the role of a few products was key in total SS-related exports. These were either highly specialised manufacturing regions or small economies to which operation of particular branches/firms was crucial. Contrary to them, mostly well-developed regions of Poland (with the exception of Lubelskie and Opolskie) had the lowest product concentration of SS-compliant exports (see first 8 regions on Fig. 12.2), signalling high differentiation of exporting products falling into SS.

Different contribution of particular products in regions' exports constitutes for their specific regional specialisation, also in the case of products in line with regional SS. Krugman specialisation index is a fairly frequently used metric to reveal cross-regional differences in the sectoral composition with a reference area. In the study, it was applied at 4-digit CN for regions' exports to reveal the extent to which regions' composition of product groups is falling into the national-wide volume of exports or the opposite (Fig. 12.3).

Table 12.1: The role of smart specialisation in exports in relative terms (LQ)

Regions	2005*	2015	change	Regions	2005*	2015	change
Regions with a relatively low share of SS related exports				**Regions with a relatively high share of SS related exports**			
(ES53) Balearic Islands	0.012	0.018	0.006	(PL43) Lubuskie	1.023	1.015	-0.008
(PL22) Śląskie	0.161	0.236	0.075	(PL12) Mazowieckie	1.095	1.117	0.022
(PL42) Zachodniopomorskie	0.277	0.278	0.001	(PL21) Małopolskie	1.178	1.143	-0.035
(ES51) Catalonia	0.312	0.379	0.067	(PL52) Opolskie	1.231	1.147	-0.084
(ES62) Region of Murcia	0.699	0.436	-0.263	(PL31) Lubelskie	1.563	1.296	-0.268
(ES70) Canary Islands	1.413	0.542	-0.871	(ES41) Castile-Leon	1.449	1.312	-0.137
(ES43) Extremadura	0.438	0.605	0.167	(ES42) Castile-La Mancha	1.053	1.384	0.331
(ES61) Andalusia	0.769	0.629	-0.140	(PL41) Wielkopolskie	1.534	1.396	-0.137
(PL61) Kujawsko-pomorskie	0.609	0.631	0.021	(ES13) Cantabria	1.322	1.424	0.102
(ES21) Basque Community	0.658	0.640	-0.018	(PL11) Łódzkie	1.712	1.474	-0.238
(PL33) Świętokrzyskie	0.823	0.694	-0.129	(ES22) Navarre	1.607	1.509	-0.098
(PL62) Warmińsko-mazurskie	1.035	0.802	-0.233	(ES52) Valencian Community	1.416	1.589	0.172
(PL32) Podkarpackie	0.516	0.888	0.373	(PL51) Dolnośląskie	1.685	1.594	-0.091
(ES23) La Rioja	0.982	0.901	-0.080	(ES12) Principality of Asturias	1.892	1.772	-0.120
(PL63) Pomorskie	1.077	0.941	-0.136	(ES24) Aragon	2.046	1.785	-0.261
(ES30) Madrid	1.013	0.962	-0.051	(ES11) Galicia	2.234	2.288	0.054
(PL34) Podlaskie	0.719	0.980	0.261				

Source: own estimation.
Information: The indices were calculated in a similar way LQ is obtained. It is the share of regional exports compliant with SS divided by its corresponding value at the national level. Thus, it reflects a relative position of regions, corresponding to the national-level heterogeneity. Regions in the table were sorted with reference to the LQ index in 2015. * The data on 2005 is hypothetical as in this year no SS were introduced. However, owing to the data, one may find the trajectories towards SS regions had over the past decade.

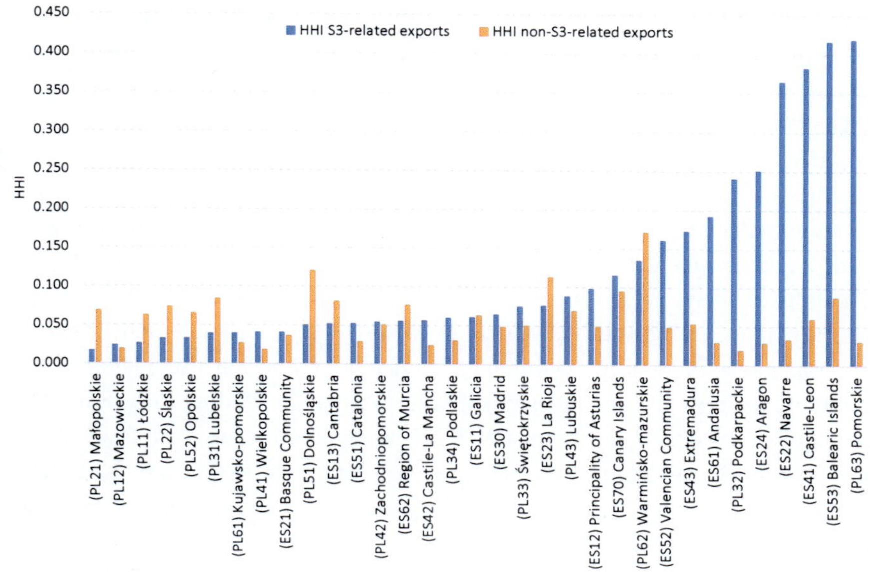

Figure 12.2: Product concentration of SS-related exports vs non-SS-related exports in regions of Spain and Poland in 2015

Source: own elaboration. Notes: Regions were sorted within their HHI SS-related exports.

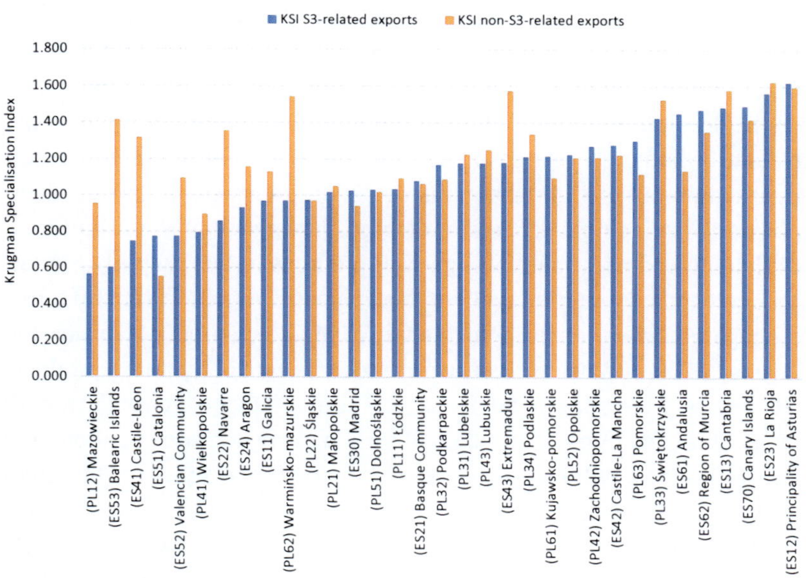

Figure 12.3: Regional specialisation (Krugman Specialisation Index – KSI) of SS-related exports vs non-SS-related exports in regions of Spain and Poland in 2015

Source: own estimates. Notes: Higher values of KSI indicates a higher level of dissimilarity with the total national export structure.

Due to the fact that the role of SS is a concern in this chapter, the index was calculated for exports (i) falling into SS and (ii) not conforming to the above, separately. Obviously, bigger regions in terms of their contribution to total (national) exports matter more, given their volume of exports; thus they simultaneously are more similar to the reference area, which is national exports.

The highest dissimilarities for SS-related exports were obtained for mainly Spanish regions Principality of Asturias, La Rioja, Canary Islands, Cantabria, Region of Murcia. On the contrary, the lowest were observed in Mazowieckie, Wielkopolskie (Poland), Balearic Islands, Castile-Leon, Catalonia, Valencian Community (Spain).

Since the share of high-tech products in exports may to some extent measure the competitiveness of regional economies, that is why another dimension of the study attempts to verify the extent to which high-tech exports falling into SS matters for total regional exports, compliant with SS. It was not an issue for a few regions of Spain (Basque Community, Extremadura, Catalonia, Balearic Islands, Canary Islands) and one in Poland (Warmińsko-mazurskie) as their share equalled null (Fig. 12.4). These were mostly small and underdeveloped economies (with the exception of Catalonia) and periphery located. On average in 2015, regions of Poland had a higher mean level of high-tech products falling into SS (8.8%), compared to its Spanish counterparts (4.9).

The highest high-tech products' share in total SS-related exports was observed in Podkarpackie, Śląskie (Poland) and Madrid, Andalusia (Spain). To some extent, the results indicated the importance of aviation valley in Podkarpackie, tech-hub in Madrid, Technological Park in Andalusia, Technological Park in Gliwice (Śląskie).

The results clearly show that only a fraction of regions can build their competitive advantages on the development of high-tech industries since, in most of the regions, the high-tech contribution to SS-related exports is negligible. These could be a result of insufficient attention put to high-tech industries in SS-priorities or their absence/ incidental appearance in regional economies. Regions having a high contribution in this respect anticipated a lower share of high-tech products in total exports, signalling the pro technological orientation of SS in these regions. Albeit, in general terms not all of these regions, had a relatively high share of high-tech products in exports. The case of Śląskie (5.9%) with below than average contribution of high-tech products in total exports proves that certain regions may build their advantages with intense use of technological-related branches. In light of this, many regions do not attempt to utilize their capabilities, even though they possess an above-average contribution of high-tech products in exports.

Detailed data on exports also enables us to verify the extent to which products created in regions can face international competition. Following Radosevic and Ciampi Stancova (2018), we treat foreign trade as a platform for verification of international competitiveness. To reveal the level of regional competitiveness, a Balasa-type revealed competitiveness index (RCA) is calculated, with a reference area of EU, which enables cross-regional comparisons without a distinction of a country of origin.

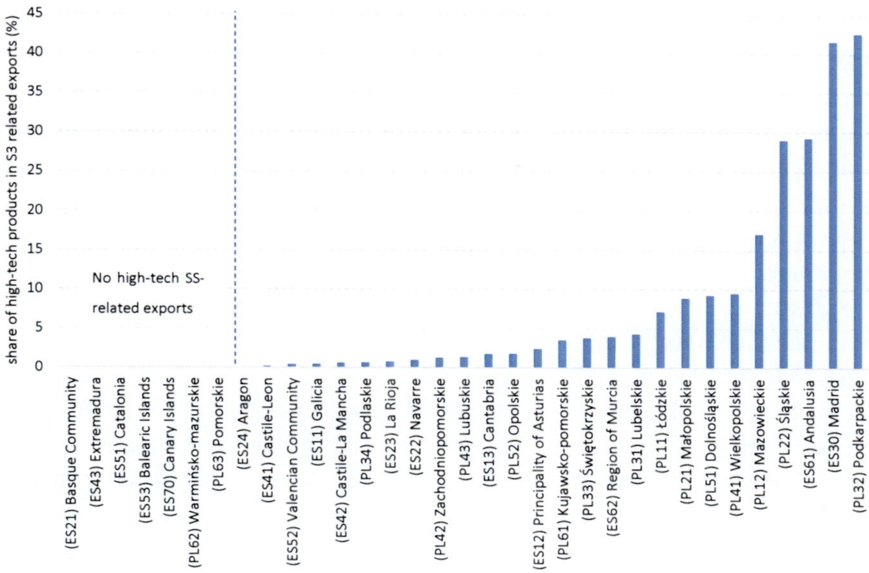

Figure 12.4: Share of high-tech products in SS-related exports in 2015
Source: own estimation.

Since particular product groups have a different contribution to regional exports, the authors decided to utilize the weighted version of RCA of the index. It corrects the possible spikes for RCA in product groups with a small export share. The calculation was carried out for 4-digit CN product groups (ca. 1,300 product groups in total).

The results show the number of product groups in exports (total), as well as the above-number for product groups having WRCA>2, WRCA>5, respectively (Table 12.2). It represents thus the number of product groups having its share in regional exports two or five times higher than on average in the whole EU. Additionally, information on the number of product groups falling into SS and having WRCA>2 or WRCA>5 is presented. Finally, by relating the number of products groups in SS-related exports to the total number of products in exports having a high weighted revealed comparative advantage, we try to show the extent to which regional SS (on the basis of export data) fit into the existing comparative advantages in exports at the European level.

The analysed regions differ substantially in terms of the number of products exported, which correlates well with the size of the economies, as well as their level of competitiveness. The highest number of product groups with WRCA >2 was a domain of Galicia, Castile-La Mancha (Spain) and Łódzkie, Dolnośląskie, Małopolskie, Wielkopolskie, Mazowieckie (Poland). Yet, these were mostly Polish regions that anticipated the highest share of SS-related product groups with RCA>2 in exports, together with Spanish Galicia. A similar situation occurred when dealing with WRCA>5.

Particularly interesting is the issue of regions having the lowest share of SS-related products in exports with WRCA>2 like the Balearic Islands, Andalusia (Spain) and Zachodniopomorskie (Poland). The regions accrued in their SS less than 10% of their product groups in exports with high competitiveness. These were mainly tourist regions, with high importance of services in their economies, which due to the type of data provided in the chapter (export of manufacturing and agricultural products) are excluded from the analysis. Thus, in the case of regions where services play a dominant role, the obtained results might be underestimated in terms of showing the real impact of SS. Similarly, mostly manufacturing regions may encounter higher values of the index.

Knowing the above limitations, we try to answer the question in which country on average the SS fit to a higher extent into the existing comparative advantages in product-related exports. In this respect, we address the correlation between the no. of product groups with WRCA > 2 in exports and corresponding no. of product groups (also with WRCA > 2) in exports compliant with SS. In theory, the higher the match between the two, the higher the R^2 representing the goodness of the fit. Scatter plots depicting the existing relations between the variables of interest are presented in figure (Fig. 12.5).

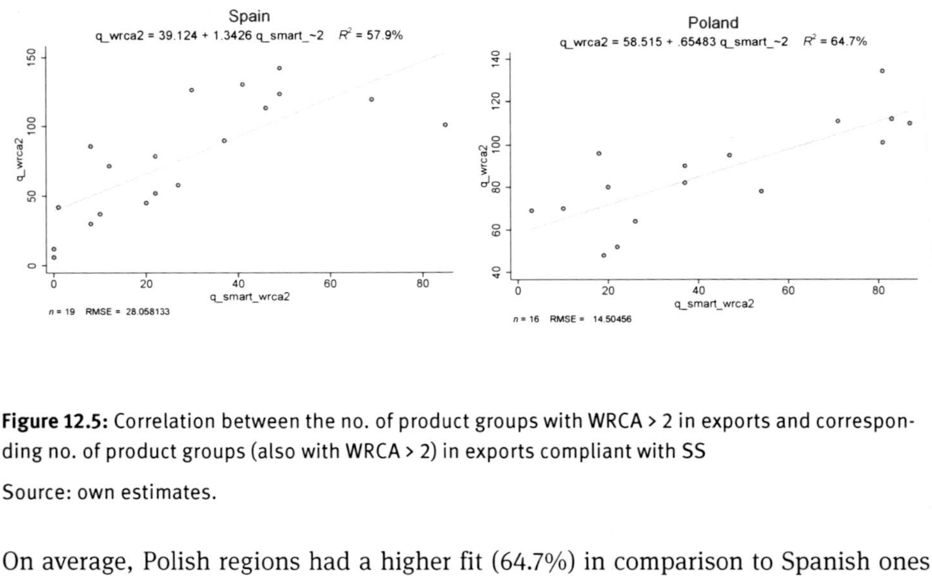

Figure 12.5: Correlation between the no. of product groups with WRCA > 2 in exports and corresponding no. of product groups (also with WRCA > 2) in exports compliant with SS

Source: own estimates.

On average, Polish regions had a higher fit (64.7%) in comparison to Spanish ones (57.9%), which signalled their higher rootedness in endogenous exporting regional potential. Once one removes two Spanish regions Ceuta and Melilla (not having SS) R^2 for Spain drops to 49.1. Obviously, the results should be treated with caution, as they do not incorporate exports of services. However, they directly show more product and export-oriented approach towards establishment of SS in Polish regions.

Finally, changes in the importance of SS in exports were calculated. Since SS were introduced at the end of the available time span, the indices presented below may be treated only as hypothetic due to data constraints. We show them only to present

Table 12.2: No. of product groups in 2015 with high WRCA in total exports and compliant with smart specialisations

Region	No. of product groups	Total exports	SS exports	SS (%)	Total exports	SS exports	SS (%)
		WRCA > 2			WRCA > 5		
(ES11) Galicia	1045	101	85	84.2	49	41	83.7
(PL11) Łódzkie	968	101	81	80.2	36	29	80.6
(PL51) Dolnośląskie	987	110	87	79.1	42	34	81.0
(PL21) Małopolskie	1017	112	83	74.1	57	42	73.7
(PL31) Lubelskie	910	78	54	69.2	35	30	85.7
(PL41) Wielkopolskie	1051	111	71	64.0	54	35	64.8
(PL12) Mazowieckie	1132	134	81	60.4	48	31	64.6
(ES42) Castile-La Mancha	957	119	69	58.0	43	20	46.5
(PL52) Opolskie	839	95	47	49.5	42	25	59.5
(ES12) Principality of Asturias	783	58	27	46.6	29	12	41.4
(PL43) Lubuskie	824	82	37	45.1	44	23	52.3
(ES13) Cantabria	653	45	20	44.4	27	14	51.9
(PL33) Świętokrzyskie	636	52	22	42.3	29	11	37.9
(ES23) La Rioja	679	52	22	42.3	26	12	46.2
(PL61) Kujawsko-pomorskie	857	90	37	41.1	44	16	36.4
(ES41) Castile-Leon	966	90	37	41.1	34	8	23.5
(ES24) Aragon	963	113	46	40.7	35	13	37.1
(PL34) Podlaskie	815	64	26	40.6	31	14	45.2
(ES52) Valencian Community	1152	123	49	39.8	52	22	42.3
(PL62) Warmińsko-mazurskie	763	48	19	39.6	26	9	34.6
(ES51) Catalonia	1205	142	49	34.5	34	15	44.1
(ES30) Madrid	1168	130	41	31.5	39	17	43.6
(ES22) Navarre	822	79	22	27.8	31	7	22.6
(ES70) Canary Islands	797	37	10	27.0	22	7	31.8
(ES43) Extremadura	733	30	8	26.7	15	6	40.0
(PL32) Podkarpackie	900	80	20	25.0	26	3	11.5
(ES21) Basque Community	1079	126	30	23.8	52	16	30.8
(PL22) Śląskie	1070	96	18	18.8	43	9	20.9
(ES62) Region of Murcia	916	72	12	16.7	36	6	16.7
(PL63) Pomorskie	909	70	10	14.3	33	7	21.2
(ES61) Andalusia	1119	86	8	9.3	51	4	7.8
(PL42) Zachodniopomorskie	923	69	3	4.3	32	0	0.0
(ES53) Balearic Islands	653	42	1	2.4	26	0	0.0

Source: own estimation.

Note: data were sorted by the 5th column.

the possible trajectories regional economies direct to as regards the share of exports compliant with SS.

Surprisingly, the mean share of SS-related exports followed two different paths in Poland and Spain (Fig. 12.6). While it increased in Poland from ca. 45.9% in 2005 to 48.1% in 2015, in Spain it followed a different trend. Mean share of exports compliant with SS decreased in Spain from 43.3% to 38.3% within the same period. The results seem to be unforeseeable as they present different approaches to changes in the role of SS. Yet, one has to keep in mind that the results of the inquiry, presented in that chapter, cover only agricultural and manufacturing products; thus the apparent decreased trend in Spanish regions may stem from their structural changes owing to shifts from the role of the first and second sector to the third sector of the economy. These needs obviously further research.

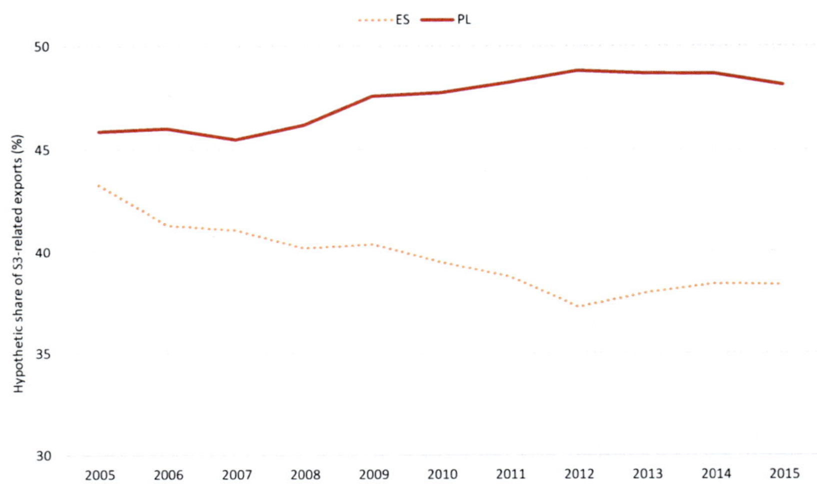

Figure 12.6: Hypothetic mean share of SS-related exports in regions of Spain and Poland between 2005 and 2015

Source: own elaboration.

12.5 Conclusions

Most of the differences between Polish and Spanish regions in terms of the role SS play in exports stem from cross-regional heterogeneity; however, few characteristics seem to be more country-specific. Generally, the mean contribution of exports in line with SS was on average higher in the case of Polish regions as compared to their Spanish counterparts, yet it is only a part of the bigger picture, due to data constraints (lack of information on exports in services). Thus, it is difficult to precisely answer the question to what extent regions utilize their export potential in terms of formulated SS.

In fact, the available data shows, however, that many regions could do better in exploiting their existing comparative advantages in exports as their number of products with revealed comparative advantages (when EU market is taken as a reference) greatly surpass the number of product groups with RCA in SS-related exports. The findings also direct to the need of higher attention put to the use of exporting data or RCAs in SS.

Since foreign trade may be treated as a platform verifying international competitiveness, local/regional authorities with the knowledge of region's RCAs, as well as other region-specific characteristics (incl. ability to generate R&D in particular activities), may increase their chances to fit into domains/industries that have strong revealed competitive advantages in the region, that could have enough critical mass to initiate positive structural shifts (i.e. with the collaboration of R&D). To date, it seems to be a neglected aspect of SS strategy as regional strategic documents and operational programmes predominantly do not incorporate this type of international activity in their priorities.

Since foreign trade is a true validator or international competitiveness, which verifies comparative advantages regions have, there is a need of higher attention put to the international aspect of competitiveness in the process of SS' formulation. This product-based approach offers a high resolution of the data needed to depict specialisations, thus gives the possibility of a precise declaration of particular SS. Secondly, it enables fairy easy post-evaluation of the already set priorities, given the availability of regional trade data in selected countries. It can also provide evidence-based information on the role of particular industries/activities regions have in terms of their competitiveness as well as to better understand the foundations of the regional competitiveness.

Part V: **Concluding remarks of the book**

The approach to the research we have decided on is not common in the literature. Analysis of exports and imports is usually performed at the country level. Theories and concepts applicable to international trade, with their strict assumptions, have been formulated with respect to countries – not to regions. Their usage to interpret exporting (and importing) activity of regions is often problematic. A scientific purist would hardly accept the application of Heckscher-Ohlin or Intra-Industry Trade (IIT) concepts to the regional level analysis. We, therefore, propose the use of a region as a small open economy concept (SOE), which bridges the regional and international economics.

An interesting process can be captured in the theoretical layer. In fact, there appears an integrated theory of localisation, factors endowment, increasing returns to scale, which is composed of New Economic Geography (NEG) (evolving into New, New Economic Geography) and international trade theory (Cieślik, 2005). Although the geographers do not always agree with the economists (Martin, 1999a; Martin, 1999b; Martin and Sunley, 2011), the framework of NEG opens many interesting possibilities helpful in interpretation and understanding of economic processes in regions. The NEG brought the issue of space into the mainstream economic theory. International economics has also opened itself to threads from other sciences, gravity being a perfect example. The discussion in the literature is pending, however, and the question often asked is if countries are flat (Krugman, 2015) or lumpy (Courant and Deardorff, 1992). We envisage that the process of bridging the gap between regional and international economics will be continued; the main reason being the growing dependence of regional economies on international relations. It shall create better, comprehensive theoretical foundations for regional export analysis.

A function of a region as an exporter has been neglected in the literature. However, which shall be underlined, the straight application of international theories to the regional level of analysis and interpretations is difficult. A good example is IIT. For instance, much is known about the consequences of IIT vs inter-industry trade. The abundant literature sheds light on the redistribution of income as an effect of international trade, the improved accesses to product variety, merits of economies of scale etc. This issue addressed to regional economies, has so far not been seriously tackled. The relationship between openness and economic growth and a region's economic situation is sophisticated, and to a great extent, ambiguous. The consequences of trade openness for regions' economic growth, as mentioned, are hard to predict. Our conclusion is that for Polish and Spanish regions, bigger openness affects growth in a positive way. The issue, however, deserves further, more formal inquiry and a question remains: how much openness is "safe", and beyond which threshold is there serious volatility brought to the regional economy? Spatial determinants and interactions shall be taken into account more seriously in international trade analysis. A good example showing the permeation of regional and international economics is Dutch Disease. It perfectly illustrates the consequences of uneven regional development through the international economics "lens".

The main prerequisite that brought our interest to the regional level of analysis is that in line with the nations' economies becoming more open, regions became more open and heterogeneous. Openness brings positive and negative consequences for them. On the one hand, it enables competitive firms to flourish and expand to new, foreign markets. On the other, over-competitive pressure eliminates less competitive firms from the market. One of the reasons to inquire into the regional economies participation in the global economy is improving the availability of statistical data. International trade theories are changing; space is more often incorporated. Space shall be treated as a factor of production (Capello, 2016), that determines the competitive position of firms and their performance on the international market. Reference to regions as SOE shows us how diversified they are in respect to the ability to participate in the global economy.

Without paying so much attention to serious, sound theoretical foundations, empirical research on regions' exports has been developing. Early works that deserve attention can be traced as early as in the 1970s for Canada and the US. Empirical research reflected, to a great extent, the evolving international economics as such. Therefore, such threads can be identified in the empirical layer, as the role of foreign direct investments (FDI), the role of the industrial base (vs intermediary function performed by the region), exports promotion, agglomeration and border effect. Recently, the shift into firms' heterogeneity can be observed, with a focus on the role of FDI, which reflects the changing international trade theory nature, incorporating firms' heterogeneity.

The taxonomy of regions depicts many aspects in which their participation in international trade differs. We treat our diagnosis as a first step towards more detailed assessments of regions' export profiles, necessary for efficient exports promotion. It can also be treated as a sort of vulnerability map, depicting possible consequences of economic shocks coming from the external economies, such as Brexit, negotiation of trade agreements, monetary integration, trade conflicts or global slowdown.

The inquiry into the determinants of foreign trade has identified orthodox and non-orthodox factors, which shall be taken into account in the formulation of regions' export strategy. The gravity model has proven its usefulness as a tool in explaining the nature of regions' foreign trade links. The concept of gravity shall be used by regional authorities more frequently than now to capture trade regularities as well as to predict the consequences of alterations of foreign trade policy, currency unions, trade costs changes and infrastructure development.

Although the domain of exports promotion, according to the EU legislation, is an exclusive competence of the EU institutions, regions possess economic policy instruments that can be used in boosting foreign sales. The effectiveness of their usage seems to be a promising subject of further research, as is in the case of the US economy (Cassey, 2008, 2010c, 2014).

Recently, smart specialisation has become the key framework through which regions shall build their unique competitive capabilities. We have identified the serious drawback of smart specialisations, which is not paying proper attention to foreign trade performance. A reason is probably a poor understanding of international competitiveness by regional authorities. Many regions of Poland and Spain could perform much better in exports, through (i) strengthening their existing comparative advantages with the intensive use of R&D within smart specialisation policy instruments, (ii) or identifying and exploiting the new domains of the unique, innovative competence.

Several policy recommendations can be formulated as regards regions' exporting activity:

1. Because of globalisation, flows of FDI and economic integration processes, regional economies will be more dependent on the external sector (exports). Therefore, the export characteristics (profiles), incl. SWOT analysis shall be prepared for each region. Such a profile shall identify a region's vulnerability to the challenges stemming from globalisation and economic shocks as well as to increase the effectiveness of exports support.
2. To do so, the foreign trade statistical data availability ought to be improved. This remark relates to Poland in particular. In Spain, a dataset on regions' exports and imports is available online; however, more information shall be provided, for instance, related to the share of foreign-owned entities in exports. For Poland, the system of data collection is highly imperfect, the better correspondence of information on exports and imports with the regional economies (industrial base) shall be worked out. According to the legal rules, a firm is obliged to report exports only if it exceeds a certain value threshold in intra-EU trade. It reduces administrative burdens for the reporting companies; however, it makes thorough inquiry difficult. As scientists, we ought to postulate to establish a more detailed statistical system for regions' firms' exports reporting, as it is crucial from the point of view of designing and implementing effective regional economic policy. Also, the data availability on services exports from regions shall be seriously improved. In Poland, a serious drawback is internal trade data unavailability, which makes border effect analysis impossible, as can be done for Spain, Australia and Canada for instance.
3. Bridging the gap between regional and international economics, in theory, is a difficult and long-term perspective process. Nonetheless, the international economics apparatus shall be more intensively used in the regional export empirical analysis. The benefits from assessing regions' exports performance, characteristics, SWOT and potential are so important that a researcher can take a risk that some of the strict assumptions of international theories and concepts applied to regions are not fulfilled.
4. Understanding the nature of the economic processes at the regional level without a serious look into a region's external economic relations is difficult or almost impossible. Many of the ongoing problems of regional economies and the structural trends thereof (particularly in the labour market) cannot be comprehensively

understood without, for instance, analysis of FDI, the motive of foreign investors' activity and their OLI advantages.

5. The external relations (exports and imports) component shall become much more important in the formulation and implementation of regions' smart specialisation strategies. We postulate that the smart specialisation strategies shall be the core platform coordinating economic policy aimed at competitiveness improvements with the focus on international activity (exports and FDI).
6. Analysis of any international trade relations in which a country is engaged, incl. trade agreements, tariff alterations or exports promotion schemes, shall refer to a country export internal diversity and lumpiness. Our research has proven that, on the one hand, exports are concentrated in a few regions; on the other hand, even if a region does not belong to the main exporters, it can still be highly open to foreign trade, which makes its economies extraordinarily vulnerable to external economic shocks. Thus, the adjustments to global economic changes are region-specific, depending on the geographic and product structures, the share of high-tech commodities, the role of FDI, firms' productivity and – last but not least – the capacity of regions' economies to adapt.
7. The experiences of other countries (the Netherlands, Australia and, Canada) show that export success in specific circumstances (relying on the extensive extraction of raw materials) can result in serious troubles, which is known as DD. It must be remembered that DD can generally stem from the unequal development of export capabilities, which may bring cost increases (for instance agglomeration and congestion costs). The regional economic policy shall consider the long-term consequences of intensive, unbalanced export potential increases. Regional policy (incl. smart specialisation schemes) shall work in favour of creating opportunities for the diffusion of exports knowledge and expertise, in order to reduce the sunk costs and risk for firms already in their initial stages of internationalisation. In other words, it is better for a regional economy to have more of exporters with lower exports to total sales ratio, that a few exporters with high export intensity.

On behalf of the research team,
Stanisław Umiński
Jarosław M. Nazarczuk

References

Abreu, M., Groot, H. L. F. de, & Florax, R. J.G.M. (2004). Space and Growth: A Survey of Empirical Evidence and Methods. *SSRN Electronic Journal*. Advance online publication. https://doi.org/10.2139/ssrn.631007

ABS (2018a). 8155.0 - *Australian industry.*

ABS (2019a). 1345.0 - *Key economic indicators, summary.*

ABS (2019b). *Data by region.* Retrieved from https://itt.abs.gov.au/itt/r.jsp?databyregion#/

ABS (2019c). 5368.0 - *International trade in goods and services, Australia, Aug 2019.*

Acemoglu, D., & Zilibotti, F. (2001). Productivity Differences. *Quarterly Journal of Economics*, *116*(2), 563–606. https://doi.org/10.1162/00335530151144104

Acosta, P. A., Lartey, E. K.K., & Mandelman, F. S. (2009). Remittances and the Dutch disease. *Journal of International Economics*, *79*(1), 102–116. https://doi.org/10.1016/j.jinteco.2009.06.007

Aghion, P., & Howitt, P. (1990). *A Model of Growth Through Creative Destruction*. Cambridge, MA: National Bureau of Economic Research.

Aghion, P., & Howitt, P. (1998). *Endogenous growth theory* (2. print). Cambridge, Mass.: MIT Press.

Aghion, P., & Howitt, P. (2009). *The economics of growth*. Cambridge (Mass.), London: MIT Press.

Aghion, P., Howitt, P., & Mayer-Foulkes, D. (2005). The Effect of Financial Development on Convergence: Theory and Evidence. *Quarterly Journal of Economics*, *120*(1), 173–222. https://doi.org/10.1162/qjec.2005.120.1.173

Aitken, B., Hanson, G. H., & Harrison, A. E. (1997). Spillovers, foreign investment, and export behavior. *Journal of International Economics*, *43*(1-2), 103–132. https://doi.org/10.1016/S0022-1996(96)01464-X

Alamá-Sabater, L., Márquez-Ramos, L., Navarro-Azorín, J. M., & Suárez-Burguet, C. (2015). A two-methodology comparison study of a spatial gravity model in the context of interregional trade flows. *Applied Economics*, *47*(14), 1481–1493. https://doi.org/10.1080/00036846.2014.997929

Alfaro, L., Chanda, A., Kalemli-Ozcan, S., & Sayek, S. (2004). FDI and economic growth: The role of local financial markets. *Journal of International Economics*, *64*(1), 89–112. https://doi.org/10.1016/S0022-1996(03)00081-3

Álvarez, I. C., Rodríguez-Pose, A., & Zofío, J. L. (2018). Does institutional quality matter for trade? Institutional conditions in a sectoral trade framework. *World Development*. (103), 72–87.

Amiti, M. (1999). Specialization patterns in Europe. *Weltwirtschaftliches Archiv*, *135*(4), 573–593.

Anderson, J. E., & van Wincoop, E. (2003). Gravity with Gravitas: A Solution to the Border Puzzle. *American Economic Review*, *93*(1), 170–192. https://doi.org/10.1257/000282803321455214

Anderson, M., & Smith, S. (1999a). Canadian Provinces in World Trade: Engagement and Detachment. *The Canadian Journal of Economics / Revue canadienne d'Economique*, *32*(1), 22–38. https://doi.org/10.2307/136393

Anderson, M., & Smith, S. (1999b). Do National Borders Really Matter? Canada-US Regional Trade Reconsidered. *Review of International Economics*, *7*(2), 219–227. https://doi.org/10.1111/1467-9396.00158

Antras, P., & Yeaple, S. R. (2014). Multinational Firms and the Structure of International Trade. In G. Gopinath, E. Helpman, & K. S. Rogoff (Eds.), *Handbooks in economics. Handbook of international economics* (pp. 55–130). Amsterdam, New York: North Holland; Elsevier.

Anwar, S., & Nguyen, L. P. (2010). Foreign direct investment and economic growth in Vietnam. *Asia Pacific Business Review*, *16*(1-2), 183–202. https://doi.org/10.1080/10438590802511031

Aray, H. (2015). Hysteresis and import penetration with decreasing sunk entry costs. *International Economics and Economic Policy*, *12*(2), 175–188. https://doi.org/10.1007/s10368-014-0269-8

Armington, P. S. (1969). A theory of demand for products distinguished by place of production. *Staff Papers - International Monetary Fund*, *16*(1), 159. https://doi.org/10.2307/3866403

Armstrong, H. W., & Taylor, J. (2000). *Regional economics and policy* (3. ed.). Oxford: Blackwell.

Asheghian, P. (2004). Determinants of Economic Growth In The United States: The Role of Foreign Direct Investment. *The International Trade Journal*, *18*(1), 63–83. https://doi.org/10.1080/08853900490277350

Asheim, B. T. (2019). Smart specialisation, innovation policy and regional innovation systems: What about new path development in less innovative regions? *Innovation: The European Journal of Social Science Research*, *32*(1), 8–25. https://doi.org/10.1080/13511610.2018.1491001

Athukorala, P.-C., & Rajapatirana, S. (2003). Capital Inflows and the Real Exchange Rate: A Comparative Study of Asia and Latin America. *The World Economy*, *26*(4), 613–637. https://doi.org/10.1111/1467-9701.00539

Australian Government (2018). *Our country*.

Australian Government (2019). *ABS Labour Force Region*. Retrieved from http://lmip.gov.au/default.aspx?LMIP/Downloads/ABSLabourForceRegion

Bachtler, J., & Mendez, C. (2007). Who Governs EU Cohesion Policy? Deconstructing the Reforms of the Structural Funds. *JCMS: Journal of Common Market Studies*, *45*(3), 535–564. https://doi.org/10.1111/j.1468-5965.2007.00724.x

Baier, S. L., & Bergstrand, J. H. (2009). Bonus vetus OLS: A simple method for approximating international trade-cost effects using the gravity equation. *Journal of International Economics*, *77*(1), 77–85. https://doi.org/10.1016/j.jinteco.2008.10.004

Bakker, J. D. (2018). International trade and regional inequality. *CEPREMAP*.

Balassa, B. (1978). Exports and economic growth. *Journal of Development Economics*, *5*(2), 181–189. https://doi.org/10.1016/0304-3878(78)90006-8

Balasubramanyam, V. N., Salisu, M., & Sapsford, D. (1996). Foreign Direct Investment and Growth in EP and is Countries. *The Economic Journal*, *106*(434), 92. https://doi.org/10.2307/2234933

Baldwin, J. R., & Brown, W.M. (2004). Regional manufacturing employment volatility in Canada: The effects of specialisation and trade. *Papers in Regional Science*, *83*(3). https://doi.org/10.1007/s10110-004-0210-6

Baldwin, R. (1999). *The Core-Periphery Model with Forward-Looking Expectations*. Cambridge, MA: National Bureau of Economic Research.

Baldwin, R., & Forslid, R. (1999). *The Core-Periphery Model and Endogenous Growth: Stabilising and De-Stabilising Integration*. Cambridge, MA: National Bureau of Economic Research.

Baldwin, R., Forslid, R., Martin, P., Ottaviano, G., & Frederic, R.-N. (2001). *The Core-Periphery Model: Key Features and effects*. Retrieved from http://econ.sciences-po.fr/sites/default/files/martinp/CPmodel.pdf

Baldwin, R., Forslid, R., Martin, P., Ottaviano, G., & Robert-Nicoud, F. (2011). *Economic geography and public policy*: Princeton University Press.

Baldwin, R., & Okubo, T. (2009). Tax Reform, Delocation, and Heterogeneous Firms. *The Scandinavian Journal of Economics*, *111*(4), 741–764.

Baldwin, R. E., & Martin, P. (2004). Agglomeration and regional growth. In V. J. Henderson & J. F. Thisse (Eds.), *Handbook of Regional and Urban Economics* (1st ed., Vol. 4, pp. 2671–2711). Elsevier.

Baldwin, Richard E., The Euro's Trade Effects (March 2006). ECB Working Paper No. 594. Available at SSRN: https://ssrn.com/abstract=886260

Baldwin, R. E., & Okubo, T. (2006). Heterogeneous firms, agglomeration and economic geography: Spatial selection and sorting. *Journal of Economic Geography*, *6*(3), 323–346. https://doi.org/10.1093/jeg/lbi020

Barham, Bradford, L., & Coomes, Olivier, T. (1994). Reinterpreting the Amazon Rubber Boom: Investment, the State, and DutchDisease. *Latin American Research Review*, *29*(2), 73–109.

Barro, R. J. (1992). Convergence. *Journal of Political Economy, 100*(2), 223–251. https://doi.org/10.1086/261816

Barro, R. J., & Sala-i-Martin, X. (2004). *Economic growth* (2nd ed.). Cambridge, Mass: MIT Press. Retrieved from http://search.ebscohost.com/login.aspx?direct=true&scope=site&db=nlebk&db=nlabk&AN=138607

Barua, A., & Sawhney, A. (2015). Development Policy Implications for Growth and Regional Inequality in a Small Open Economy: The Indian Case. *Review of Development Economics, 19*(3), 695–709. https://doi.org/10.1111/rode.12154

Basu, P., Chakraborty, C., & Reagle, D. (2003). Liberalization, FDI, and Growth in Developing Countries: A Panel Cointegration Approach. *Economic Inquiry, 41*(3), 510–516. https://doi.org/10.1093/ei/cbg024

Batabyal, A. A., & Nijkamp, P. (2015). *The region and trade: New analytical directions*. New Jersey: World Scientific.

Battersby, B., & Ewing, R. (2005). International trade performance: the gravity of Australia's remoteness. The Treasury.

Beaulieu, E. (2000). The Canada-U.S. Free Trade Agreement and labour market adjustment in Canada. *Canadian Journal of Economics/Revue Canadienne d'Economique, 33*(2), 540–563. https://doi.org/10.1111/0008-4085.00028

Begg, I. (1999). Cities and Competitiveness. *Urban Studies, 36*(5-6), 795–809. https://doi.org/10.1080/0042098993222

Behrens, K. (2005). Market size and industry location. Traded vs non-traded goods. *Journal of Urban Economics, 58*(1), 24–44. https://doi.org/10.1016/j.jue.2005.01.002

Behrens, K., Lamorgese, A., Ottaviano, G. I. P., & Tabuchi, T. (2004). Testing the home market effect in a multi-country world: the theory. *CEPR Discussion Paper*. (4468).

Behrens, K., & Thisse, J.-F. (2007). Regional economics: A new economic geography perspective. *Regional Science and Urban Economics, 37*(4), 457–465. https://doi.org/10.1016/j.regsciurbeco.2006.10.001

Behrman, Jack, N. (1972). *The Role of International Companies in Latin America: Autos and Petrochemicals*. Lexington, MA: Lexington Books.

Beine, M. A. R., Bos, C. S., & Coulombe, S. (2009). Does the Canadian Economy Suffer from Dutch Disease? *SSRN Electronic Journal*. Advance online publication. https://doi.org/10.2139/ssrn.1504565

Ben-David, D., & Loewy, M. B. (2002). Trade and the Neoclassical Growth Model. *Journal of Economic Integration, 18*(1), 1–16. https://doi.org/10.2139/ssrn.359262

Benedictis, L. D. (2005). Three Decades of Italian Comparative Advantages. *The World Economy, 28*(11), 1679–1709. https://doi.org/10.1111/j.1467-9701.2005.00752.x

Benhabib, J., & Spiegel, M. (1994). The role of human capital in economic development evidence from aggregate cross-country data. *Journal of Monetary Economics, 34*(2), 143–173.

Bensassi, S., Márquez-Ramos, L., & Martínez-Zarzoso, I. (2012). Economic Integration and the Two Margins of Trade: The Impact of the Barcelona Process on North African Countries' Exports. *Journal of African Economies, 21*(2), 228–265.

Bentivogli, C., Ferraresi, T., Monti, P., Paniccià, R., & Rosignoli, S. (2018). *Italian regions in global value chains: an input-output approach* (Questioni di Economia e Finanza, Occasional Papers Banca D'Italia No. 462).

Berube, A., & Parilla, J. (2012). *Metro Trade. Cities Return to their Roots in the Global Economy*. Washington: The Brookings Institution.

Bhagwati, J. N. (1974). *Illegal Transactions in International Trade. Theory and Measurement*: Elsevier.

Biles, J. J. (2004). Export-oriented Industrialization and Regional Development: A Case Study of Maquiladora Production in Yucatán, Mexico. *Regional Studies, 38*(5), 517–532. https://doi.org/10.1080/0143116042000229294

Bils, M., & Klenow, P. J. (2000). Does Schooling Cause Growth? *American Economic Review, 90*(5), 1160–1183. https://doi.org/10.1257/aer.90.5.1160

Blomstrom, M., Lipsey, R., & Zejan, M. (1992). What Explains Developing Country Growth? Advance online publication. https://doi.org/10.3386/w4132

Blomström, M., Globerman, S., & Kokko, A. (2002). Regional Integration and Foreign Direct Investment. In J. H. Dunning (Ed.), *Regions, Globalization, and the Knowledge-Based Economy* (pp. 109–130). Oxford University Press. https://doi.org/10.1093/0199250014.003.0006

Boldrin, M., & Canova, F. (2001). Inequality and convergence in Europe's regions: Reconsidering European regional policies. *Economic Policy, 16*(32), 206–253. https://doi.org/10.1111/1468-0327.00074

Borensztein, E., Gregorio, J. de, & Lee, J.-W. (1998). How does foreign direct investment affect economic growth? *Journal of International Economics, 45*(1), 115–135.

Boschma, R., & Iammarino, S. (2009). Related Variety, Trade Linkages, and Regional Growth in Italy. *Economic Geography, 85*(3), 289–311. https://doi.org/10.1111/j.1944-8287.2009.01034.x

Boschma, R. A., & Fritsch, M. (2009). Creative Class and Regional Growth: Empirical Evidence from Seven European Countries. *Economic Geography, 85*(4), 391–423. https://doi.org/10.1111/j.1944-8287.2009.01048.x

Bosker, M., Brakman, S., Garretsen, H., & Schramm, M. (2010). Adding geography to the new economic geography: Bridging the gap between theory and empirics. *Journal of Economic Geography, 10*(6), 793–823. https://doi.org/10.1093/jeg/lbq003

Bossak, J. (2000). Międzynarodowa konkurencyjność gospodarki kraju i przedsiębiorstwa: Zagadnienia teoretyczne i metodologiczne. In J. Bossak & W. Bieńkowski (Eds.), *Konkurencyjność gospodarki Polski w dobie integracji z Unią Europejską*. Warsaw: SGH.

Bottazzi, L., & Peri, G. (2003). Innovation and spillovers in regions: Evidence from European patent data. *European Economic Review, 47*(4), 687–710. https://doi.org/10.1016/S0014-2921(02)00307-0

Bradley, J. (2009). *Debata na temat polityki spójności i funduszy strukturalnych, in: Polityka spójności w obliczu wyzwań XXIw.: Materiały z konferencji, Ministerstwo Rozwoju Regionalnego*. Warszawa.

Bradley, J., Morgenroth, E., & Untiedt, G. (2003). *Macro-regional evaluation of the Structural Funds using the HERMIN modelling framework: Paper for presentation at the 43rd Congress of the European Regional Science Association*. University of Jyväskylä, Finland.

Bradley, J., & Zaleski, J. (2003). Modelling EU accession and structural fund impacts using the new Polish HERMIN model. In W. Welfe (Ed.), *Modeling EU accession and Structural Fund impacts using the New Polish HERMIN model: Proceedings of the 7th Conference of the International Association AMFET.*

Bradley, J. F. N., Zaucha, J., Brodzicki, T., Ciołek, D., Komornicki, T., Mogiła, Z., . . . Zaleski, J. (2017). *Territorial cohesion: A missing Link between Economic Growth and Welfare*. Lessons from Baltic Tiger. Gdańsk: Uniwersytet Gdański. Katedra Makroekonomii.

Brainard, S., Lael (1993). A Simple Theory of Multinational Corporations and Trade with a Trade-Off Between Proximity and Concentration. *NBER Working Papers, National Bureau of Economic Research*. (4269), 1–45. Retrieved from http://www.nber.org/papers/w4269.pdf

Brakman, S., Garretsen, H., & Schramm, M. (2004). The strategic bombing of German cities during World War II and its impact on city growth. *Journal of Economic Geography, 4*(2), 201–218. https://doi.org/10.1093/jeg/4.2.201

Brakman, S., Garretsen, H., Gorter, J., van der Horst, A., & Schramm, M. (2005). *New Economic Geography, Empirics, and Regional Policy* (No. 56).

Brakman, S., & van Marrewijk, C. (2013). Lumpy countries, urbanization, and trade. *Journal of International Economics, 89*(1), 252–261. https://doi.org/10.1016/j.jinteco.2012.05.004

Branstetter, L. (2006). Is foreign direct investment a channel of knowledge spillovers? Evidence from Japan's FDI in the United States. *Journal of International Economics*, *68*(2), 325–344. https://doi.org/10.1016/j.jinteco.2005.06.006

Breinlich, H., Ottaviano, G. I.P., & Temple, J. R.W. (2014). Regional Growth and Regional Decline. In *Handbook of Economic Growth* (Vol. 2, pp. 683–779). Elsevier. https://doi.org/10.1016/B978-0-444-53540-5.00004-5

Britton, J. N. H. (2002). Regional Implications of North American Integration: A Canadian Perspective on High Technology Manufacturing. *Regional Studies*, *36*(4), 359–374. https://doi.org/10.1080/00343400220131133

Brodzicki, T. (2015). Shallow determinants of growth of Polish regions. Empirical analysis with panel data methods. *Collegium of Economic Analysis Annals*. (39), 25–40.

Brodzicki, T. (2016a). An econometric analysis of the determinants of Poland's intra-industry-trade. In K. Gawlikowska-Hueckel & S. Umiński (Eds.), *An analysis of Poland's foreign trade in the light of the latest theoretical concepts: Implications for economic policy at a time of crisis* (pp. 128–133). Warsaw: Scholar Publishing House; Wydawnictwo Naukowe „Scholar".

Brodzicki, T. (2016b). Intra-industry trade theories. In K. Gawlikowska-Hueckel & S. Umiński (Eds.), *An analysis of Poland's foreign trade in the light of the latest theoretical concepts: Implications for economic policy at a time of crisis* (pp. 87–93). Warsaw: Scholar Publishing House; Wydawnictwo Naukowe „Scholar".

Brodzicki, T. (2017a). Internationalisation and Innovation Intensities of Polish Manufacturing Firms: A Close Nexus? *Entrepreneurial Business and Economics Review*, *5*(1), 91–109. https://doi.org/10.15678/EBER.2017.050106

Brodzicki, T. (2017b). The Role of Openness in Regional Economic Growth. The Case of Polish and Spanish NUTS-2 Regions. *Roczniki Kolegium Analiz Ekonomicznych*. (47), 43–64.

Brodzicki, T., Jurkiewicz, T., Márquez-Ramos, L., & Umiński, S. (2019). Patterns and determinants of the horizontal and vertical intra-industry trade of regions: Panel analysis for Spain & Poland. *Applied Economics*, *44*(2), 1–20. https://doi.org/10.1080/00036846.2019.1676871

Brodzicki, T., Márquez-Ramos, L., & Umiński, S. (2018). The Investigation into Determinants of Regional Exports Base: Panel Analysis for Spanish and Polish Regions. *Entrepreneurial Business and Economics Review*, *6*(1), 135–151. https://doi.org/10.15678/EBER.2018.060108

Brodzicki, T., & Umiński, S. (2017). A gravity panel data analysis of foreign trade by regions: The role of metropolises and history. *Regional Studies*, *52*(2), 261–273. https://doi.org/10.1080/00343404.2017.1296123

Bronzini, R., & Piselli, P. (2009). Determinants of long-run regional productivity with geographical spillovers: The role of R&D, human capital and public infrastructure. *Regional Science and Urban Economics*, *39*(2), 187–199. https://doi.org/10.1016/j.regsciurbeco.2008.07.002

Brown, W. M., & Anderson, W. P. (2002). Spatial markets and the potential for economic integration between Canadian and U.S. regions. *Papers in Regional Science*, *81*(1), 99–120. https://doi.org/10.1111/j.1435-5597.2002.tb01224.x

Brülhart, M. (2001). Evolving geographical concentration of European manufacturing industries. *Weltwirtschaftliches Archiv*, *137*(2), 215–243.

Brülhart, M. (2011). The spatial effects of trade openness: A survey. *Review of World Economics*, *147*(1), 59–83. https://doi.org/10.1007/s10290-010-0083-5

Brülhart, Marius, Carrère, Céline, Robert-Nicoud, Frédéric (2018). Trade and towns: heterogeneous adjustment to a border shock. *Journal of Urban Economics*, *105*, 162–175.

Buckley, P. J., Clegg, J., Wang, C., & Cross, A. R. (2002). FDI, Regional Differences and Economic Growth: Panel Data Evidence from China. *Transnational Corporations*, *11*(1), 1–28.

Budd, L., & Hirmis, A. (2004). Conceptual Framework for Regional Competitiveness. *Regional Studies*, *38*(9), 1015–1028. https://doi.org/10.1080/0034340042000292610

Camacho, P., Carmen, M. d., & Zou, B. (2004). The Spatial Solow Model. *Economics Bulletin*, *18*(2), 1–11.

Cantwell, J. (1995). The globalisation of technology: What remains of the product cycle model? *Cambridge Journal of Economics*, *12*(1), 155–174. https://doi.org/10.1093/oxfordjournals.cje.a035301

Cantwell, J., & Iammarino, S. (2001). The technological relationships between indigenous firms and foreign-owned MNCs in the European regions. Retrieved from https://www.econstor.eu/handle/10419/115288

Cantwell, J., & Iammarino, S. (2010). Multinational Corporations and the Location of Technological Innovation in the UK Regions. *Regional Studies*, *34*(4), 317–332. https://doi.org/10.1080/00343400050078105

Cantwell, J., & Piscitello, L. (1999). The emergence of corporate international networks for the accumulation of dispersed technological competences. *Management International Review*, *39*(1), 123–147. Retrieved from http://www.jstor.org/stable/40835813

Capello, R. (2016). *Regional economics* (Second edition). *Routledge advanced texts in economics and finance: Vol. 27*. Abingdon, Oxon, New York, NY: Routledge.

Carkovic, M., & Levine, R. E. (2002). Does Foreign Direct Investment Accelerate Economic Growth? *SSRN Electronic Journal*. Advance online publication. https://doi.org/10.2139/ssrn.314924

Cassey, A. J. (2006). State export data: origin of movement vs. origin of production. *Munich Personal RePEc Archive*, *2006*(3352), 1–49. Retrieved from https://mpra.ub.uni-muenchen.de/3352/1/MPRA_paper_3352.pdf

Cassey, A. J. (2008). California's Exports and the 2004 Overseas Office Closures. *School of Economics Sciences Working Paper Series*. (WP 2008-28), 1–24. Retrieved from http://faculty.ses.wsu.edu/WorkingPapers/Cassey/CalifExports_WP2008-28.pdf

Cassey, A. J. (2010a). Analyzing the export flow from Texas to Mexico. *Staff Papers Federal Reserve Bank of Dallas*. (11), 1–16. Retrieved from http://hdl.handle.net/2376/5845

Cassey, A. J. (2010b). State Export Behavior and Barriers. *School of Economics Sciences Working Paper Series*. (WP 2010-14), 1–34. Retrieved from http://faculty.ses.wsu.edu/WorkingPapers/Cassey/WP2010-14.pdf

Cassey, A. J. (2010c). State Trade Missions. *School of Economics Sciences Working Paper Series*. (WP 2010-13), 1–29.

Cassey, A. J. (2011a). Does the Type of Exports Affect the Odds that an Overseas Office Exists? *American Journal of Agricultural Economics*. (93(2)), 457–462. https://doi.org/10.1093/ajae/aaq163

Cassey, A. J. (2011b). State Foreign Export Patterns. *Southern Economic Journal*, *78*(2), 308–329. https://doi.org/10.4284/0038-4038-78.2.308

Cassey, A. J. (2012). California's exports and the 2004 overseas office closures. *Economic Inquiry*, *50*(3), 641–651. https://doi.org/10.1111/j.1465-7295.2010.00337.x

Cassey, A. J. (2014). The Location of US States' Overseas Offices. *Review of International Economics*, *22*(2), 310–325. https://doi.org/10.1111/roie.12109

Cassey, A. J. (2016). The Destinations of State Trade Missions. *CESifo Economic Studies*, *62*(3), 547–571. https://doi.org/10.1093/cesifo/ifv026

Cassey, A. J., & Lee, K. (2015). Export trends in Washington State: Volume 7. *Washington State University Extension*, *2015*(7), 1–8. Retrieved from http://cru.cahe.wsu.edu/CEPublications/FS190E/FS190E.pdf

Cassey, A. J., & Schmeiser, K. N. (2013). The agglomeration of exporters by destination. *The Annals of Regional Science*, *51*(2), 495–513. https://doi.org/10.1007/s00168-012-0538-9

Cassey, A. J., Schmeiser, K. N., & Waldkirch, A. (2016). Exporting Spatial Externalities. *Open Economies Review*, *27*(4), 697–720. https://doi.org/10.1007/s11079-016-9394-z

CESE (2011). *Opinion of the European Economic and Social Committee on a Comprehensive European International Investment Policy, Document CESE 1184/2011), paragraphs: 5.4., 5.5.* (No. CESE 1184/2011), par. 5.4., 5.5.

Chaney, T. (2008). Distorted Gravity: The Intensive and Extensive Margins of International Trade. *American Economic Review, 98*(4), 1707–1721. https://doi.org/10.1257/aer.98.4.1707

Chao, C.-C., Hazari, B. R., Laffargue, J.-P., Sgro, P. M., & Yu, E. S. H. (2006). Tourism, Dutch Disease and Welfare in an Open Dynamic Economy. *The Japanese Economic Review, 57*(4), 501–515. https://doi.org/10.1111/j.1468-5876.2006.00400.x

Charron, N., Dahlberg, S., Holmberg, S., Rothstein, B., Khomenko, A., & Svensson, R. (2016). The Quality of Government EU Regional Dataset, version Sep16. *University of Gothenburg: The Quality of Government Institute, http://www.qog.pol.gu.se.*

Chen, J., & Fleisher, B. M. (1996). Regional Income Inequality and Economic Growth in China. *Journal of Comparative Economics, 22*(2), 141–164. https://doi.org/10.1006/jcec.1996.0015

Choe, J. I. (2003). Do Foreign Direct Investment and Gross Domestic Investment Promote Economic Growth? *Review of Development Economics, 7*(1), 44–57. https://doi.org/10.1111/1467-9361.00174

Chowdhury, A., & Mavrotas, G. (2005). *FDI and growth: A casual relationship. Research paper: 2005/25.* Helsinki: UNU/WIDER.

Churski, P. (2008). *Czynniki rozwoju regionalnego i polityka regionalna w Polsce w okresie integracji z Unią Europejską. Seria Geografia: Vol. 79.* Poznań: Wydawn. Naukowe UAM.

Ciampi, C. (Ed.) (1995). *Enhancing European Competitiveness: First Report to the President of the Commission, the Prime Ministers and Heads of State.* Rome.

Ciccone, A. (1996). Productivity and the Density of Economic Activity. *American Economic Review, 86*(1), 54–70.

Cieślik, A. (2005). *Geografia inwestycji zagranicznych. Przyczyny i skutki lokalizacji spółek z udziałem kapitału zagranicznego w Polsce.* Warszawa: Wydawnictwa Uniwersytetu Warszawskiego.

Cieślik, A. (2008). Wpływ przedsiębiorstw międzynarodowych na fragmentaryzację produkcji i handel wewnątrzgałęziowy Polski z krajami OECD. *Gospodarka Narodowa, 206*(10), 1–21. Retrieved from http://gospodarkanarodowa.sgh.waw.pl/p/gospodarka_narodowa_2008_10_01.pdf

Cieślik, A. (2017). Determinants of MNE Activity in Poland: The Case of Firms from EU-15. *Entrepreneurial Business and Economics Review, 5*(1), 151–167. https://doi.org/10.15678/EBER.2017.050109

Cieślik, A., & Rokicki, B. (2010). Wpływ inwestycji drogowych na rozwój polskich regionów. In B. Jóźwik & P. Zalewa (Eds.), *Spójność ekonomiczno-społeczna regionów Unii Europejskiej: / redakcji Bartosz Jóźwik, Piotr Zalewa ; T. 1. Spójność ekonomiczno-społeczna jako doświadczenie i wyzwanie dla Europy.* Lublin: Wydawn. KUL.

Ciołek, D., & Brodzicki, T. (2016). Determinanty produktywnosci polskich powiatow. *Bank i Kredyt, 47*(5), 463–494. Retrieved from nbp.pl/content/2016/05/bik_05_2016_04_art.pdf

Ciołek, D., & Brodzicki, T. (2017). Spatial Dependence Structure of Total Factor Productivity in Polish Local Administrative Districts. *Acta Universitatis Lodziensis. Folia Oeconomica, 3*(329). https://doi.org/10.18778/0208-6018.329.06

Ciżkowicz, P., Rzońca, A., & Umiński, S. (2013). The determinants of regional exports in Poland – a panel data analysis. *Post-Communist Economies, 25*(2), 206–224. https://doi.org/10.1080/14631377.2013.787741

Ciżkowicz, P., & Opala, P. (Eds.) (2011). *Uwarunkowania krajowej i międzynarodowej konkurencyjności województwa lubelskiego.* Warszawa: Wydawnictwo Ernst & Young.

Clark, D. P., Sawyer, W. C., & Sprinkle, R. L. (2005). Revealed Comparative Advantage Indexes for Regions of the United States. *Global Economy Journal, 5*(1). https://doi.org/10.2202/1524-5861.1033

Coe, D. T., & Helpman, E. (1995). International R&D spillovers. *European Economic Review, 39*(5), 859–887. https://doi.org/10.1016/0014-2921(94)00100-E

Coe, D. T., Helpman, E., & Hoffmaister, A. W. (1997). North-South R & D Spillovers. *The Economic Journal, 107*(440), 134–149.

Combes, P.-P., & Lafourcade, M. (2001). Transport Cost Decline and Regional Inequalities: Evidence from France. *Centre for Economic Policy Research*. Retrieved from https://cepr.org/active/publications/discussion_papers/dp.php?dpno=2894

Combes, P.-P., & Lafourcade, M. (2011). Competition, market access and economic geography: Structural estimation and predictions for France. *Regional Science and Urban Economics, 41*(6), 508–524. https://doi.org/10.1016/j.regsciurbeco.2011.03.012

Combes, P.-P., Mayer, T., & Thisse, J.-F. (2008). *Economic Geography: The Integration of Regions and Nations*. New Jersey: Princeton University Press. Retrieved from https://ebookcentral.proquest.com/lib/gbv/detail.action?docID=827797

Commission, E. (1999). *Sixth Periodic Report on the Social and Economic Situation of Regions in the EU*: European Commission Brussels.

Corden, W. M. (1984). Booming Sector and Dutch Disease Economics: Survey and Consolidation. *Oxford Economic Papers, 36*(3), 359–380.

Corden, W. M., & Neary, J. P. (1982). Booming Sector and De-Industrialisation in a Small Open Economy, *92*(368), 825–848.

Cordes, A., Gehrke, B., Rammer, C., Römisch, R., Schliessler, P., & Wassmann Pia (2016). *Identifying Revealed Comparative Advantages in an EU Regional Context* (Research Report No. 42). Retrieved from The Vienna Institute for International Economic Studies; Wiener Institut für Internationale Wirtschaftsvergleiche website: http://wiiw.ac.at/identifying-revealed-comparative-advantages-in-an-eu-regional-context-dlp-3967.pdf

Cortes, M. (2007). *Composition of trade between Australia and Latin America: gravity model.* Department of Economics, University of Wollongong.

Costa-i-Font, J., & Tremosa-i-Balcells, R. (2003). Spanish Regions and the Macroeconomic Benefits of the European Monetary Union. *Regional Studies, 37*(3), 217–226. https://doi.org/10.1080/0034340032000065389

Coughlin, C. C. (2004). The increasing importance of proximity for exports from US states. *Federal Reserve Bank of St. Louis Review, November/December 2004, 86*(6), 1–18. Retrieved from https://files.stlouisfed.org/research/publications/review/04/11/Coughlin.pdf

Coughlin, C. C., & Cartwright, P. A. (1987). An examination of state foreign export promotion and manufacturing exports. *Journal of Regional Science, 27*(3), 439–449. https://doi.org/10.1111/j.1467-9787.1987.tb01172.x

Coughlin, C. C., & Fabel, O. (1988). State Factor Endowments and Exports: An Alternative to Cross-Industry Studies. *The Review of Economics and Statistics, 70*(4), 696–701. https://doi.org/10.2307/1935836

Coughlin, C. C., & Mandelbaum, T. B. (1990). Accounting for Changes in Manufactured Exports at the State Level: 1976-86. *Federal Reserve Bank of St. Louis Review.* (72), 3–14. Retrieved from https://research.stlouisfed.org/publications/review/90/09/Accounting_Sep_Oct1990.pdf

Coughlin, C. C., & Mandelbaum, T. B. (1991). Measuring State Exports: Is There a Better Way? *Federal Reserve Bank of St. Louis Review, July/August 1991,*(73), 65–79.

Coughlin, C. C., & Novy, D. (2013). Is the International Border Effect Larger than the Domestic Border Effect? Evidence from US Trade. *CESifo Economic Studies, 59*(2), 249–276. https://doi.org/10.1093/cesifo/ifs002

Coughlin, C. C., & Pollard, P. S. (2001). Comparing Manufacturing Export Growth Across States: What Accounts for the Differences? *Federal Reserve Bank of St. Louis Review, January/February 2001,*(83), 25–40. Retrieved from https://research.stlouisfed.org/publications/review/01/0101cc.pdf

Coughlin, C. C., & Wall, H. J. (2003). NAFTA and the changing pattern of state exports. *Papers in Regional Science*, *82*(4), 427–450. https://doi.org/10.1007/s10110-003-0122-x

Coulombe, S. (2003). *International trade, interprovincial trade, and Canadian provincial growth*: Industry Canada, Ottawa, ON.

Coulombe, S. (2007). Globalization and Regional Disparity: A Canadian Case Study. *Regional Studies*, *41*(1), 1–17. https://doi.org/10.1080/00343400601099698

Coulombe, S. (2013). The Canadian Dollar and the Dutch and Canadian Diseases. *SPP Research Papers*, *6*(30), 1–16. Retrieved from https://www.policyschool.ca/wp-content/uploads/2016/03/canadian-dollar-dutch-disease-coulombe.pdf

Courant, P. N., & Deardorff, A. V. (1992). International Trade with Lumpy Countries. *Journal of Political Economy*, *100*(1), 198–210. https://doi.org/10.1086/261813

Crescenzi, R., & Rodríguez-Pose, A. (2008). Infrastructure endowment and investment as determinants of regional growth in the European Union. *EIB Papers*, *13*(2), 62–101.

Cronovich, R., & Gazel, R. (1998). Do Exchange Rates and Foreign Incomes Matter for Exports at the State Level? *Journal of Regional Science*, *38*(4), 639–657. https://doi.org/10.1111/0022-4146.00114

Cupitt, R. T., & Reid, M. (1991). State Government International Business Promotion Programs and State Export of Manufactures. *State and Local Government Review*, *23*(3), 127–133. Retrieved from http://www.jstor.org/stable/4355020

Davis, D., & Weinstein, D. (1996). *Does Economic Geography Matter for International Specialization?* Cambridge, MA: National Bureau of Economic Research.

Davis, D., & Weinstein, D. (1998). *Market Access, Economic Geography, and Comparative Advantage: An Empirical Assessment*. Cambridge, MA: National Bureau of Economic Research.

Davis, D., & Weinstein, D. E. (2008). A Search For Multiple Equilibria In Urban Industrial Structure. *Journal of Regional Science*, *49*(1), 29–65. https://doi.org/10.1111/j.1467-9787.2008.00545.x

Davis, D. R., & Weinstein, D. E. (2002). Bones, Bombs, and Break Points: The Geography of Economic Activity. *American Economic Review*, *92*(5), 1269–1289. https://doi.org/10.1257/000282802762024502

Davis, D. R., & Weinstein, D. E. (2003). Market access, economic geography and comparative advantage: An empirical test. *Journal of International Economics*, *59*(1), 1–23. https://doi.org/10.1016/S0022-1996(02)00088-0

Davis, D. R., Weinstein, D. E., Bradford, S. C., & Shimpo, K. (1997). Using International and Japanese Regional Data to Determine When the Factor Abundance Theory of Trade Works. *American Economic Review*, *87*(3), 421–446.

Davoudi, S., Zaucha, J., & Brooks, E. (2016). Evolutionary resilience and complex lagoon systems. *Integrated Environmental Assessment and Management*, *12*(4), 711–718. https://doi.org/10.1002/ieam.1823

DeKaser, R. J., & Sneddon Little, J. (1994). Explaining New England's Export Performance: 1987 to 1993. *Federal Reserve Bank of Boston New England Economic Review, November/December 1994*, 43–59. Retrieved from https://www.bostonfed.org/publications/new-england-economic-review/1994-issues/issue-november-december-1994/explaining-new-englands-export-performance-1987-to-1993.aspx

Delsol, C. (1993). *Le principe de subsidiarité. Que sais-je? Vol. 2793*. [Paris]: Presses universitaires de France.

DFAT (2019a). *Australia's Free Trade Agreements (FTAs).*

DFAT (2019b). *Australia's total goods & services trade.*

DFAT (2019c). *Trade and investment at glance 2019*. Retrieved from https://dfat.gov.au/about-us/publications/trade-investment/trade-at-a-glance/trade-investment-at-a-glance-2019/Documents/trade-and-investment-at-a-glance-2019.pdf

DFAT (2018). *Australia's trade by states and territories.*

Dijkstra, L. (2017). *My region, my Europe, our future: Seventh report on economic, social and territorial cohesion*. Luxembourg: Publications Office of the European Union.

Dixit, A. K., & Stiglitz, J. E. (1997). Monopolistic competition and optimum product diversity. *American Economic Review*, *67*(3), 297–308.

Dixon, R. J. (1973). Regional Specialisation and Trade in the United Kingdom: a Test of Some Hypotheses. *Scottish Journal of Political Economy*, *20*(2), 159–170. https://doi.org/10.1111/j.1467-9485.1973.tb00878.x

Do, Q.-T., & Levchenko, A. A. (2006). Trade, Inequality, and the Political Economy of Institutions. *IMF Working Paper*. (WP/06/56), 1–52. Retrieved from https://ssrn.com/abstract=892947

David H., Dorn, D., & Hanson, G. H. (2013). The China Syndrome: Local Labor Market Effects of Import Competition in the United States. American Economic Review, 103(6), 2121–2168.

Dollar, D. (1992). Outward-Oriented Developing Economies Really Do Grow More Rapidly: Evidence from 95 LDCs, 1976-1985. *Economic Development and Cultural Change*, *40*(3), 523–544. https://doi.org/10.1086/451959

Domański, R. (2013). *Gospodarka przestrzenna: Podstawy teoretyczne* (Wyd. 1, 4 dodr). Warszawa: Wydawnictwo Naukowe PWN.

Doppelhofer, G., Miller, R., & Sala-i-Martin, X. (2000). *Determinants of Long-Term Growth: A Bayesian Averaging of Classical Estimates (BACE) Approach*. Cambridge, MA: National Bureau of Economic Research.

Dreger, C., & Herzer, D. (2013). A further examination of the export-led growth hypothesis. *Empirical Economics*, *45*(1), 39–60. https://doi.org/10.1007/s00181-012-0602-4

Dubé, J., & Polèse, M. (2015). Resource Curse and Regional Development: Does Dutch Disease Apply to Local Economies? Evidence from Canada. *Growth and Change*, *46*(1), 38–57. https://doi.org/10.1111/grow.12064

Dufort, J., & Murray, F. (2004). Impact of the Exchange Rate Appreciation on Québec Export and GDP Growth. *Ministère du Développement Economique et Régional et de la Recherche*, 1–46. Retrieved from http://collections.banq.qc.ca/ark:/52327/bs47327

Dühr, S. (2005). Potentials for polycentric development in Europe: The ESPON 1.1.1 project report. *Planning Practice and Research*, *20*(2), 235–239. https://doi.org/10.1080/02697450500414728

Dungey, M., Fry-Mckibbin, R., & Volkov, V. (2020). Transmission of a Resource Boom: The Case of Australia. *Oxford Bulletin of Economics and Statistics*, *82*(3), 503–525. https://doi.org/10.1111/obes.12352

Dunning, J. H., & Lundan, S. M. (2008). *Multinational enterprises and the global economy* (2nd ed.). Cheltenham, UK, Northampton, MA: Edward Elgar.

Duque, J. C., Ramos, R., & Suriñach, J. (2005). What Have We Learned from the Changeover to the Euro? Lessons for Accession Countries from Catalonian Firms. *Eastern European Economics*, *43*(1), 34–58. https://doi.org/10.1080/00128775.2005.11041098

Dwyer, L., Pham, T., Jago, L., Bailey, G., & Marshall, J. (2014). Modelling the impact of Australia's mining boom on Tourism: a classic case of Dutch Disease. *Journal of Travel Research, 55(2)*, 233–245.

Dziemianowicz, W., & Peszat, K. (2014). Smart specialisations for voivodeships – the first steps toward improvement? *Miscellanea Geographica - Regional Studies on Development*, *18*(1). https://doi.org/10.2478/mgrsd-2014-0012

Easterly, W., Kremer, M., Pritchett, L., & Summers, L. H. (1993). Good policy or good luck? *Journal of Monetary Economics*, *32*(3), 459–483. https://doi.org/10.1016/0304-3932(93)90026-C

Eaton, J., & Kortum, S. (2001). Technology, trade, and growth: A unified framework. *European Economic Review*, *45*(4-6), 742–755. https://doi.org/10.1016/S0014-2921(01)00129-5

Eaton, J., & Kortum, S. (2002). Technology, geography, and trade. *Econometrica*, *70*(5), 1741–1779.

Ederveen, S., Gorter, R., Mooij, R. de, & Nahuis, R. (2002). *Funds and Games. The Economics of European Cohesion Policy*. The Hague.

Edwards, S. (1998). Openness, Productivity and Growth: What do We Really Know? *The Economic Journal, 108*(447), 383–398.

Eff, E. A., & Livingston, S. G. (2007). Is there a rural/urban export gap? *Journal of Regional Science, 47*(2), 339–363. https://doi.org/10.1111/j.1467-9787.2007.00512.x

Eichengreen, B., & Irwin, D. A. (1998). The Role of History in Bilateral Trade Flows. In J. A. Frankel (Ed.), *National Bureau of Economic Research project report. The regionalization of the world economy* (pp. 33–62). Chicago: University of Chicago Press. Retrieved from http://www.nber.org/chapters/c7819

Erickson, R. A. (1978). Purchasing Patterns and the Regional Trade Multiplier. *Growth and Change, 9*(2), 49–51. https://doi.org/10.1111/j.1468-2257.1978.tb00370.x

Erickson, R. A. (1989). Export Performance and State Industrial Growth. *Economic Geography, 4*(65), 280–292.

Erickson, R. A., & Hayward, D. J. (1991). The International Flows of Industrial Exports from U.S. Regions. *Annals of the Association of American Geographers, 81*(3), 371–390. https://doi.org/10.1111/j.1467-8306.1991.tb01700.x

Estrin, S., Meyer, K. E., Wright, M., & Foliano, F. (2008). Export propensity and intensity of subsidiaries in emerging economies. *International Business Review, 17*(5), 574–586. https://doi.org/10.1016/j.ibusrev.2008.04.002

Eswaran, M., Kotwal, S., Ramaswami, B., & Wadhwa, W. (2007). How Does Poverty Decline? Evidence from India, 1983-1999. *Indian Statistical Institute Discussion Papers in Economics*. (07-05).

European Commission (2010a). *COM(2010) 612 Final version (Communication from the Commission to the European Parliament, the Council, the European Economic and Social Committee and the Committee of the Regions).*

European Commission (2010b). *Communication from the Commission to the European Council. Europe 2020. A Strategy for Smart, Sustainable and Inclusive Growth*. Brussels.

European Commission (2010c). *Communication from the Commission, Europe 2020. A strategy for smart, sustainable and inclusive growth*. Brussels.

European Commission (2011). *Official Journal of the EU (2011/C 132/04), Opinion of the European Economic and Social Committee on 'Energy supply: what kind of neighbourhood policy do we need to ensure security of supply for the EU?'.*

European Commission (2012). *Communication from the Commission to the European Parliament, The Council, The European Economic and Social Committee and The Committee of the Regions: A Stronger European Industry for Growth and Economic Recovery*. COM/2012/0582. Brussels.

Fagerberg, J. (1988). International Competitiveness. *The Economic Journal, 98*(391), 355. https://doi.org/10.2307/2233372

Fardmanesh, M. (1991). Dutch disease economics and oil syndrome: An empirical study. *World Development, 19*(6), 711–717. https://doi.org/10.1016/0305-750X(91)90205-V

Feenstra, R. C., Inklaar, R., & Timmer, M. P. (2015). The Next Generation of the Penn World Table. *American Economic Review, 105*(10), 3150–3182. https://doi.org/10.1257/aer.20130954

Felice, E., & Vecchi, G. (2015). Italy's Modern Economic Growth, 1861–2011. *Enterprise & Society, 16*(2), 225–248. https://doi.org/10.1017/eso.2014.23

Fidrmuc, J., & Martin, R. (2011). FDI, Trade and Growth in CESEE Countries, Focus on European Economic Integration. *Oesterreichische Nationalbank (Austrian Central Bank)*. (1), 70–89.

Fieleke, N. S. (1970). The Kennedy Round. Impact of Tariff Reductions on New England Manufacturing. *Growth and Change, 1*(2), 3–10. https://doi.org/10.1111/j.1468-2257.1970.tb00101.x

Findlay, R. (1995). *Factor proportions, trade, and growth. The Ohlin Lectures: Vol. 5*. Cambridge, Mass.: Massachusetts Institute of Technology.

Florida, R. (1995). Toward the learning region. *Futures, 27*(5), 527–536. https://doi.org/10.1016/0016-3287(95)00021-N

Florida, R. L. (2005). *The flight of the creative class: [the new global competition for talent]* (1. ed.). New York, NY: HarperBusiness.

Foray, D., David, P., & Hall, B. (2009). *Knowledge for growth: Prospects for science, technology and innovation*: Selected papers from Research Commissioner Janez Potočnik's Expert group.

Foray, D. (2014). *Smart Specialisation: Challenges and opportunities for regional innovation policies: Opportunities and Challenges for Regional Innovation Policy*: Routledge.

Foreign Affairs and International Trade Canada (2012). *Canada's State of Trade.*

Forsgren, M. (2008). *Theories of the Multinational Firm: A Multidimensional Creature in the Global Economy*. Cheltenham, UK, Northampton, MA, USA: Edward Elgar.

Forslid, R., & Okubo, T. (2010). Spatial Relocation with Heterogeneous Firms and Heterogeneous Sectors. *CEPR Discussion Paper*. (8117).

Forslid, R., & Okubo, T. (2018). *Trade, Location and Multiproduct Firms* (RIETI Discussion Paper Series No. 18-E-075), pp. 1–24.

Forslid, R., & Okubo, T. (2019). Trade, Location and Multiproduct Firms.

Frankel, J., & Romer, D. (1996). *Trade and Growth: An Empirical Investigation*. Cambridge, MA: National Bureau of Economic Research.

Frankel, J. A., & Romer, D. (1999). Does Trade Cause Growth? *American Economic Review*, *89*(3), 379–399. https://doi.org/10.1257/aer.89.3.379

Fujita, M., & Gokan, T. (2005). On the evolution of the spatial economy with multi-unit · multi-plant firms: The impact of IT development. *Portuguese Economic Journal*, *4*(2), 73–105. https://doi.org/10.1007/s10258-005-0043-5

Fujita, M., & Krugman, P. (2003). The new economic geography: Past, present and the future. *Papers in Regional Science*, *83*(1), 139–164. https://doi.org/10.1007/s10110-003-0180-0

Fujita, M., Krugman, P. R., & Venables, A. (2001). *The spatial economy: Cities, regions, and international trade* (1. paperback ed.). Cambridge, Mass.: MIT Press.

Fujita, M., & Mori, T. (2005). Frontiers of the New Economic Geography *Papers in Regional Science*, *84*(3), 377–405. https://doi.org/10.1111/j.1435-5957.2005.00021.x

Fujita, M., & Thisse, J.-F. (2004). *Economics of agglomeration: Cities, industrial location, and regional growth* (transferred to digital printing). Cambridge: Cambridge Univ. Press.

Fujita, M., & Thisse, J.-F. (2006). Globalization and the evolution of the supply chain: who gains and who loses? *International Economic Review*, *47*(3), 811–836. https://doi.org/10.1111/j.1468-2354.2006.00397.x

Gajewski, P., Gawlikowska-Hueckel, K., & Umiński, S. (2009). Szanse i zagrożenia związane z przyjęciem euro przez Polskę w ujęciu regionalnym. In NBP (Ed.), *Raport na temat pełnego uczestnictwa Rzeczypospolitej Polskiej w trzecim etapie Unii Gospodarczej i Walutowej. Projekty badawcze, cześć II.* (pp. 11–86). Warszawa: NBP.

Gajewski, P., & Tchorek, G. (2017). What drives export performance of firms in Eastern and Western Poland? *European Planning Studies*, *25*(12), 2250–2271. https://doi.org/10.1080/09654313.2017.1355890

Gale, H. F., JR. (1998). Rural manufacturers in the export market. *Rural development perspectives*, *13*(2), 24–30.

Gale, H. F., JR., McGranahan, D. A., Teixeira, R., & Greenberg, E. (1999). Rural Competitiveness: Results of the 1996 Rural Manufacturing Survey. *Agricultural Economics Reports*. (776). Retrieved from http://purl.umn.edu/34077

Gallego, N., & Llano, C. (2017). Trade and spatial agglomeration: how spatially concentrated are inflows in the importing country. Paper presented during ETSG 2017 conference in EUI, Florence, Italy.

Gallup, J. L., Sachs, J. D., & Mellinger, A. D. (2016). Geography and Economic Development. *International Regional Science Review*, *22*(2), 179–232. https://doi.org/10.1177/016001799761012334

Garretsen, H., & Martin, R. (2010). Rethinking (New) Economic Geography Models: Taking Geography and History More Seriously. *Spatial Economic Analysis*, *5*(2), 127–160. https://doi.org/10.1080/17421771003730729

Gaston, N., & Trefler, D. (1997). The Labour Market Consequences of the Canada-U.S. Free Trade Agreement. *Canadian Journal of Economics/Revue Canadienne d'Economique*, *30*(1), 18. https://doi.org/10.2307/136358

Gawlikowska-Hueckel, K. (2005). Polityka regionalna – rozwój, finansowanie i przyszłość. In Z. Brodecki (Ed.), *Regiony*. Warszawa.

Gawlikowska-Hueckel, K., & Szlachta, J. (Eds.) (2014). *Wrażliwość polskich regionów na wyzwania współczesnej gospodarki: Implikacje dla polityki rozwoju regionalnego*. Warszawa: Wolters Kluwer; Wolters Kluwer Polska.

Gawlikowska-Hueckel, K., & Umiński, S. (2009). *Handel zagraniczny Małopolski 2008*. Kraków: Urząd Marszałkowski Województwa Małopolskiego. Departament Transportu i Społeczeństwa Informacyjnego.

Gawlikowska-Hueckel, K., & Umiński, S. (2011). Handel zagraniczny województwa lubelskiego. In P. Ciżkowicz & P. Opala (Eds.), *Uwarunkowania krajowej i międzynarodowej konkurencyjności województwa lubelskiego* (pp. 137–229). Warszawa: Wydawnictwo Ernst & Young.

Gawlikowska-Hueckel, K., & Umiński, S. (2013a). Competitiveness at the Regional Level: Export Oriented Approach for Poland. *Yearbook of the Institute of East-Central Europe*, *11*(6), 133–158. Retrieved from http://www.iesw.lublin.pl/rocznik/pliki/Rocznik_2013-205.pdf

Gawlikowska-Hueckel, K., & Umiński, S. (2013b). Competitiveness at the regional level: export-oriented approach for Poland. In B. Jóźwik & T. Stępniewski (Eds.), *Central and Eastern Europe: convergence, integration and security* (pp. 131–156). Lublin.

Gawlikowska-Hueckel, K., & Umiński, S. (Eds.) (2016). *An analysis of Poland's foreign trade in the light of the latest theoretical concepts: Implications for economic policy at a time of crisis*. Warsaw: Scholar Publishing House; Wydawnictwo Naukowe „Scholar".

Gawlikowska-Hueckel, K., & Zielińska-Głębocka, A. (2004). *Integracja europejska: Od jednolitego rynku do unii walutowej. Academia Oeconomica*. Warszawa: C. H. Beck.

Gerbet, P. (2016). *Reform of the Community budget: the Delors Packages*. Retrieved from http://www.cvce.eu/obj/reform_of_the_community_budget-en-ad39fbfd-ede4-454d-bcea-553ae7170535.html

Gianelle, C., Kyriakou, D., Cohen, C., & Przeor, M. (2016). Implementing smart specialisation strategies. *A Handbook. European Commission.*

Giesecke, J. (2007). *Slow Growth in Australia's South-Eastern Regions: Are They a Victim of 'Dutch Disease*. Paris: Joint Congress of the European Regional Science Association (47th Congress) and ASRDLF (Association de Science Régionale de Langue Française, 44th Congress),.

Gil, S., Llorca, R., & Serrano, J. A. M. (2008). Measuring the impact of regional export promotion: The Spanish case. *Papers in Regional Science*, *87*(1), 139–146. https://doi.org/10.1111/j.1435-5957.2007.00155.x

Gil-Pareja, S., Llorca-Vivero, R., Martinez-Serrano, J. A., & Oliver-Alonso, J. (2005). The Border Effect in Spain. *The World Economy*, *28*(11), 1617–1631. https://doi.org/10.1111/j.1467-9701.2005.00749.x

Gil-Pareja, S., Llorca-Vivero, R., & Martínez-Serrano, J. A. (2006). The border effect in Spain: The Basque Country case. *Regional Studies*, *40*(4), 335–345. https://doi.org/10.1080/00343400600725186

Gil-Pareja, S., Llorca-Vivero, R., Martínez-Serrano, J. A., & Requena-Silvente, F. (2015). Regional export promotion offices and trade margins. *Review of World Economics*, *151*(1), 145–167. https://doi.org/10.1007/s10290-014-0199-0

Glejser, H., Jacquemin, A., & Petit, J. (1980). Exports in an Imperfect Competition Framework: An Analysis of 1,446 Exporters. *The Quarterly Journal of Economics*, *94*(3), 507. https://doi.org/10.2307/1884582

Glickman, N. J., & Woodward, D. P. (1989). *The New Competitors: How Foreign Investors are Changing the U.S. Economy?* New York: Basic Books.

Głąbicka, K., & Grewiński, M. (2005). *Polityka spójności społeczno-gospodarczej Unii Europejskiej*. Warszawa: Elipsa.

Golladay, F. L., & Sandoval, A. D. (1972). Optimal development policy in an open regional economy: a programming analysis. *Journal of Regional Science*, *12*(2), 185–198. https://doi.org/10.1111/j.1467-9787.1972.tb00342.x

González Rivas, M. (2007). The effects of trade openness on regional inequality in Mexico. *The Annals of Regional Science*, *41*(3), 545–561. https://doi.org/10.1007/s00168-006-0099-x

Gorzelak, G. (2014). Wykorzystanie środków Unii Europejskiej dla rozwoju kraju - wstępne analizy. *Studia Lokalne i Regionalne*, *57*(3), 5–25.

Gómez Prieto, J., Demblans, A., & Palazuelos Martínez, M. (2019). *Smart Specialisation in the world, an EU policy approach helping to discover innovation globally*. Publications Office of the European Union. Luxembourg.

Grasjo, U. (2008). University-educated Labor, R&D and Regional Export Performance. *International Regional Science Review*, *31*(3), 211–256. https://doi.org/10.1177/0160017608319335

Greenaway, D., Hine, R., & Milner, C. (1995). Vertical and Horizontal Intra-Industry Trade: A Cross Industry Analysis for the United Kingdom. *The Economic Journal*, *105*(433), 1505–1518. https://doi.org/10.2307/2235113

Grossman, G. M., & Helpman, E. (1995). *Innovation and growth in the global economy* (5. printing). Cambridge, Mass.: MIT Press.

Guerrieri, P., & Iammarino, S. (2006). Euro-Commentary. The Rise of 'Many Mezzogiorni': An Empirical Assessment of the Internal Differentiation of Italian Southern Regions. *European Urban and Regional Studies*, *13*(2), 167–178. https://doi.org/10.1177/0969776406060829

Guttmann, S., & Richards, A. (2006). *Trade openness: an Australian perspective*. Australian Economic Papers, 45(3), 188-203. https://onlinelibrary.wiley.com/doi/epdf/10.1111/j.1467-8454.2006.00287.x

Hansen, H., & Rand, J. (2006). On the Causal Links between FDI and Growth in Developing Countries. *The World Economy*, *29*(1), 21–41. https://doi.org/10.1111/j.1467-9701.2006.00756.x

Hansen, J. D., & Zhang, J. (2010). A Kaldorian approach to regional economic growth in China. *Applied Economics*, *28*(6), 679–685. https://doi.org/10.1080/000368496328425

Hanson, G. H. (1994). Localization Economies, Vertical Organization and Trade. *NBER Working Paper*. (4744).

Hanson, G. H. (1996). Localization Economies, Vertical Organization, and Trade. *American Economic Review*, *86*(5), 1266–1278.

Hanson, G. H. (2001). Scale economies and the geographic concentration of industry. *Journal of Economic Geography*, *1*(3), 255–276.

Harilal, K. N., & Joseph, K. J. (2003). Stagnation and Revival of Kerala Economy: An Open Economy Perspective. *Economic and Political Weekly*, *38*(23), 2286–2294. Retrieved from www.jstor.org/stable/4413657.

Hassink, R., & Gong, H. (2019). Six critical questions about smart specialization. *European Planning Studies*, *27*(10), 2049–2065. https://doi.org/10.1080/09654313.2019.1650898

Hausner, J. (2013). Konkurencyjna Polska. Jak awansować w światowej lidze gospodarczej. *Fundacja Gospodarki i Administracji Publicznej, Kraków.*

Head, K., & Mayer, T. (2014). Gravity Equations: Workhorse, Toolkit, and Cookbook. In G. Gopinath, E. Helpman, & K. S. Rogoff (Eds.), *Handbooks in economics. Handbook of international economics* (pp. 131–195). Amsterdam, New York: North Holland; Elsevier.

Head, K., Mayer, T., & Ries, J. (2004). Home Market Effects, Market Size and Location Strategies. In J.-L. Mucchielli & T. Mayer (Eds.), *Multinational Firms' Location and the New Economic Geography*. Edward Elgar Publishing.

Heid, B., Larch, M., & Yotov, Y. (2017). Estimating the Effects of Non-Discriminatory Trade Policies within Structural Gravity Models. *CESifo Working Paper Series*. (6735), 1–37.

Hejazji, W., & Safarian, E. (1999). Trade, Foreign Direct Investment, and R&D Spillovers. *Journal of International Business Studies*, *30*(3), 491–511.

Helliwell, J. F. (1996). Do National Borders Matter for Quebec's Trade? *The Canadian Journal of Economics*, *29*(3), 507. https://doi.org/10.2307/136247

Helliwell, J. F. (2000). *How much do national borders matter?* Brookings Institution Press.

Helliwell, J. F., Lee, F. C., & Messinger, H. (1999). *Effects of the Canada-United States Free Trade Agreement on Interprovincial Trade*: Industrie Canada.

Helpman, E. (1984). A Simple Theory of International Trade with Multinational Corporations. *Journal of Political Economy*, *92*(3), 451–471. https://doi.org/10.1086/261236

Helpman, E., & Krugman, P. R. (1985). *Market structure and foreign trade: Increasing returns, imperfect competition, and the international economy*. Cambridge, Mass.: MIT Press.

Helpman, E., & Krugman, P. (1985). *Market Structure and International Trade. Increasing Returns, Imperfect Competition and the International Economy*. Cambridge, MA: MIT Press.

Helpman, E., Melitz, M., & Yeaple, S. (2003). *Export versus FDI*. Cambridge, MA: National Bureau of Economic Research.

Helpman, E., Melitz, M. J., & Yeaple, S. R. (2004). Export Versus FDI with Heterogeneous Firms. *American Economic Review*, *94*(1), 300–316. https://doi.org/10.1257/000282804322970814

Herzer, D., & Nowak-Lehnmann D., F. (2006). What does export diversification do for growth? An econometric analysis. *Applied Economics*, *38*(15), 1825–1838. https://doi.org/10.1080/00036840500426983

Hillberry, R. (1998). Regional trade and "the medicine line": The national border effect in U.S. commodity flow data. *Journal of Borderlands Studies*, *13*(2), 1–17. https://doi.org/10.1080/08865655.1998.9695516

Hirose, K., & Yoshida, Y. (2018). Where at home do exporters produce and export? *The World Economy*, *41*(6), 1596–1639. https://doi.org/10.1111/twec.12588

Howitt, P. (2000). Endogenous Growth and Cross-Country Income Differences. *American Economic Review*, *90*(4), 829–846. https://doi.org/10.1257/aer.90.4.829

Hufbauer, G. (1966). *Synthetic Materials and the Theory of International Trade Hardcover – 1966*. Cambridge, Mass.: Harvard University Press.

Hufbauer, G. (1970). The Impact of National Characteristics & Technology on the Commodity Composition of Trade in Manufactured Goods. In R. Vernon (Ed.), *The Technology Factor in International Trade* (pp. 145–231). New York: National Bureau of Economic Research.

Huggins, R., Izushi, H., & Thompson, P. (2013). Regional Competitiveness: Theories and Methodologies for Empirical Analysis. *Journal of CENTRUM Cathedra (JCC): The Business and Economics Research Journal*, *6*(2), 155–172. https://doi.org/10.7835/jcc-berj-2013-0086

Hummels, D. L. (1999). Toward a Geography of Trade Costs. *SSRN Electronic Journal*. Advance online publication. https://doi.org/10.2139/ssrn.160533

Hymer, Stephen, H. (1972). The multinational corporation and the law of uneven development. In J. N. Bhagwati (Ed.), *Economics and world order from the 1970's to the 1990's* (1st ed., pp. 113–140). New York, London: Free Press; Collier Macmillan.

Hymer, Stephen, Herbert (1960/1976). *The international operations of national firms: A study of direct foreign investment*. Cambridge, MA: The MIT Press.

Iacobucci, D., & Guzzini, E. (2016). Relatedness and connectivity in technological domains: Missing links in S3 design and implementation. *European Planning Studies*, *24*(8), 1511–1526. https://doi.org/10.1080/09654313.2016.1170108

Iammarino, S., & McCann, P. (2013). *Multinationals and economic geography: Location, technology and innovation*. Cheltenham, U.K: Edward Elgar Pub. Ltd.

Iamsiraroj, S. (2016). The foreign direct investment–economic growth nexus. *International Review of Economics & Finance*, *42*, 116–133. https://doi.org/10.1016/j.iref.2015.10.044

Iamsiraroj, S., & Ulubaşoğlu, M. A. (2015). Foreign direct investment and economic growth: A real relationship or wishful thinking? *Economic Modelling*, *51*, 200–213. https://doi.org/10.1016/j.econmod.2015.08.009

International Trade Centre (2016). *Investing in Trade Promotion Generates Revenue - A study of Trade Promotion Organizations*. Switzerland.

Irwin, D. A., & Terviö, M. (2002). Does trade raise income? *Journal of International Economics*, *58*(1), 1–18. https://doi.org/10.1016/S0022-1996(01)00164-7

Jacobs, J. (1970). *The economy of cities*. *Vintage books: Vol. 584*. New York: Vintage Books.

Jaffe, A. B., Trajtenberg, M., & Henderson, R. (1993). Geographic Localization of Knowledge Spillovers as Evidenced by Patent Citations. *Quarterly Journal of Economics*, *108*(3), 577–598. https://doi.org/10.2307/2118401

Jayachandran, G., & Seilan, A. (2010). A Causal Relationship between Trade, Foreign Direct A Causal Relationship between Trade, Foreign Direct Investment and Economic Growth for India. *International Research Journal of Finance and Econo*. (42), 74–88.

Jensen, C. (2002). Foreign direct investment, industrial restructuring and the upgrading of Polish exports. *Applied Economics*, *34*(2), 207–217. https://doi.org/10.1080/00036840010025641

Johansson, S., & Karlsson, C. (2007). R&D accessibility and regional export diversity. *The Annals of Regional Science*, *41*(3), 501–523. https://doi.org/10.1007/s00168-007-0122-x

Kamas, L. (1986). Dutch disease economics and the Colombian export boom. *World Development*, *14*(9), 1177–1198. https://doi.org/10.1016/0305-750X(86)90119-1

Kanbur, R., & Venables, A. (2005). Rising Spatial Disparities and Development. *United Nations University Policy Brief*. (3).

Kannapiran, C. A., & Fleming, E. M. (1999). *Competitiveness and comparative advantage of tree crop smallholdings in Papua New Guinea*.

Kaufmann, D., Kraay, A., & Mastruzzi, M. (2011). The Worldwide Governance Indicators: Methodology and Analytical Issues. *Hague Journal on the Rule of Law*, *3*(02), 220–246. https://doi.org/10.1017/S1876404511200046

Kawecka-Wyrzykowska, E. (Ed.) (2009). *Polityki gospodarcze Unii Europejskiej*. Warszawa: Szkoła Główna Handlowa w Warszawie - Oficyna Wydawnicza.

Keller, W. (2002). Trade and the Transmission of Technology. *Journal of Economic Growth*, *7*(1), 5–24. https://doi.org/10.1023/A:1013461025733

Keller, W. (2004). International technology diffusion. *Journal of Economic Literature*, *42*(3), 752–782.

Kepaptsoglou, K., Karlaftis, M. G., & Tsamboulas, D. (2010). The Gravity Model Specification for Modeling International Trade Flows and Free Trade Agreement Effects: A 10-Year Review of Empirical Studies. *The Open Economics Journal*, *3*(1), 1–13. https://doi.org/10.2174/1874919401003010001

Ketterer, T. D., & Rodríguez-Pose, A. (2018). Institutions vs. 'first-nature' geography. What drives economic growth in Europe's regions? *Papers in Regional Science*, *97*, S25-S62. https://doi.org/10.1111/pirs.12237

Knox, R. H. (2001). *Canada's agreement on internal trade: It can work if we want it to*: Certified General Accountants Association of Canada.

Koenig, P. (2009). Agglomeration and the export decisions of French firms. *Journal of Urban Economics*, *66*(3), 186–195. https://doi.org/10.1016/j.jue.2009.07.002

Koenig, P., Mayneris, F., & Poncet, S. (2010). Local export spillovers in France. *European Economic Review*, *54*(4), 622–641. https://doi.org/10.1016/j.euroecorev.2009.12.001

Koitsiwe, K., & Adachi, T. (2015). Australia mining boom and Dutch Disease: analysis using VAR method. *Procedia Economics and Finance*, *30*, 401–408.

Komornicki, T., & Szejgiec, B. (2015). Spatial diversity of Polish export linkages. *Geographia Polonica*, *88*(1), 173–178. https://doi.org/10.7163/GPol.0011

Komornicki, T., & Szejgiec, B. (2017). Przekształcenia przestrzennego rozmieszczenia obszarów koncentracji eksportu – od okresu transformacji systemowej do rzeczywistości pokryzysowej. *Przegląd geograficzny*.

Korbutowicz, T. (2016). Polityka konkurencji Unii Europejskiej a Strategia Europa 2020. *Studia Ekonomiczne. Zeszyty NaukoweUniwersytetu Ekonomicznego w Katowicach*. (269), 140–151.

Kounetas, K., & Napolitano, O. (2018). Modeling the incidence of international trade on Italian regional productive efficiency using a meta-frontier DEA approach. *Economic Modelling*, *71*, 45–58. https://doi.org/10.1016/j.econmod.2017.11.020

Krammer, S. M.S. (2017). Science, technology, and innovation for economic competitiveness: The role of smart specialization in less-developed countries. *Technological Forecasting and Social Change*, *123*, 95–107. https://doi.org/10.1016/j.techfore.2017.06.028

Krugman, P. (1979). Increasing Returns, Monopolistic Competition and International Trade. *Journal of International Economics*, *9*(4), 469–479. https://doi.org/10.1016/0022-1996(79)90017-5

Krugman, P. (1980a). Scale Economies, Product Differentiation, and the Pattern of Trade. *The American Economic Review*, *70*(5), 950–959.

Krugman, P. (1980b). Scale Economies, Product Differentiation, and the Pattern of Trade, American Economic Review. *The American Economic Review*, *70*(5), 950–959.

Krugman, P. (1987). The narrow moving band, the Dutch disease, and the competitive consequences of Mrs. Thatcher. *Journal of Development Economics*, *27*(1-2), 41–55. https://doi.org/10.1016/0304-3878(87)90005-8

Krugman, P. (1990). *Rethinking International Trade*. Cambridge, MA: The MIT Press.

Krugman, P. (1991a). *Geography and trade* (London). *Gaston Eyskens lecture series*. Leuven: MIT Press.

Krugman, P. (1991b). Increasing Returns and Economic Geography. *Journal of Political Economy*, *99*(3), 483–499. https://doi.org/10.1086/261763

Krugman, P. (1998). What's New about the New Economic Geography? *Oxford Review of Economic Policy*, *14*(2), 7–17.

Krugman, P. (2010). The New Economic Geography, Now Middle-aged. *Regional Studies*, *45*(1), 1–7. https://doi.org/10.1080/00343404.2011.537127

Krugman, P. (2015). Interregional and International Trade: Different Causes, Different Trends? In P. Nijkamp, A. Rose, & K. Kourtit (Eds.), *Regional Science Matters: Studies Dedicated to Walter Isard* (pp. 27–34). Springer.

Krugman, P., & Elizondo, R. L. (1996). Trade policy and the Third World metropolis. *Journal of Development Economics*, *49*(1), 137–150. https://doi.org/10.1016/0304-3878(95)00055-0

Krugman, P., & Venables, A. (1995). The seamless world: a spatial model of international specialization. *NBER Working Paper*. Advance online publication. https://doi.org/10.3386/w5220

Kukucha, C. J. (2009). *The provinces and Canadian foreign trade policy*: UBC press.

Lall, S., & Mohammad, S. (2007). Foreign ownership and export performance in the large corporate sector of India. *The Journal of Development Studies*, *20*(1), 56–67. https://doi.org/10.1080/00220388308421888

Landreth, H., Szeworski, A., Godłów-Legiędź, J., Dzionek-Kozłowska, J., & Colander, D. C. (2013). *Historia myśli ekonomicznej* (Wyd. 2 uzup., 5 dodr). Warszawa: Wydawnictwo Naukowe PWN.

Lee, C.-C., & Chang, C.-P. (2009). FDI, Financial Development, and Economic Growth: International Evidence. *Journal of Applied Economics*, *12*(2), 249–271. https://doi.org/10.1016/S1514-0326(09)60015-5

Lee, J.-W. (1993). International Trade, Distortions, and Long-Run Economic Growth. *Staff Papers - International Monetary Fund*, *40*(2), 299. https://doi.org/10.2307/3867316

Leichenko, R., & Silva, J. (2004). International Trade, Employment and Earnings: Evidence from US Rural Counties. *Regional Studies*, *38*(4), 355–374. https://doi.org/10.1080/03434002000213897

Leichenko, R. M., & Coulson, E. N. (1999). Foreign Industrial Exports and State Manufacturing Performance. *Growth and Change*, *30*(4), 479–506. https://doi.org/10.1111/j.1468-2257.1999.tb00042.x

Leichenko, R. M., & Erickson, R. A. (1997). Foreign Direct Investment and State Export Performance. *Journal of Regional Science*, *37*(2), 307–329. https://doi.org/10.1111/0022-4146.00056

Leong, C. K. (2013). Special economic zones and growth in China and India: An empirical investigation. *International Economics and Economic Policy*, *10*(4), 549–567. https://doi.org/10.1007/s10368-012-0223-6

Lessmann, C. (2013). Foreign direct investment and regional inequality: A panel data analysis. *China Economic Review*, *24*, 129–149. https://doi.org/10.1016/j.chieco.2012.12.001

Levine, R., & Renelt, D. (1992). A Sensitivity Analysis of Cross-Country Growth Regressions. *The American Economic Review*, *82*(4), 942–963.

Lewandowski, J. P. (1996). Sources of U.S. Regions Manufacturers Export Performance. *Middle States Geographer*. (29), 49–56.

Linder, S. B. (1961). *An Essay on Trade and Transformation*. Uppsala: Almqvist & Wiksells Boktryckeri AB.

Linders, G.-J. M., Burger, M. J., & van Oort, F. G. (2008). A rather empty world: The many faces of distance and the persistent resistance to international trade. *Cambridge Journal of Regions, Economy and Society*, *1*(3), 439–458. https://doi.org/10.1093/cjres/rsn019

Lindert, P. H. (1986). *International economics* (8th ed.). Homewood, Ill.: Irwin.

Liu, X., Song, H., & Romilly, P. (1997). An empirical investigation of the causal relationship between openness and economic growth in China. *Applied Economics*, *29*(12), 1679–1686. https://doi.org/10.1080/000368497000000043

Llano-Verduras, C., Minondo, A., & Requena-Silvente, F. (2011). Is the Border Effect an Artefact of Geographic Aggregation? *Working Papers in Applied Economics, Universitat de Valencia, WPAE-2011-08*.

Llop, M., & Manresa, A. (2007). Analysis of Linear Multipliers in an Open Regional Economy. *Regional Studies*, *41*(4), 421–428. https://doi.org/10.1080/00343400701281824

Lombardía, M. J., & Sperlich, S. (2012). A new class of semi-mixed effects models and its application in small area estimation. *Computational Statistics & Data Analysis*, *56*(10), 2903–2917. https://doi.org/10.1016/j.csda.2012.01.015

Lovely, M. E., Rosenthal, S. S., & Sharma, S. (2005). Information, agglomeration, and the headquarters of U.S. exporters. *Regional Science and Urban Economics*, *35*(2), 167–191. https://doi.org/10.1016/j.regsciurbeco.2003.09.002

Lucas, R. E. (1988). On the mechanics of economic development. *Journal of Monetary Economics*, *22*(1), 3–42. https://doi.org/10.1016/0304-3932(88)90168-7

Lucas, R. E. (1990). Why Doesn't Capital Flow from Rich to Poor Countries? *The American Economic Review*, *80*(2), 92–96.

Łaźniewska, E., Gorynia, M., & Chmielewski, R. (2012). *Konkurencyjność regionalna: Koncepcje, strategie, przykłady*. Warszawa: Wydawnictwo Naukowe PWN.

Ma, A. C. (2006). Geographical Location of Foreign Direct Investment and Wage Inequality in China. *The World Economy*, *29*(8), 1031–1055. https://doi.org/10.1111/j.1467-9701.2006.00812.x

Macmahon, F. (1996). *Looking the gift horse in the mouth: The impact of federal transfers on Atlantic Canada*. Halifax: AIMS.

Majkowska-Szulc, S. (2016). Legal conditioning of the development of export by Polish enterprises within the framework of EU economic policy. In K. Gawlikowska-Hueckel & S. Umiński (Eds.), *An analysis of Poland's foreign trade in the light of the latest theoretical concepts: Implications for economic policy at a time of crisis* (pp. 190–202). Warsaw: Scholar Publishing House; Wydawnictwo Naukowe "Scholar".

Makhoul, B., & Otterstrom, S. M. (1998). Exploring the accuracy of international trade statistics. *Applied Economics, 30*(12), 1603–1616. https://doi.org/10.1080/000368498324689

Mankiw, G., Romer, D., & Weil, D. (1992). A Contribution to the Empirics of Economic Growth. *Quarterly Journal of Economics, 107*(2), 407–437.

Marin, D. (1992). Is the Export-Led Growth Hypothesis Valid for Industrialized Countries? *The Review of Economics and Statistics, 74*(4), 678. https://doi.org/10.2307/2109382

Markusen, J. (1984). Multinational, multi-plant economies, and the gains from trade. *Journal of International.* (16), 205–266.

Márquez-Ramos, L. (2015). The relationship between trade and sustainable transport: A quantitative assessment with indicators of the importance of environmental performance and agglomeration externalities. *Ecological Indicators, 52*, 170–183. https://doi.org/10.1016/j.ecolind.2014.11.023

Márquez-Ramos, L. (2016a). Port facilities, regional spillovers and exports: Empirical evidence from Spain. *Papers in Regional Science, 95*(2), 329–351. https://doi.org/10.1111/pirs.12127

Márquez-Ramos, L. (2016b). Regionalism, subnational variation and gravity: A four-country tale. *Investigaciones Regionales.* 35, 7–36.

Márquez-Ramos, L. (2016c). The Role of Institutional Environment in International Trade. The Case of Spanish Regions. *REGION, 3*(2), 125–140. https://doi.org/10.18335/region.v3i2.147

Márquez-Ramos, L., Florensa, L. M., & Recalde, M. L. (2015). Economic Integration Effects on Trade Margins: Sectoral Evidence from Latin America. *Journal of Economic Integration, 30*(2), 269–299.

Márquez-Ramos, L., Martínez-Zarzoso, I., Suárez-Burguet, C. (2011). Determinants of deep integration: examining socio-political factors. *Open Economies Review*, 22(3), 479–500. https://doi.org/10.1007/s11079-009-9132-x

Marrewijk, C. (2008). Intra-industry trade. In A. J. Glass, R. S. Rajan, K. A. Reinert, & L. S. Davis (Eds.), *The Princeton Encyclopedia of the World Economy.* Princeton University Press.

Marshall, A. (1890). *Principles of Economics.* London: Macmillan.

Marshall, A. (1919). *Industry and Trade: A Study of industrial technique and business organization; and of their influences on the condition of various classes and nations.* London: Macmillan.

Marshall, A., & Marshall, M. P. (1879). *The Economics of Industry.* London: Macmillan.

Martin, P., & Ottaviano, G. (1996). Growth and Agglomeration. (12).

Martin, R. (1999a). Critical survey. The new 'geographical turn' in economics: Some critical reflections. *Cambridge Journal of Economics, 23*(1), 65–91. https://doi.org/10.1093/cje/23.1.65

Martin, R., & Sunley, P. (2011). The new economic geography and policy relevance. *Journal of Economic Geography, 11*(2), 357–369. https://doi.org/10.1093/jeg/lbq042

Martin, R. (1999b). The new 'geographical turn' in economics: some critical reflections. *Cambridge Journal of Economics, 23*(1), 65–91.

Martin, R. L. (2003). A study on the factors of regional competitiveness. *A draft final report for The European Commission Directorate-General Regional Policy, Cambridge: University of Cambridge.*

Martincus, C. V. (2010). Spatial effects of trade policy: Evidence from Brazil. *Journal of Regional Science, 50*(2), 541–569. https://doi.org/10.1111/j.1467-9787.2009.00617.x

Martinez-Galarraga, J. (2014). Market potential estimates in history: a survey of methods and an application to Spain, 1867-1930. *EHES Working Papers in Economic History.* (51), 1–53. Retrieved from http://www.ehes.org/EHES_No51.pdf

Matsen, E., & Torvik, R. (2005). Optimal Dutch Disease. *Journal of Development Economics*, *78*(2), 494–515.

Mayer, T., & Ottaviano, G. I. P. (2008). The Happy Few: The Internationalisation of European Firms. *Intereconomics*, *43*(3), 135–148. https://doi.org/10.1007/s10272-008-0247-x

Mayer, T., & Zignago, S. (2011). Notes on CEPII's distances measures: the GeoDist Database. *CEPII Working Paper*. (2011-25), 1–47. Retrieved from http://www.cepii.fr/pdf_pub/wp/2011/wp2011-25.pdf

McCallum, J. (1995). National borders matter: Canada-US regional trade patterns. *American Economic Review*, *85*(3), 615–623.

McCalum, J. (1995). National Borders Matter: Canada-U.S. Regional Trade Patterns. *American Economic Review*, *85*(3), 615–623. Retrieved from http://www.jstor.org/stable/2118191

Melitz, J., & Toubal, F. (2014). Native language, spoken language, translation and trade. *Journal of International Economics*, *93*(2), 351–363. https://doi.org/10.1016/j.jinteco.2014.04.004

Melitz, M. J. (2003). The Impact of Trade on Intra-Industry Reallocations and Aggregate Industry Productivity. *Econometrica*, *71*(6), 1695–1725. https://doi.org/10.1111/1468-0262.00467

Melitz, M. J., & Redding, S. J. (2014). Heterogeneous Firms and Trade. In G. Gopinath, E. Helpman, & Rogoff Kenneth (Eds.), *Handbook of International Economics. Handbook of International Economics* (Vol. 4, pp. 1–54). Amsterdam: Elsevier. https://doi.org/10.1016/B978-0-444-54314-1.00001-X

Mello, L. (1999). Foreign Direct Investment-Led Growth: Evidence from Time Series and Panel Data. *Oxford Economic Papers*, *51*(1), 133–151.

Mello, L. R. de (1997). Foreign direct investment in developing countries and growth: A selective survey. *The Journal of Development Studies*, *34*(1), 1–34. https://doi.org/10.1080/00220389708422501

Midelfart-Knarvik, K. H., & Overman, H. G. (2002). Delocation and European integration: Is structural spending justified? *Economic Policy*, *17*(35), 321–359. https://doi.org/10.1111/1468-0327.00091

Mitchell, W., & Bill, A. (2006). The Two-speed Australian Economy - the Decline of Sydney's Labour Market. *People and Places*, *14*(4), 14–24.

Moreno, R., Paci, R., & Usai, S. (2016). Spatial Spillovers and Innovation Activity in European Regions. *Environment and Planning A: Economy and Space*, *37*(10), 1793–1812. https://doi.org/10.1068/a37341

Mudambi, R., Li, L., Ma, X., Makino, S., Qian, G., & Boschma, R. (2018). Zoom in, zoom out: Geographic scale and multinational activity. *Journal of International Business Studies*, *49*(8), 929–941. https://doi.org/10.1057/s41267-018-0158-4

Murphy, T., Hicks, J., Morrison, M., Basu, P., & Ranshaw, D. (2019). The Importance of Regional Export Development and a Specialised Local Supply Chain on the Development of Australia's Regions. *Economic Papers*, *38*(2), 131–143. https://doi.org/10.1111/1759-3441.12238

Nacewska-Twardowska, A. (2013). Polityka handlowa UE a Strategia Europa 2020. *Prace Naukowe Uniwersytetu Ekonomicznego we Wrocławiu*. (305).

Nair-Reichert, U., & Weinhold, D. (2001). Causality Tests for Cross-Country Panels: A New Look at FDI and Economic Growth in Developing Countries. *Oxford Bulletin of Economics and Statistics*, *63*(2), 153–171. https://doi.org/10.1111/1468-0084.00214

Naudé, W. A., & Matthee, M. (Febr. 2007). *The geographical location of manufacturing exporters in South Africa. Research paper / UNU-WIDER: Vol. 2007,09*. Helsinki, Finnland: UNU World Inst. for Development Economics Research (UNU/WIDER).

Nazarczuk, J. M., & Umiński, S. (2018a). The geography of openness to foreign trade in Poland: The role of special economic zones and foreign-owned entities. *Bulletin of Geography. Socio-economic Series*, *39*(39), 97–111. https://doi.org/10.2478/bog-2018-0007

Nazarczuk, J. M., Umiński, S., & Brodzicki, T. (2019). Determinants of the spatial distribution of exporters in regions: The role of ownership. *The Annals of Regional Science*, *43*(8), 103. https://doi.org/10.1007/s00168-019-00947-6

Nazarczuk, J. M., Umiński, S., & Gawlikowska-Hueckel, K. (2018). The Role of Specialisation in the Export Success of Polish Counties in 2004-2015. *Entrepreneurial Business and Economics Review*, *6*(2), 91–109. https://doi.org/10.15678/EBER.2018.060205

Nazarczuk, J. M., Umiński, S., & Jurkiewicz, T. (2020). Foreign ownership as a neglected factor in regions' smart specialisation exports. *Journal of Business Economics and Management*, *21*(3), 826–850. https://doi.org/10.3846/jbem.2020.12425

Nazarczuk, J. M., Umiński, S., & Márquez-Ramos, L. (2020). Vulnerability to the consequences of Brexit: evidence for Polish and Spanish regions. *E+M Ekonomie a Management*, *23*(1), 34–49. https://doi.org/10.15240/tul/001/2020-1-003

Nazarczuk, J. M., & Umiński, S. (2018b). The impact of special economic zones on export behaviour: Evidence from polish firm-level data. *E+M Ekonomie a Management*, *21*(3), 4–22. https://doi.org/10.15240/tul/001/2018-3-001

Nazarczuk, J. M., & Umiński, S. (2019). *Foreign trade in special economic zones in Poland*. Olsztyn: Wydawnictwo Uniwersytetu Warmińsko-Mazurskiego.

Neary, J. P. (Ed.) (1986). *Natural resources and the macroeconomy*. Cambridge/Mass.: MIT Pr.

Nelson, R. R., & Phelps, E. S. (1966). Investment in Humans, Technological Diffusion, and Economic Growth. *The American Economic Review*, *56*(1/2), 69–75.

Nitsch, V. (2000). National borders and international trade: Evidence from the European Union. *Canadian Journal of Economics/Revue Canadienne d'Economique*, *33*(4), 1091–1105. https://doi.org/10.1111/0008-4085.00055

Nocke, V. (2006). A Gap for Me: Entrepreneurs and Entry. *Journal of the European Economic Association*, *4*(5), 929–956.

Noponen, H., Markusen, A., & Driessen, K. (1997). Trade and American cities: Who has the comparative advantage? *Economic Development Quarterly*, *11*(1), 67–87.

North, D. C. (1955). Location Theory and Regional Economic Growth. *Journal of Political Economy*, *63*(3), 243–258. https://doi.org/10.1086/257668

Obstfeld, M., & Rogoff, K. (2000). The Six Major Puzzles in International Macroeconomics: Is There a Common Cause? *NBER Macroeconomics Annual*, *15*, 339–390. https://doi.org/10.1086/654423

OECD (1992). *Programme on Technology and the Economy*. Paris: Organization for Economic Cooperation and Development Paris.

OECD (2002). Intra-industry and intra-firm trade and the internationalization of Production. *OECD Economic Outlook*. (71), 159–170. Retrieved from https://www.oecd.org/eco/outlook/2752923.pdf

OECD (2009). Regional Policy Challenges, New Issues and Good Practices. Retrieved from http://www.oecd.org/regional/ministerial/42532004.pdf

OECD (2013). *Territorial Reviews: Antofagasta, Chile 2013*: OECD.

Ohmae, K. (1999). *The borderless world: Power and strategy in the interlinked economy. Management lessons in the new logic of the global marketplace* (Rev. ed.). New York: Harper-Business.

OIR (2011). *Regional Challenges in the Perspective of 2020 - Phase 2: Deepening and Broadening the Analysis: Final report*. Vienna/Heisdorf/Bonn. Retrieved from http://www.et2050.eu/docs/Regions2020_2ndPart.pdf

Okubo, T. (2009). Trade liberalisation and agglomeration with firm heterogeneity: Forward and backward linkages. *Regional Science and Urban Economics*, *39*(5), 530–541. https://doi.org/10.1016/j.regsciurbeco.2009.03.005

Orłowski, W. M. (1996). *Droga do Europy: Makroekonomia wstępowania do Unii Europejskiej. Z Prac Zakładu Badań Statystyczno-Ekonomicznych. Studia i Prace*. Warszawa: Główny Urząd Statystyczny. Zakład Badań Statystyczno-Ekonomicznych.

Ott, M. (1988). Have US exports been larger than reported? *Federal Reserve Bank of St. Louis Review, September/October 1988*, 3–23. Retrieved from https://research.stlouisfed.org/publications/review/88/09/Exports_Sep_Oct1988.pdf

Ottaviano, G. I. P. (2011). 'New' new economic geography: Firm heterogeneity and agglomeration economies. *Journal of Economic Geography, 11*(2), 231–240. https://doi.org/10.1093/jeg/lbq041

Ottaviano, G. I. P. (2008). Infrastructure and economic geography: An overview of theory and evidence. *EIB Papers*. (6).

Paluzie, E., Pons, J., & Tirado, D. A. (2001). Regional Integration and Specialization Patterns in Spain. *Regional Studies, 35*(4), 285–296. https://doi.org/10.1080/00343400125457

Papyrakis, E., & Raveh, O. (2014). An Empirical Analysis of a Regional Dutch Disease: The Case of Canada. *Environmental and Resource Economics, 58*(2), 179–198. https://doi.org/10.1007/s10640-013-9698-z

Petrakos, G., Kallioras, D., & Anagnostou, A. (2011). Regional convergence and growth in Europe: Understanding patterns and determinants. *European Urban and Regional Studies, 18*(4), 375–391. https://doi.org/10.1177/0969776411407809

Pietrzyk, I. (2004). *Polityka regionalna Unii Europejskiej i regiony w państwach członkowskich*. Warszawa: PWN.

Polasek, W., & Sellner, R. (2011). Does globalization affect regional growth? Evidence for NUTS-2 regions in EU-27. *Economics Series, Institute for Advanced Studies*. (266).

Porter, M. E. (1990). *The competitive advantage of nations*. New York: The Free Press.

Porter, M. E. (1998). *Competitive advantage: Creating and sustaining superior performance*. New York: Free Press.

Porter, M. E. (2010). *Strategia konkurencji: Metody analizy sektorów i konkurentów. Klasyka Zarządzania. Złota Kolekcja*. Warszawa: Wydawnictwo MT Biznes.

Posner, M. (1961). International Change and Technical Change. *Oxford Economic Papers, 13*(3), 323–341. https://doi.org/10.1093/oxfordjournals.oep.a040877

Productivity Commission (2017). *Rising protectionism: challenges, threats and opportunities for Australia*. Canberra.

Proença, I., Sperlich, S., & Savaşcı, D. (2015). Semi-mixed effects gravity models for bilateral trade. *Empirical Economics, 48*(1), 361–387. https://doi.org/10.1007/s00181-014-0891-x

PWC (2017). *Diagnoza potencjału MŚP z Warszawskiego Obszaru Funkcjonalnego w zakresie internacjonalizacji: Raport końcowy*. Warszawa.

Radosevic, S., & Ciampi Stancova, K. (2018). Internationalising Smart Specialisation: Assessment and Issues in the Case of EU New Member States. *Journal of the Knowledge Economy, 9*(1), 263–293. https://doi.org/10.1007/s13132-015-0339-3

Rahman, M. M. (2009). *Australia's global trade potential: evidence from the gravity model analysis*. St. Hugh's College, Oxford University.

Redding, S. J. (2010). The empirics of new economic geography. *Journal of Regional Science, 50*(1), 297–311. https://doi.org/10.1111/j.1467-9787.2009.00646.x

Redding, S. J. (2016). Goods trade, factor mobility and welfare. *Journal of International Economics, 101*, 148–167. https://doi.org/10.1016/j.jinteco.2016.04.003

Rehner, J., Baeza, S. A., & Barton, J. R. (2014). Chile's resource-based export boom and its outcomes: Regional specialization, export stability and economic growth. *Geoforum, 56*, 35–45. https://doi.org/10.1016/j.geoforum.2014.06.007

Rivera-Batiz, L. A., & Romer, P. M. (1991). Economic Integration and Endogenous Growth. *The Quarterly Journal of Economics, 106*(2), 531. https://doi.org/10.2307/2937946

Rodríguez-Pose, A., Tselios, V., Winkler, D., & Farole, T. (2013). Geography and the Determinants of Firm Exports in Indonesia. *World Development*, *44*, 225–240. https://doi.org/10.1016/j.worlddev.2012.12.002

Rodrik, D. (2002). Institutions, Integration, and Geography: In Search of the Deep Determinants of Economic Growth. *Working Papers*. Retrieved from http://j.mp/2oGu20g

Romalis, J. (2007). Market Access, Openness and Growth. Advance online publication. https://doi.org/10.3386/w13048

Romer, P. M. (1986). Increasing Returns and Long-Run Growth. *Journal of Political Economy*, *94*(5), 1002–1037.

Romer, P. M. (1990). Endogenous technological change. *Journal of Political Economy*, *98*(5), 71–102.

Ross, M. L. (1999). The Political Economy of the Resource Curse. *World Politics*, *51*(2), 297–322. https://doi.org/10.1017/S0043887100008200

Sachs, J., Bajpai, N., & Ramiah, A. (2002). Understanding regional economic growth in India. *Asian Economic Papers*, *1*(3), 32–62.

Sachs, J., & Warner, A. (1995). *Economic Convergence and Economic Policies*. Cambridge, MA: National Bureau of Economic Research.

Samuelson, P. A. (1954). The Transfer Problem and Transport Costs, II: Analysis of Effects of Trade Impediments. *The Economic Journal*, *64*(254), 264. https://doi.org/10.2307/2226834

Santos Silva, J.M.C., & Tenreyro, S. (2011). Further simulation evidence on the performance of the Poisson pseudo-maximum likelihood estimator. *Economics Letters*, *112*(2), 220–222. https://doi.org/10.1016/j.econlet.2011.05.008

Santos Silva, J., & Tenreyro, S. (2006). The Log of Gravity. *Review of Economics and Statistics*, *88*(4), 641–658. https://doi.org/10.1162/rest.88.4.641

Sapir, A. (2003). *An Agenda for a Growing Europe. Making the EU Economic System Deliver: Report of an Independent High-Level Study Group established on the initiative of thePresident of the European Commission*. Brussels.

Sassen, S. (2009). The specialised differences of cities matter in today's global economy. In S. Whimster (Ed.), *Reforming the city. Responses to the global financial crisis* (pp. 209–236). London: Forumpress. Retrieved from http://www.saskiasassen.com/PDFs/publications/The-Specialised-Differences.pdf

Savasci, D. (2011). *Three Studies on Semi-mixed Effects Models*. Dissertation presented for the degree of Doctor of Philosophy at the Faculty of Economic Sciences of the Georg-August-Universität Göttingen, pp. 1–106.

Schumpeter, J. A. (2013). *Theorie der wirtschaftlichen Entwicklung: Eine Untersuchung über Unternehmergewinn, Kapital, Kredit, Zins und den Konjunkturzyklus* (9. Aufl.). Berlin: Duncker & Humblot. Retrieved from https://ebookcentral.proquest.com/lib/zbw/detail.action?docID=1370361

Scott, B. R. (1985). US competitiveness: Concepts, performance, and implications. *US competitiveness in the world economy*, 13–70.

Serra, M. I. (2006). Regional Convergence in Latin America. *IMF Working Paper*. (6/125). Retrieved from http://lib.myilibrary.com/detail.asp?id=382864

SGS Economics and Planning. (2018). Economic performance of Australia's cities and regions.

Shafiullah, M., Selvanathan, S., & Naranpanawa, A. (2017). The role of export composition in export-led growth in Australia and its regions. *Economic Analysis and Policy*, *53*, 62–76. https://doi.org/10.1016/j.eap.2016.11.002

Shafiullah, M., Selvanathan, S., Naranpanawa, A., & Chai, A. (2019). Examining Dutch disease across Australian regions. The World Economy, 42(2), 590–613. https://doi.org/10.1111/twec.12720

Siebert, H. (1969). *Regional Economic Growth. Theory and Policy*. Scranton: International Textbook Company.

Simmie, J. (2002). Trading Places: Competitive Cities in the Global Economy. *European Planning Studies*, *10*(2), 201–214. https://doi.org/10.1080/09654310120114490

Sjöholm, F. (1999). Productivity Growth in Indonesia: The Role of Regional Characteristics and Direct Foreign Investment. *Economic Development and Cultural Change*, *47*(3), 559–584. https://doi.org/10.1086/452419

Smith, T. R. (1989). Regional Exports of Manufactured Products. *Federal Reserve Bank of Kansas City Economic Review*, *January 1989*(25), 21–31. Retrieved from https://www.kansascityfed.org/PUBLICAT/ECONREV/econrevarchive/1989/1q89smit.pdf

Sneddon Little, J. (1990). New England's Links to the World Economy. *Federal Reserve Bank of Boston New England Economic Review, November/December 1990*, 33–50. Retrieved from http://www.bostonfed.org/economic/neer/neer1990/neer690c.pdf

Solow, R. M. (1956). A Contribution to the Theory of Economic Growth. *The Quarterly Journal of Economics*, *70*(1), 65–94.

Soukiazis, E., & Antunes, M. (2011). Is foreign trade important for regional growth? Empirical evidence from Portugal. *Economic Modelling*, *28*(3), 1363–1373. https://doi.org/10.1016/j.econmod.2011.02.023

Stabler, J. C., & Howe, E. C. (1988). Service exports and regional growth in the postinudstrial era. *Journal of Regional Science*, *28*(3), 303–305. https://doi.org/10.1111/j.1467-9787.1988.tb01084.x

Sterlacchini, A. (2008). R&D, higher education and regional growth: Uneven linkages among European regions. *Research Policy*, *37*(6-7), 1096–1107. https://doi.org/10.1016/j.respol.2008.04.009

Stevens, P. (2003). Resource Impact: Curse or Blessing? A Literature Survey. *Journal of Energy Literature*, *9*(1), 1–42.

Storper, M. (2011). Why do regions develop and change? The challenge for geography and economics. *Journal of Economic Geography*, *11*(2), 333–346. https://doi.org/10.1093/jeg/lbq033

Su, Y., & Liu, Z. (2016). The impact of foreign direct investment and human capital on economic growth: Evidence from Chinese cities. *China Economic Review*, *37*, 97–109. https://doi.org/10.1016/j.chieco.2015.12.007

Sun, H. (2001). Foreign Direct Investment and Regional Export Performance in China. *Journal of Regional Science*, *41*(2), 317–336. https://doi.org/10.1111/0022-4146.00219

Sun, H., Hone, P., & Doucouliago, H. (1999). Economic openness and technical efficiency: A case study of Chinese manufacturing industries. *The Economics of Transition*, *7*(3), 615–636. https://doi.org/10.1111/1468-0351.00028

Sun, H., & Parikh, A. (2010). Exports, Inward Foreign Direct Investment (FDI) and Regional Economic Growth in China. *Regional Studies*, *35*(3), 187–196. https://doi.org/10.1080/713693805

Swan, T. W. (1956). Economic Growth and Capital Accumulation. *Economic Record*, *32*(2), 334–361. https://doi.org/10.1111/j.1475-4932.1956.tb00434.x

Szlachta, J. (1992). Interwencjonizm państwa w przebiegu procesów rozwoju regionalnego w świetle doktryny neokeynesowskiej i neoliberalnej. In B. Winiarski (Ed.), *Polityka regionalna w warunkach gospodarki rynkowej*. Wrocław, Warszawa, Kraków: Ossolineum.

Szlachta, J. (2010). Wpływ kryzysu końca pierwszej dekady XX wieku na europejska politykę spójności. In A. Harańczyk & T. Kudłacz (Eds.), *Wyzwania regionalnego i przestrzennego rozwoju Polski na początku XXI wieku: Księga jubileuszowa dedykowana profesorowi Zygmuntowi Szymli*. Kraków: Wydawnictwo Uniwersytetu Ekonomicznego.

Szlachta, J. (2012). Strategia Europa 2020 a europejska polityka spójności po 2013 roku. *Prace i Materiały Instytutu Rozwoju Gospodarczego SGH*. (88), 231–253. Retrieved from https://ssl-kolegia.sgh.waw.pl/pl/KAE/struktura/IRG/publikacje/Documents/pim88_9.pdf

Takatsuka, H., Zeng, D.-Z., & Zhao, L. (2015). Resource-based cities and the Dutch disease. *Resource and Energy Economics*, *40*, 57–84. https://doi.org/10.1016/j.reseneeco.2015.01.003

Tang, S., Selvanathan, E. A., & Selvanathan, S. (2008). Foreign Direct Investment, Domestic Investment and Economic Growth in China: A Time Series Analysis. *World Economy*, *31*(10), 1292–1309. https://doi.org/10.1111/j.1467-9701.2008.01129.x

Teixeira, A. C. (2006). Transport policies in light of the new economic geography: The Portuguese experience. *Regional Science and Urban Economics*, *36*(4), 450–466. https://doi.org/10.1016/j.regsciurbeco.2006.01.002

The Economist (2013). Metropolitan Trade. The humming trade between American towns, *October 26th*, (US Section). Retrieved from http://www.economist.com/news/united-states/21588405-humming-trade-between-american-towns-open-cities

The World Bank (2010). *Global Economic Prospects 2010*: The World Bank.

Thissen, M., Diodato, D., & van Ort, F. (2013). Integration and Convergence in Regional Europe: European Regional Trade Flows from 2000 to 2010. Retrieved from http://www.pbl.nl/sites/default/files/cms/publicaties/PBL_2013_European%20Regional%20Trade%20Flows%20from%202000-2010_1036.pdf

Thissen, M., Lankhuizen, M., & Jonkeren, O. (2015). *Multi-regional trade data for Europe in 2010. Project for the Institute for Prospective Technological Studies* (No. 1753). The Hague, pp. 1–39.

Thompson, P., & Fox-Kean, M. (2005). Patent Citations and the Geography of Knowledge Spillovers: A Reassessment. *The American Economic Review*, *95*(1), 450–460.

Tiebout, C. M. (1956). Exports and Regional Economic Growth. *Journal of Political Economy*, *64*(2), 160–164.

Todtling, F. (1997). Strategic Reactions of Firms in Austrian Regions to Change in Central and Eastern Europe. *European Urban and Regional Studies*, *4*(2), 171–182. https://doi.org/10.1177/096977649700400205

Tödtling, F., & Trippl, M. (2005). One size fits all? *Research Policy*, *34*(8), 1203–1219. https://doi.org/10.1016/j.respol.2005.01.018

Tomaszewski, K. (2007). *Regiony w procesie integracji europejskiej*. Kraków: Oficyna a Wolters Kluwer business.

Tomiura, E. (2003). Changing economic geography and vertical linkages in Japan. *Journal of the Japanese and International Economies*, *17*(4), 561–581. https://doi.org/10.1016/S0889-1583(03)00063-7

Torvik, R. (2001). Learning by doing and the Dutch disease. *European Economic Review*, *45*(2), 285–306. https://doi.org/10.1016/S0014-2921(99)00071-9

Townsend, J. (2007). Do tariff reductions affect the wages of workers in protected industries? Evidence from the Canada-U.S. Free Trade Agreement. *Canadian Journal of Economics/Revue Canadienne d'Economique*, *40*(1), 69–92. https://doi.org/10.1111/j.1365-2966.2007.00400.x

Trippl, M., Zukauskaite, E., & Healy, A. (2019). Shaping smart specialization: The role of place-specific factors in advanced, intermediate and less-developed European regions. *Regional Studies*, *35*(4), 1–13. https://doi.org/10.1080/00343404.2019.1582763

Turnbull, C., Sun, S., & Anwar, S. (2016). Trade liberalisation, inward FDI and productivity within Australia's manufacturing sector. *Economic Analysis and Policy*, *50*, 41–51.

Umiński, S. (Ed.) (2010). *Eksport oraz bezpośrednie inwestycje zagraniczne firm województwa pomorskiego*. Sopot: PBS DGA; Ośrodek Badań Integracji Europejskiej Uniwersytetu Gdańskiego.

Umiński, S. (2012). *Rozważania nad naturą, przyczynami oraz konkurencyjnością działalności eksportowej w ujęciu regionalnym dla Polski*. Gdańsk: Wydawnictwo Uniwersytetu Gdańskiego; Uniwersytet Gdański.

Umiński, S. (2014). Integration of Poland's regions with the European Union – assessment of intra industry trade relations. *European Integration Studies*, *8*, 93–98. https://doi.org/10.5755/j01.eis.0.8.6770

Umiński, S. (2016). The regionalisation of commercial policy and of export-related analyses. In K. Gawlikowska-Hueckel & S. Umiński (Eds.), *An analysis of Poland's foreign trade in the light of the latest theoretical concepts: Implications for economic policy at a time of crisis* (pp. 212–231). Warsaw: Scholar Publishing House; Wydawnictwo Naukowe "Scholar".

US Department of Commerce (2013). *Exports from manufacturing establishments: Preliminary estimates for 2011*. Washington: DC: Department of Commerce.

Usui, N. (1996). Policy adjustments to the oil boom and their evaluation: The Dutch disease in Indonesia. *World Development*, *24*(5), 887–900. https://doi.org/10.1016/0305-750X(96)00008-3

Vamvakidis, A. (1999). Regional Trade Agreements or Broad Liberalization: Which Path Leads to Faster Growth? *IMF Staff Papers*, *46*(1), 42–68.

Vamvakidis, A. (2002). How Robust is the Growth-Openness Connection? Historical Evidence. *Journal of Economic Growth*, *7*(1), 57–80. https://doi.org/10.1023/A:1013418610712

Venables, A., & Krugman, P. (1990). Integration and the competitiveness of peripheral industry. In C. J. Bliss (Ed.), *Unity with diversity in the European economy: The Community's southern frontier*. Cambridge: Cambridge Univ. Press.

Vernon, R. (1966). International investment and international trade in the product cycle. *The Quarterly Journal of Economics*, *80*(2), 190. https://doi.org/10.2307/1880689

Volpe Martincus, C., & Blyde, J. (2013). Shaky roads and trembling exports: Assessing the trade effects of domestic infrastructure using a natural experiment. *Journal of International Economics*, *90*(1), 148–161. https://doi.org/10.1016/j.jinteco.2012.11.001

Wacziarg, R., & Welch, K. H. (2003). Trade Liberalization and Growth: New Evidence. *NBER Working Paper*. (10152).

Wade, J. (2007). Researchers keen to avoid 'Dutch Disease' in Queensland. Australian Mining.

Wei, K., Yao, S., & Aying, L. (2007). Foreign Direct Investment and Regional Inequality in China. *SSRN Electronic Journal*. Advance online publication. https://doi.org/10.2139/ssrn.1023897

Westerlund, J., & Wilhelmsson, F. (2011). Estimating the gravity model without gravity using panel data. *Applied Economics*, *43*(6), 641–649. https://doi.org/10.1080/00036840802599784

Western Australian Planning Commission (2015). Great southern regional planning and infrastructure framework part A: regional strategic planning. Perth.

Wilson, B. (2016). Smart specialization and innovation: A view from beyond Europe. International Association of Science Parks and areas of Innovation, 1–7. Retrieved from http://researchbank.rmit.edu.au/view/rmit:42535

Wilson, B. (2018). *Smart Specialisation in Asia and Oceania, an inspiration for place-based innovation: An Australian perspective*. Seville (Spain). Retrieved from the first global workshop on Smart Specialisation from the EU to the World. 25 September 2018. website: https://s3platform.jrc.ec.europa.eu/-/smart-specialisation-from-the-eu-to-the-world?inheritRedirect=true&redirect=http%3A%2F%2Fs3platform.jrc.ec.europa.eu%2Fhome

Wolf, H. C. (2000). Intranational Home Bias in Trade. *Review of Economics and Statistics*, *82*(4), 555–563. https://doi.org/10.1162/003465300559046

WTO (2018): Australia and the WTO.

Wu, Y. (2000). Productivity, Growth and Economic Integration in the Southern China Region. *Asian Economic Journal*, *14*(1), 39–54. https://doi.org/10.1111/1467-8381.00099

Xu, Z. (2000). Financial development, investment, and economic growth. *Economic Inquiry*, *38*(2), 331–344. https://doi.org/10.1111/j.1465-7295.2000.tb00021.x

Yoshida, Y. (2008). Intra-Industry Trade Between Japan and Korea: Vertical Intra-Industry Trade, Fragmentation and Export Margins. *Discussion Paper Faculty of Economics, Kyushu Sangyo University*. (32). Retrieved from http://econpapers.repec.org/paper/kyudpaper/32.htm

Yu, J., Zhao, C., & Ming, L. (2006). Industry Agglomeration in China: Economic Geography, New Economic Geography and Policy. *Economic Researchch Journal*. (4). Retrieved from http://en.cnki.com.cn/Article_en/CJFDTotal-JJYJ200604007.htm

Zaucha, J. (2007). *Rola przestrzeni w kształtowaniu relacji gospodarczych: Ekonomiczne fundamenty planowania przestrzennego w Europie Bałtyckiej*. Gdańsk: Fundacja Rozwoju Uniwersytetu Gdańskiego.

Zaucha, J. (2008). Ziemia i przestrzeń w procesie wytwarzania. Ewolucja spojrzenia. In P. Kulawczuk & E. Kwella (Eds.), *Stymulowanie rozwoju społeczno-gospodarczego* (pp. 53–72). Sopot: Fundacja Rozwoju Uniwersytetu Gdańskiego.

Zaucha, J., Brodzicki, T., Ciołek, D., Komornicki, T., Mogiła, Z., Szlachta, J., & Zaleski, J. (2015). *Terytorialny wymiar wzrostu i rozwoju*: Difin.

Zaucha, J., & Ciołek, D. (2014). Potencjał rozwojowy polskich regionów. Międzynarodowe i wewnątrzregionalne zróżnicowania poziomu rozwoju polskich regionów oraz determinanty lokalizacji gospodarczej. In K. Gawlikowska-Hueckel & J. Szlachta (Eds.), *Wrażliwość polskich regionów na wyzwania współczesnej gospodarki: Implikacje dla polityki rozwoju regionalnego* (pp. 141–157). Warszawa: Wolters Kluwer; Wolters Kluwer Polska.

Zawalińska, K., Giesecke, J., & Horridge, M. (2010). *The Regional Economic Consequences of Less Favoured Area Support: A Spatial General Equilibrium Analysis of the Polish LFA Program* (Centre of Policy Studies and the Impact Projects No. G-211). Melbourne: Monash University. *General Paper*, pp. 1–33.

Zestos, G. K., & Tao, X. (2002). Trade and GDP Growth: Causal Relations in the United States and Canada. *Southern Economic Journal*, *68*(4), 859. https://doi.org/10.2307/1061496

Zhang, X., Xing, L., Fan, S., & Luo, X. (2008). Resource abundance and regional development in China1. *Economics of Transition*, *16*(1), 7–29. https://doi.org/10.1111/j.1468-0351.2007.00318.x

Zielińska-Głębocka, A. (2012). *Współczesna gospodarka światowa: Przemiany, innowacje, kryzysy, rozwiązania regionalne*. Warszawa: Oficyna a Wolters Kluwer business.

Zucker, G, L., Darby, R, M., Armstrong, & Jeff (1998). Geographically Localised Knowledge: Spillovers or Markets. *Economic Inquiry*, *36*(1), 65–86. https://doi.org/10.1111/j.1465-7295.1998.tb01696.x

List of Figures

List of Tables

Index of Subject